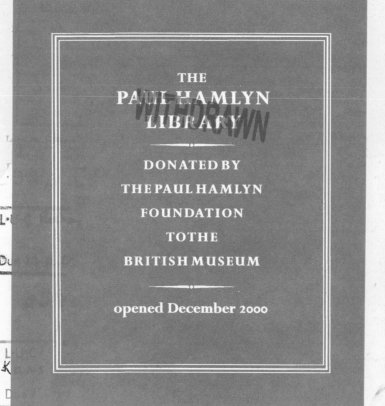

The History of Civilization
Edited by C. K. OGDEN, M.A.

The Ægean Civilization

The History of Civilization

In the Section of this Series devoted to PRE-HISTORY AND ANTIQUITY *are included the following volumes :—*

I. Introduction and Pre-History

* An asterisk indicates that the volume does not form part of the French collection "L'Évolution de l'Humanité".

A full list of the SERIES *will be found at the end of this volume.*

The
Ægean Civilization

By

GUSTAVE GLOTZ

*Member of the Institute of France and Professor of Greek History
at the University of Paris*

WITH EIGHTY-SEVEN ILLUSTRATIONS, THREE
MAPS IN THE TEXT AND FOUR PLATES

LONDON
KEGAN PAUL, TRENCH, TRUBNER & CO., LTD.
NEW YORK : ALFRED A. KNOPF
1925

C

20192

Translated by

M. R. DOBIE AND E. M. RILEY

Printed in Great Britain by Stephen Austin & Sons, Ltd., Hertford.

FOREWORD

THE EARLIEST MEDITERRANEAN CIVILIZATION

*I*N *the preceding volumes of the Évolution de l'Humanité emphasis is laid upon the the importance of the excavations and the value of archæological documents in the study of pre-historic and proto-historic times.*[1] *The victories of the naturalists and physicists, who wrest their secrets from life and matter, have their pendant in the calling up by J. de Morgan, Schliemann, and Evans of whole civilizations and peoples from the earth. Where documents of another nature exist, archæology supplies additional information of great value ; but there are fragments of past history which for the most part can only be reconstructed by the aid of stones and similar mute witnesses which, neverthe-less, have been made to speak.*

We have seen something of the Hittite[2] *civilization and of that of the Mitanni. The present volume is devoted entirely to the civilization revealed by Evans in excavations in Crete dating from* 1900 *and by earlier excavations dating from* 1876 *on the mainland of Greece and in Asia Minor. The earliest Mediterranean civilization, with Crete as its centre and Knossos as its focus, has now taken shape and assumed its place in history.*

Fresh links are caught up in this logical, manifold, and persistent development which, sometimes helped and sometimes hindered by circumstances, tended not only to improve life but also to draw men together in a certain conception of an improved life. Various causes—identity of needs,[3] *diffused sociality,*

---

[1] *See Forewords to J. de Morgan,* Prehistoric Man (*and also pp.* 10–11, 22 *ff.*), *and to L. Delaporte,* Mesopotamia, *both in* The History of Civilization.

[2] " *A more searching study will be required, in the light of the amazing results of recent excavations and the deciphering of the archives discovered at Boghaz-Keui . . . if we are to determine exactly the part played by the Hittites in Palestine* " (*Kreglinger,* La Religion d'Israël, *p.* 32).

[3] *See J. de Morgan, " La Notion innée du Progrès dans l'Humanité," in the* Revue de Synthèse historique, *vol. xxxv.*

imitation [1]—*operating before the Empires and later side by side with imperialism, produced vast and more or less homogeneous human groups, and, in some measure, a humanity. The basin of the Mediterranean, and more especially the Ægean region, were by their conformation adapted to this unification of life and culture. Before it was Romanized, before it was Hellenized, the ancient world was Ægeanized. But the factor which contributed to this unity, in an even greater degree, it seems, than the nature of the environment,*[2] *was the nature of a certain population which was able to benefit by Oriental influences but possessed original qualities of its own and unique faculties for civilization, by which it radiated a potent influence.*[3]

It was doubtless a branch of a Mediterranean *race, preceding the Indo-Europeans in its historical rôle and foreign to the Semites. Since the activity of the Ægeans has become manifest that of the Phœnicians, which there had been a tendency to exaggerate,*[4] *has appeared correspondingly diminished. Phœnicia did not come to the front until about the XIth century, after the fall of the Minoan power ; its supremacy in the Mediterranean dates from about* 1100 *to* 800. *In the IXth century the Greeks renewed Ægean traditions and little by little drove back the Phœnicians. Ægæo-Hellenic expansion, moreover, proceeded along different lines from Phœnician. The Phœnicians cared only for gain, to compass which they did not shrink from violence and cunning. " Contact with the Phœnicians made the Greeks feel for the first time the profound difference between themselves and the Semites of Asia. The Homeric poems are not lacking in allusions to this rivalry with the Phœnician, who is always represented as a dishonest trader, cheap-jack, and kidnapper of slaves.*[5] *All the gaudy show displayed in front of his ships*

[1] *See the Forewords to* L. Febvre, A Geographical Introduction to History, *and to* A. Moret, From Tribe to Empire, *in this series.*

[2] " *Here the sea does not separate : it unites. From the beginning it assumed the character that it was destined to retain through history—that of a Greek lake."* Ad. Reinach, L'Hellénisation du monde antique, *p.* 13. *Glotz contrasts this maritime civilization with the " local and terrestial " character of the Egyptian and Asiatic civilizations,* p. 394.

[3] *Monsieur C. Autran, in a book containing some interesting and contestable hypotheses, justly points out that the history of the origins of civilization has long been confined " to the narrow limits of Egypt and Mesopotamia ", and that it has been too exclusively the work of Egyptologists and of enthusiastic Semites unduly attached to the traditions of the " sacred books ".* (" Phéniciens ", essai de contribution à l'histoire antique de la Méditerranée, *note, p.* 8.)

[4] Movers, Clermont-Ganneau, V. Bérard, Siret, *etc.*

[5] *This does not include the oldest portions of the Homeric poems, which are prior to the rivalry in question.*

*is only there for the purpose of attracting human merchandise
to be sold afar. It is he who sows terror along the sea-routes
and lies in wait by straits and sounds for navigators who lack
the foresight of Odysseus."* [1] *The antithesis must not be strained.
Nevertheless, the Ægeans and the Greeks, in general, exported
their products honestly ; and they sent out swarms of colonists.
Maritime trade and colonization were " great novelties in the
history of the world." Here was a process of dissemination
very different from mass migration, imperialist conquest, and
" Punic " thalassocracy,* [2] a means, as it has aptly been expressed,
of conquering the world without conquest.* [3]*

*The present work proceeds, as is fitting, from the outside
to the inside. To a certain extent it follows the order in which
the resurrection of the period has been attempted, starting with
objects, relics of the past, the framework and decoration supplied
by them, and arriving gradually at the intimate life, the institutions, and the mental requirements of the people.*

*In this volume will be found a corroboration and a complement
of Moret's* From Tribe to Empire : *the clans will be seen to
split up into families and, under the town system, into individuals,
regrouped, however, under a leader—a leader of leaders who,
on attaining the power of a Minos, contributed in a remarkable
degree to the spread of Ægean civilization. This royalty was
all the more powerful and influential for the reason that, while
creating unity, it did not smother either local self-government or
individual initiative.*

*Furthermore, this book continues and completes de Morgan's
volume on* Prehistoric Man : *it follows the progress of craftman-
ship in exact and illuminating fashion. The practical reasoning
power (the humble origins of which we beheld in animal life,
together with its decisive development in prehistoric times) was
served by the Ægeans with ingenious inventions.*

[1] *Ad. Reinach, op. cit., p.* 40.
[2] *On the Phoenicians, see A. Reinach, op. cit., pp.* 66 ff. ; *also Pittard,*
Race and History, *special chapter, Moret,* From Tribe to Empire, *and Jardé,*
The Formation of the Greek People, *all in this series. For writing, see Glotz,
p.* 371. *On the hypothesis of an Ægean origin of the Phœnicians (C. Autran),
see note in Moret, op. cit.*
[3] *It was the Egyptians who invented the " protectorate ". See Moret,* From
Tribe to Empire.

But perhaps the most striking thing about them is their æsthetic sense. It was no doubt innate but received a peculiar refinement from the conditions of their environment and life (conditions which we shall emphasize in connexion with Greek art). " Frescoes recalling the naturalism of Japanese paintings, painted stucco reliefs of unsurpassed realism, hard stones and gems, objects of ivory and steatite chiselled with a fineness unparalleled until the Renaissance, pottery affording patterns to all modern lovers of fired earthenware and rare faience, jewellery of floral design, enriched with enamel as well as with precious stones, such as our Laliques are only just beginning to make anew : such are the masterpieces with which the Minoans adorned their dwellings for nearly a thousand years." [1] *The development of dress, furniture, and various forms of luxury, those minor arts which, in the life of peoples, have from an early stage played a considerable part, which have diffused delightfulness over all the objects with which man (and still more woman, for the satisfaction of man) adorns and surrounds himself and which have created, as it were, the æsthetic atmosphere of civilization—this development is here already of an extreme, perhaps excessive, importance, calculated to give rise to doubts and criticisms later on among the blasé and the thoughtful.*

The Ægeans, who brought into art everything, also cultivated the arts properly so called. They had leisure and they embellished it. They experienced to the highest degree the joy of creation. They combined the elements of reality with liberty and fantasy, or they reproduced reality with an ingenuity of invention and marvellous versatility. Modern civilization, though ignorant of them for so long, owes much to their artistic experience which through the Middle Ages and the Renaissance was sometimes lost and always found again.

Concerning their literature and science one can only make conjectures, for their writing and language remain for us an alluring riddle. Crete awaits its Champollion. But their religion is known to us, thanks to monuments of all kinds. The chief features of this religion, at the culmination of its original evolution, are the position given to woman—to fruitful and beneficent maternity—and to the bull—the male principle, the vigorous begetter—the sense of universal life, the anthropo-

---

[1] *Ad. Reinach, op. cit., p. 5.*

*morphic imagination, the part played by the priestess in worship,
the importance of daily or seasonal ceremonies and of games.
The festivals which afforded communion with the goddess and
the ceremonies by which the dead were honoured, were the
occasion of " contests which were to give birth to a national
athletic tradition and to the lyric and dramatic art of future
times."* [1]

*This volume was to have been written by Adolphe Reinach.
I cannot omit here an expression of homage to this admirably
gifted young man, who won for himself, at an early age, a position
of great scientific authority in the distinct but associated realms
of archæology, epigraphy, ethnography, and the history of religions,
whose learning was prodigious and who knew how to master
the abundance of his knowledge.*

*He had sketched the plan of his book. He would have written
it with joy, for the subject was after his own heart. " That
marvellous Minoan civilization, brought to light twenty years
since by the excavations in Crete, was not merely one of those
splendid meteors which vanish without leaving a trace. From it
the sacred spark fell upon the Hellenic hearth. In spite of many
transformations, Greece has reaped its heritage ; the further
science advances the more it realizes that Ionian Greece bears
to Minoan Greece almost the same relation as the Italian
Renaissance bore to the Græco-Roman civilization."* [2]

*A few days before war broke out, in July, 1914, he wrote to
me as follows : " As soon as I return, I shall start working at
this book without a break. In answer to your call I am giving up
a campaign of excavation in Egypt and I am putting off my
thesis till the Greek Calends (unless I decide to work it in among
the threads that I shall try to gather up for you). I cannot
do more, and I think I may say that few of your collaborators
will sacrifice as much."*

*He was soon to make the full sacrifice for France. At the
end of August, 1914, in the Ardennes, as lieutenant of dragoons,*

---

[1] *See p. 289.*
[2] *Op. cit., p. 5. I have made a point of borrowing certain passages from this*
Hellénisation du monde antique, *a collective work, the plan and several
important chapters of which are the work of Adolphe Reinach.*

he disappeared in a heroic charge with a few of his men, bent on preventing the retreat of his troop.

Gratitude is due to Gustave Glotz for having consented to succeed him, although he had already accepted another task forming part of this work, and for having produced in a comparatively short time a book which will prove a veritable revelation to many. Hitherto documentary works have been written on the excavations in the Ægean region and on certain aspects of this renascent past. There has been no complete picture such as Glotz gives us. The rise and spread of this civilization, going back fifty centuries and practically unknown to us yesterday, the part played by Crete and its relations with the Mediterranean world, receive a treatment which one would be tempted to call final if Gustave Glotz had not taken pains to point out the gaps in our present knowledge and had he not appealed for further study and research.

In this work sound and comprehensive scholarship is quickened by penetrating vision and a profound sense of life ; it is clothed in a style amazingly rich and picturesque. Ingenious comparisons with modern life help the reader to understand a distant past. Moreover, this curious civilization perpetually invites the historian to make such comparisons : the royalty of the fleur-de-lys, the virgin mother, Our Lady of the Mountain or of the Waves, the plastic symbols, the number three or the cross, the " Parisienne " of Knossos, the boxers, and the toreadors, bring very close to us a life separated from our own by thousands of years. It seems to us to be eminently the gift of the best historians of to-day to discern in the history of civilization what is the same and what is different, what transitory and what eternal.

HENRI BERR.

LIST OF ILLUSTRATIONS

Plates

CONTENTS

BOOK III : RELIGIOUS LIFE

BOOK IV : ARTISTIC AND INTELLECTUAL LIFE

ÆGEAN CIVILIZATION

INTRODUCTION

I The Mediterranean and the Ægean

THE valley of the Nile and the steppes of Mesopotamia had emerged long centuries before from barbarism, the savage tribes of the continent of Europe had still before them long centuries of stagnation in thick darkness, when the civilization which was to be that of the future was born on the shores of the Mediterranean. Hitherto the only men of any account in the world had been land-dwellers living on boundless plains, where great rivers assisted the creation of continuous oases, where nature raised no obstacle to uniformity of manners and customs, where, over a vast surface, towns and villages could be united under the sceptre of one king. For the first time scattered peoples appeared in little islands or mountain cantons, keenly attached to self-government, dispersed in cities barely accessible from the interior but facing the sea, always ready to launch out on every trail in the world. The Mediterranean was to exercise a decisive influence on the destinies of humanity.

Stretching between the burnt deserts of the tropics and the frozen regions of the North, the great sea-basin serves in every way as a means of transition between these two zones. Between the masses of the old continent it inserts a little cut-up continent with a special character of its own, due to its scattered nature and its hybrid features. Thanks to the extraordinary way in which land and water are mingled, and to the gulfs which everywhere split it up into haphazard bays and peninsulas prolonged in chains of islands, it possesses a wonderful wealth of coastline and incomparable facilities of communication ; but also, by its intermediate position, and the infinite consequences of that position, it shares in the climate, the flora and fauna, the culture, and the industries of the zones on either side of it. The men who take up their

B

abode on its shores will be in an excellent position for receiving
from the great nations of the South and the East such elements
of their civilization as are adaptable to their own needs, for
welding them into a whole, which retains its originality by
its very variety, and for sending forth their merchandise
and their ideas to the distant lands of the North and the West.

The advantages common to the whole basin of the
Mediterranean are concentrated in a pre-eminent degree
and assume an outstanding importance in the eastern section.
The Ægean Sea marks the point where the basin of the sea
branches north-east as the Bosphorus and the Euxine and
south-east as the Levant, which in its turn leads on the one
side to the Nile and the Red Sea and on the other towards
the Euphrates and the Persian Gulf. It is there that the
three parts of the world washed by the Mediterranean come
closest to one another and it is there that the nations have
learnt to distinguish them. There Europe and Asia
throw out towards each other, opposite to Africa, peninsulas
barely separated by narrow sounds and almost united by
archipelagos. There upheavals of the most violent character
have produced the most chaotic jumble of depressions and
heights, of marine trenches and rocky islands, of plains and
mountains. There on lofty slopes the change from the dry
heat of the South to the moist coolness of the North is most
abrupt and the vegetation presents the greatest variety.

There, above all, is the focus where races and civilizations
most readily concentrated, where they were refined by the
most fruitful contrasts, and where the irradiation of their
influence was most intense. When Zeus, in order to mark
the centre of the earth, released two eagles at the extremities
of the sky and ordered them to fly towards each other, they
met in Hellas.

It is necessary, therefore, before studying the earliest
of the Mediterranean civilizations, to examine more thoroughly
the influence which the sea, the land, and the climate exercised
upon the men who created that civilization. When we have
seen the characteristic features of the Mediterranean in general
revealed particularly strongly on the shores of the Ægean,
we shall understand better how a civilization, born on the
island lying nearest both to Asia and to Egypt, spread over
the neighbouring countries of Europe, and, after having

conquered the Greeks, roused from their lethargic slumber the barbarians of the remotest shores.

The Sea.—Most beautiful of all the seas, the Mediterranean, with its waves of transparent azure, has also proved in history the most useful and beneficent. Consider its general situation, its endless ramifications. It is ready for every kind of service. Europe, worn down into peninsulas, extends three of them into its midst. Of these three the most remarkable is the eastern one, the Balkan peninsula. Near its base in the trunk of the continent it is continued by a fourth peninsula, Asia Minor, which runs out to meet it, and it has an appendage in the Hellenic peninsula which, cleft by the Gulf of Corinth, itself terminates in a last peninsula, the Peloponnese. Thus the Ægean Sea is wonderfully carved out between the coasts of Thrace, Asia Minor, and Greece. In the North-East, two straits, which are veritable sea-rivers, link it with the Euxine, while bold promontories ensure communication between the European and Asiatic coasts. From Greece and Asia Minor little peninsulas advance towards each other like the abutments of bridges, having the innumerable islands for their piers. Several archipelagoes in parallel lines stake out the path from Europe to Asia. Right to the South, from Cape Malea to the peninsula of Knidos, a last row of islands closes the Ægean Sea with a curved barrier, which not only is a link between Europe and Asia but curves down as far as Crete so as to approach Africa also. Thus a large lake, regularly supplied with inlets, stretches from the straits which lead to the Hyperborean regions to the waves which are borne by currents towards the strand of Egypt. Fretting away the mountains which frame it, the sea has scooped out on every side deep gulfs, bays of sinuous outline, channels easy of access, and an uninterrupted succession of precipitous cliffs, of harbours, and of creeks. There is no region in the world which, in proportion to the area of the land, presents such a highly developed coastline.

Man, in these countries, is irresistibly attracted by the sea. Here the oar seems as necessary to him as the plough or the shepherd's crook. On every side there is land at no great distance, inviting men to exchange their surplus goods for others which they lack. There is no coast from which an island is not visible. The mariner can scud along towards a succession of bournes which are always in sight. There is no distance between them. Long voyages can be made without any feeling that one is lost between the sky and the water. While, on a voyage eastwards or westwards, chains of islands serve to mark the ports of call, a crossing northwards or southwards is facilitated by the movements of the sea ; in the middle a great current flows from North to South, flanked by counter-currents that skirt the coasts of Greece and Asia Minor from South to North. Whichever direction he takes, the navigator finds wonderful facilities along his path.

But he must beware of the wind. The atmospheric system of the Mediterranean varies very much with the seasons. From spring to autumn the alternation of breezes enables the fisherman to put out in the evening and return in the morning without danger. At the same time the winds from the North assert themselves until they become absolute masters. These are the so-called Etesian winds which, with powerful breath, blow the vessels from the Cyclades towards Crete and from Crete towards Egypt. But in winter the succession of sea and land breezes disappears in a general tumult. Barometric variations lead to violent and local inrushes of air at all times. Aiolos instals his windbags on every coast and opens them all together. The winds blow against each other, come into collision, and, lashing up a tempest, produce a short, irregular, and irresistible swell, or set prodigious masses of water whirling in dreadful cyclones. Gloomy Notos pours down rain in waterspouts without preventing clear Boreas from bringing snow and hail. Among blinding downpours, abrupt veerings of the wind, shattering waves, lowering skies, and sudden spells of darkness, the intrepid mariner loses sight of the north-star. Too late he perceives that to hoist sail would be fatal and that his oars are useless.

Navigation, therefore, in the Mediterranean, and particularly in the Ægean Sea, is governed by imperative rules. The " Nautical Instructions " drawn up by Hesiod were dictated to him by the experience of centuries. Long before, the man of the Ægean had learnt the art of battling with the elements and of submitting to nature in order to subdue her to his desires. The Ægean Sea became the naval school from which lessons were handed on to all the nations of the world. While the civilized peoples of the Nile, Euphrates, and Tigris and the barbarous tribes of Europe confined their efforts to river craft, the inhabitants of a country with but a scanty provision of navigable river-mouths were led on by way of fishing and coasting to lengthy voyages ; they fixed the principles of nautical science and built fleets which for centuries ensured their empire of the sea.

" Hydrophobic " civilizations might develop in other lands ; here an " amphibious " civilization flourished. The influence of the Ægean Sea was so powerful that all the races which ruled successively upon its shores were stamped with the same imprint ; the Cretans of the prehistoric period created the first thalassocracy that ever existed ; the Hellenes had hardly taken up their abode on the shores that were to hold them for ever before they were transformed into sailors. Penned up in their islands or their mountain enclosures, all these men own the sea as their common fatherland. " Peoples of the Sea "—that is the name which is given to them in Egypt. Wherever their ships can penetrate they are at home. It costs them nothing to change their dwelling-place. From North to South, from East to West, Hellenes and pre-Hellenes move freely about the Mediterranean. From one end to the other, they make it their own sea. Without going away from the coast they occupy its circumference, " like frogs round a pond," as Plato says. They trade where they will, they take up their abode where they can. Maritime trade and colonization, great novelties in the history of the world, come from the Ægean.

The Surface of the Land.—The land has contributed no less than the sea to the moulding of these peoples. All the windings of the coastline show the unevenness of the surface inland. Heights and plains are intermingled in indescribable confusion. There are no spacious plains save that of Thessaly. If ever a valley attains any length it is hemmed in by mountains all the way. Thus the Ægean world is broken up into an infinity of fragments, islands of restricted size, or cantons almost hermetically closed save on the side facing the sea.

Each of these islands and cantons has its own life. Nowhere else has nature placed side by side so many distinct compartments. There are as many states as there are habitable

centres. A few thousand men owning a few fields on the
plain, some woods and pastures in the mountains, a mound
serving as a refuge in case of danger, a market for home
exchanges, and a port for communication with the rest of the
world ; that is all, and there we have the framework of a self-
governing and sovereign community.

A structure which inevitably entails an utter lack of political
unity exposes a people to invasions. Every time the warlike
tribes of the Balkans yield to the attractions of the South
they are able to creep or to break in without meeting any
strong resistance, and thus the primitive population is
swallowed up in successive incursions of Greek tribes.
But though it is not without dangers, the spontaneous
particularism which sprang up on the shores of the Ægean
produces an ample harvest of benefits. In this infinite variety
of little communities all natural gifts develop with ease ;
in this atmosphere of absolute freedom men realize all their
faculties. The Ægean, from one end to the other, tingles
with an inexhaustibly fruitful vigour. The spirit of
independence which animates towns and individuals urges
them to a constant rivalry fraught with serious drawbacks
and immense advantages. Competition, the source of progress,
rises here from the very womb of the earth.

But the diversity of individual and collective efforts could
only be welded into a higher civilization through the help
of the sea. It was the sea that gave the mountains their
special value. In the great plain-lands all is monotony.
The same soil and the same climate produce the same plants
and the same animals in every part. The men, sunk in
natural surroundings that are always the same, perpetually
reproduce an unvarying type. Gestures and thoughts petrify
into immutable traditions. In mountainous countries the
valleys differ according to their lie, their altitude and their
geological composition. Each has its individuality, its own
products, and its own life. But, when the mountains tower
up in the middle of a continent, the scattered centres are
separated by such a barrier and their intercourse is so infrequent
that neighbouring populations are hardly acquainted with
each other and never succeed in deriving profit from their
diversity. On the one hand, uniformity of civilization makes
facilities of intercourse valueless ; on the other hand, lack of

intercourse renders varied civilization sterile. Here, however, we have a country where the mountains encounter on all sides the " liquid plain " ; it is cut up into an infinite number of compartments and groups which, however, share everything together. Here the disadvantages, which are, moreover, inherent in the natural advantages, disappear. Self-government is in no way an enforced isolation ; constant relations and daily exchanges excite continual comparisons and assist the development of a civilization unifying all the contrasts in one supreme harmony.

The Climate.—The Mediterranean countries include the hottest part of the temperate zone. On the whole, a gentle heat prevails there. This exquisite climate is at its kindliest in the Ægean countries. During the season which should be torrid, and during the hours when the sun is at its height, the sea-breeze blows. All through the burning dog-days the Etesian winds bring ever renewed coolness. Nevertheless, the Ægean countries do not by any means rejoice in eternal spring. In spite of all, they have scorching Libya for one of their neighbours and the bleak Balkans for another. At different points of the same latitude they present fairly violent contrasts. The seasons are quite distinct here. The fresh winds of summer do not prevent a dryness that lasts for months. Winter brings weeks of heavy rain and days of frost. The continual changes of altitude bring correspondingly abrupt changes of temperature ; a few hours' walk transports the traveller from the tropics to the cold regions.

One can imagine the effects produced by this climate upon man. The populations of the North devote an enormous measure of their work and their resources to a perpetual struggle against cold and bad weather ; in the tropical regions the drowsy uniformity of the heat relaxes the springs of human energy. The peoples of the intermediate regions do not have to become hardened in all-absorbing and costly struggles nor, on the other hand, need they grow incurably soft. Neither the summer drought nor the winter rain diminishes their activities. The alternations of heat and cold fortify and temper their bodies. A type of man is produced who is vigorous and firm, supple and wiry, spare and active. These are physical qualities, but they have their moral and intellectual value.

Nowhere has man fewer material exigences to contend with than on the Mediterranean. With the bracing air he breathes he has no need of heavy and substantial food. A cake or bowl of barley-soup, a handful of olives and figs, a couple of onions or a clove of garlic are all the Ægean asks as food for the day. He is naturally a vegetarian. He likes fish, but he eats meat only on feast-days, after the sacrifice. His ordinary drink is water. Although wine abounds he never drinks it neat. His clothing is neither thick nor tight. In prehistoric Crete it covers the waist and loins but leaves the torso completely exposed, at all events the chest. As this dress does not hamper a man's freedom of movement, his carriage is upright, easy, and of natural and unconscious majesty. The housing question is considerably simplified by the sun. None of the rooms are air-tight ; closed apartments are only used for sleeping purposes. The greater part of the day is spent in the open air. The men are outside all day long ; the women stay at home but are not imprisoned between four stifling walls. A spacious courtyard surrounded by colonnades which open at the back into sparsely furnished little rooms is all that is required for home life.

A life so easy as this enables everyone to enjoy the leisure which, in countries of unceasing labour and continual strain, is the privilege of the few rich. Why should one labour for ever ? Pleasures abound on all sides and can be had for the mere stretching out of the hand. Each one participates according to his tastes in the gaiety which overspreads the whole of nature. Powers of observation are sharpened by a curiosity ever on the alert ; vision becomes surer and intelligence quicker. Apprehension is swift. Ideas detach themselves instantly from objects ; though subtle they remain precise. They arise from all sides and suit all. It is in the fresh air that the spirit bloweth where it listeth.

These idlers, who do not need to be specialists in order to be connoisseurs, owe to the mildness of the climate another benefit—the sense of beauty. Open-air life and the lightness of their attire are a perpetual inducement for the Ægeans to dance and to practise gymnastic exercises. The eye teaches the hand to imitate the forms and movements of the bodies which it is accustomed to behold in all attitudes. Dancing furthers the lyric art, both music and words. On the shores of the Ægean art and poetry assume at birth a character both original and ineradicable. In this airy land, beneath a cloudless sky, shapes stand out distinctly ; lines keep their sharpness to the farthest limits of vision ; distant objects seem nearer and it is easy to understand why painters in these parts were so long in discovering the laws of perspective. There is no shading off of colours or of lines. Colours are not merged together in greys but stand out in vigorous contrast. Upon men with a sense of the beauty of things such natural surroundings had a powerful influence.

The Products.—On the whole the soil of the Ægean countries is poor. The smallest plot of cultivable land acquires an inestimable value. Where it is in any way possible to use the plough the question of water straightway arises. Lying between the northern zone, where west winds bring rain at all seasons, and the zone of the deserts, which suffers from drought all the year round, the Mediterranean zone is characterized by wet winters and dry summers. In the Ægean countries the drought lasts for about four months. The winter rains are brief but violent. The waters under the earth are renewed in a few days, sometimes in a few hours.

The conditions of rainfall determine the circumstances peculiar to Mediterranean flora. Northwards, grass and deciduous trees cover vast areas with spontaneous vegetation, and cultivation on a large scale is easy. Southwards, the only form of vegetation is confined to oases and, at that, is very stiff and thorny. The Mediterranean countries suit small plants that can sprout during the autumnal rains and ripen in the spring. Forests take the form of copses through which the light penetrates freely. The trees and shrubs that can be cultivated successfully are those with long roots, enabling them to suck up the moisture hidden away in deep places. But in the Ægean world, more than anywhere else, geological differences and the variations of altitude and temperature prevent any unity in the distribution of vegetation and cultivable ground. It is impossible for plants to spread over large surfaces. All expansion in the mass is denied to them. Here there is no question of anything but autonomy and variety.

The Ægean countries will never be storehouses of agricultural products. There the realm of agriculture must always be enlarged by odd scraps, by adding where possible waste land to the good ground in the valleys, by organizing the defence of the fields that have been wrested from the mountains, and above all by fetching water by artificial means. Gushing springs have to be diverted into canals, wells have to be bored and rain-water collected in cisterns. The drainage of all the water is effected with wonderful skill. Homer delights in describing the work of the fountain-maker, the flow of water filling the runnels, the murmur of the rushing stream, the joyous clamour of the little cascades. But the exuberance of vegetation in well-watered nooks must not be allowed to give a false impression of natural fertility and richness in the Ægean countries. It has been necessary everywhere to beguile the earth and the water, to think out methods suitable for each separate square yard, to cherish each plant with special solicitude, to practise ingenuity, to acquire the gift of invention, and to make of agriculture a kind of art. Wheat yields little, barley more, while farinaceous and aromatic products and condiments abound. The cultivation of trees and shrubs is successful, provided that ditches for watering them are kept up step for step. This is the native country of the vine. Long before it was consecrated to Dionysos it was the joy of prehistoric peoples. In the time of the Cretans the olive-tree was already supplying the finest of oils and from the earliest ages fruit that was good to eat was obtained by caprification from the fig-tree.

So much ground being unfit for cultivation, cattle-raising holds an important place in rural economy. The cattle spend almost the whole year out of doors and hardly know what stalls are. In winter they are kept in the pastures of the plains. Before the hot weather comes the flocks and herds make for the mountains in an endless string. This system of seasonal migrations is characteristic of pastoral life all along the Mediterranean ; it stands midway between the sedentary methods of temperate countries and the nomadism of the deserts. In the Ægean basin this system is carried to such a pitch that in the remotest times the Cretan shepherds had their winter village down below and their summer village up above.

In other countries it sometimes happens that insufficient productivity of the land is made up for by mineral resources and by industries. This is not at all the case in the Ægean world. During the Stone Age it was not always possible to find the flint which was of such great service in central and western Europe. Fortunately obsidian, which served the same purpose, was obtainable, though only on one island. At the time when the Cretans of prehistoric times knew bronze they could easily procure copper. They had to get their tin from distant parts. But nature, while refusing these peoples prompt riches, showered upon them the materials proper to artistic expression. They had only to make a gash in the earth where limestone abounded in order to extract admirable building stones, blocks of gypsum and tufa, soft to the chisel yet resisting the weather and, better still, the most beautiful marbles in existence. They had only to stoop down in the clayey valleys in order to obtain an inexhaustible supply of wonderfully fine and plastic potter's earth. In love with beauty, they had within their reach all they needed in order to realize it.

Supposing that the Ægean population becomes dense and neither industry nor agriculture and cattle-raising can satisfy its needs any longer—what is to be done then ? Trade. Is the land insufficient ? They turn to the sea. There is always a surplus stock of wine and oil left over from the last harvest. They carry it away, putting that of the finest quality, the most delicious vintage, into the most elegant vases with the best decorations. In exchange, they bring back metals and cereals. From island to island, from anchorage to anchorage, they go where necessary. Lying at the juncture of the ways which lead to the ends of the earth, the Ægean Sea links up all the peoples of antiquity. The roads only serve for bringing down the goods to the coast and feeding the sea trade of which the Ægean is the centre. Happy poverty, forcing the Ægeans at all times to turn the Mediterranean into one great market for the disposal of their goods and the spreading of their ideas !

From whatever point of view one considers the basin of the Mediterranean, it appears as the natural receptacle of a civilization which derives from it its special characteristics ;

from whatever point of view one considers the basin of the
Ægean, it accentuates with remarkable force the features
which distinguish the Mediterranean in its entirety and
thereby appoints itself the cradle of the aforesaid civilization.
What strikes one elsewhere in great countries of the East
is hugeness and uniformity ; production, power, and even
beauty are all matters of quantity. Here, the continual
diversity of nature leaves no room anywhere for large
agglomerations of plants, animals, or men. In no matter
what sphere, in politics as well as in art, it is impossible to
add sameness to sameness indefinitely. Here is the triumph
of autonomy and individualism, the free blossoming of natural
gifts with no other restriction than the necessity of a harmonious
organization. Nevertheless, in the narrow limits of a city
or an island, a civilization of this kind runs the risk of
exhausting its sap too soon and dying prematurely. But
then there is the sea, the great benefactress. By her means,
the Ægeans go out and seek the wealth and observe the
manners of other men. Thanks to her, they can settle in
distant lands, increase their country by numberless colonies
and, giving their civilization eternal youth, can carry it to
the confines of the known world. In sum, the " Greek
miracle ", nay, the Ægean miracle, is the effect produced
by a unique conjuncture of natural circumstances upon men
capable of profiting by it.

II The Excavations

Before the first years of this century we had no notion
of what Greece could have been like before the Greeks
were there. Like the ancient writers, we uttered such names
as Pelasgians, Carians, and Leleges, but it was only by an
effort of the imagination or by a retrospective interpretation
of historical facts and legends that we managed to go back
beyond Homeric times. True, we knew of some traces of
a very distant past, but we could not explain them. Curious
looking vases had come from Melos to the museum at Sèvres
and from Kephallenia to that at Neuchâtel [1] ; the excavations
at Ialysos and Kameiros in Rhodes had revealed deep strata
containing all kinds of objects which had no connexion with

[1] RA. 1900, i, 128 ff.

ancient Greece[1]; Fouqué had unearthed at Thera and
Therasia cities which had been buried by an eruption which
was supposed to have occurred before 2000 B.C.[2] Nobody
knew what all this was. Archæologists shook their heads
distrustfully.

From 1875 Schliemann, with Homer haunting his mind,
astonished the world by his splendid discoveries. Under his
triumphant spade Troy, Mycenæ, and Tiryns were reborn.[3]
But Schliemann thought that he had found the treasure of
Priam in the " Burnt City ", and never dreamed that Priam's
city was Troy VI, not Troy II, and that therefore the stratum
contemporary with the *Iliad* covered more than a thousand
years of history. He shook with emotion before the tombs
in which he thought he saw the bones of Agamemnon and
Klytaimnestra, but he should have said, with Horace,
" *Vixere fortes ante Agamemnona multi.*" In reality, at
Mycenæ, at Vapheio, and at many another point,[4] a whole
civilization was emerging from the darkness of centuries.
But what place did the Mycenæan civilization have in the
whole Ægean world ? What was its origin ? Was it the
end of a world or the beginning, dawn or dusk ?

Many had already foretold the importance which Crete
would assume in the history of pre-Hellenic societies.[5] In
1878 a merchant of Candia, prophetically named Minos
Kalokairinos, had established the site of Knossos and made
interesting remarks about it.[6] Schliemann visited the site
in 1886, and would have been glad to conjure up the shade
of Idomeneus. The French School at Athens tried to organize
excavations in 1891 and 1892. Crete attracted attention
more and more. Rapid explorations confirmed predictions.
Even in those early days archæologists were discovering
to their astonishment a Neolithic period (at Miamou)[7] and

---

[1] Furtwaengler, **XXX,** 1 ff., 80 ff. ; Perrot, **LXVII,** 463 ff.
[2] **XXVI,** 94 ff. ; cf. Renaudin, BCH. 1922, 113 ff.
[3] **LXXII-LXXIX ;** cf. **X.**
[4] Tsountas, 'Εφ., 1888, 197 ff. ; 1889, 129 ff. ; at Epidauros (Staïs,
Δελτίον, 1886, 155 ff.), at Aigina ('Εφ., 1895, 234 ff. ; cf. 1910, 177 ff. ;
Furtwaengler, *Aegina*, 370 ff., 435 ff.), at Amyklai (Tsountas, 'Εφ., 1892,
1 ff.).
[5] Milchhoefer, *Anfaenge der Kunst in Griechenland* (1883), 122–37 ; cf.
45 ff., 174 ff., 201 ff., 216 ff. ; Perrot, **LXVII** (1894), 458 ff.
[6] Stillman, *Arch. Inst. of America*, 1881, 47 ff.
[7] Taramelli, AJA. 1897, 287 ff.

a Chalcolithic period (at Hagios Onouphrios),[1] the fine vases
of the Kamares grotto,[2] and the funerary baths of Anogia
and Milatos.[3] Even then Evans was classifying the " pictographs " of a pre-Hellenic culture. Then it was, in 1900
to be exact, that the heroic age of the Cretan discoveries
commenced.

From 1900 to 1905, in a series of campaigns which form
an epoch in prehistoric archæology and have been supplemented
by discoveries of a more detailed nature, Evans has won a
king's share—Knossos.[4] He has brought to light a collection
of monuments without its like in the world, the Great Palace,
the Little Palace, the Royal Villa, and, further off, the
necropolis of Zapher Papoura and the royal tombs of Isopata.
By daring strokes of intuition, which are sometimes strokes
of genius, he has called up a society which began to exist in
the sixth millenium before Christ and progressed continuously
until it reached its apogee in the second millennium.

While he was achieving this magnificent work other British
scholars were working in the East of the island. Hogarth
explored the sacred grotto of Psychro[5] and the port of Zakro,[6]
while Bosanquet, Dawkins, and Myres explored Palaikastro
and its environs, including the Neolithic site of Magasa and
the sanctuary of Petsofa.[7] At the same time the Italians,
who had previously visited the Kamares grotto, took in hand
the plain of the Messara in the South. Near the mouth of
the Lethaios, Pernier, Halbherr, Savignoni, and Paribeni
cleared the palace of Phaistos,[8] which vied with that of Knossos,
and the palace of Hagia Triada,[9] which was smaller but was
full of works of art. The region of the Eastern isthmus was
reserved by the Americans ; Seager made important discoveries

---

[1] Evans, **XII**, 112 ff.
[2] Mariani, MA. vi (1895), 331 ff. ; Taramelli, loc. cit., 1901, 437 ff. ;
cf. Dawkins and Laistner, BSA. xix, 5 ff.
[3] Orsi, MA. i (1890), 203 ff., 208 ff.
[4] BSA. vi–xi ; **XVI ; XVIII ; XX ;** cf. **XIV, XIX.**
[5] BSA. vi, 94 ff. See, for the neighbouring town, Dawkins, ib., xx, 1 ff.
[6] Ib., vii, 121 ff. ; JHS. xxii, 76 ff., 333 ff.
[7] BSA. viii, 286 ff. ; ix, 274 ff., 356 ff. ; x, 192 ff. ; xi, 258 ff. ; Suppl.
Paper, i (1923).
[8] Pernier, MA. xii (1902), 8 ff. ; xiv (1904), 313 ff. ; Savignoni, ib.,
501 ff. ; Halbherr, MIL. xxi, v (1905), 248 ff. ; RL. 1905, 365 ff. ; 1907,
257 ff. ; Pernier, RL. 1908, 642 ff. ; ASI. 1914, 356 ff.
[9] Halbherr, MA. xiii (1903), 5 ff. ; MIL. loc. cit. ; cf. Paribeni, MA. xiv
(1905), 677 ff. ; xix (1908), 141 ff. ; Savignoni, ib., xiii, 77 ff.

Map I.—Pre-Hellenic Crete.

at Vasiliki, Pachyammos, Pseira and, above all, Mochlos,[1] Miss Boyd unearthed a whole town at Gournia,[2] and Miss Hall brought to light the cemetery at Sphoungaras.[3] The Cretans were inspired to emulation. In the Messara, Xanthoudidis attacked the *tholos* or bee-hive tombs (Koumasa,[4] Kalathiana,[5] Platanos,[6] etc.). In the East he discovered a large house of a singular type at Chamaizi,[7] and tombs of the period which closes the Bronze Age at Mouliana,[8] and he unearthed a sanctuary-palace at Nirou Chani near Candia.[9] Hatzidakis has devoted himself to the district near Knossos. He has explored the dwelling of a potentate at Tylissos,[10] a palace near a port at Mallia,[11] and a sacred grotto at Arkalochori.[12] This long list is only a brief résumé. According to Homer, Crete contained a hundred cities. Only half the island has yet been explored, and already more than a hundred sites prove that the poet did not exaggerate. The visitor to the Candia Museum, where most of the Cretan finds are kept, comes out marvelling.

All this time another civilization was coming to light in the Cyclades, different from both the Cretan and the Mycenæan cultures, but presenting remarkable points of resemblance to both. Even before the great Cretan discoveries the tombs of Amorgos,[13] Paros,[14] Siphnos,[15] and Syra [16] had yielded rich collections of vases, weapons, and statuettes, and at Chalandriani and at Hagios Andreas fortifications had been cleared similar to those of Troy, Mycenæ, and Tiryns.[17] Then came Naxos.[18] In Euboia pottery was found at Manika

[1] **LXXX-LXXXIII.**
[2] **XL.**
[3] **XXXIV.**
[4] Παναθήναια, Jan. 1905, Oct. 1906 ; cf. MA. xix, 207.
[5] JS. 1910, 127.
[6] ΑΔ, ι, ii (1915), 60 ff. ; ιι, ii (1916), 25 ff. ; cf. ιv, ii (1918), 16 ff.
[7] 'Εφ., 1906, 117 ff.
[8] Ib., 1904, 21 ff.
[9] BCH. 1920, 400.
[10] 'Εφ., 1912, 197 ff. ; cf. **XXXVIII.**
[11] ΑΔ. ii, 167. Excavations continued by Renaudin (BCH. loc. cit.).
[12] BSA. xix, 35 ff.
[13] Duemmler, AM. 1886, 15 ff., 209 ff. ; Tsountas, 'Εφ., 1898, 137 ff.
[14] Tsountas, loc. cit., cf. AM. 1919, 1 ff.
[15] Id., ib., 1899, 73 ff., 130 ff.
[16] Id., ib., 77 ff. ; Blinkenberg, MAN. 1896, 1 ff.
[17] 'Εφ., 1899, 118, 130 ff., pl. vii, 1, figs. 17–18.
[18] Stephanos, **LXXXV ;** Πρ., 1906, 86 ff. ; 1908, 114 ff. ; 1909, 209 ff. ; 1910, 270 ff.

which enables us better to establish the relations between
the Cyclades and the mainland.[1] Above all, the question
of Cretan and Mycenæan influences, which first arose in
connexion with the old finds at Thera and Rhodes, was solved
by the excavations at Delos,[2] and still more at Melos. On
this island the obsidian quarries have been found which
supplied the whole Ægean world for thousands of years,
and at Phylakopi three towns, one on the top of the other,
have been unearthed.[3] When light was thrown upon the
civilization of the mainland by the discovery of its relations
with the Cyclades and still more with Crete, archæologists
found that they could distinguish two great periods—the
" Mycenæan " period, in which external influences predominate,
and an earlier or " pre-Mycenæan " period, in which they are
hardly perceptible. To determine them better, excavations
were carried on with energy in the Peloponnese. At Mycenæ
itself Schliemann's discoveries were supplemented by
Tsountas[4] and further developed by Wace.[5] At Tiryns
the German School obtained good results.[6] In the neighbourhood Waldstein explored the Heraion[7] and Volgraff Argos.[8]
More recently the French School excavated Schoinochori[9]
and the Crown Prince of Sweden Asine.[10] Not far from
Vapheio and Amyklai there was found on the hill of the
Menelaeion the Mycenæan town which was succeeded by
Sparta.[11] The island of Kythera was recognized to be one of
the points by which Crete communicated with the mainland.[12]
The western coast proved to have been fringed with ports
belonging to wealthy chiefs—Tragana, near Pylos in Messenia,[13]
and Kakovatos, near Pylos in Elis.[14] Finally, the Gulf of
Corinth is surrounded by prehistoric sites—in the North

[1] Papavasileiou, **LXV.**
[2] Courby, *Expl. de Délos*, v (1912), 63 ff. ; CRAI. 15th Dec., 1922.
[3] **XXI ;** cf. BSA. iii, 35 ff., 71 ff. ; xvii, 1 ff.
[4] **LXXXIX.**
[5] *Times, Lit. Sup.*, 24th June, 19th Aug., 13th Oct., 1920, 26th Oct., 1922 ; BCH. 1921, 506 ff. ; cf. Rodenwaldt, JAI. 1919, 87 ff. ; **LXXI.**
[6] AM. 1905, 151 ff. ; 1907, 1 ff. ; 1911, 198 ff. ; 1913, 78 ff. ; 329 ff. ; cf. *AΔ*, ii, ii (1916), 15 ff. ; **LXX.**
[7] **XCII,** i, 41 ff., 79 ff. ; ii, 74 ff., 91 ff.
[8] BCH. 1904, 364 ff. ; 1906, 1 ff. ; 1907, 139 ff.
[9] Ib., 1920, 386 ff. ; 1921, 100 ff.
[10] CRAI. loc. cit ; BCH. 1921, 295 ff.
[11] 'Εφ., 1889, 130 ff. ; BSA. xv, 109 ff. ; xvi, 4 ff.
[12] Staïs, *AΔ*, i, 191 ff.
[13] Skias, *Πρ.*, 1909, 274 ff. ; Kourouniotis, 'Εφ., 1914, 98 ff.
[14] K. Mueller, AM. 1908, 295 ff. ; cf. 1909, 269 ff. ; 1913, 97 ff.

c

at Delphi,[1] whither according to the legend men came from Knossos by the port of Pylos, and in the East all over Corinthia. By numerous excavations, for example at Zygouries and Korakou,[2] the Americans have shown the early importance of the country of the Isthmus.

Indeed, Central Greece is not at all cut off from the Peloponnese, at any rate during the greater part of the prehistoric centuries; the same civilization, known as the " Helladic " civilization, is supreme in the Mycenæan and pre-Mycenæan periods from Cape Malea to Mount Othrys. Attica, although hidden behind Mount Parnes, comes within this sphere. It contains a great number of sites which the Athenians used to call " Pelasgian ".[3] One may mention Nisaia, the islet Minoa, Salamis, Eleusis, the Acropolis of Athens, Thorikos and, further inland, Spata, Menidi, and Aphidna. While the barren land of Attica was divided among a multitude of petty chieftains, the fat fields of Bœotia even in those early days saw a powerful king enthroned on the hills of Thebes, and from the palace discovered by Keramopoullos [4] we learn that he was the Kadmos of legend. On a rocky islet in Lake Kopaïs rose the fortified palace of Gla.[5] On the other side of the lake there were four towns in succession at Orchomenos.[6] The whole valley of the Kephissos, both in Bœotia and in Phokis, is full of pre-historic settlements. The most important are crowded round Chaironeia and Elateia. There we find the posts of Drachmani, Manesi, and Hagia Marina, where Sotiriadis obtained the essential data for Helladic history and chronology.[7] The Spercheios valley, with Lianokladi, belongs to the same civilization.[8] Further afield we find Helladic and Mycenæan remains in Akarnania and in Aitolia, especially at Thermos.[9] Further still comes the whole range of the Ionian Islands. The discoveries of Kavvadias at Kephallenia[10] and of Doerpfeld

---

[1] Perdrizet, *Fouilles de Delphes*, v, 1 ff.
[2] AJA. 1922, 298 ff. ; Blegen, **III** ; cf. Blegen and Wace, BSA. xxii, 176 ff.
[3] See **XXXII** ; cf. **XXV**, 6–9 ; **XXXI** ; **L.**
[4] **XLI.**
[5] De Ridder, BCH. 1894, 271 ff. ; cf. Noack, **LXII**, 19 ff.
[6] Schliemann, **LXXXIII** ; Bulle, **V** ; *AΔ*, i (1914), 51 ff.
[7] REG. 1912, 253 ff.
[8] **XCI**, 171 ff.
[9] Rhomaios, *Πρ.*, 1908, 95 ff. ; *AΔ*, i, 225 ff. ; ii, 179 ff.
[10] CRAI. 1909, 382 ff. ; 1911, 6 ff. ; *Πρ.*, 1912, 115 ff., 247 ff.; cf. **VII,** 355 ff.

at Leukas[1] prove uninterrupted occupation since the Neolithic Age. Moreover, the finds at Kephali,[2] in the extremity of Kerkyra, seem to point to a radiation of even this early culture towards Illyria and Italy.

Beyond Mount Othrys, Thessaly in its turn entered the domain of prehistoric archæology. The fine discoveries of Tsountas at Dimini and Sesklo set the example.[3] After many explorations, Wace and Thompson[4] were able to outline a general picture of Thessalian civilization. According to this, Thessaly for many centuries had connexion only with the Balkans. In consequence, the excavations conducted in Macedonia by the British and French[5] during the last war are of very great interest, for they partly fill the enormous lacuna which existed in pre-history between Thessaly and the region extending towards the Danube.

In Europe the background on which we see the illuminated circle of Ægean civilization is still very dim as soon as we leave Argolis ; in Asia Minor we are faced almost everywhere with inky darkness. We know the six towns which succeeded each other on the hill of Hissarlik until the Trojan War,[6] but the civilization there revealed is clearly of a European type, despite certain commercial relations with the Ægean world, and proves that the Hellespont was never an obstacle to intercourse. At Yortan there is nothing which recalls either the Isles or Hellas. It is no doubt possible that the native populations of Asia Minor, for example, the Carians, were subjected to Mesopotamian, and, above all, to Hittite influence; if we like we may even suppose, on the strength of some vague indications, that they passed on something of it to the Ægeans. But the excavations which should elucidate this problem are sadly lacking. Those which have been carried out so far, at Miletos[7] and at Phokaia,[8] only prove that, either as traders or as colonists, the Cretans and the Mycenæans arrived late

[1] *Briefe ueber Leukas-Ithaka*, i–vi; Velde, ZE. 1912, 852 ff.; 1913, 1156 ff.
[2] JAI. 1913, ii, 106 ff.
[3] **LXXXVIII;** cf. Arvanitopoullos, Πρ., 1907, 166 ff.; 1908, 163 ff., 180 ff., 212 ff.; 1909, 153 ff.; BCH. 1920, 395.
[4] **XCI.**
[5] Gardner and Casson, BSA. xxiii, 10 ff.; L. Rey, BCH. 1917–19.
[6] **LXXIV–LXXVI, X.**
[7] Wiegand, *Abh. der Berl. Akad.*, 1908, 7 ff.
[8] Sartiaux, CRAI. 1921, 122.

in these lands, as they arrived late in Cyprus and in Syria,
in Italy and in Sicily.

III Chronology

Despite so many lacunæ, it will be seen that an enormous
quantity of monuments of different kinds has risen from
the earth in the Ægean lands, and in Crete more than everywhere else. Therefore, before we can enter into the life of
societies which are yet little known, it is indispensable that
we should know the order in time of the palaces and cities,
the weapons, vases, seals, frescoes, and all the objects of
art which constitute the chief part of our data. We must
proceed to a chronological classification of the strata and
their contents.

To guide us in the Cretan Labyrinth we are offered a guiding
clue by Evans.[1] He attaches the whole of this civilization,
from the moment when it emerges from Neolithic Limbo
to the legendary king of Knossos, Minos, and calls it the
MIÑOAN civilization. There are three main Minoan ages—
Early Minoan (E.M.), Middle Minoan (M.M.), and Late Minoan
(L.M.). Each of these ages is subdivided into three periods,
I, II, and III.

Evans has justified his classification by exhibiting it on
the ground. He has dug a specimen trench at Knossos in
the Western Court of the palace. An analysis of this vertical
section [2] shows the following layers above the virgin rock.

Neolithic			6·43 metres.
		E.M.I	·33
	E.M. 1·33 metres	E.M.II	·56
		E.M.III	·44
Minoan and later layers 5·33 metres.		M.M.I	none at this point.
	M.M. 1·50 metres	M.M.II	·50
		M.M.III	1·00
	L.M. and later layers		2·50

[1] **XIV, XIX.**   [2] BSA. x, 19, fig. 7.

Many objections may be made to this system. First of all, the very term "Minoan" may give rise to misunderstandings. It has the advantage of being non-committal in respect of the ethnological question ; but it has this drawback, that if it is extended beyond Crete to the whole of the Ægean countries it suggests a unity which did not exist until after the fall of Minos, and if it is confined to Crete itself it traces back to the very beginning of things a political system which was only remembered at all by the Greeks because it was comparatively recent. However, taking everything into account, since the authority of Evans has invested the word with such respectability, we shall not deny ourselves the use of it, on the understanding that we confine it to Crete and that even in Crete we apply it especially to the period of the hegemony of Knossos. To avoid any complications from false or premature hypotheses we shall use simply "Ægean" for what belongs to the Ægean world in general and "Cretan" for what belongs to Crete.

The proposed divisions and subdivisions are seductive in virtue of their symmetry, which calls for no effort of the memory, so to speak. Evans, it is clear, combines the data of the stratification with the universal laws of evolution and the requirements of the human mind when he assumes with such regularity a period of growth leading to a period of apogee, followed by a period of decadence and transition. He now goes so far as to introduce the ternary system into the Neolithic Age.[1] Nevertheless, since his scholarly conscience has always taken into account new discoveries and well-founded objections, he has not been too uncompromising in the exact delimitation of the periods, and has not hesitated to modify the hard lines of his system. He has, for example, placed after the Neolithic Age proper a "sub-Neolithic" Period, forming part of E.M.I, and he divides each of the three M.M. periods, L.M.I, and L.M.III into phases *a* and *b*.

But it is not only between the Neolithic Age and the Early Minoan Period that the line separating the main epochs is less definite than the system supposes and requires amendment. Evans' sub-Neolithic Period is the beginning of the Chalcolithic Age, the Age of Copper, which extends over E.M.I and II ; but with E.M.III the appearance of bronze

[1] **XX**, 35 ff.

certainly requires that the commencement of a new age should be indicated. Moreover, the absence of any M.M.I objects in the specimen trench is all the more significant because the most characteristic fact of this period, the building of the First Palaces at Knossos and Phaistos, dates from the second phase *b* of the period; consequently phase *a* might be placed at the end of E.M. at least as fairly as at the beginning of M.M. Similarly, it is difficult to detach M.M.III *b*, which built the Second Palaces and saw all the arts start in a new direction, from the following period, in which the palaces shone in all their glory and the arts made good their promise. Again, L.M.II, which has left no trace whatever in many sites, including some of the most important, like Phaistos and Tylissos, and did not last more than half a century, can hardly be considered anything but the final phase of L.M.I. Lastly, between L.M.II and L.M.III the destruction of Knossos and the ruins covering all the island mark a new state of things—Crete has lost her supremacy.

Therefore, without breaking with an accepted practice or abandoning the logical and mnemonical advantages of the classification proposed by Evans, we would propose the following arrangement.[1]

Neolithic Age.
Chalcolithic Age = E.M.I and III.

Bronze Age
- First Bronze Age = E.M.III and M.M.I*a*.
- First Palace Age = M.M.I*b* and M.M.II, with M.M.III*a* attached.
- Second Palace Age = M.M.III*b* and L.M.I and II.
- Mycenæan Age = L.M.III.

This chronological system must be brought into line with those of the Cyclades and of the mainland.

The Cyclades offer no difficulty. They show no trace of a Neolithic population, although the obsidian at Melos was worked at a very early date. But it has been generally agreed to apply to the CYCLADIC civilization, age for age and period for period, the same classification as for the Minoan —E.C.I, II, and III, M.C.I, II, and III, L.C.I, II, and III.

Things on the mainland are much more complicated. There is no sign of Neolithic civilization in the Peloponnese any more than in the Cyclades. But it existed for a very long

[1] The arrangement to which we are led is almost identical with that proposed by Franchet, **XXVII**, 12.

time in Thessaly, where it had two periods—*Thessalian I*, lasting until the final century of E.M.II or E.C.II, and *Thessalian II*, extending roughly to the middle of M.M.I or M.C.I. It is not till then that there begins in Thessaly the Chalcolithic Age, or *Thessalian III*. The use of bronze and relations with the Ægean only come with *Thessalian IV*, which is contemporary with the whole of the Late Minoan Period.

Central Greece had been partly attached to the Thessalian civilization during the first Neolithic Period, but at the time of Thessalian II it became more and more closely connected with the Helladic civilization.

The HELLADIC civilization begins at the same time as that of the Cyclades. But its development is much slower. Early Helladic I (E.H.I) continues until the moment when central Greece begins to look southwards, E.H.II only commences towards the last quarter of E.M.II, and E.H.III commences about the last third of E.M.III. Shortly after the appearance of Thessalian III, about the middle of M.M.I, a new age is announced in Greece. Henceforward the periods of the Helladic civilization will correspond with those of the Minoan, but the former is so much behind that M.H.I finishes with M.M.II, and M.H.II with M.M.III. They are completely on a level only during the last three Late Helladic Periods. But we must make a grouping of the Helladic Periods as we have done with the Minoan. With M.H.II the great days of Mycenæ begin and the relations of the mainland with Crete develop, and therefore a division must be made there between *Pre-Mycenæan* and *Mycenæan*. Furthermore, the Mycenæan Age must be divided into (i) the period in which it is under Minoan influence, the *Early Mycenæan* (M.H.II, L.H.I, and L.H.II = M.M.II, L.M.I, and L.M.II), and (ii) the period in which it absorbs Crete, the *Late Mycenæan* (L.H.III = L.M.III).

The relative chronology which we obtain by the comparison of the objects discovered in the Ægean can fortunately be made into an absolute chronology by the comparison of these objects with those of countries of which we can read the writing and so fix certain dates. We have here a mute archæology, but a speaking archæology comes to its help. Egypt was in almost constant relations with prehistoric Crete. If an Egyptian object of certain date is found in a determined stratum of an Ægean site it communicates its date to that stratum. If an Ægean object is found in Egypt in a dated monument, or bears the cartouche of a Pharaoh, it gives an approximate date to the class to which it belongs.[1] Thus we obtain a series of partial conclusions which confirm each other by continual counter-checks.

At Knossos, on the boundary of the Neolithic and Sub-Neolithic strata, a flat-necked vase of syenite was found,[2] of a type which is only found in Egypt and is only known there in the pre-dynastic period and under the two first dynasties, that is before 2895 B.C. Other vases of hard stone of the same origin have been found in later strata, but they can only have reached Crete at the time of the earliest dynasties —a porphyry vase which must belong to the IInd Dynasty,[3] and some diorite bowls similar to those of the IVth and Vth Dynasties found in the tomb of King Seneferu (2840–2829) and in a temple of King Sahura (2673–2661).[4] Now it was on such models as these that the Cretan stone-cutters carved the beautiful vases of Mochlos in E.M.II.[5] Further evidence for the beginning of the early Minoan Period is supplied by some bowls with feet found in a sub-Neolithic stratum, which are made of a clay which is not Cretan, and are of a type which is found at Abydos under the Ist Dynasty, that is about the end of the fourth millennium.[6] E.M.II, while it takes us back with some stone vases to the IVth Dynasty (2840–2680), brings us with other vases,[7] with certain faience beads,[8] and with some button-shaped seals[9] down to the VIth (2540–2390). This long duration quite agrees with the evidence of the strata. It will be remembered that the three Early Minoan strata are 33, 56, and 44 centimetres thick.

---

[1] The reader might here be referred to the chapter on the " International Relations " of the Ægean world (Book II, Chap. V) ; but it seems desirable to set forth in one place the whole of the chronological data which have been obtained from those relations, with further information and in more precise detail.

We adopt the chronology generally accepted to-day for Egypt, the " reduced " chronology, which is supported by Ægean evidence.

[2] **XX**, figs. 28, 31.
[3] Ib., fig. 32.
[4] Ib., figs. 54–5.
[5] **XXV**, 168–9.
[6] **XX**, fig. 17.
[7] Ib., figs. 60–1.
[8] Ib., fig. 53.
[9] Cf. **XXV**, 155.

Since the two first require about six centuries, it is fair to allot two of these to E.M.I (3000–2800) and four to E.M.II (2800–2400).[1] For the same reason three may be assigned to E.M.III (2400–2100). And indeed the Cretan seals of this period often bear the same designs as the "Egypto-Libyan" seals of the period from the end of the VIth Dynasty to the end of the XIth (2390–2000).

M.M.I*a* is dated at Platanos by a Babylonian cylinder of hæmatite[2] and M.M.I*b* at Psychro by a scarab.[3] The cylinder represents divine personages of whom the type and costume are not known in Chaldæa before the time of Khammurabi (2123–2081). Since it can be placed among the earliest examples of its kind, and since the pottery accompanying it is of the kind which immediately preceded the First Palaces, it fixes the foundation of these palaces about 2000. The scarab is of a type peculiar to the Egypt of the XIIth Dynasty (2000–1788). But on the one hand it cannot be much later than M.M.I*a*, because it bears a representation of a vase which by its shape belongs to that period ; on the other hand, it comes very close to M.M.II by the beauty of the work executed on hard stone. Therefore M.M.I*b* can hardly be longer than M.M.I*a*, and one may allow two centuries for the whole period (2100–1900).

These dates are confirmed by those of the following period. The days have come when Crete exports the magnificent vases of Kamares and the beautiful work of her goldsmiths and armourers. About 1900 the tombs of the three daughters of Amenemhat II (1935–1903) receive jewels and a dagger of a style which predominates in M.M.II.[4] At Kahun the most ancient pottery of M.M.II arrives while they are working at the pyramid of Senusert II (1903–1887) and the most recent arrives under the first kings of the XIIIth Dynasty, down to about the middle of the XVIIIth century. At Abydos (Fig. 34) the purest Kamares ware is associated with cylinders of Senusert III (1887–1849) and Amenemhat III (1849–1801). Knossos supplies a counter-check : under the ruins of the First Palace there lay a diorite statuette [5] which Egyptologists assign to the end of the XIIth Dynasty or the beginning

---

[1] Cf. **XX**, 70, 102.   [2] Ib., fig. 146.
[3] Ib., fig. 147.   [4] **IV**, 221–2, 268.
[5] **XX**, fig. 220.

of the XIIIth.   Thus the Middle Minoan Period begins about 2100, and the history of the First Palaces is confined between 2000 and 1750.

For the third Middle Minoan Period we have no such abundance of synchronisms as for the previous two.   Relations with Egypt cease abruptly.   But this very fact is significant. The rupture is due to the misfortunes which rained on Egypt in the last century of the XIIIth Dynasty (1788–1660) and to the invasion of the Hyksos (1675–1580).   Moreover, we have first-class evidence for the date of the end of M.M.IIIa, in the shape of vases of that time which were found at Knossos with an alabaster lid bearing the cartouche of King Khian,[1] whose accession is placed about 1633.[2]

With the Late Minoan Period and the XVIIIth Dynasty, on the other hand, there begins an epoch in which the relations of Egypt with Crete, and soon after with the Ægean world, are suddenly so active that we obtain precise dates on every side.   The comparison of the weapons deposited in the tomb of Aahhetep, the mother of Aahmes, with the famous daggers of Mycenæ [3] shows that the limit between the Middle Minoan and Late Minoan Periods coincides with the accession of the new dynasty (1580).   A whole series of vases of Egyptian alabaster, placed in the royal tomb at Isopata, has a parallel in a series found in the tombs at Abydos with objects dating from the juncture of the XVIIth and XVIIIth Dynasties or with scarabs of Thothmes III (1501–1447).[4]   In Egypt L.M.I vases are found in burials of the first half of the XVth century,[5] and the paintings show the " Keftiu " bringing vases of similar types (Fig. 35).   Cartouches of Amenhetep III (1415–1380) are found all over the Ægean at the end of L.M.II and the beginning of L.M.II.   From then onwards Mycenæan pottery abounds in Egypt.[6]   At Tell el-Amarna the palace of Akhenaten (1380–1362) is full of it.   At Gurob, whither L.M.I ware came under Thothmes III, L.M.III stirrup-vases are found in masses with the cartouches of the last kings of the XVIIIth Dynasty down to Tutankhamen (1362–50) and also with those of the kings of the XIXth Dynasty down to Rameses II (1300–1234), Meneptah (1235–24), and Seti II

[1] Ib., fig. 304b.
[2] R. Weill, Rec. des Mém., vi (1915), 47.
[3] Cf. XX, figs. 537–8.
[4] XVI, pl. xcix ; cf. XXV, 173–4.
[5] XXV, 160–1.
[6] Ib., 161 ff.

CRETE	CYCLADES	PELOPONNESE	CENTRAL GREECE	THESSALY
NEOLITHIC (6000 ?–3000)	—	—	—	—
E.M.I (3000–2800)	E.C.I	E.H.I (3000–2500)	THESSALIAN I (NEOLITHIC I) (3500–2500)	THESSALIAN I (NEOLITHIC I) (3500–2500)
E.M.II (2800–2400)	E.C.II			
E.M.III (2400–2100)	E.C.III	E.H.II (2500–2200)	THESSALIAN II (NEOLITHIC II) (2500–2000)	THESSALIAN II (NEOLITHIC II) (2500–2000)
M.M.I (2100–1900)	M.C.I	E.H. III (2200–2000)		
M.M.II (1900–1750)	M.C.II	M.H.I (2000–1750)	THESSALIAN III (CHALCOLITHIC) (2000–1580)	THESSALIAN III (CHALCOLITHIC) (2000–1580)
M.M.III (1750–1580)	M.C.III	M.H.II		
L.M.I (1580–1450)	L.C.I	L.H.I	THESSALIAN IV (BRONZE) (1580–1200)	THESSALIAN IV (BRONZE) (1580–1200)
L.M.II (1450–1400)	L.C.II	L.H.II		
L.M.III (1400–1200)	L.C.III	L.H.III		

CRETE groupings:
- CHALCO-LITHIC
- BRONZE
  - First Bronze Age (2400–2000)
  - First Palaces (2000–1750)
  - Second Palaces (1700–1400)

CYCLADES groupings:
- CHALCO-LITHIC
- BRONZE

PELOPONNESE groupings:
- CHALCOLITHIC
- BRONZE
  - Pre-Mycenæan
  - Early Mycenæan (Creto-Mycenæan)

CENTRAL GREECE groupings:
- PRE-HELLENIC
- ACHAIANS

LATE MYCENÆAN (MYCENÆAN EXPANSION) (1400–1200)

(1218–14). Thus we can date L.M.I from 1580 to 1450, L.M.II from 1450 to 1400, and L.M.III from 1400 to 1200.

The table on page 27 summarizes the general outlines of the chronology of Ægean civilization.

IV Historical Survey of the Ægean Peoples

Before we fit the Ægean civilization into the framework which we have described above, we still have to place it in its historical setting. The enterprise is a perilous one. Until the day when it becomes possible to decipher the many tablets which Crete has left us the history of the Ægean is only pre-history. It is based on mute documents. By looking at buildings and tombs, the articles with which they are furnished, and the scenes depicted by painters and sculptors, we come to some knowledge of the character of the population and its life, material, economic, social, religious, and artistic. We may even find points of comparison in the other societies of the same epoch, or instructive commentaries in the legends of the Greece which was to be. But what idea can we form of the events which favoured or disturbed the development of civilization ? Over this essential question hangs an inexorable silence. At the best we sometimes trace between two successive strata the marks of fire and destruction, or perhaps certain changes, more or less abrupt, which interrupt the regularity of development. At the best the Egyptian documents mention at rare intervals the " peoples of the sea " or the Keftiu, or tradition has saved for the Greeks a few vague memories of their precursors. Nevertheless we must endeavour, with these rare and meagre sources of information, to see what were, from the Stone Age to Hellenic times, the peoples of the Ægean, and especially those Cretans who made their island the true centre of the prehistoric Mediterranean.

It is in Crete that we must start. When the companions of Æneas are bidden by the god to return to the cradle of their race—" *Antiquam exquirite matrem* "—Anchises has no doubts

> " *Creta Jovis magni medio jacet insula ponto,*
> *Mons Idæus ubi et gentis cunabula nostræ* . . .
> *Ergo agite* . . . *et Cnossia regna petamus.*" [1]

[1] Virgil, *Æneid*, iii, 94 ff.

Let us too go to Crete, the ancient mother, and seek at Knossos
the cradle of a civilization which enabled the Greeks to create
the civilization which has become ours.

The great island stands at the centre of the eastern Mediterranean—μέσῳ ἐνὶ οἴνοπι πόντῳ, as Homer [1] said, whom
Virgil has copied. The advantages of its position caught the
eye of Aristotle at a day when historical conditions hardly
allowed him to profit by them.[2] " It seems made by nature
to rule over Greece. Its situation is remarkably fine. It
dominates the sea around which all the Greeks are settled.
On one side it is a short way from the Peloponnese, on the
other it faces the part of Asia about Cape Triopion and Rhodes."
If we add that it is at equal distance from Troy and the mouths
of the Nile, from the Argive Gulf and Cyrenaïca, from Cyprus
and Sicily, from Syria and Italy, and that it is thus the land
nearest to all three continents, we may conclude with Aristotle,
" That is why Minos held the empire of the sea and conquered
or colonized the islands." With all these facilities for receiving
products and influences from outside, or for itself acting on
other countries, it owes to its insular position the benefits of
independence and that security for the morrow which inspires
fertile initiative and audacity of the spirit. This little world,
which could so easily be thrown open or closed, according to
its needs, was itself to supply, on pain of falling short of its
destiny, the resources required to feed a sufficiently dense
population or to obtain elsewhere what was lacking. With a
length of 260 kilometres and a maximum breadth of 57, Crete
has an area of 8,000 square kilometres. It is large enough not
only to draw the small islands into its orbit but to live on itself.
Three mountain ranges—Dikte with the Lasithi Mountains
(the ancient Aigaion) in the East, Ida in the centre, and the
White Mountains in the West—reduce the habitable surface,
but supply the wealth of their forests and their pastures.
Thanks to numerous valleys it is possible to grow corn, vines,
and olives close up to the high summits. The sea enters into
the depressions enough to form isthmuses which ensure easy
communication between North and South. In the centre,
however, it has spared two plains running East and West—
that in the North which is overlooked by Mount Iouktas, and

---

[1] *Odyssey*, xix, 172.   [2] *Politics*, ii, 7, 2.

is watered in the middle by the Kairatos, the river of Knossos, and in the South the Plain of the Messara, where the Lethaios runs, the river of Phaistos. Homer once more tells us what the great island was before his day : " Fair, fat, well-watered, it has men beyond numbering and ninety cities."

Neolithic Age (6000 ?–3000)

Of all the Ægean lands, Crete is that which presents the most ancient civilization. It was not, however, inhabited so early as many other regions of the globe. In the age when Greece and Asia Minor were not yet separated by the sea, the vast Ægean world was the domain of monstrous beasts, but there is no sign yet of the presence of man. He first appeared there after the cataclysm. Otherwise, the Ægean regions would all have been populated together from the Palæolithic Age. As it was, they were only peopled later, one after the other, by immigrations of different populations. Crete itself, which comes at their head, does not appear in pre-history until the Neolithic Age.

In those times, men first lived in caves or in shelters beneath rocks. Then they built round mud huts with stone floors, such as the " hut-foundation " discovered at Phaistos, or else they adopted the rectangular form of house made of unhewn stones. The sea, by which they had come, held them to its shores. They scarcely practised any agriculture ; no grinders have been found in their dwellings. Gleaning, stock-breeding, hunting, and fishing were their chief means of existence ; the remains of their food consist of shells and bones of sheep, cattle, hares, and boars.

Gradually they abandoned the use of sandstone and lime-stone for their tools and axes, and adopted hard stones such as serpentine, jadeite, and hæmatite, which they polished carefully. Their weapons and tools were of bone, horn, and stone. To complete their equipment they had obsidian. This vitreous rock, which is easily split into fine blades with sharp edges and is therefore suitable for the manufacture of knives, razors, and arrow-heads, did the same duty in Ægean lands as the flint in northern Europe. They brought it from Melos, which possesses excellent quarries. The pottery, which at first was very coarse and badly baked, was later decorated with incised lines, filled in with a white substance, and was finely polished by hand. Spindle weights and bobbins show how the women were employed. The idols of clay, and later of steatite, represent a steatopygous goddess who symbolizes fertility. The absence of any tomb or skeleton indicates that the dead were buried close to the surface, perhaps beneath the dwellings.

In this way the peoples of Crete lived for long ages, progressing slowly but continuously. While the women kept the house, spinning and weaving, and the men fed the flocks, ranged the woods, or braved the sea, the huts fell to pieces beneath the weather, new huts were built over them to fall in their turn, and from year to year, from century to century, from millennium to millennium, the earth was covered by deep layers, by which to-day we measure the slow passage of time.

CHALCOLITHIC OR CRETO-CYCLADIC PERIOD (3000–2400)

Three thousand years went by. Towards the end of the fourth millennium a great change took place all over the basin of the Ægean. Already, perhaps about 3500, the culture common to the Danubian countries and southern Russia had penetrated into Thrace, into Macedonia, and into Thessaly, and in its slow advance it was to reach Leukas, to conquer Phokis and Bœotia, and even to gain a point on the Gulf of Corinth. Despite local variations, the unity of this civilization is attested by pottery of gay and brilliant colour which is found in the *toumbes* of Macedon and the *magoulas* of Thessaly, and as far as the round houses of Orchomenos I. But the two Neolithic cultures, that of Crete and that of the mainland, nowhere came into contact. Between the two lay the desert mass of the Peloponnese and the whole breadth of a sea of islands still uninhabited. But about 3000 it was no longer so.

In the Ægean and in all the East there is a vast movement of peoples. The Peloponnese and the Cyclades emerge from nothingness ; the whole Ægean world is populated. Of what race were these first inhabitants ? Whether we call them Pelasgians, as the later Greeks generally did, or Carians, as Thucydides would have it, they were probably already of very different origins ; in different islands they had long heads or short heads, so that it would seem that in one place a Mediterranean stock predominated, and in the next an Asiatic. In any case they were not Hellenes, nor even Aryans, and they did not come from the continent of Europe by way of Thessaly, for the Thessalian civilization alone remained untouched by these upheavals. Certainly their arrival has some connexion with the migrations which about this time were changing the face of nearer Asia. Near the Hellespont the hill of Hissarlik is inhabited for the first time. Cyprus, where the Stone Age has left no trace whatever, is invaded by peoples who at first live by fishing on the coast and later penetrate inland towards the mines. In Syria, Byblos enters into relations with Egypt. In the land of Canaan the Neolithic Age comes to an end. In all this seething movement Greece is shaping itself, long before the Greeks, with all the indefiniteness of first beginnings.

At the same time, another civilization announces its arrival. Metal appears. The various uses of stone are not all suddenly abandoned, and obsidian will serve for a long time yet for the manufacture of knives, scrapers, and especially arrow-heads. But the principal weapons and pointed or cutting tools are now made of copper, while jewels are made of gold and silver. So the Age of Stone is ended, but the Age of Bronze has not yet begun ; between the two lies the Copper or Chalcolithic Period.

The new civilization will be supreme in Crete during the five or six centuries of E.M.I and II. It is fairly probable that the transformation of industry there was not merely the result of internal development. The great island could not completely escape the repercussion of the migrations which, near or far, were upsetting the world. It may have been at this time that the aboriginal population mingled with certain short-headed elements. Some groups of immigrants seem to have landed on the northern coast of the island, especially in the dependent islets. At Mochlos have been found both the oldest fragment of copper and the oldest tombs of the Cycladic type ever discovered in Crete. But the mass of the population was not affected ; on the contrary, it absorbed the aliens. In spite of the appearance of metal no abrupt break is to be seen in Crete at the beginning of the Chalcolithic Period ; evolution proceeds continuously. Dwellings capable of housing a large number of persons, and tombs which held hundreds of bodies point to a system of family collectivity. From E.M.I the decoration of the houses testifies to plenty and security. On the vases, which first began to be painted about 3000, bright colours are laid on dark backgrounds, and later dark colours on light backgrounds. Seals marked with ideographic signs prove conditions of existence far beyond the simple needs of a primitive society. In E.M.II progress is still more definite. The potter produces " mottled ware " from his kiln. The metal-worker perfects the form of his copper triangular dagger, and reproduces it in silver. The carving of stone and ivory is full of promise. The jewels and vases of hard stone, heaped up in the tombs, bear witness to a sure taste and an advanced art, and at the same time to lavish opulence. Whence this wealth came is told by the clay boats offered *ex voto*. The Cretans were beginning to be excellent seamen. They brought marble idols from the Cyclades, and sailed to Egypt to fetch ivory and all kinds of objects, which were imitated in the island, especially idols of a particular type and precious vases of syenite. Thanks to the Etesian winds, which brought the ships home from the North or sent them out to the South, two influences made themselves felt in the island. A glance at the map will show on what points of Crete trade and prosperity must first have concentrated—on the eastern and southern coasts. And this is where the most numerous and richest settlements of the period are found—in the East the ports of Zakro and Palaikastro, but above all the islet of Mochlos and the sites of the isthmus, from Gournia and the copper veins of Chrysokamino to Vasiliki, and in the south the sites of the Messara, marked by their bee-hive tombs, Hagia Triada, Hagios Onouphrios, Kalathiana, Platanos, Koumasa, and many others.

It is not surprising, therefore, that the Cyclades from the very first played an important part in Chalcolithic civilization. Between the two continents which were becoming populated on the East and on the West they ensured communication between the great island of the South and the Acropolis of Troy, which commanded the region of the Bosphorus. They rise brilliantly from the darkness which enveloped them. Melos sends its obsidian to the furthest shores of the eastern Mediterranean. Neighbouring islands draw out inexhaustible treasures from their mines and quarries. Paros and Naxos exploit their marble and carve it into figurines, vases, and *pyxides*. It is to be supposed that Seriphos, rich in lead and

copper, and Siphnos, the Eldorado of the Cyclades, contribute
to the supply of the Ægeans in metals. The weapons of
Amorgos are as good as those of contemporary Crete, and are
perhaps better than they. Pottery still has a rustic air, but
it takes on original shapes and borrows the spiral motive from
the peoples of the North. But, cramped on their rocks, the
islanders can only make a livelihood by travelling afar, without
ceasing, in search of profitable barter. They become the
brokers of the producing countries. Wherever they go they
leave their little idols behind them. Certain pots of the
Cyclades and Crete have handles pierced in a way which is
special to Troy I ; whatever the origin of the process may be,
they have their interest in the general diffusion. Syra, the
central island, becomes in this way the commercial capital
of the archipelago. The long thin ship with long oars which is
painted on its vases has documentary value, for it is a record
of the fleet which was the first, with that of the Cretans, to
range a European sea. In sum, if we wished to give the
Chalcolithic Period of the Ægean a less vague title, we should
call it the Creto-Cycladic Period.

During this period the Peloponnese, which had become
populated at the same time as the Cyclades, remained in close
relations with them. The only part of the country which is
of any account at this time is the peninsula which runs out to
meet the Cyclades, namely Argolis, and indeed not the whole of
Argolis, but the isthmus which lies between the gulf stretching
towards Melos and the Gulf of Corinth. There, from Tiryns to
Corinth, was the seat of a civilization which borrowed largely
from the Cyclades and was also in contact with central Greece.
But through its distance from the centre of things the mainland
was slow to make the progress which leads us to divide the
Chalcolithic Age in the islands into two periods, and E.H.I
lasted without notable change for half a millennium.

FIRST BRONZE AGE (2400–2000) AND FIRST CRETAN HEGEMONY
(2000–1750). PRE-MYCENÆAN PERIOD (2500–1600)

About the XXVth century we notice for the second time an
intense fermentation in Europe and Asia. From the Balkan
Peninsula new invasions start. About this time the Hittites
establish themselves on the plateau of Cappadocia. A Thraco-

Phrygian population sets up a second town of Troy on the ruins of the first. Another wave pours over Thessaly. The consequence is an abrupt and complete break between the northern countries and central Greece, and Mount Othrys becomes for centuries an impassable barrier.

Thessaly, held by the advanced guard of the Balkan peoples, henceforth looks towards the North. Its *megaron* houses are of the plan which prevails in Troy II. Its figurines represent a type of which the forehead is prolonged in the nose, with a pointed stomach and thick thighs. Its stagnant civilization makes progress in one thing only; the high towns become fortified.

Central Greece, on the other hand, is thrown on the South. From the valley of the Spercheios to Cape Malea all lands will be united by a common civilization. A great road leads from the sources of the Kephissos by the Isthmus of Corinth to the Gulf of Argos, and is continued by paths into Laconia and into Elis. Orchomenos II is surrounded by a perfect escort of new cities; near old Tiryns settlements appear on the Aspis of Argos and on the Acropolis of Mycenæ; Corinthia profits by its good position to blossom into prosperous sites. The ash-pits or *bothroi* which are characteristic of the houses of Orchomenos II reappear at Gonia and Korakou; the glazed pottery of Hagia Marina does not extend northward beyond Lianokladi, now a frontier post, but spreads to the South into Argolis, and even further, all over the Peloponnese. While Thessaly remains in ignorance of the use of metal, Hellas passes from the Chalcolithic Age (E.H.II) to the Bronze Age (E.H.III).

From now onward the importance of the Cyclades declines. The new peoples of the mainland are able to defend themselves, as the fortifications of the Troad and Argolis show; they are even able to attack, as is proved by those of Chalandriani in Syra and of Hagios Andreas in Siphnos. Between Hellas and Crete the civilization of the Cyclades is stifled for want of room. The islanders vainly increase their efforts; they still export a few flat pans or palettes of clay to Phokis and marble figurines to Corinthia, and even to Caria; they still import glazed pots from the mainland and two-handled cups from Troy; they succeed in introducing bronze to the mainland, and the mainland motive of the spiral to Crete. For all that their decline is rapid and complete. Only one of the Cyclades escapes—

Melos, not so much because of its obsidian, which is being supplanted more and more by metal, but thanks to its intermediary position between Argolis and Crete. While Syra relapses into obscurity a new city arises at Phylakopi.

What contributed to this displacement towards the South of the centre of gravity of the Ægean world was the economic change which once again supplemented the political change. Relations with the Nile valley were increasing in importance. Under the VIth Dynasty (2540–2390) they were very active. As soon as trade with Egypt became really profitable Crete had an advantage over the Cyclades for which nothing else could make up.

Still more remarkable was the effect produced by an industrial revolution. The Bronze Age was beginning. It was not that the Ægeans had been completely ignorant of the alloying of copper and tin in the Copper Age. Wherever the two ores exist together man has known how to make bronze almost as soon as copper, for copper requires a temperature of 1,200 degrees centigrade to fuse, and 228 degrees are sufficient for tin. But there was no tin in the Cyclades and Crete, any more than in Cyprus and Asia Minor, and what bronze they had was imported as a luxury article. Soon after the middle of the third millennium all this was changed. The traders of the Ægean went to fetch tin, if not in the countries where it was produced, at any rate on the neighbouring coasts. Now the precious deposits were not so very numerous in the regions accessible from the Mediterranean. They existed in Etruria, in Gaul, in Spain, and in Cornwall. There were some also in the Erzgebirge, and the caravans could bring the tin to the shores of the Adriatic as well as the amber which came from still further. By the West or by the North this trade was concentrated in the Ionian Sea. It was just at this time that the first civilization of the Sikels, which shows evidence of connexion with the Ægeans, was born, and that we notice a sudden awakening down the whole length of western Greece. This stream of trade could flow into the Ægean Sea by Crete alone. Half-way between Cyprus, the Copper Island, and the sea by which the tin came, opposite the Cyclades, equidistant from Egypt and the Troad, Crete was wonderfully placed to attract the manufacture of bronze and to distribute its products. Draw a line from the west coast of Cyprus to the point in the

Ionian Sea at which the routes of the Tyrrhenian Sea and of the Adriatic converge ; this line goes through Crete longitudinally and is bisected by it. Measure the distance from Knossos to Troy; it is exactly that from Zakro to the mouths of the Nile. The bronze industry, then, was to give Crete an experience in technique which it would extend to all other industries, and thereby the island would soon be producing masterpieces of every art. At the same time, in order to ensure the arrival of the raw materials which it needed and the export of its manufactured goods, to maintain its supremacy at sea Crete would have to organize a powerful navy. The Bronze Age was to be for about ten centuries the age of the Cretan thalassocracy.

While Crete thus raised itself above all rivals, in Crete itself a displacement of wealth and power was preparing during E.M.III (2400–2100). Little by little the central portion of the island contested the supremacy of the eastern district, and the same time saw the first decline of the sites where once the clans of the South had so proudly heaped treasures in their great *tholos* tombs. Trade and industry became general, and society underwent a transformation. In the plain round Knossos enormous jars were made to hold oil. The potter altered his style and acquired new colours. The growing length of the daggers testifies to the advance made in metal-working. *Pyxides*, idols, a bit of pumice-stone from Melos, the spiral motive, all indicate that Crete was in constant relations with the Cyclades, and button-seals prove a similar connexion with Egypt. Already Knossos boasted vast buildings with a sanctuary, magazines, and a great tower, a whole congeries which has been called the " Pre-Palace ".

At the beginning of the Minoan Period the decline Middle of eastern Crete becomes manifest. This country, which once seemed to be on the way to hastening social development and weakening the clan system, takes on a rustic, backward appearance. Mochlos is abandoned, Zakro loses its importance. The peasants live in patriarchal groups in dwellings like that of Chamaizi, which are spacious and easy to defend, but bear every sign of poverty. In the middle of M.M.II the potters maintain the types of the preceding period. Even the revered shrines of Mount Dikte, like that of Petsofa, have a mean, provincial, decayed air. Supremacy belongs once and for all to the central region.   There the clans are absorbed into larger groupings, and the *tholos* tombs are closed for ever.   This phenomenon was perhaps encouraged by the influence of Amphiktionies, whose religious centres were the high places of Petsofa and Mount Iouktas and the sacred caves of Psychro, Skoteino, and Kamares ; in any case it is connected with the development of the urban system.   A town is founded at Mallia, and acts as a connecting point between the two parts of the island. But the big towns are found near the sea, at the end of valleys connecting the north and south coasts—Knossos on the Cycladic front, facing Melos and Argolis, and Phaistos, whence down to the days of the *Odyssey* " the dark-prowed ships were borne to Egypt by the force of the wind and the wave ".[1]

Towards the middle of M.M.I (about 2000) the period of the First Palaces begins.   The princes of Knossos, Phaistos, and Mallia built themselves dwellings suitable to their opulence, grandiose systems of apartments, workshops, magazines, and sanctuaries.   At Knossos the palace, situated on a slight eminence, is protected by a powerful surrounding wall dominated by a keep.   That of Phaistos stands in the mountains and needs no fortifications.   At Mallia, on the edge of the sea, the walls are in places 2·30 metres thick.   Often rearranged during their two centuries and a half of existence, these palaces were adorned with a profusion of colonnades and frescoes. Under the protection of its kings Crete worked with ardour and produced with exuberance.   Private people had houses with several stories.   The armourers made their daggers longer, varied their forms and beautified them with chased ornament.   The potters now had the wheel and made clay as thin as metal, vitrified it into barbotine and faience, and adorned it with gorgeous polychrome—the " Kamares " of M.M.II is one of the loveliest wares that ever came out of a royal factory.   The goldsmiths collaborated in the execution of vases with gold mountings.   The engravers applied their art to gems, on which they cut portraits of men and figures of beasts.   From the primitive ideographs a hieroglyphic script was developed in M.M.I, and it was simplified in M.M.II.   The overseas trader extended his connexions.   From M.M.I onward, Egypt was not the only country with which he dealt ; he

---

[1] *Odyssey*, iii, 296 ff.

brought spices from Cyrenaïca, he sent vases of steatite and terra-cotta to Argolis and Phokis, and a lord of Platanos obtained possession of a Babylonian seal. In M.M.II the Cretans did still better. They sent Kamares ware as far as Upper Egypt, and obtained for the king of Knossos a statuette of an Egyptian dignitary. They exported their precious pottery to Melos, Delos, Thera, and far-away Cyprus. Their silver vases arrived at Byblos at a time when a period of Ægean influence was beginning in Canaan. A great and beautiful civilization was blossoming forth.

Yet the side on which it should have extended quite naturally, the European mainland, was that on which it made the slowest progress during the whole period of the First Palaces. The reason was that when this period was commencing (2000) the continents were once more thrown into confusion by invaders. The Aryans left the shores of the Caspian and swarmed in every direction. They made their way into Turkestan, Iran, and India, and one tribe, the Mitanni, made a salient across the Tigris and Euphrates. The whole East felt the repercussions of this drive. The accession of the XIIth Dynasty (2000) was distinguished by hard struggles for the defence of Egypt, Canaan was born to a new life, shortly afterwards Troy II, the " Burnt City ", was buried under two yards of debris, on which a simple village then arose, and in 1926 the Hittites subdued Babylonia. In Europe, too, it seems almost certain that peoples of Aryan origin arrived at this time. While the Proto-Latins were making their way towards Italy a race related to the Illyrians, the Hellenic race, made its appearance in the Balkan Peninsula. Soon the Achaians entered Thessaly, drove the old Pelasgian population into the surrounding hills, and installed themselves in the central region which was to keep their name. They were acquainted with metal, and Thessaly entered the Chalcolithic Age. But the bulk of these bands crossed the barrier of Othrys. Bit by bit, from Mount Olympos to Olympia, the whole of Hellas was conquered. The Early Helladic Period ended in the destruction and burning which marked the path of the invader. The chiefs of a warlike minority established themselves in the midst of the pre-Hellenic populations, and at once Hellas broke completely with the past.

But the new-comers were a strong, intelligent, assimilating race. After having destroyed they set themselves to reconstruct. Above Orchomenos II rose Orchomenos III ; Corinthia was repopulated ; and a second settlement succeeded the first on the Aspis of Argos. The position of the Kadmeia was not neglected. Attica, hitherto almost completely isolated behind Parnes, was attached to the great Bœotian road. New sites were occupied in the Peloponnese, of which a large number were in Argolis, around the growing Mycenæ. Still better, the barrier of Othrys fell, and Thessaly was opened to commercial intercourse. Into this vast dominion the Achaians brought with them a civilization which did not lack vitality, a trunk full of sap which, with proper grafting, could bear fine fruit. From Thessaly to Elis a special type of house became predominant, with an apse and a rectangular *megaron* with a fixed hearth, and at the same time a special type of pottery appears, the Minyan ware with metallic forms.

But this " Nordic " civilization was soon transformed under the influence of the native inhabitants and foreigners. The use of bronze spread on the mainland as it had never done before, and, though the arrow-heads are still of stone, we see, as we pass from Thessaly to the Peloponnese, flint giving way to obsidian and the primitive hafted type to the more developed barbed type. From the XXth century matt-painted pottery made its way on the mainland, and a vase-painter of Drachmani in Phokis copied a M.M.I jug from Knossos. The relations of the mainland with the Cyclades became more and more intensive. At the beginning of the period Melos suffered from the general disturbance, and Phylakopi I disappeared. But Phylakopi II almost at once was importing Minyan ware as well as Kamares. Through the Cyclades the civilization of Crete would be able to reach and penetrate the civilization of the mainland. At the end of the first period following the Achaian invasion the Helladic chronological system would correspond exactly with the Cycladic and the Minoan. It seems as if we were on the eve of the Creto-Mycenæan epoch. Yet it did not commence until half a century later.

For in Crete M.M.II ended in disaster. All the palaces which challenged the centuries were laid low in one evil day. At Knossos the royal potteries were buried under a layer of ashes, while in another quarter everything remained in its place beneath the fallen walls. Phaistos, Mallia, Tylissos had the same fate. What had happened ? An invasion, as on the mainland ? Some have suggested that Asiatics came and drove the old population into the western part of the island. But no people of Asia can have had at that time a fleet capable of conquering the empire of the sea, and a foreign invasion would have brought profound changes very different from those which we actually find. It is more likely that we have before us an internal revolution, which, moreover, broke out after an earthquake, a sign from the gods. Was it the revenge of eastern Crete ? It is very possible. Crete was covered with strongholds, and a faience mosaic of M.M.II represents war-scenes round a Cretan city. Lastly, if the figure which we have on a seal is a portrait of a M.M.II king, that king was not of the dolichocephalic type, which is becoming predominant in Crete, and we may imagine a revolt against an ethnic minority. Whether the rising was regional, feudal, or national, in any case it brought a new dynasty into power. This line at once asserted its authority by the introduction of a new writing, a linear script, of which certain signs are derived from hieroglyphs more ancient than those of M.M.II. The shock had been too violent for the normal course of things to be resumed without delay. Half a century went by, a period of expectation and transition.

SECOND CRETAN HEGEMONY (1700–1400)
EARLY MYCENÆAN PERIOD (1600–1400)

About 1700 Crete appears again, more beautiful and more brilliant. It rises to its apogee, and there maintains itself for three centuries.

On the site of the destroyed palaces the kings of Knossos and of Phaistos built new palaces. A prince's villa rose at Hagia Triada and the houses of lords at Tylissos. Eastern Crete awoke once more. In the capitals all was splendour. At Knossos an extensive enclave of cists was reserved for the treasury, numerous offices were set up with their seals and their archives and their inventories, and royal factories catered for cultivated tastes with masterpieces of pottery, sculpture, and marquetry. The monumental stairways, the colonnades of cypress wood, the frescoes and the reliefs of painted stucco which covered the walls of the great halls were the setting to a luxurious court life, in which feasts followed receptions, and the great nobles mingled with the ladies in their décolleté bodices, and the king, rising from a banquet, left a table laden with precious plate to sit down to a game-board starred with jewels. Under the ægis of the Minoses, the blessings of peace and ease were disseminated by strong and respected authority and stern justice. The factories could work, for there was no lack of custom. Industry made wonderful progress. The potter, aided by the quick-rotation wheel, made one happy experiment after another, the faience-worker produced low relief and high, the bronze-worker cast statuettes and, combining the goldsmith's craft with his own, executed admirable chased and inlaid daggers. Existence was so agreeable and nature so kindly that the artist put away the child's play of polychrome and indulged in images of reality. On frescoes, vases, and seals he took delight in representing lilies and reeds, bulls and wild goats, dolphins and flying-fish, and ladies adorned in rich stuffs and jewellery. Even the goddess is not forgotten, but appears in the fashion of the day with a flounced dress.

After all this youthful impetuosity which marks the second phase of M.M.III comes, about 1580, the rich maturity of L.M.I. The palaces had been remodelled, and their appearance was more majestic than ever. In the great courts in front of them theatres with stone tiers were built. The king of Knossos added a Little Palace to the Great Palace, and built a tomb for his line at Isopata ; the villa at Hagia Triada was remodelled on an enormous scale and filled with masterpieces ; new palaces were built at Nirou Chani and Gournia. Eastern Crete took more and more part in the general prosperity. The vases which it manufactured or bought are among the finest of the period. The sacred cave of Psychro attracted so many pilgrims that a town was built in the neighbourhood. Art, powerful and chastened, takes on a classic appearance, so that in this respect the XVIth and XVth centuries are for Crete what the VIth and Vth are for Greece. There are happy discoveries without end. Beside the big fresco the miniature fresco appears. The mural decorator heightens the relief of his painted stucco and achieves works of a magnificent style. Scenes of intense vitality are finely chiselled on steatite vases. Certain ivory statuettes set off with gold are marvels. The goldsmith adds iron to the precious metals. The forges produce socketed spear-heads, huge basins, swords decorated like trinkets, pretty bronze statuettes, and gorgeous repoussé vases. Naturalism, which has attained full command of its methods, gives to vase-painting a noble freedom, in no wise hampered by the imitation of mural painting.

But Crete had not yet by any means arrived at political unity. Minos still had to cope with rival cities or rebellious vassals. At the end of M.M.III Knossos had been surprised ; pillagers flung themselves on the stone cists which contained the most precious objects of the treasury and in their haste left behind the hammers which they had used to break them open. A keen look-out had to be kept. In the following period the other palaces of Crete vied in splendour with that of Knossos, and a seal from Zakro shows that the chiefs still possessed strongholds (Fig. 73d). Nevertheless, the resources at the disposal of Minos continued to increase. The doors of the royal magazines had to be widened to admit gigantic oil-jars ; a high official was placed over the granary ; the arsenal was full to bursting with arrows and chariots. About 1450 the palace of Phaistos was destroyed, that of Hagia Triada was set on fire, and the houses of the lords of Tylissos fell into ruin. Fifty years were to pass before any of these cities would be reborn from its ashes, and in the East Gournia fell into complete decline.

During these fifty years of L.M.II (1450–1400) Knossos enjoyed undivided supremacy. Minos built a throne-room, where he sat as high priest, and a villa with a basilica, where he sat as chief judge. His tribunal earned a name for severity which was to survive. His scribes composed a new script for the sole use of the royal administration. Since there were no longer any fortifications in the island which could oppose his omnipotence, he no longer needed to keep up those of Knossos ; for external defence he relied on his fleet. It was still a great age for art, but it had lost the naïve spontaneity and fruitful audacity of old. The artist worked for his master, to order. The triumph of the " Palace style " was not confined to writing alone. The official painters portrayed the king adorned with fleurs-de-lys and more than human in size, the griffins watching over his sacred person, and the procession of messengers bringing gifts to the Pharaoh of the Keftiu. Naturalism grew conventional, and the finest vases reproduced the pompous

ordering of architectural ornament, and at last fell into the
elegant preciosities of rococo—" Louis Quatorze " was followed
by " Louis Quinze ". Almost all the notable works of the
period, not only the frescoes but the beautiful vases of stone
or enamelled terra-cotta, the *rhytons* set with precious materials,
the bronze ewers, and the chased rapiers were destined for the
king of Knossos, his ministers, and his courtiers.

Such a brilliant civilization could not develop in an island
without constant intercourse with countries overseas ; it was
the product of a thalassocracy. Now about 1700, when the
Cretans were once more in a position to scour the seas, the
market which had once been their great source of wealth was
closed to them for many years. Egypt fell a prey to the
Hyksos. Broken up, impoverished, and inhospitable, it had
no longer any attraction. In the last third of the XVIIth
century Khian seems to have tried to resume intercourse, but
in vain. Not till after 1580, when the XVIIIth Dynasty had
restored national unity and prosperity, did the Cretans begin
once more to take the road to Egypt, little by little. They knew
how to make themselves welcome. Henceforward they were
distinguished from the other Ha-unebu under the name of
Keftiu. They offered " gifts " in order to obtain the right to
trade ; they even built on the island of Pharos a port from
which their goods went up the Nile.

But during the long interruption of relations with Egypt the
Cretan sailors had not resigned themselves to inactivity.
Cut off from the South, they turned their energies in every
other direction. As early as M.M.III a Babylonian cylinder
reached Knossos, and a disk covered with foreign characters
came to Phaistos. At the beginning of the Late Minoan Period
the horse, come from the East, landed on the island. Cyprus,
which had already received Ægean pottery in M.M.II, was
much exploited by the Cretans. Syria had for a long time
been visited by the ships of the Keftiu when the Pharaohs
gave them free access to the country, allowing them presently
to establish settlements from which Ægean goods spread
to the interior. But it was above all in the North, in the
countries occupied since 2000 by the Achaians, in Hellas
which was opened more and more to external influences, that
from 1700 onwards Cretan civilization poured in a mighty flood.

For some time past significant facts had been observed on

the mainland. Formerly grey Minyan ware had gone from
North to South, from Orchomenos to the Peloponnese; now
the yellow Minyan of Argolis, of Nordic forms covered with a
southern slip, took the opposite direction. The matt-painted
wares were now covered with exotic ornament. The Cretans,
driven out of Egypt, were seeking compensation elsewhere.
They found it in Hellas, and it was magnificent.

Suddenly, towards the end of the XVIIth century, Argolis
undergoes a general transformation. The cultivation of the
vine and olive is learned. Everything becomes Cretanized.
The ladies dress in fashions of Knossos. In sanctuaries of
Cretan type the Cretan goddess is installed, with her usual
animals, attributes, and ritual objects; all the ceremonies and
all the games celebrated in her honour on the island accompany
her to the continent. The princes' dwellings are adorned with
frescoes and filled with precious vases and jewels in which there
is scarce a trace of Helladic inexperience. Is it the effect of an
armed invasion, of an immigration *en masse*? No. The mass
of the population has not changed. The Achaians still testify
to their northern origin by their beard, by their drawers and
sleeved *chiton*, by their isolated *megaron* and fixed hearth.
Their chiefs, greedy as they are for exotic and luxurious
novelties, still keep a rude way of life. From their fortresses
on the heights they overlook the roads frequented by foreign
merchants. and allow them free passage in exchange for
honourable gifts. When they have castles or tombs built they
impress all the hands needed to carry the gigantic blocks of
stone. They delight in war and raids, fine weapons and chariots.
By land and sea they go, carrying off cattle and women ; but
above all they need gold, plenty of gold, to decorate their lair
with gorgeous things, and to hold festivals followed by long
banquets. The sudden metamorphosis of Argolis appears
then to be the result of sporadic and peaceful colonization.
Elsewhere, on certain coasts of the Ægean, and in the far
countries of the Levant and the West, Cretans could instal
themselves as masters and impose their dominion ; but in
Argolis they doubtless confined themselves to making the
natives accept the blessings of a superior civilization.

A palace rose on the Acropolis of Mycenæ, and another on
the rocks of Tiryns. These edifices, which were of the mainland
type, had their walls covered with Cretan paintings, but the

subjects were battle and the chase. They held riches which
increased every day, and attracted round them a growing
population. So the lords of these places were constantly
concerned with securing their defence. The walls were extended
as the towns built below the palaces grew larger. For each
Late Helladic Period there is at Tiryns a corresponding
extension of the fortified circuit—first the *Oberburg* on the top,
with its jagged wall and two big towers, and then the *Mittelburg*
on the slope. At Mycenæ the system of defence organized
in the middle of the XVth century takes in the lower slopes,
including the circle of the royal necropolis. The mighty and
redoubtable kings demanded that the fine things which had
been their pride in this life should still be their joy in the next.
The Shaft Graves of Mycenæ have preserved to our day the
remains of the princes who first dwelled in the palace of the
upper town ; when Schliemann came to disturb their rest they
were there, with gold masks over their faces, with their long
swords, their heavy jewels, and their cups of gold and silver.
Their successors were not content with mere graves for such
treasures as these ; towards the end of L.H.I they began to
build magnificent domed tombs in the lower town.

This Creto-Mycenæan civilization prevailed on the mainland
during the two centuries which may be assigned to the Early
Mycenæan Period (1600–1400). It gradually reached every
land in Hellas. Along the great road from Argolis to Corinthia
more than twenty sites have yielded, at the very least, pottery
of which the ornament proves Cretan connexions. All the
shores of the Peloponnese were visited by the strangers, and
at many points they established factories or branches. By
way of Kythera, where they deposited steatite vases, they
came to Laconia. There the lords of Vapheio eclipsed those
of the neighbouring towns and vied with those of Mycenæ.
They had their bee-hive tomb, in which they were buried first
with wonderful gold L.M.I cups, and then with vases imitating
the Palace style. The two Pyloses, that in Messenia and that
in Elis, became cities in the second half of the XVIth century.
They had extensive relations with the Gulf of Corinth and with
the Adriatic, down which the amber came to them. Their
wealth attracted the Cretans, who brought their swords and
their fine vases and picked up the information which they
needed themselves to navigate to more distant lands.

Soon central Greece was finally attached to the mixed civilization which had conquered the Peloponnese. The Cretans landed at Krissa, and took their goods and their religion to Delphi. Palace style vases arrived in Aigina, at Chalkis in Euboia, and, no doubt from there, at Thebes and Orchomenos. Mainland imitations of the same style reached Athens and Thorikos, Iolkos and Volo. By land the Mycenæan progress was slower, but regular and irresistible. Corinthia, at the centre of communications, became more prosperous than ever, and its potters were soon to make a name for themselves by replacing Minyan ware by Ephyrean. In L.M.I Attica was conquered.

Further north new bands had arrived in the Balkans and, mingling with various elements picked up on the way, the Aiolians had installed themselves in Thessaly and Bœotia. Far from being an obstacle to the expansion of the southern civilization they staked out the road which it was to follow. Bœotia took on a new appearance. At Thebes, on the Kadmeia, a palace arose of which the greatness is witnessed by many precious objects, while the central court, the frescoes of personages in Cretan costume and the water-conduits point to the presence of a foreign architect and foreign artists. Operations were set on foot for the draining of Lake Kopaïs, and on a rock-island in the lake the fortified palace of Gla was built. Orchomenos no longer exported its Minyan pottery, but none the less it attained a size which it had not yet known, in a Fourth City. Lastly, by the roads of Phokis and by the ports of the Pagasetic Gulf, Thessaly came under the universal influence. About 1580 it had learned the use of bronze and the potter's wheel. About 1450 it received vases of Mycenæan or Cretan style, to the very foothills of Olympos.

MYCENÆAN HEGEMONY (LATE MYCENÆAN) (1400–1200)

In this continual expansion the part played by Cretan traders and colonists was for a long time predominant. But it tended to diminish as the pupils learned to do without their masters, and the power of the mainland chiefs increased. There remained to the Cretans the immense superiority which they enjoyed through their empire of the sea. But even here the Achaians were doing their apprenticeship. When they arrived in Greece they had not even known what the sea was, and had borrowed a pre-Hellenic word (θάλασσα) to designate it. Little by little the " briny " (ἅλς) opened roads to them, and became a " passage " (πόντος). At first the warriors took to piracy ; about 1600 the kings of Mycenæ and Tiryns ordered Cretan artists to engrave exploits of this kind on a silver vase or a gold ring. Then the advantages of peaceful barter were recognized ; about 1500 amber came regularly by the Adriatic to Pylos. Then Cretans and Achaians worked together, combining their science of navigation and their geographical knowledge. But a day came when the peoples grew tired of paying tribute to the Cretan thalassocracy. The Mycenæans no longer needed middlemen to carry their vases to Egypt and, above all, to the western seas. On their side the Pharaohs judged it to be to their political and commercial interest to dispense with the Keftiu and to enter into direct relations with the peoples of the " Circuit ". The kings of Mycenæ on many occasions received objects of glass and faience marked with the cartouche of Amenhetep II (1447–1420) and Amen-hetep III (1415–1380), and responded with consignments of fine vases. These gifts are perfect documents of diplomatic history. They announce an event of first magnitude—the rising of the Mycenæan world against Crete which had con-verted and transformed it, a recoil which was to destroy the power of Knossos.

Since Crete had shed its fortifications it had been at the mercy of a surprise attack. One day of weakness, and the island was conquered. It was. About 1400 the glorious palace of Knossos was overthrown. It was swift and dreadful, a thunderbolt. On the very eve a gang of workmen had been employed with heaps of limestone before them and their materials scattered about ; the sculptor and the lapidary of the king had been busy in their shop roughing out a stone *amphora* and putting together a rare piece of marquetry. As the enemy were beating at the gates some tried to rush the king into the Throne Room, to obtain divine protection for him by a last desperate anointing ; they had not the time, and the ritual vessels of alabaster remained there on the floor. While the flames devoured the palace the looters carried off everything that was not withheld from their grasp by the collapse of the walls. The catastrophe was universal ; Gournia, Pseira, Zakro disappeared ; Palaikastro went up in flame.

It was no internal revolution this time. Evans would attribute all this destruction to a revolt of the plebs against the monarchy. But everything testifies to the arrival of a new population in Crete. The Egyptian documents mention the Keftiu no more. Suddenly short-headed men prevail over the long-headed men who had hitherto been preponderant. From beneath the Dorian speech which was implanted in Crete two centuries later, a few elements emerge of the speech which was that of the Peloponnese also before the Dorian invasion. Many Achaian place-names can only have been introduced into the island at this epoch. Every characteristic of the mainlanders is now found in Crete. The men are no longer clean-shaven. A carved sceptre handle portrays a crowned head with the beard and up-turned moustache of the Mycenæan kings ; if it is not the Idomeneus of legend it is one of his predecessors.[1] For the first time there appears in Crete the northern house with a *megaron* ; the chiefs who rebuild Hagia Triada and Gournia will have no other. Funerary architecture is transformed, and the bee-hive tomb and the rock chamber are adopted. Even the beliefs to which Crete had converted the Mycenæans come back to her in a primitive, childish form.

The island which had been mistress of the Mediterranean had become a distant dependency of the mainland. The jewel of the Ægean was to lose all its lustre. Subjected to foreign domination, what was left of the old inhabitants after massacre and emigration vegetated in poverty. When, at the end of a half-century, a few groups of men took possession of Knossos, they could only set up mean hovels in the ruins of the palace. The Royal Villa had been spared by the conqueror ; they let it fall into ruin and did no more than rig up a few shelters in it. A chapel, 1·50 metres in length and breadth, was sufficient for religious needs. The ancient tomb of the kings was violated, and became a common burial pit. Phaistos, Hagia Triada, Tylissos, and Mallia, destroyed by the king of Knossos in the days of his omnipotence, and Gournia and Palaikastro destroyed by the invaders, were reborn, but only to drag out a mediocre existence. The occupation of an islet like Pseira had no *raison d'être* except in a time of sea-power ; the islet was abandoned. Where a population no longer feels safe it withdraws from the coast into the mountains. All over Crete civilization goes back.

[1] Unless it is a forgery. See p. 397 and Fig. 5.

E

There is no trace of mural painting after 1400. Clay supplants stone and metal in the manufacture of vessels. The idols are lamentably crude or repulsively gross. In vase-painting taste is maintained for some time yet, for the space of a generation ; then the naturalistic design degenerates into mere patterns of lines. In all this melancholy decay there is only one consoling feature; these islanders still have intellectual needs and do not give up writing.

It is on the mainland, in Argolis—the Pharaohs had shown foresight—that the centre of gravity of the Ægean world is henceforth to be found. At Mycenæ a second palace, much more spacious than the first, retains the traditional *megaron*, but with all the embellishments of Cretan architecture, the great court giving light to the rooms and corridors, the great pillared hall, the broad stairways rising to the private apartments, lavish use of imported gypsum, and paintings on the walls and on the stone flooring. At Tiryns too, the palace is rebuilt on a new plan and magnificently decorated. The fortifications become imposing in size—who knows what menace might come out of the North ? At Mycenæ obstructions are accumulated about the Lion Gate. At Tiryns the defence is improved by a covered gallery, and a third enclosure, the *Unterburg*, is constructed at the foot of the Acropolis.

But while the Achaians of Argolis assumed the mastery of the Ægean world the civilization which they had assimilated and transformed to their own use extended further than it had ever gone. Everywhere, in this, the Mycenæan Age *par excellence*, we see the same bee-hive tombs and rock chambers, the same types of stirrup-vases, the same carved ivories, the same jewels of glass paste, the same daggers, and the same swords. Provinces with more or less different civilizations are merged in one common civilization. It is indeed a *koine* which is commencing.

Its domain is immense. New settlements multiply in the Peloponnese, and the city of Menelaos arises as a pendant to the city of Agamemnon. At Spata, Menidi, and twenty other sites in Attica little principalities swarm. Thebes grows greater. Orchomenos becomes the city whose opulence is compared by the heroes of the *Iliad* to that of Egypt, and we still see its magnificence in the high dome and painted ceiling of the royal tomb. Beyond Phokis Aitolia and Akarnania with the Ionian

Islands form the western front of the new Hellas. Beyond Thessaly Macedonia detaches itself from the barbarism of the north ; its population deserts the *toumbes* of the plain and builds stone houses on the terraces, to which come Mycenæan goods. These henceforward are the advanced posts of the Ægean world on the mainland. The Hellas thus formed is the Hellas of the *Iliad*, and the *Catalogue of Ships*, which enumerates its peoples, is a veritable chapter of political geography.

But the Mycenæans by no means halted at the sea. They had conquered the great island of the South and the intermediate station of Melos ; many other lands invited their mercantile and warlike activities. For these operations by sea Crete was a powerful help to them. It had always had sailors ; the general impoverishment drove men to emigrate. Thanks to its Achaian chiefs Crete had a half share in most of the enterprises of piracy, trade, and colonization. At Rhodes the Creto-Achaians founded cities which at once entered into relations with the Egypt of Amenhetep III and rapidly became prosperous. Cyprus received a swarm of colonists speaking a dialect similar to that of the future Arcadians and using a script like that of the Cretans ; they brought to Paphos the cult of the goddess and to the whole island an art which remained faithful to its origins while assuming a local character. From the islands the wave broke on to the neighbouring mainland. From the beginning of the XIVth century a population of Danauna or Danaans was settled on the coast of Syria. The dialect of Cyprus spread in Pamphylia. While the Cretans and the Achaians of the Peloponnese kept access to the Mæander and the Cayster to themselves, the Aiolians went across the sea in a straight line, and occupied the coast between Mount Ida and Mount Olympos. Miletos, Ephesos, and Phokaia received colonists. The Ægeans thus entered into direct relations with the interior of Asia Minor ; a Hittite cylinder and sphinx reached Tiryns and Hagia Triada. In the West the Mycenæan *diaspora* produced less intensive effect but extended to even greater distances. By way of Pylos and Kerkyra the traders and colonists reached the land of the Messapians and the island of the Sikels. They brought liparite from the Aiolian Islands, deposited ingots of Cypriot copper in Sardinia, and introduced their goods and their ideas to distant Iberia. For the first time the Mediterranean played fully the civilizing part for which it was destined, and the Ægeans, already mingled with Greeks, called the barbarians of all its shores to a higher life.

Glorious though the spectacle may be which is presented by the Mycenæan civilization if we consider only its extent, it gives the impression of a backward movement if we compare its quality with that of its predecessor. We know what Crete had become. Elsewhere, it is true, there is the superiority of wealth ; Mycenæ is more than ever the city " full of gold ", and the poet speaks with enthusiasm of the riches heaped in the houses of Orchomenos. New classes attain to a certain ease of life. Hence came real progress. Industry had a plentiful supply of raw materials. Metals were so abundant that obsidian was given up altogether, and the Third City of Phylakopi merely languished. Even tin became so common that the bronze of Thebes contained over eighteen per cent. of it. Iron alone was still lacking, or rather was only known as a precious metal. Furthermore, technical knowledge was diffused everywhere and maintained at a fairly high level. The potters used the wheel as far as Macedonia. A potter's workshop has been found at Zygouries, and a foundry at Enkomi. The lords of Tiryns and Thebes established kilns near their palaces, as once the kings of Knossos and Phaistos had done. The king of Mycenæ even had his lapidary and his faience-worker. The fresco-painters had nothing to do in Crete but they found work from Tiryns to Orchomenos. Unfortunately nothing made up for the lack of inspiration. The Cretanized Achaians were after all not Cretans. From one civilization to the other there was no break in the curve, but it was a descending curve. Without their masters the pupils were nothing more than good workmen, and they were succeeded by mediocre workmen. Weapon-making kept longest the qualities which it had acquired, because material and technique were the most important factors in it, and a warlike society supplied customers who were both numerous and exacting. But in general industry was concerned with wholesale production. As overseas trade opened new markets, it worked more and more for export and descended to the level of ruder peoples. Art grew vulgar and degenerate. It was a characteristic sign of the intellectual decline that writing was very rarely used, and tablets were wanted nowhere outside of Crete.

The Achaians had lost none of their warlike ardour. The extension of the Mycenæan civilization was not due to purely moral or economic influences, peaceful exchange and colonization by mutual consent. Immigration was conducted by force of arms. According to the circumstances the ships went off laden with merchandise or with warriors. When they established themselves on one shore, they went further, in search of adventures and plunder. Danauna were no sooner in Syria than they threatened Byblos. For big enterprises the Achaian peoples combined and, mixing themselves in the quarrels of the natives, found among them allies whom they carried along with them by land and sea. Nevertheless for more than a century the Hittites and the Egyptians were able to make themselves respected. This was the time when Amenhetep III was still sending to Mycenæ gifts marked with his cartouche, when Akhenaten surrounded himself with foreigners at Tell el-Amarna, and when the first Pharaohs of the XIXth Dynasty (after 1300) allowed the vases of the Ægeans to go up as far as Nubia. But in the XIIIth century the Hittites suffered the defeat of Kadesh (1295). Among the warriors who had followed them there were many from the Troad and the neighbouring regions, the Iliuna (men of Ilion), the Dardenui (Dardanians), the Masa (Mysians), the Pedasa (men of Pedasos), and the Kirkisha (men of Gergis), not to mention the Lukki (Lycians) and the Danauna (Danaans). It was a good opportunity to fall upon Troy; about 1280, three generations after the death of Minos, the Achaians united for an expedition of which the memory was to remain alive among the Aiolians of the neighbourhood. Half a century later (1229) Egypt itself was attacked. The " Akaiwasha of the countries of the sea ", with the Tursha (Tyrsenians) of Lemnos, Lukki, and Shakalesha (Cicilians), came and joined the Libu (Libyans) to invade the Delta; but they were crushed at Piari. The era of triumphant expansion was ended.

THE DORIAN INVASION (1200)

By dispersing themselves the Achaians had grown dangerously weak. In going off to every shore of the Mediterranean they left many gaps behind them. Gradually bands of the same race, speaking a dialect of the same language, came out of Illyria and made their way across Pindos, ever pressing further towards the South. The Dorians were coming into history.

About 1200, this slow infiltration turned into an invasion. Perhaps it was repelled for a time ; the forts of the Mycenæans must have done the duty which was expected of them. But the Herakleidai returned victoriously with their armies of three tribes. Some followed the roads of the west and occupied Epeiros, Aitolia, Akarnania, and Elis ; the others, advancing by the east, subdued Phokis, Corinthia, Argolis, Laconia, and Messenia. In the Peloponnese the Achaians were compelled to submit or to take refuge in the uplands of Arcadia. After the mainland the turn of the southern islands came ; Melos and Thera, Crete, and then Karpathos, Kos, and Rhodes fell a prey to the conquerors.

The savagery of this inroad everywhere sent the peoples flying terror-stricken. There was wild turmoil and jostling. The conquered sought new homes at any cost, and themselves became terrible to others. The commotion was general. " The isles were without rest ", says a document of Rameses III ; and so were the continents. Many Achaians sought a refuge with their brothers in Attica. A strong current of emigration bore on the whole of Asia Minor and transformed its civilization. Ionia received Achaians from every land, including, doubtless, people from Pylos. Delos became the religious centre of this Attic-Ionian Achaia. About the same time the Mushki, Phrygians, fell on the Hittites and took their capital, Pteria ; it was the end of a power which had counter-balanced that of the Pharaohs and held back that of the Assyrians. A dynasty of Herakleidai became masters of Lydia. And then a mass of Ægeans, including Pelesati or Kheretim (Cretans) and Zakari (Teukrians or men of Zakro) appeared on the borders of Egypt. They had come by land and by sea, with their women and children heaped in ox-wagons. " No people had stood before them." Rameses III managed to stop them at Magadil, but could not prevent them from establishing themselves in the country which received from the Pelesati the name of Palestine (1193).

What happened to the Mycenæan world after the invasion of 1200 can in no way be compared to what had happened to Crete two hundred years before. The Achaians, adapted to the Cretan civilization, had preserved its heritage, although they allowed it to diminish. The Dorians, coming from the wilds of Albania, destroyed all that remained of it. Their path from Corinth to Sparta was marked by a trail of ruins. In Crete the ports were abandoned for the heights of the interior, and the wretched remains of Knossos were given to the flames. This time all was indeed over for the city which had once been the mistress of the Mediterranean ; over the blackened ruins, buried by the centuries, three thousand years were to pass in the silence of death. All this devastation was the sign not of a local and temporary storm but of a universal and final cataclysm. The beautiful bronze civilization went under when iron appeared. The submission of Crete to the Achaians was the conquest of Greece by Rome— *capta ferum victorem cepit* ; the advent of the Dorians was the barbarian invasions, the Middle Ages, to be followed by the Renaissance.

BOOK I

MATERIAL LIFE

CHAPTER I

THE PHYSICAL TYPE

IN order to distinguish the different races of humanity
anthropologists scrutinize the shape of the head.
Craniometry determines the *cephalic index*, the relation of
the breadth of skulls to their length, and from this standpoint
the races are divided into three categories : the *dolichocephalic*
or long-headed men, the *brachycephalic* or short-headed,
and the *mesocephalic* or medium-headed. This process is,
to be sure, somewhat crude. It is supplemented by an
examination of the general shape of the skull and particularly
of its curvature. Even then craniometry still leaves room
for doubts, but in default of other information one cannot
afford to ignore the indications supplied by it, and its voice
must be heard along with that of archæology with its objects
representing human figures. We can at least try to check
them one against the other.[1]

It seems to have been established by Sergi and his school
that in prehistoric times, before the arrival of the Indo-
Europeans, there was in existence a Mediterranean race
with a long head, an oval face, short stature, dark skin, and
wavy black hair. In Europe the Iberians and the Ligurians
belonged to this type, and in Africa the Libyans and the
Egyptians. Asia Minor, on the other hand, was inhabited
by a decidedly brachycephalic population.[2] Were the Ægeans
a branch of either of these races or were they a cross between
the two ?

[1] See Boyd and Dawkins, BSA. vii, 150–5 ; Duckworth, ib., ix, 344–55 ;
C. H. Hawes, ib., ix, 296 ; xiv, 258 ff. ; Mackenzie, xii, 230 ff. Cf. Sergi,
MIL. xxi, 252 ; AJA. 1901, 315–18 ; Modestov, **LV,** 106 ff. ; Hawes, **XXXIX,**
22–6 ; von Luschau, ZE. 1913, 307–93.
[2] Sergi, **LXXXIV ;** cf. Koerte, AM. 1899, 1 ff. ; Evans, **XX,** 6–7.

More than a hundred skulls from Cretan sites have been available for measurement. A large majority are dolichocephalic. But if we consider the facts more closely and if, instead of taking the figures obtained as a whole, we split them up according to period, we arrive at the following percentages :—

	DOLICHO-CEPHALIC.	MESO-CEPHALIC.	BRACHY-CEPHALIC.
E.M. I, II, and III	55%	35%	10%
M.M. I and II .	66·6%	25·6%	7·7%
L.M. III . .	12·5%	50%	37·5%

The following conclusions can be drawn from this table :—

(i) From the Copper Age to the end of the Bronze Age during the whole course of the centuries in which the continuous development of a single civilization can be traced in Crete, the long-headed type is seen to predominate. The bulk of the Cretans were of Mediterranean stock. The predominant race, however, is intermixed with a brachycephalic race, perhaps of Asiatic origin. This minority may represent the survivors of an original population massacred by the predominant race, but more probably they were immigrants coming, very likely, from the Cyclades, where, during the Copper Age, *dolichocephali* were to be seen on Syra and *mesocephali* on Naxos, but *brachycephali* on Paros, Oliaros, and Siphnos.[1] This mixture was responsible for a fairly large number of mesocephalic half-breeds.

(ii) The long head made great progress in Crete during the centuries from the Early Minoan Period to the Middle Minoan. Was this the result of mixed marriages or were new conditions of life sufficient to alter the type of the immigrant element ? The whole time the predominant race, as is usual, can be seen progressively eliminating the others. Its superiority increases from 55 per cent. to two-thirds of the total population while the proportion of short-heads and half-breeds is decreased by a quarter. The descendants of the intruders are more and more completely absorbed by the aboriginal race.

(iii) The revolution which was to bring to an end the Bronze Age and the Minoan civilization was preceded by a marked

[1] Stephanos, **LXXXV**, 225.

change in the population. There was a tremendous falling off in the number of long-heads, the proportion being reduced from two-thirds to one-eighth, and a corresponding increase of short-heads and medium-heads. Such a change could be due only to one cause, an invasion of short-headed warriors. It marks the arrival of the Hellenes. The greater number of the old inhabitants, particularly the men, were massacred or fled. The women who remained were shared among the conquerors and founded a race of half-breeds. This last conclusion, although it fits in with craniometrical and historical data, is unfortunately based upon too small a number of measurements. But observations among the Cretans of to-day confirm in a striking manner those made upon the skulls of 3,000 years ago.[1] The island has known many rulers, but Byzantines, Saracens, and Venetians, with their few garrisons, have none of them succeeded in altering the Cretan type, while the influence of the Turks is barely perceptible. At bottom the race has remained what the Achaians and, after them, the Dorians made of it. The *mesocephali* are in a majority. The dolichocephalic type of the Minoan Age persists at the western extremity of the island and on isolated heights. The most impenetrable region, the haunt of the Sphakiots, harbours most of the *brachycephali* and is precisely the district that has preserved most completely the speech and the warlike spirit of the Dorians.

This long predominance of the *dolichocephali* and this sudden intrusion of *brachycephali* are phenomena by no means peculiar to Crete. Craniometrists have discovered them in all the neighbouring regions of the Ægean. In the Troad, during the period of the first three cities, twelve skulls out of sixteen are long and only one short, while at Mycenæ and Nauplia, at the time of the Achaians, not one out of three skulls is long, and in Attica, at the end of the Mycenæan epoch, out of six skulls one is long and three are short. Further afield, Italy and Sicily also experience the substitution of short heads for the long heads of the Mediterranean race. It is, therefore, a question of general migrations. The ousting of the long-heads by the short-heads is known in history as the driving back of the Mediterranean race by the Indo-Europeans.

[1] Hawes, **XXXIX**, 24–5 ; BSA. xiv, 258 ff., pl. xv, xvi.

A few skeletons and a few tibias are, fortunately, not our only evidence for the physical type of the Cretans. We possess enough paintings, reliefs, figurines, and engraved stones to show us how they saw themselves, while the paintings on the Egyptian tombs tell us how they appeared in the eyes of strangers.

Like the Mediterraneans in general they were of small stature. Measurements taken from the bones that have been unearthed give an average height of 1·62 metres. At Zapher Papoura the Carpenter's Grave, in which the dead man lies stretched out in an uncrouched position, measures 1·65 metres. This average is 5 centimetres less than that of the present type, which has been improved by the admixture of Greek blood. The Minoans have often been compared to the Japanese, and this is an important point of resemblance.

Though the race lacks that imposing stature which gives an impression of muscular strength, it makes up for this deficiency in wiry suppleness. The type of man to be seen on so many of the frescoes of Knossos is truly a fine one. His bearing is graceful. Accustomed to gymnastic exercises and great lovers of athletic games, the Cretans of prehistoric times set even greater store by a slim figure than the Cretans of to-day. They held themselves in as tightly as possible by means of a stout belt. A slender waist was characteristic of the race. Egyptian art well renders this peculiarity of the Keftiu. (Fig. 35.) Conversely, Minoan art takes care not to attribute it to strangers—to the Egyptian priest, for instance, who appears in a procession with a sistrum in his hand. (Plate II, 2.) But when the Cretan artist is representing his own people, he delights in reproducing their slenderness of waist, exaggerating it sometimes to a degree that is an affront to nature, as on certain seals of sketchy design where the bodies appear to be cut in two. This device is intended to express agility and sprightliness. By a curious coincidence it is to be found also in Japanese art.

Minoan painters always represented their men with bronzed complexions and their women with white skins. This difference must not be attributed purely and simply to an artistic convention. The women were little exposed and led a sheltered life, in the shade. The men, who lived out of doors and went almost naked, were tanned by the blazing sun and the sea-winds. When the Greeks from the north, whose ideal of manly beauty was represented by the " fair-haired " Achaian Achilleus, beheld for the first time these exceedingly bronzed Mediterraneans, they called them all without distinction the " Redskins ", *Phoinikes*. Before they applied this name solely to the Punites, who were to keep it as " Phœnicians ", they gave it to the Carians and even to the Cretans. Is not Europé, the mother of Minos, a daughter of Phoinix ?

Tattooing, which is universally practised by primitive communities, and is perpetuated by the primitive members of advanced communities, was known among all the Neolithic populations of the Ægean. Crete was no exception. At Phaistos a figurine of a steatopygous woman is marked with a little cross on one side.[1] In the metal age the custom

Fig. 1.—Painted limestone head from Mycenæ. Mainland type with tattooing.

survived in the Cyclades and in Argolis, where faces are often marked with horizontal lines of red dots, with vertical or oblique lines, or with circles of dots around a central point. (Fig. 1.)[2] In the tombs, within reach of the dead, were placed the tools and vessels required for this ritual operation, such as needles or awls, vases containing red or blue pigment, and palettes. But in Crete there is no trace of tattooing after the Stone Age. Certain small vases, discovered in Cretan tombs and houses, and mistaken for paint pots, were

[1] **LVII,** fig. 117.
[2] '*Εφ*., 1902, pl. i: cf. **VIII,** i, fig. 230 ; **LXVII,** fig. 336 ; **IV,** 123.

really receptacles for offerings.[1] The very most that may
be supposed is that the Cretans placed a stigma upon the faces
of their slaves.   This would explain the fact that the Cup-
Bearer, a brachycephalic type, has a blue mark carefully
painted on his temple (Fig. 53), though it is probable that
he is a foreigner bringing tribute.   This haste to get rid of
marks disfiguring the face is an early sign of the æsthetic
sense.   The Greeks too were to begin by cutting patterns
on their skin.   At Sparta, and also at Phaistos, there are
steatopygous idols adorned in this barbarous manner.   But
the Greeks were not slow in leaving this practice to immigrants
living apart, like the Kylikranes of Oite, to Thracians and to
slaves.   From the beginning of the Minoan period Crete
presents the same superiority over the Cyclades, and it can
be said of her, as of classical Greece, that " she was too keenly

FIGS. 2, 3.—Cretan types (M.M.II and III).

alive to the beauty of the human body to mar it with the
livid stains of tattooing ".[2]

In the course of time and in proportion as the long head
gained ascendancy in Crete, two types of face prevailed
successively among the men.   During the Middle Minoan
Period a prominent chin, an aquiline nose, and short hair
were characteristic.   Later, the face became more angular,
the nose larger, and the hair long and curly.   This is not
a proof that Crete was inhabited first of all by a purely Asiatic
people and conquered at the end of the Middle Minoan Period
by invaders—the Keftiu of the Egyptians and the Eteocretans
of the Greeks.   Neither craniometry nor archæology authorizes
so decisive a demarcation.   There are particulars more

[1] Xanthoudidis, BSA. xii, 12.
[2] Perdrizet, ARW. xiv, 77.

important than the shape of the nose or the arrangement
of the hair. The figurines from Petsofa, which date from
M.M.I, have their heads almost close-shaven, but the preter-
naturally small waist and the smooth cheeks which were to
characterize the Keftiu are already present. Moreover,
the two portraits of Cretans (Figs. 2 and 3) which, with their
pointed chins, their full lips, their long noses continuing the
line of the forehead and their short hair covered by a turban,
have more in common than any others known to us, belong
respectively to the two periods between which it was proposed
to set a gulf. One is engraved on a seal of M.M.II, the other
is taken from a statuette which cannot be earlier than M.M.III.[1]
The differences to be observed in the male type may be due
simply to a change of fashion and of artistic ideal. It is more
probable, however, that it bears some relation to the continuous
development of the aboriginal race and to the dynastic
revolution which appears to have resulted from it about 1750.

It must further be noted that as far as the hair is concerned
the change is not radical. As usual, Society set the example.
On the steatite vases of L.M.I from Hagia Triada the king,
with ringlets hanging down to his waist, faces an officer whose
hair is cut short (Fig. 27), while the harvesters passing in
procession have turbans on their heads, with the exception
of the leader whose shoulders are covered with floating tresses.
(Plate II, 2.) In most cases, however, the hair is long and
waves over the shoulders or the breast. The courtier
simpering before the ladies, the flute-player taking part in
divine service, the cowboy leaping over the bulls, the boxer
in the gymnasium, and the fisherman returning from the
beach all wear their hair long. Often, too, they have small
ringlets on the crown of the head or across the forehead.
The distinctive trait of the Cretans in the eyes of strangers
was a triple tuft of hair standing up in a crest. By this mark
the Keftiu in the Egyptian paintings could be recognized
at first glance. (Fig. 35.) After the XVIth century, at
any rate, the Cretans did not cut their hair. Doubtless they
shared with so many other peoples the belief that long hair
was the seat and the token of manly strength.

With their long hair the Cretans had no liking for beards.
They are all clean-shaven. Certain very old figurines, which

[1] **XVII,** figs. 124–5 ; **LXXXII,** fig. 21.

represent men with pointed chin-tufts, must have been copied from Egyptian models. When bearded warriors are portrayed in battle-scenes on objects which are purely Cretan they are foreigners, either mercenaries or enemies. An archer with a pointed beard, on a sealing, has a Semitic nose and is not dressed in the Cretan loin-cloth but in short drawers. (Fig. 8.) The Minoans themselves always remained faithful to a fashion dating from the Neolithic Age. Hence the extraordinary paraphernalia of razors and tweezers contained in their tombs.

Unlike the Cretans, the Mycenæans of ancient times, or at any rate their chiefs, took pains to preserve the attribute of manhood. The famous gold masks found in the Shaft Graves bear witness to many variations of this fashion. Two princes without beards are counter-balanced by two others,

FIG. 4.—A king of Mycenæ. Gold mask.

one with a moustache but no beard and the other, the most famous of all, with both moustache and beard. (Fig. 4.) Later the upper lip was shaved and the beard retained, sometimes in a point and sometimes in a fringe.[1] The Mycenæans, however, did not always reject Minoan fashions. At Tiryns, on the frescoes of the First Palace, the men wear their hair at half-length, and have their faces shaven. Elsewhere bearded Mycenæans are to be seen with their heads framed in curls ;[2] these are the " long-haired " Achaians of the *Iliad*, κάρη κομόωντες Ἀχαιοί. In their turn the Dorians were to earn the epithet of men " with floating manes " and their descendants, the Spartiates of Thermopylai, still prepare for battle by combing their long hair.

[1] **LXVII,** figs. 371–3 ; 380–2 ; 241, 497.
[2] **LXX,** 6 ; **LXVII,** figs. 381–2.

Since the Cretans were always clean-shaven, how does it happen that the head of a man carved on a stag's antler by a Cretan artist wears a beard and an up-turned moustache and thus bears a striking resemblance to one of the gold masks dug up at Mycenæ? (Figs. 4 and 5.) [1, 2]

The portrait is that of a person of consequence. Over his thick and flowing locks he wears a crown. This Cretan king of Mycenæan appearance can only be an Achaian. He is not a contemporary of the kings buried on the Acropolis of Mycenæ but one of their descendants established in Crete. Neither Minos nor Agamemnon, might he not be Idomeneus?

FIG. 5.—An Achaian king of Crete. Horn sceptre-handle.

The physical type of the women, like that of the men, bears no resemblance whatsoever to the features and forms of Greek art. The famous profile in which the nose is a prolongation of the forehead is unknown. From a vertical forehead the nose springs abruptly, often with a slightly bumpy outline and still more frequently with an impudently *retroussé* tip. The eyes are wide open. The well-shaped mouth has full, red lips. A row of kiss-curls is arranged across the forehead; little curls of the ringlet type dangle in front of the ears; the bulk of the hair, confined by a ribbon, is divided into long tresses which stream over the shoulders

[1] JHS. 1920, 176 ff., and pl. vi.
[2] But see corrections and additions, p. 397. This may be a forgery.

and down the back. The body with its swelling bosom, slender waist, and curving hips is all sinuous lines. The very irregularities of this type lend it a bold grace, a piquant and

FIG. 6.—Head of a young girl, called the " Parisienne ". Fresco from Knossos.

voluptuous charm, an indefinable sprightliness which has earned for one of the fresco portraits the name of " the Parisienne ". (Fig. 6.) [1]

[1] BSA. vii, 57, fig. 17.

CHAPTER II

DRESS AND ADORNMENT

CRETAN dress[1] is known to us through objects of all kinds representing human figures. Among men's costumes there is no great diversity; women's vary extraordinarily. The Minoans of both sexes, however, are always dressed differently from the Greeks. We must forget the costumes of classical antiquity and seek instead points of comparison with modern peoples, at any rate in the matter of feminine fashions.

As far back as our documents take us it can be established that the inhabitants of Crete span and wove wool. Stuffs have not been preserved in the Ægean countries as they have elsewhere in torrid soils and in peat-bogs. All that has been found is a mere scrap or two of cloth in the tombs of Zapher Papoura and Mycenæ. It is none the less certain that spinning and weaving were already known in the Neolithic settlements. This is proved by the discovery of countless spindle-whorls.

Before clothing themselves in wool, however, men and women for a long time had only the skins of animals, which, almost of necessity, were made into garments of identical form. In hot countries they served solely to cover the sexual organs and were worn not for protection but for concealment, in answer to a religious idea rather than to a physical need. The same kind of tailed skirt that clothed the women of Cogul during the Reindeer Epoch appears in Crete in representations of ritual scenes.[2] Rounded in front, it has exactly the outline of a halved skin and the appendage attached to it is the tail of the animal itself. This ancestral garment is reverentially retained, in skin or cloth, in religious observances. On the Hagia Triada sarcophagus (Fig. 50) the bearers of offerings

---

[1] See Perrot, **LXVII**, 752 ff.; Myres, BSA. ix, 363 ff.; Mackenzie, ib., xii, 233 ff.; Deonna, **IX**; Rodenwaldt, **LXX**, 7 ff., 76 ff.; Fimmen, **XXV**, 185 ff.

[2] See L. Fougerat, *La Pelleterie et le vêtement de fourrure dans l'antiquité*, Paris and Lyons (1914), 48, fig. 25; 227-8, figs. 82-3.

and the priestesses are girt with spotted panther-skins ; on intaglios and seals a skirt of the same shape, but of more pliant material, is worn by all participants in sacred ceremonies.

The origins of Minoan costume explain many things. When a people that has not yet discovered the art of weaving carries a pious horror of nakedness to the point of covering certain parts of the body with furs, a feeling of such intensity is bound to become hereditary. In Crete the men left the upper part of their bodies bare and the women showed their breasts, but both men and women always covered themselves round the hips. Complete nakedness was only to appear with another race. It was not until after the Dorian invasion that man dispensed with all concealments and the modesty of the pre-Hellenes passed for a prejudice of barbarians.[1] The Minoans also borrowed from their remotest ancestors the very principle of their costume, which always hangs from the waist. They kept the primitive garment but made it in cloth and altered it in other respects. Shortened, it becomes no more than a waistcloth, convenient for practical life and particularly for violent exercise, for which purpose it is accordingly borrowed by athletic women. Lengthened, it forms a skirt, an essentially feminine dress, which is, however, worn also by men as a ceremonial dress in palaces and holy places.

I MASCULINE DRESS

The simplest costume is a kind of pocket attached to the girdle and serving as a suspensor. (Plate II, 2.) This article has the appearance, especially in profile, of a kind of sheath such as was known to the Libyans of antiquity and to the Western Europeans of the Renaissance. But it is rarely sufficient by itself ; it is worn along with the loin cloth which generally makes it superfluous.

The waistcloth was used by all the peoples of the Mediterranean. The *schenti* of the Egyptians was a waist-cloth in its simple form ; the *subligaculum* or *subligar*, which was the forerunner of the tunic in Italy and was retained for a long time by both male and female peasants, was a waistcloth fastened in the form of drawers. Among the

[1] Herodotus, i, 10 ; cf. Thucydides, i, 6.

Ægeans it is the usual costume of the men, which we see worn
by tillers of the fields and fishermen, by athletes and warriors,
by high dignitaries and princes.   But the cut of it varies
considerably according to the material used, which may be
either pliable or stiff and may even be leather.   Sometimes
it envelops the thighs and even the knees in the form of
a short skirt and sometimes it is very much cut away at the
sides, so as to fall in two aprons.   (Figs. 7, 63.)[1]   At the back
it generally comes to a point which is sometimes elongated
and turned up like an animal's tail.   (Fig. 58.)   By way

Fig. 7.—Cretan of M.M.I. Figurine from Petsofa.

of exception we see two waistcloths placed one above the
other, forming flounces and coming halfway down the thigh
with a double point in front and behind.[2]   The wall-paintings
show us what a luxurious article the ceremonial waistcloth
can be made.   The Keftiu painted on the Egyptian tombs
of the XVth century (Fig. 35) wear over their variegated
costume a band, stiff with braidings and embroideries, which
falls obliquely down to the knees.
  In the Cyclades the Cretan form of waistcloth is worn.
But on the mainland it is caught together and transformed

[1] Fig. 7 is after BSA. ix, pl. ix.
[2] MA. xiii, 43, fig. 40.

into a pair of drawers or short breeches. A statuette from
Kampos in Laconia[1] shows how the idea of this transformation
originated. The waistcloth, fastened to the girdle behind,
is passed between the legs and joined up to the girdle in front.
The shape thus obtained by folding a piece of stuff was afterwards made permanent by cutting and sewing. There are
close-fitting drawers to be seen on representations of figures
from Crete, but they are worn either by foreigners (Fig. 8)[2]
or by demons to whom the artist wanted to give an exotic
look. (Fig. 73e.) Among the Mycenæans, on the contrary,
drawers are the usual costume for men.

Both waistcloth and drawers had to be fastened round
the waist by a belt. The Cretans early acquired the habit
of drawing it very tight. The Cup-bearer (Fig. 53) has what

FIG. 8.—Foreign archer. Bas-relief in steatite from Knossos.

appears to be a padded belt plated with metal. Some fragments of copper plating found in the necropolis at Phaistos
perhaps formed part of a belt. Such articles could be extremely
valuable. On one fresco richly dressed young men wear
round their waists girdles decorated with rosettes and spirals
and painted in white and yellow, showing that they were made
of silver and gold. Sometimes the metal plating is missing.
On a bronze figure a broad band of rough material can be seen
wrapped twice round the waist. (Fig. 63.) Cloth, too,
lent itself to luxury, just as much as metal. On an Egyptian
tomb the girdles of the Keftiu are represented by two long
stiff, figured ribbons arranged in large loops on the hips.

[1] **LXVII**, fig. 355.
[2] BSA. vii, 44, fig. 13.

The belt, whether of metal or cloth, is drawn excessively tight : the Cretan man laces himself as tightly as the young spark of the XVIth century with his busks.

As a general rule the Cretan is naked from the waist upwards. Certain personages, however, represented on the objects, have the upper part of the body protected by a sort of cassock. This garment sometimes appears to be made of overlapping pieces like scales of metal. (Plate II, 2.) It might, therefore, be taken for a cuirass. But it is often wide enough for the arms to remain inside, and it never appears in any but religious scenes. A sure proof that this garment is a kind of ritual cope is the fact that it is to be seen in the hands of a woman dressed in the skirt with the animal's tail, in the presence of a double axe floating in the air.[1]

The long gown, made in one piece and reaching to the feet, was, like the mantle, a ceremonial costume for men. It was worn only by princes, high dignitaries and priests, as in our day it is worn by professors, ecclesiastics, and men of law. It was made in bright colours and richly embroidered. In a procession [2] four official personages, whose bronzed skin reveals their sex, are to be seen clothed in this fashion. On the Hagia Triada sarcophagus (Fig. 50) a flute-player and a lyre-player are dressed in exactly the same way as the women taking part in the sacrifice or the dead man to whom the funeral tributes are being offered—that is to say, in tunics reaching from the neck to the calves or ankles.

Meanwhile, the waistcloth was adequate only in warm weather. In the mountains at all times of the year and on the plains during the rains and in winter, a long garment was obviously needed over it. The Ægeans have always had a cloak made from the skins of animals and the *diphthera* made of thick wool. A figurine from Petsofa even wears a kind of short cloak which has been likened with some justice to the Scots plaid.[3] The chariot-drivers are invariably wrapped in a long cloak which anticipates that worn later by the Greek charioteers.

The Cretans often go bare-headed. Several kinds of head-dresses, however, are known to them. Those who do not

[1] JHS. xxii, 78, fig. 5.
[2] BSA. vi, 12 ff.
[3] BSA. ix, pl. x, 11 ; cf. Myres, ib., 365–6.

wear their hair long frequently wear a turban or a tam-o'-shanter cap. (Figs. 2 and 3 ; Plate II, 2.) On one man's head (Fig. 64) there is a large flat round hat, apparently made of skin and resembling in shape a lady's hat of a certain kind found at Petsofa and still more similar to the Greek *petasos*.

As a general rule the Cretans put on shoes to go out of doors. The word "sandal" (σάνδαλον) is not Greek but pre-Hellenic. Most of the time the men wear very high buskins or half-boots reaching to the calves. The masculine statuettes of Petsofa (Fig. 7) are all shod well above the ankles

FIG. 9.—The Warrior Vase, found at Mycenæ. Late Period.

in boots painted white, showing that they were made of white or pale buff leather like that still used by the Cretans of to-day for making their famous boots. Half-boots of the same kind but coloured red this time, like Russian leather, and with thongs wrapped round the leg seven times, are to be seen on a fresco from Orchomenos. The Cretans, being great walkers and devoted to the *palæstra*, needed shoes both for the road and for the race-track. The toreadors, in particular, needed them in order to jump to the ground without hurting themselves. The great personages of the court do not appear barefoot in public. In the Egyptian paintings the envoys of Minos wear shoes or sandals of fine workmanship fastened by broad straps reaching above the ankles. Beads were sometimes used to adorn the shoe-straps, showing the wealth of ornament which was lavished upon these articles of dress. Shoes, however, do not appear to have been indispensable on all occasions. The fishermen would have found them decidedly in the way, and some of the boxers do not wear them. Inside the houses and in the sanctuaries people go barefoot. In the palaces the steps of the outer stairways are very much worn, while the inner staircases and all the pavements, even those of delicately rose-tinted cement, are still in a good state of preservation. The Cretans, therefore, put their shoes on only just as they were going out. Later the Greeks did the same thing. Homer's heroes only put on their " beautiful shoes " when they are going on a journey or into battle and, long afterwards, we see the Wingless Victory untying her sandals after the conflict.

The Mycenæans, who adopted the Cretan footgear, refused to accept the fundamentals of Cretan costume. Instead of waistcloths they wear drawers. Instead of leaving the upper part of their bodies bare they wear a short-sleeved *chiton* gathered in at the waist by a belt and ending in stiff skirts reaching halfway down the thighs. (Fig. 9.) This difference in masculine dress is one of the most striking manifestations of the distinction between the Cretan and the mainland races.

II Feminine Dress

Among the continual changes of fashion the Minoan ladies never achieved the noble pose which the folds of floating veils and the natural hang of soft draperies were to give to the women of Greece and Rome. On the contrary, their chief characteristic, to the great surprise of those beholding them for the first time, is the occidental *cachet* of their costumes, which sometimes look as if they had been copied from the latest Paris models. Certain ladies of Knossos, Hagia Triada, and Pseira instantly give an extraordinary impression of luxury and of studied elegance by the gay patterns of their materials and the richness of their ornaments. The colours are harmonized or contrasted ; the most varied designs are combined with graceful effect, and the material is embellished

with a profusion of pleats and puffs, multicoloured laces
and embroideries. But still more astonishing are the shapes
assumed by the two component parts of the dress—the skirt
and the bodice. Their cut continually reminds us of the most
distinctive and sometimes of the most extravagant fashions
which have been devised from the time of the Renaissance
up to the present day.

Such resemblances would be inexplicable were they not
due to a common descent and a parallel, though not simultaneous, development. There was a time, long before the

FIG. 10.—Cretan lady of M.M.I. Figurine from Petsofa.

age of metal, when the races destined to inhabit the Ægean
region and those who were to people Western Europe dressed
in the same fashion. From Neolithic, perhaps even Palæolithic
dress, Minoan costume and modern costume were evolved
at a quicker or a slower rate of progress. With certain
differences, due to climate or to individual caprice, the Ægeans
during a period of two thousand years introduced into
feminine costume the changes which took the peoples of the
North, retarded by the prolonged ascendancy of Greek and
Roman fashions, three thousand years longer to effect. The
dressmakers of the Minoan period and those of to-day, both

compelled to make clothes hanging from the waist, have only succeeded in satisfying the eternal coquetry of woman by giving to creations which are necessarily independent the same forms and the same details of ornament.

The origin of the skirt as a prolongation of the primitive waistcloth is sometimes recalled by the apron worn over it or by a polonaise very much cut away at the sides. (Fig. 62 ; Plate III, 2.)[1]

As a general rule the skirt appears alone. It is always tight at the waist and clinging round the hips but, beyond that, it is capable of infinite variations. The oldest known pattern, appearing on seals as far back as E.M.III, is clearly shown on a figurine from Petsofa. (Fig. 10.) The material is striped, the cut plain, and the shape that of a bell. To obtain a respectable diameter for the skirt recourse was had to stiffening it with horizontal hoops. Indeed, in later examples the bands of embroidery on the skirt form a cone so stiff and wide that we must imagine them held out by canes or metal ribs, just as whalebone was used in the crinoline. We see from the figurines from Palaikastro that the vogue of the stiff skirt persisted in the provincial towns until the Late Minoan Period. Possibly it was not without influence on religious sculpture. It may have contributed to the idea of making the statuettes of goddesses on a cylindrical base.

From M.M.III onwards the skirt becomes narrower at the bottom. The statuettes of the Serpent Goddess and of her priestess (Fig. 62 ; Plate III, 2) show two specimens of very different make. In the first example the plain material is divided into a score of horizontal bands by encircling rows of braid and it is edged with a strip of cross-work. The same use of a flat piece of stuff, but this time without the tiers of braid, is to be found in a skirt of the same period, which is lengthened by the addition of a deep pleated frill, and in a short skirt with trimming round the hem. (Fig. 46.) As for the priestess, her skirt represents a fashion which was to last as long as the Minoan civilization, namely, the flounce.

The flounces are sewn on to the skirt and cover this foundation entirely from the hips downwards. At first they were all of equal depth, and were subsequently narrowed as their

[1] JHS. **xxii**, 78, fig. 4 ; *AΔ*, iv, 53, fig. 3 ; BSA. **x**, 217–18, fig. 6*g–k*.

number was increased from five or six to a dozen. (Fig. 40.) On the skirt of the priestess, or the Serpent Goddess, they form a chess-board pattern in alternate rows of brown and fawn squares and brown and pale blue squares. From the Late Minoan period the prevailing shape is that of the composite skirt, on which the flounces are set at intervals with the foundation-skirt showing in between in bands, and at the same time finished in a point in front so as to accentuate the shape. The most remarkable and gorgeous example of this mode is to be found on a fresco from Hagia Triada : upon a material with a pattern of white crosses set off with red, alternating with blue crosses, two sets of flounces, composed of white, blue, red, and brown rectangles, are affixed one above the knee and the other below, the joins being hidden by a binding of red on a white ground.[1] The great period of the palace, Late Minoan II, brings a more sober fashion into favour : only the lower part of the skirt is trimmed with flounces finishing in a point in front.[2]

Unlike the men, the women of the mainland adopted the fashions of Knossos with enthusiasm. In the Pre-Mycenæan Period this was not yet the case. The third Shaft Grave at Mycenæ, where some dowager faithful to the modes of yester-year was buried, contained jewels, the like of which have not been found in Crete—pins which, with their enormous length and their heavy heads of rock crystal, cannot have been used for the hair, and must have held together a costume similar to the *peplos*. But the Mycenæan ladies of the new generation were not slow in preferring the becoming fashions from over the sea. They would have no others. The close-fitting bell-shaped skirt is therefore to be found in Mycenæ with the same varieties of style and trimming as in Crete. But the special favourite in Argolis is the composite skirt with the flounces. The immensity of the flounces and the extreme stiffness of their hooping in some instances recall a model which is rare in Crete.[3] On the great frescoes from Tiryns and Thebes the skirt is composed of beautiful multi-coloured flounces alternating with strips of the original fabric. (Figs. 11, 12.)[4] On a gem from Mycenæ it is surmounted

---

[1] MA. xiii, pl. x ; cf. 43, fig. 38 ; JHS. loc. cit., figs. 2, 8.
[2] See Rodenwaldt, **LXX,** 78.
[3] **LXVII,** fig. 343.
[4] **LXX,** pl. viii ; **XLI,** fig. 193.

by an enormous balloon-like puff or "bustle".[1] The skirt introduced at the court of Knossos in the spacious days of L.M.II was still more popular, and found its way even to Laconia. (Figs. 38, 39.)

Not all the types of skirt which we have had under review, including the bell-skirt of the Knossian goddess in faience, and the divided skirt of the ladies of fashion painted on the walls of the palaces, would suffice to give a true impression of the supreme grace bestowed upon apparel by artistic

FIGS. 11, 12.—Women in ceremonial costume, taking part in a procession. Frescoes from Tiryns and Thebes.

weaving. But we have representations of them that leave nothing to be desired either in accuracy or charm. These are the skirts in faience suspended as votive offerings in a chapel at Knossos. (Fig. 43.) Upon a greenish-white ground divided in two by a wavy line, such motives as a sheaf of slender flowers or a row of crocuses are rendered in purple brown.[2] These are in exquisite taste. The same cannot quite be said for the fashions of Phylakopi, which seek more after

[1] **XIII**, 164, fig. 44.
[2] BSA. ix, 82, fig. 58.

magnificence. The skirt adorned with two gaudy swallows with outspread wings among floral devices in white, red, and yellow, is a good example.[1]

Above the waist Ægean fashions are untroubled by our standards of modesty. In this respect the seductive ladies of the Minoan court declare themselves descendants of the women represented in Neolithic figurines. They do not expose the whole of the torso as the goddesses and priestesses sometimes do, but their bodices conceal practically nothing of their chests. At the end of E.M.III, and during the first two Middle Minoan Periods, the bodice finishes in a Medici collar at the nape of the neck but is open to the waist in front. (Fig. 10.) In M.M.III the collar disappears, the low neck remaining. The bodice is laced only below the breasts. This was the fashion which spread from Crete to Tiryns, Mycenæ, and Thebes. (Figs. 11, 12.) But during the Palace Period at Knossos court dress is completed by a transparent chemisette. The young girl known as the " Parisienne " (Fig. 6) wears a bodice held in position by a ribbon passing under the arms and tied at the nape of the neck in a large knot, the ends of which hang down like a " Watteau back ". She also wears a transparent front trimmed with narrow blue and red ribbons. The Dancing Woman (Fig. 52) wears a yellow bolero edged with embroidery over a chemisette rounded at the base of the neck. At all times and in all places the forearms are bare. The bodice has short sleeves, sometimes close-fitting, sometimes puffed, and sometimes even of the leg-of-mutton type.

The women certainly had the right to tight-lace themselves just as much as the men. They did it sometimes by means of a corset. The Serpent Goddess and the ladies on the frescoes from Tiryns and Thebes do not wear girdles. To make their skirts fit so tightly round the hips, to achieve such a slenderness of waist, and to make their bare breasts stand out as they do, they needed a framework of metallic strips. In the majority of cases, however, the juncture of the skirt and the bodice is marked by a belt. The women of M.M.I roll it twice round their waist and let the ends hang down in front to the bottom of the skirt, the oddest effect being produced when the girdle is thickly padded. This

[1] XXI, fig. 61.

double belt with two hanging ends is not unrelated to that
worn in the west during the Stone Age. Possibly, among the
Ægeans, it was a legacy from that period. In any case the
belt composed of two padded rims, one above the other, but
without hanging ends, remained in fashion for a long time
and votive specimens of it have been found in faience with
floral decoration. It was decided, however, to simplify this
great belt by getting rid of one of the two rims. This fashion
existed in Crete, but seems to have been more popular on the
mainland.[1] On a ring from Mycenæ, however, women have
their waists and hips encircled by a belt with three padded rims.
(Fig. 38.)

The long robe, all in one piece, is worn by women as well
as by men only for certain ceremonies. The religious character
of this costume is apparent from the Hagia Triada sarcophagus,
where the women who wear it are performing ritual acts, and
from an intaglio where the goddess seated between lions is
entirely enveloped in a cope which hides her arms.[2]

Like the men, too, the women put on the long cloak for
chariot-driving. For other occasions they throw over their
shoulders a sleeveless mantle or tippet made of skin.[3]

Being more stay-at-home than the men, the women were less
frequently shod; but they, too, wore sandals, shoes, and high
boots, according to the occasion. It has been remarked that
some of the women's shoes are fitted with heels.[4]

The ladies of fashion in Crete gave a lot of thought to
their hats. The figurines of Petsofa inspired Myres to a whole
chapter on hats.[5] It is like a visit to a milliner at the beginning
of the Middle Minoan Period. The smartest and the oddest
shapes follow one another in amusing variety. Here we have
a hood almost the length of the face it frames. Here we have
a " sailor ", there a three-cornered hat trimmed with rosettes
and finished with some curly adornment, either feathers or
lace. Several other hats have the distinctive elegance of
white trimming on a black shape. Side by side with these
models, which might belong to our own times, it is surprising
to find the *polos* of the Tanagra statuettes, and particularly

[1] MA. xiii, 40, fig. 34; **XIII,** figs. 44, 51, 58, 63, 64.
[2] Fig. 50; **XIII,** fig. 45.
[3] JHS. xxii, 76, pl. vi, 10.
[4] **LVII,** fig. 151.
[5] BSA. ix, 370–2; see pl. **xi,** 15, 20, **xx,** 36, viii; cf. *AΔ.* iv, 53, fig. 3.

an enormous head-dress shaped like a horn which has the strangest appearance imaginable (Fig. 10). Still more disconcerting are the hats or bonnets to be seen on the heads of goddesses, priestesses, and genii. The War Goddess (Fig. 46) has her head covered with an oriental tiara. The Serpent Goddess (Fig. 62) is increased in stature by a kind of shako. Worshippers wear toques of inordinate height. More frequently one comes across a kind of tam-o'-shanter or flat turban, generally set off by an aigrette or a flower with three spikes (Fig. 37). On the head of the sphinx this cap is adorned either with a large plume set in the middle or with a long tail floating in the breeze. It is quite possible that the tiara and the turban, before they were reserved for divine or priestly images, were worn by women.

III ADORNMENT

The dress of rich Minoans and Mycenæans was enhanced by sumptuous adornments. Both Crete and the mainland displayed great luxury in the matter of jewels which did not serve to satisfy feminine coquetry alone. A quantity of objects of gold have been found in the tombs upon skeletons of men. Very many of the rings were made for large fingers and the broad bezels, upon which scenes of battle or of the chase are so often engraved, served as seals. Bracelets and necklaces were worn almost equally by both sexes.

A male figurine from Petsofa has a jewel painted in white on its left arm. On the left wrist of a chieftain buried at Zapher Papoura three intaglio gems were found, one agate, one onyx, and one cornelian. Their presence in that place is explained by the heavy bracelet discovered in the fourth Shaft Grave at Mycenæ. Frequently the men even adorn both their wrists. Often, too, they wear two bracelets on the same arm. The Cup-bearer (Fig. 53) has on his left wrist a thin bangle in which is set a large stone with watered markings, an agate, and on the same arm, around the biceps, a broad circlet with a double rim. If fashions on the mainland were similar to those followed in Crete, certain differences can, nevertheless, be observed between them. From Mycenæ we have beautiful specimens of chased gold. In Crete, on the frescoes, varied colours and rich designs show not only the fineness of the chasing, but also the combination of precious metals and stones. The women were not likely to be behind the men in adorning themselves with bracelets. One has only to look at the Dove Goddess (Fig. 42) ; on either wrist she wears a fine circlet set with a large gem and on either arm a string of precious stones. Besides this, actual specimens are not lacking.

But Cretan men and women of all ranks like above all to display necklaces on their bare chests. There is practically not one site in the island that has not yielded large quantities of beads made of common stones. The tombs of "the common people " in the necropolis of Phaistos contained an abundance of examples. For more valuable necklaces they threaded beads of steatite, of *kyanos*, a blue paste imitation of lapis-lazuli, of agate, of amethyst, of cornelian, of rock-crystal, or else of small plaques of metal pierced in the centre. The rows of beads are broken up by pendants of different designs, such as flowers, birds, bulls, lions, and human figures. A lady of Pseira wears two necklaces, one of yellow beads of gold, with festoons hanging from them, and the other of blue beads of *kyanos*. The Dove Goddess wears across her chest a fourfold necklace composed of three rows of beads and one row of little triangular plaques. One of the "Ladies in Blue" displays every variety of jewel that could be got together, strung in five rows. The courtier strutting on the Knossos fresco wears a necklace painted in white, and so does the commoner from Petsofa. The Chieftain from Hagia Triada (Fig. 27) has a triple necklace and the King from Knossos (Fig. 57) wears majestically, from shoulder to shoulder, a broad golden chain of fleurs-de-lys. This masculine fashion spread from Crete to the other islands and to the mainland.

Ought we to be surprised that men who covered themselves with bracelets and necklaces stuck pins into their long hair and twisted strings of beads in it ? Sometimes they have a very elaborate *coiffure*. As for the women, their hair was tricked out fantastically during the Middle Minoan Period. During the Late Minoan Period it assumes a more natural appearance, with waved tresses hanging down the back and kiss-curls on the forehead. These capillary erections had to be held in position and enhanced by sticking in pins and threading in fillets. From all the sites of the Ægean a considerable number of hair-pins has been collected. Some are of copper and others of gold. The simplest had heads twisted into spirals. But at an early date the people of Mochlos had golden pins surmounted by daisies and other flowers. At Mycenæ the pins are as costly as they are varied. Several end in richly chased plaques of gold or balls of quartz or rock-crystal. Others have heads representing animals either in relief or in the round. A well-known pin from Troy II is surmounted by a stand holding six little jugs. As a rule the largest and the most valuable, such as those discovered in the third Shaft Grave at Mycenæ, belonged to women. In the tomb of Isopata, however, a beautiful golden corkscrew pin was found, an ornament for a king, while several pins from the fourth Shaft Grave are finished off with the heads of wild animals, such designs being dear to princes who were lovers of the chase. The Chieftain from Hagia Triada (Fig. 27) also wears in his long curls a trinket ornamented with large beads. But this style of ornament suits the women still better. They pass their tresses through rings or mingle spirals of gold filigree with their curls. Above all they affect fillets which are some-times simple ribbons of gold, but more often veritable diadems. Those from Mochlos are covered with a profusion of leaves and flowers, so that these delicate coronets are pretty examples of the goldsmith's craft. On the Miniature Fresco from Knossos the ladies of the palace, with their hair knotted at the nape of the neck, curled on the forehead and hanging in ringlets from the temples, wear diadems of gold and resemble, it has been said, the beauties who excited admiration at the court of the Empress Eugénie. The princesses of Mycenæ were not a whit behind those of Crete. Their tombs contained a large assortment of little plaques cut in the shape of leaves and fitted with hinges by means of which they were fastened to the diadems. The great ladies of Cyprus were conspicuous for the same kind of luxury. Lastly in Troy, in the " Treasure of Priam ", there was an imposing head-dress which has become famous ; with its sixty-four little chains from which the same number of little plaques in the form of idols hang down over the shoulders and the forehead, this orna-ment is picturesque in the extreme, and of quite Oriental magnificence.

The women, every one of them, even the least affluent,

wore other jewels of all kinds. Ear-rings are extremely varied in shape. Some are made of wire or thin strips of metal fashioned into spirals, others of plaques cut into half-moons and ornamented with rosettes. A large number of pendants and studs for the ears have been discovered. Many of the rings are too small for a man's fingers, for instance the famous ring from Mochlos (Fig. 41) engraved with the image of a goddess sailing in a boat.

CHAPTER III

ARMS AND ARMOUR

I DEFENSIVE ARMOUR

THE Shield. For the chase as for war, the Cretans had defensive weapons. The chief was a great shield.[1] None has been preserved, not even in part. For this great shield was not made of metal, or it would have been too heavy to carry. It was made of hide, and on a relief vase (Fig. 27) it terminates in an appendage, the tail of the animal. If it was not considered sufficient to take any skin and shape it roughly, an ox-hide was stretched on a wooden frame so as to retain its natural shape. Thus a gigantic piece of armour was obtained, a wall of hide, allowing nothing to show but the head and feet. When the Greek epic poets sang the paladins of old time they showed them, as does the Cretan vase, hidden by their shield up to the neck ; but one can understand that none but Aias had the strength to wield a panel of six ox-hides, over 260 pounds in weight.

The Cretans learned early to modify, lighten, and beautify the rudimentary form of the primitive shield. The most popular type was circular. As a rule, the two sides were deeply indented at the middle, so as to produce the bilobate or figure-of-eight shield (Fig. 13).[2] The advantage of greater lightness brought with it a serious disadvantage in that the narrow part of the shield gave less protection to the body; that is why the heroes of the *Iliad* are so often wounded in the side or thigh. Another fairly common type is the narrow oblong semi-cylindrical shield, curved at the top. Its length varies ; it covered the body to the ankles or protected only the trunk (Figs. 74, 45).

---

[1] See Reichel, **LXVIII ;** Helbig, JOEI. 1909, 1–70, figs. 1–4 ; von Lichtenberg, **XLIX,** 74–7 ; A. Reinach, RHR. 1909, ii, 161 ff., 309 ff. ; 1910, i, 197 ff.

[2] BSA. viii, 77, fig. 41 ; cf. our fig. 14.

Except the smaller type of shield all these weapons were too heavy to be carried long on the left arm. On the march the shield was hung round the body by a shoulder-sling ; it could always be seized in good time by the grip fixed in the centre. To make this motion easier the warrior who bore a spear carried his shield on his right side (Fig. 13). Since the sword must be drawn from its sheath with the right hand, it did not allow the use of the shield ; still less did the bow. The shield is exclusively the defensive arm of the spearman (Figs. 71, 74).

Towards the end of the Mycenæan Period the older forms are reduced. At the same time a new type appears, much smaller and lighter. It has the form of a circle, slightly indented. On the Warrior Vase (Fig. 9) it is painted alternately yellow

FIG. 13.—Warriors on the march. Sealing from Knossos.

and blue-grey, in imitation of leather and metal. Even on the march this round convex shield remains attached to the left forearm. In action the indented part is raised to the chin, and the shield then covers the body from the neck to the knees.

Finally the Ægean world took late to a target which was perfectly round and so small that, despite its metal covering, it was easy to handle. From Assyria it came to Cyprus with the cuirass in the XIVth century, in time to become part of the Greek panoply of the Homeric epoch.

Thus it appears that the heroes of the *Iliad* bore two kinds of shield, sometimes the great hide shield " like a tower " (ἠΰτε πύργος), " which envelops a man " (ἀμφιβρότη), and covers him " to his feet " (ποδηνέκης) and sometimes a small round target of metal (χάλκεον). Gradually, by a development which extended over the whole Homeric period, the first of these types disappeared before the second. No doubt the shield of Achilleus was immense, although entirely of metal ; but the work of the divine blacksmith is a poetic creation, in which confused memories seem to summarize the very history of the shield.

The Helmet. The helmet was not greatly used in Crete. Athletes wore it fairly often, but hunters and warriors only rarely. On the mainland, on the other hand, the helmet was usually worn, at least in war. No doubt it was unbearable for marching on the island on account of the heat, while it had nothing but advantages in colder countries.

Some archæologists have it that the Mycenæan helmet was always made of leather covered with metal plates and shaped like a cap, leaving the face exposed. As a matter of fact there was a fair variety of types of helmet in the Ægean world.

The helmet of the first type is made of plaited straps ; the conical form which it usually has is produced by a series of horizontal circles lying one above the other and laced together. The warriors were fond of a long tail attached to the tip (Fig. 13). With this type we may associate a helmet which at first sight presents considerable differences and is of uncertain origin. It appears most often on ivory heads from Mycenæ, Spata, and Enkomi, and on bronzes which are found from Phœnicia to Crete and from Argolis to Thessaly. This too is conical in shape, but not so high, and has at the top a large knob ; it is covered with a metal casing which is divided into zones by circles, and it is held on by a broad bandage which goes under the chin and forms cheek-guards. The zones of the head-piece were often set with boar's tusks. In the tombs of warriors from Crete to Thessaly, shaped and perforated teeth of this kind have been found surviving from leather helmets. This kind of tiara was a fairly effective piece of armour.

But a better piece of work was the bell-shaped helmet made entirely of metal. It appears at the end of M.M.II with a crest-piece, a long mane, and cheek-guards.[1] A L.M.I cup (Fig. 14) [2] shows us this fine example of Cretan armour. The head-piece is composed of strips of metal riveted together ; the lowest

[1] **XX,** figs. 227*b*, 228*m*, 229*c* ; cf. figs. 228*l*, 229*b* ; **LXXI,** pl. i, 1 ; iii, 11.
[2] **XVIII,** 27, fig. 37*b*.

strip projects so as to form a visor ; the neck-guard and cheek-guards give a rare elegance and also perfect efficacity. Athletes wore a helmet, with or without cheek-guards (Fig. 58). Warriors who carried a bow or a sword seldom had their head covered, but the spearmen, with their shield, also bore a helmet with floating crest. Even when the men-at-arms do not wear it, it glitters on the head of the officer (Fig. 27).

At the end of the Mycenæan period the helmet changes, like the shield. On the Warrior Vase (Fig. 9) there are two kinds : (i) a low close-fitting cap bristling with what is perhaps the hair of an animal, and (ii) a casque pointed at each end, and flattened in the middle, with a long mane dangling behind.

The Cuirass. Since the great shield was enough to protect the trunk, the cuirass was for long unknown in the Ægean

Fig. 14.—Figure-of-eight shield and helmet. Painted cup from Isopata.

panoply. The great cloak or cassock of scales or imbrications which appears on Cretan objects is too big for a cuirass and, moreover, it is only worn by priests or worshippers during the accomplishment of a rite (Pl. II, 2). The scraps of coarse cloth which have been found in graves among weapons were sticking to sword-blades, and must have been remnants of sheaths. Only once in Minoan Crete does a representation of a cuirass appear ; it is drawn on a tablet from Knossos. But this was probably brought as tribute from abroad.[1] It was not Crete, but Cyprus, which had the cuirass first, at the same time as the little round target,[2] and Cyprus brought it into the Ægean. Cyprus, which introduced its cuirass to the Achaians, still sent fine specimens to the kings of the Peloponnese in Homeric times.

[1] **XVII,** fig. 42.
[2] **XXXVII,** fig. 80.

The Leg-Pieces. So long as the great shield and the high boots were worn no further protection was needed for the legs. Leg-pieces or greaves seem unknown to the Cretans. They make their appearance on the mainland. They consist of bands of cloth or leather (Fig. 9). The great lords kept them on with garters of precious metal. The Shaft Graves contained many of these objects in gold, and one was still round the bone of a leg. The puttees and leggings are thus the prototype of the metal leg-pieces which were made in Cyprus at the end of the Bronze Age.

II OFFENSIVE WEAPONS

In the Stone Age everywhere man has the sling and bow for distant fighting and the axe and dagger for close combat. But in the Bronze Age the Ægeans made great progress in offensive armament. While the Egyptians, a peaceable and conservative people, remained attached to the oldest traditions in war, the Cretans perfected the arrow, transformed the stone-headed spear into redoubtable weapons for thrust and throw, and made the stoutest daggers and the finest swords of the day.

The Sling. The sling seems to have quite disappeared from Crete. But both Cretans and Mycenæans had intercourse with peoples who used it (Fig. 68). Bullets of stone and clay have been found in nearly every site in Macedonia, Thessaly and Phokis ; at Troy, too, some have been found, two of bronze, and the others of stone.

Arrows. The Ægeans of the Neolithic Age made arrow-heads of flint and obsidian. The Cretans gave up the use of stone for this manufacture early, but long after Crete had begun to use bronze continental Greece was still ignorant of metal or found it too expensive to be willing to make despised weapons of it.

The peoples who used obsidian for their arrows brought the required material from outside, but worked it themselves. The precious flakes were sent from Melos (Fig. 15) ; but in the masses of rubbish lying about the quarries and workshops of Phylakopi not a single piece has been found which resembles an arrow-head, either finished or roughed out. This proves that the island did not export manufactured weapons. Various experiments were therefore made in all parts, but in all parts a limited number of recognized types was adopted sooner or later.

In Crete the arrow-heads, both of obsidian and of flint, were at first of a clumsy, rough type. Then came the barbed or hooked type, invented in order to make the arrow stick in the wound. On the mainland this type succeeded another, which it did not drive out—the triangular type with a haft. All over the Peloponnese specimens of very fine workmanship show the preponderance of the barbed type, in flint and in obsidian. In Attica the two types and the two materials are equally frequent. Further north both types are found, but only in flint. In Thessaly the hafted type holds its ground throughout the Neolithic Age, and the barbed type does not appear before the Bronze Age, which corresponds to the Late

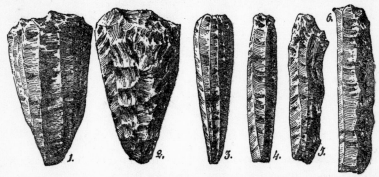

Fig. 15.—Obsidian cores and blades.

Minoan Period. Thus the use of bronze did not cause the stone arrow-heads to disappear, and the further one goes from Crete the longer this primitive manufacture persists. But, just because the tradition lasted so long, the cutters of flint and obsidian developed a barbed type which was as remarkable for its delicacy and beauty as for its penetrating power.

When the bronze-founders of Crete came to manufacture arrow-heads, they confined themselves at first to copying the models supplied by the stone-cutters. However, with the easier methods of casting they invented a mixed type, which combined the advantages of the barbs, which could be made at a more acute angle in metal, with those of a strong butt which could itself be made to terminate in two small barbs. This type supplanted the simple hafted type and spread concurrently with the simple barbed type (Fig. 16). The sure hand of the Cretan metal-worker is in marked contrast to the hesitation shown in the arrow-heads of Phylakopi II and of Thebes. Moreover, on the mainland the bronze arrow-head appears late and hardly spreads at all. At Kakovatos only one bronze head is found for more than forty of flint ; the whole of Thessaly has yielded only a few specimens in metal.

In imitating their stone models the bronze workers did not make their arrow-heads longer ; indeed they made them shorter. There are stone heads as long as 55 millimetres from Kakovatos and 66 millimetres from Dimini. The maximum length of the bronze heads is 42 millimetres at Phylakopi and 50 millimetres in Crete and at Thebes. They are usually so small that some have denied that such arrow-heads could be used as weapons of war. But, small though its head may be, the arrow is a terrible weapon in the hands of a stout bowman.

FIG. 16.—Bronze arrow-heads from Zapher Papoura.

It is not a rare occurrence to find human and animal bones pierced by flint arrow-heads. The Assyrians, Parthians, and Scythians hunted big game with no other arm than the bow. With their pointed heads and acute edges the Ægean arrows bit deep, and when an attempt was made to pull the weapon out of the wound the barbs tore the flesh horribly. With the Cretans and with the Mycenæans the bow was an arm both for hunting and for war (Figs. 8, 68, 71).

The stock of arrows which has been found at Knossos was certainly part of a military store. Among the hundreds of arrow-heads and the remains of the chests from which they had been strewn over the ground were found the sealings once fixed to the chests. We are in the stores of an arsenal. Tablets give us the inventories. Some record stocks of arrows, while others bear a statement of ibex-horns. The *Iliad* tells us for what these horns were used when it relates how Pandaros the Lycian had a bow made from the horns of a wild goat ;

the *Odyssey* tells us, in the story of Odysseus slaying the suitors, what could be done with such a weapon. So the arrows preserved in the arsenal of Knossos were not intended for hunters alone. The Cretan archers of classical antiquity had for ancestors the Kheretim or Cherethites who formed the guard of the Jewish kings and, long before that, the soldiers of Minos.

The Spear. All over the world man has had the idea of fixing a stone point to the end of a shaft, thus obtaining a weapon which he could throw to a distance or hold in his hand for close combat.

When the metal-founders of the Ægean produced the bronze spear-head, they gave it the form of a blade with a rib down the middle, terminated by a tongue or bored with a hole on each side of the rib. This blade was fixed in a cleft in the shaft, either by the tongue which was held in place by rivets, or with the aid of bindings run through the two holes. These two types are well known to us from specimens from Amorgos, Cyprus, and eastern Crete, but often when we have before us a triangular blade with rivet-holes we may ask ourselves whether it was a spear-head or a dagger. It is probable that the type with rivets was earlier than the type with two holes, for not only was the method of fixing it clumsier but the surviving specimens of it are shorter and thicker. For example, there is a spear-head with three rivets from Amorgos only 4·5 centimetres long, thus recalling stone originals, and, although it is true that another of the same type is as much as 25 centimetres long and 8 millimetres thick, those of the type with holes are never less than 17·4 centimetres and sometimes reach 31 centimetres in length, while their thickness does not exceed 2 millimetres.[1] In this way the methods proper to metal-working supplanted mere imitation of work in stone.

But a time came when it was felt that the cleft end of the shaft must be protected, and the fastening of the tang strengthened. On the mainland the upper half of the blade was furnished with a hollow rib on each face, running up to the point, and the lower part was pierced with two holes ; the two prongs of the cleft shaft were driven into the hollows of the ribs and the flat portion was made fast with nails. But

[1] AM. 1886, 21 ff., No. 7 ; De Ridder, *Bronzes de la Soc. Arch. d'Ath.,* 97, Nos. 491, 494.

this was not how the Ægeans arrived at the type of spear-head with a socket. First they hammered a broad tang into a tube round the shaft.[1] Progress consisted in making one casting of the blade and a closed conical socket. To these socketed spear-heads the armourers gave a beautiful shape. Before the end of the Middle Minoan Period they had types which were 28 and even 33 centimetres in length, the blade being 15 or 13 centimetres. The length of the blade was hardly increased in later years ; 13·5 centimetres was the maximum for the small type, and 17 centimetres for the large ; but the socket was sometimes increased, so that a total length of 34 centimetres has been known.[2]

The shapes vary considerably. Great antiquity may be assigned to the triangular type, in which the spear-heads resemble the oldest daggers. We may also regard the barbed or winged type as very old (Fig. 13) ; it reproduces the form so often given to arrow-heads. The fine specimens found at Zapher Papoura[3] may be divided into three types : (i) the long, straight type, very narrow, in which the socket and the blade are of the same breadth and the central rib continues the line of the socket towards the point ; (ii) the type with an oval blade on a rather narrower socket ; (iii) the type with a leaf-shaped blade much broader than the socket. It is in this last form, which was used very extensively at the end of the Mycenæan Period, that we must imagine the spear which the heroes of the *Iliad* carried, with its point (αἰχμή) fixed on the oaken shaft (δόρυ, μελίη) by means of a socket (αὐλός) of which the rim is sometimes held in a ferrule (πόρκης).[4]

So far we have spoken simply of " spear-heads " to avoid cumbrousness. The same point would do for a hand-weapon or a missile, a lance or a javelin.   In the presence of an actual specimen it is often impossible to say whether it was thrown at a distance or wielded at close quarters. Even the representations of figures do not decide the question for us ; for the javelin could be very long and serve for both purposes (Fig. 71). There are, however, points from 6 to 8·5 centimetres in length which are too big for arrows, and too small for lances,[5]

---

[1] See **LXXXII,** fig. 45, xx, 10–12 ; **LXVII,** fig. 552 ; **XL,** pl. iv, 48.
[2] **XVI,** figs. 56–7, 113.
[3] Ib., fig. 113.
[4] See Cuq, DA. *Hasta,* 34.
[5] **XVIII,** 6, figs. *a–c* ; 15, No. 3*e* ; BSA. vi, 110, fig. 42, Nos. 2, 4, 8, 11.

and these must have been specially intended for javelins. Furthermore, on the Warrior Vase (Fig. 9) some of the figures carry long spears, armed at each end, which must be lances, while the others brandish very short spears as one would a missile. Finally it is to be noted that the frescoes of Tiryns constantly represent persons carrying two spears. It is thus that Odysseus and his supporters, when about to give battle to the suitors, take care to provide themselves each with two javelins,[1] and the warriors buried in the ancient tombs of Athens always have spear-heads buried with them in pairs. For close combat they would not have needed two, but they did not want to remain unarmed after throwing one.

Whether lance or javelin, the weapon of the Ægeans is never of the size of which we hear later. When the Homeric poems describe a spear as " long " or " gigantic " we know what that means from the weapons of Hektor and Aias— one is eleven cubits (5½ yards) and the other is twice as long. We should believe that it was poetic exaggeration, were it not that the Chalybes, according to Xenophon, handled spears of fifteen cubits, or 7½ yards, and the Macedonian *sarissa* was at least 14 feet and perhaps 7 yards. The Cretans and Mycenæans had nothing like this. On the objects representing persons, the shaft of the warrior is generally slightly shorter or slightly taller than the man who carries it (Figs. 13, 45) ; it was therefore between 5 and 6 feet. For hunting boar and lion, however, shafts were used which were much taller than men, and must have been over 6½ feet.[2]

Whether they have a long spear or a short, warriors and hunters carry the shield or dispense with it without there being any apparent reason for the difference. There is the same variety in the way in which men carry their arms on the march.

The Dagger. Although it is often hard to distinguish spear-heads from daggers, it is certain that Neolithic civilization had attained perfection in the art of cutting a thrusting weapon with two edges. The bronze-worker inherited fine models which he had only to copy.

The first metal daggers were cast in copper. In Crete they date from E.M.II, but they are already of a perfected type

---

[1] *Odyssey*, xxii, 101 ff., 251 ff., 272 ff.
[2] Fig. 71 ; **XX,** fig. 541*a*.

which goes back earlier.[1] The blade of this period is short and flat ; a broad butt without tang, bored with rivet holes, gives it an isosceles form. In the oldest examples the length varies from 6 centimetres to 12·4 centimetres, and the maximum breadth from 2·8 centimetres to 5·3 centimetres.[2] At the end of the Early Minoan Period the Cretan metal-workers attain a more formidable length—15·4 centimetres at Mochlos, 18 centimetres at Vasiliki, and 20 centimetres in the cave of Arkalochori. From this cave indeed we have much longer blades, but they are so narrow and thin that they can only be votive *simulacra*, models for the armourers of the next world.[3] Without leaving eastern Crete we find the triangular dagger again in M.M.I on figurines from Petsofa (Fig. 7). Attached almost horizontally to the belt in front, it is as long as the fore-arm with closed fist, half of this length being the handle. The blade has a rib down the middle, and is very broad at the base. The hilt, fastened with two rivets, and sometimes embellished with chased or inlaid decoration, ends in a button-shaped pommel. This is the perfection of the type which the Copper Age handed down to the Bronze Age.

In spite of the progress accomplished the metal-workers of Crete were in no way pre-eminent at that time. The triangular dagger of copper exists in the Cyclades. Amorgos even had blades 24 centimetres long.[4] In Cyprus [5] development had been so rapid that the primitive type is no longer found even in the oldest strata. It is replaced by new types. First the blade, growing steadily longer, was inserted in the handle by a tang ; then a stouter form of tang or shaft was beaten down over the end of the handle in a hook, the shoulders of the blade were rounded, and the willow-leaf form of the dagger was produced—the especially " Cypriot " dagger. At Troy II a great variety in the manufacture of daggers was reached fairly early.[6] In short, the armourers of Crete did not surpass those of the Cyclades towards the end of the Early Minoan Period, and when they had bronze at their disposal they still remained long centuries without beating

[1] Evans, **XX**, 68.
[2] MIL. xxi, v, fig. 24, pl. x ; **LXXXII,** fig. 12.
[3] Ib., fig. 44 ; **XL**, 49 ; BSA. xix, 45, fig. 8, Nos. 4, 8, 20.
[4] AM. 1886, 23, 26, 38; Beilage i, 6 ; 1891, 48, figs. 3, 4 ; 'Eϕ., 1898, pl. xii, 8 ; **LXXXV,** 224 ; 'Eϕ., 1899, 121, pl. x, 43.
[5] See Myres, **LXI ;** Dussaud, **XI,** 259-64, fig. 185.
[6] **X,** 421, Nos. 1, 3 ; 329 ; 344–5, figs. 262–4.

those of Cyprus and of Troy. But, while the other Ægeans allow their armourer's art to sink into a decline, and the Troad never produces anything resembling a sword, and the master-piece of the Cypriots, a weapon 47 centimetres long, hardly deserves this name, we shall see to what perfection the Cretans will attain.

They did not do it without endless experiments. Progress was slow, but continuous. It can be seen as early as M.M.I. It is enough to compare with the dagger of the Petsofa figurines that which is worn by a person carved on a contemporary ivory (Figs. 7, 25). The weapon is long, with the handle reduced to a minimum ; it is slender from one end to the other ; on account of its length it is worn at the side. The specimens preserved tell the same story ; the blade grows longer and slenderer, and ends in a very fine point, without growing broader, and even growing narrower, at the butt ; thus it obtains a more graceful appearance, and loses the triangular outline. At Mochlos the new type at once appears with a maximum breadth of 5 centimetres and a length of 22·5 centimetres. At Hagia Triada it is represented by examples with and without tangs ; one of them has a total length of 25·5 centimetres, of which 22 centimetres go to the blade.[1] A slender dagger from Amorgos of the same date has exactly the same length as the specimens from Mochlos and Hagia Triada, and the same breadth at the butt as the latter, viz. 3·5 centimetres.[2] But already there was in the Palace of Phaistos a founder's matrix which turned out blades 4 centi-metres broad at the base, and 31·5 centimetres long.[3] In M.M.I, then, the triangular dagger had been made narrower and much longer ; in M.M.II and III [4] shapes were multiplied and diversified, and even the rudiments of slightly flanged projecting shoulders were introduced, but the length revealed by the Phaistos mould was not exceeded.

From the Late Minoan Period the armourers of Crete began to give their types a variety which was ever producing new forms, and, while they continued to supply stilettoes of ordinary size, they made large daggers which grew longer and longer.

[1] **LXXXII,** fig. 45, xi, 22 ; MA. xiv, pl. xliv, 11, 7.
[2] 'Εφ., 1898, 189, pl. xii, 6.
[3] MA. loc. cit., 467, 469–70, fig. 75a.
[4] **XL,** pl. xliv, 6, 8–10 ; **XIII,** 68–70, fig. 54.

At Gournia [1] the blades, whether slender, shaped like oval leaves, or tongue-shaped, are not more than 17·8, 20·6, or 22 centimetres in length ; but a triangular type with a broad flat rib and three big rivets in the old style shows some remarkable specimens ; one example with a short tang, 6 centimetres broad at the butt, is 35·3 centimetres long ; another, 6·5 centimetres broad, has a length of 36·7 centimetres, which with the tang (now lost) must have come well up to 42 centimetres.

The arms found in the cemetery of Zapher Papoura have the same variety of forms and exceed the dimensions which could be assigned to a mere dagger. Without them, the results obtained by the armourers of Knossos would only be known by the daggers represented on a tablet, which pass from the triangular form to the diamond leaf form by the intermediate " spear-head " form.[2] But the four specimens from Zapher Papoura,[3] by their form and by their size, summarize the whole history of the dagger in Crete. The first, which recalls the old Early Minoan form, is only 19·2 centimetres long and 5 centimetres broad at the butt. The second, of which the blade, slightly indented in the middle and wider towards the ends, is ornamented along the edges with a triple groove, is 23 centimetres long, of which 6·5 centimetres go to the handle. The third, of the sub-triangular type, has a hilt 8·8 centimetres long, bordered by a metal flange and ending in a large knob ; it has a total length of 37 centimetres. The fourth and last is something quite new ; projections on the blade turned down towards the point form the guard of a hilt 8 centimetres in length, plated with ivory, solidly riveted and ending in a broad conical pommel ; the total length this time is 42 centimetres.

The Sword. However, to transfix an enemy who is covered by an enormous shield, a dagger—even such a dagger as these—was not sufficient. What was wanted, to pierce over the shield, was a thrusting weapon of some length, with a blade strengthened by the enlargement of the rib, sharp cutting edges, a sharp point, and a hilt just long enough to be easily handled and strong enough to stand the shock of blows—in

---

[1] Ib., pl. iv, 49–61.
[2] BSA. viii, 94, fig. 54.
[3] **XVI,** 62c, 86a, 95e, 14s ; cf. our fig. 17.

fact, a sword. Cyprus, we have seen, made good long daggers of 47 centimetres. It is not much, we shall see, in comparison with what Mycenæ and Crete can produce from the end of M.M.III.

We shall here make use, with certain modifications, of the chronology of the Creto-Mycenæan swords which has been established by Evans and Déchelette.[1] We shall distinguish seven types. The first two are those in which the sword still appears only as a highly developed dagger :

(i) The type with a very narrow blade, rounded shoulders, *a short thin tang* with small rivets, and a separate hilt of doubtful solidity ;

(ii) The similar type which has, however, a broader blade and butt, widely projecting shoulders and *a long, broad, flat hilt-plate* with big rivets.

These two types were combined by leaving the blade as slender as before, while accentuating the projection of the shoulders so as to make them into a kind of guard ; thus was obtained :

(iii) The type with rounded perpendicular projections in the form of a *cross.*

Instead of standing at right angles these projections could stand obliquely, and thus we have :

(iv) The type with wings turned up like *horns* ;

(v) The same type, more developed, in the form of *hooks* turned down towards the blade.

Lastly there are two types, not closely connected with the preceding, which are frequently found over a considerable part of Europe :

(vi) The type with a flat tang, with the *edges flanged* to hold the plating of the hilt, and *rounded shoulders;*

(vii) The short type with a flat tang, with *flanges* on the edges of the hilt, a flat triangular pommel and a *triangular butt* to the blade.

All these types are found at Mycenæ. The two first are frequent in the oldest graves of the Acropolis. The cruciform type is found with the short-tanged type before it is mixed with the horned type. From the horned type, which gains the upper hand, the hooked type is derived late. Lastly, the

---

[1] **XVI,** 495 ff. ; **VIII,** ii, i, 212 ff.

H

two types with metal flanges appear just before the end of the Mycenæan civilization. Whereas type (i) is as yet represented only by a dagger of 37·5 centimetres, type (ii) has already reached a length of 77·5 and even 85 centimetres.[1] The three types of the good period keep up the size, from 50 to 66 centimetres.[2] There is no sign yet of decadence in the long sword of type (vi).[3] But the triangular type of the last period not only shows a retrogression towards the primitive form of the dagger, but goes back to a length of 37·5 centimetres.[4]

In Crete we see the manufacture of the sword pass through the same phases and produce even more remarkable results. In L.M.I the Cretans knew the two types without guard. They remained faithful to the oldest type long after they had perfected it, for a sword of this type, 53 centimetres long, was buried in the same tomb as one of the horned type (Fig. 17, Nos. 44*a*, *b*). As for the second type, it is represented by examples, of which one must have been quite 70 centimetres long.[5] We recognize it also on a relief vase (Fig. 27) where its length clearly exceeds half the height of a man. But the Cretans did not go on for long making a weapon of which the guard was inadequate. In L.M.II and III the cruciform type was popular. It was used for short swords ; the specimens from Zapher Papoura are between 50 and 63 centimetres (Fig. 17, No. 36*i*). At the same time, the Cretan armourer showed his incomparable excellence by the use he made of the horned type. With its upturned wings, this form was better adapted than any other to cover and enclose the hand which had to fight with a heavy rapier.[6] The two swords of the horned

---

[1] 'Εφ., 1897, 105, pl, vii, 3 ; **LXXII,** figs. 445*a*, 448. A sword from Kakovatos, of the first type, is 92 cm. long (AM. 1909, 298–9, fig. 14).

[2] 'Εφ., 1897, pl. viii, 1, 2, 5 ; 1891, pl. ii, 5.

[3] Ib., 1897, pl. viii, 3 ; **VIII,** ii, i, fig. 65, 8.

[4] 'Εφ., loc. cit., 4.

[5] **XVIII,** 4, figs. 7, 8.

[6] Since the Cretan and Mycenæan warriors had the long and the short sword at the same time one might ask what special use they made of them. The appearance of both in the same grave has led some to suppose (Burrows, **VI,** 88) that warriors used the rapier to attack and the short sword to parry, like our XVIth century duellists. Another hypothesis (A. Reinach, DA., *Pugio,* 763) regards the short sword as a " dague de miséricorde ", used to finish off the wounded. But never, in any battle-scene, do we see two swords in the hands or at the belt of a combatant. The fact is that when a warrior's family buried several weapons in his tomb, for example, a sword with a spear or arrows, they wished him to be as richly furnished in death as in life ; they certainly did not expect him to handle all the weapons in his panoply simultaneously.

type found at Zapher Papoura in company with short swords measure 91·3 centimetres and 95·5 centimetres respectively

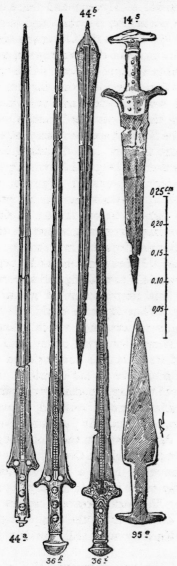

FIG. 17.—Daggers and swords from Zapher Papoura. (After Evans, **XVI,** fig. 109.)

(Fig. 17, Nos. 44a, 36h). These are indeed masterpieces, which show gloriously the superiority of the metal-smiths who worked

for the master of Knossos.   Such an art can only deteriorate
(Fig. 17, No. 14s).

Between the swords of Mycenæ and those of Crete, be they
long or short, the connexion is certain and obvious.   How is it
to be explained ?   So long as the Cretans needed to arm themselves only in order to make their voyages in complete security
they did not trouble to have rapiers, which would have been
a nuisance if anything ; good stout daggers of various sizes
and short swords were sufficient and more useful.   But from
the moment when the Minoans had vassals and customers on
the mainland in the North it was necessary to give them a sword
which would ensure to them the advantage in battles on land
and would enable them to keep the northern peoples respectful.
Although the rapier appears at Mycenæ many centuries
before it is found at Knossos there is no proof that it was
manufactured in Argolis before it was in Crete.   The very
continuity of the improvements added to the oldest types
testifies to a regular development in a straight line.   Moreover,
the synchronism of this development at Mycenæ and in Crete
from M.M.III onwards is so striking and so complete that there
must have been one single centre of manufacture, at least
at the beginning.   That Mycenæ could play such a part is
unlikely.   There is no evidence which allows us to see in
Argolis a first-class metal-working centre, and the arms which
were the pride of its chieftains are enriched with ornaments
which are not at all native to the country.   On the contrary,
all the decoration of the daggers and swords, whether they were
found on the mainland or on the island, is borrowed from the
most authentic processes and the purest motives of Minoan art.
There is nothing curious even in the fact that no rapier earlier
than L.M.II has come to light in Crete, for, if we have no actual
specimens, we have at least a representation from L.M.I
(Fig. 27).   On the other hand it is very significant that the
tombs of Zapher Papoura received rapiers, and the most
beautiful of all, directly after the conquest of the island by
the Achaians.   Knossos was still working for the folk of
Mycenæ.

The success of the bronze swords of Crete is attested in
every country of the prehistoric world.   They were imported
and soon after imitated everywhere.   At Gezer, in Palestine,
a sword of the horned type has been found with Ægean

pottery. At Rhodes there are swords of the cruciform type.[1]
In the West the Ægean blade of the earliest type was retained
for a long time for the manufacture of rapiers, witness the fine
specimen found at Massolivieri.[2] The Ægean models even
penetrated far into the continent. But at the time of the
decline of Crete all peoples manufactured swords with metal
flanges. The round-shouldered type not only served as model
for the first iron swords forged by the Greeks; it is also widespread in Egypt, the whole Balkan Peninsula, Hungary, and
the whole of Italy.[3] The type with the triangular blade, the
last which was known to the Bronze Age in Crete and at
Mycenæ, appears at Karpathos, Corinth, Athens, Thebes, and
Dodone; and it appears too from Egypt to Italy, where it was
passed on to the iron-worker.[4] It is therefore difficult to make
any positive statement on the origin of the types invented
towards the end of the Mycenæan age; they prove, in any
case, that the long undisputed superiority of Crete was over.

[1] **XVI**, 497, note *d*; cf. **XXX**, pl. D, 11, 13; Worsae, MAN. 1880, 131.
[2] **XVI**, 497–8.
[3] Ib., 501–2.
[4] Ib.; **VIII**, ii, i, 213.

CHAPTER IV

THE HOUSE AND THE PALACE [1]

I THE ORIGINS OF ÆGEAN ARCHITECTURE

THE earliest dwellings in which men have sheltered themselves are caves. In the mountainous regions which border the Mediterranean, nature everywhere offered these refuges to the peoples of the Neolithic Age. The Greeks did not lose the memory of these forefathers who " dwelt, like frail ants, under the ground, in the depths of caves where the sun did not reach ".[2] They knew that Polyphemos, living on the mountain in company with his sheep and goats, in a cave which he closed every night with a huge rock, was the type of the men—Kyklopes or Troglodytes—who knew no laws and did not till the fields.[3] Many of these rock dwellings are known—the cave of Choirospilia in Leukas, and the rock shelters of Miamou, Skalaes, and Magasa in Crete.

Very early the tribes of the Neolithic Age learned to build, hollowing out caves which were too small, or reducing clefts which gaped too widely with artificial walls. They soon learned to build huts of a wattle of reeds or branches covered with clay. The floor of these huts was at first made of beaten earth, and then it was given some kind of stone paving. These " hut-floors " have been found almost everywhere on the mainland, and there is one in Crete at Phaistos.[4] These dwellings were too fragile to resist the violence of storms and the injuries of time ; on the same spot, and with the same materials, others were built, and yet others. From century to century the accumulated debris raised the level of the soil. In this way the Neolithic stratum at Knossos reached a depth of between 6 and 8 metres.

[1] See Mackenzie, BSA. xi, 181–223 ; xii, 216–57 ; xiii, 423–46 ; xiv, 343–422 ; Doerpfeld, AM. 1905, 257 ff. ; 1907, 575 ff. ; Noack, **LXI I**, **LXIII** ; Leroux, **XLVI**, ch. I–IV ; Fimmen, **XXV**, 39–54.
[2] Æschylus, *Prometheus*, 452–3.
[3] *Odyssey*, ix, 106 ff.
[4] MA. xix, 141 ff.

The cave of primitive times is recalled by many survivals in the Ægean type of hut and, later, of house. The cave was situated on a height ; and, just as the shrine was installed for choice in a cave and the tomb was for a long time dug in the rock, the house was built on the side of a slope and required for its foundations an artificial terrace. The cave was chosen with an opening towards the East in order that its darkness might be dispelled, as in the cave of Polyphemos, " by the first rays of the daughter of the morning, Dawn with the rosy fingers " ; at Magasa a Neolithic house has the same exposure as the rock shelter.[1] But it was above all the actual shape of the hut and of the house which recalled the round interior of the cave.

All over the Mediterranean world the Neolithic Age was acquainted with the round straw hut.[2] At Sesklo in Thessaly round huts were built for at least a thousand years ; on Leukas and at Mycenæ the tombs were in enclosures surrounded by circular walls. At Orchomenos the lowest stratum contains only circles of superimposed stones ; these once served as the foundations of walls of unbaked brick which sloped inwards so as to form a dome between seven and eight metres high.[3] A box from Melos represents the seven round houses of a *genos* grouped round a court with a covered entrance.[4] It was better to collect the *genos* under one roof ; at Tiryns, in the second half of the third millennium, above an older stratum of round huts, a great rotunda was built, itself enclosing circular constructions.[5] In Italy the form of the terramara huts was perpetuated in cinerary urns ; similar Early Minoan urns have been found at Phaistos and Pyrgos.[6] So, too, in the lower strata of Knossos traces have been found of round buildings, walls with rounded corners. But the rotunda which the pre-Hellenic peoples of Crete built longest and with a special devotion was the *tholos* or beehive tomb.

From the circular form the oval or elliptical form was derived. At Orchomenos the stratum of the circular houses was covered,

---

[1] BSA. xi, 263, fig. 2.
[2] See Mackenzie, BSA. xiv, 345 ff. ; Modestov, **LV,** 163, 330 ; Leroux, **XLVI,** 2 ff.
[3] **LXXXVIII,** 155 ff. ; **XXV,** fig. 49 ; **V,** 19 ff.
[4] **IV,** i, 11.
[5] AM. 1913, 84 ff. ; 334 ff.
[6] Cf. **XXV,** fig. 30 ; **XX,** fig. 82.

after 2500, by a stratum of elliptical houses.[1] The advance from the one type to the other is general, and is found in Thessaly and also in Italy. This transformation is explained by the necessity for enlarging the round house in order to gather together the members of the group who had hitherto lived in huts placed side by side. The construction of a common roofing for several round huts, or, as at Tiryns, of several roofs on the same rotunda, was too complicated ; it was easier to extend the same roofing over two half-huts, two apses, placed at the required interval, and more commodious rooms were obtained by means of straight partition walls. But it is in Crete that the most remarkable example of the elliptical type was found, in the house at Chamaizi (Fig. 23).[2] The longer axis is over 22 metres, and the shorter is over 15. The ground floor, formerly surmounted by a storey, contains a dozen rooms, which received a certain amount of light from a small central court. The rooms in the two apses are naturally irregular ; the others are almost rectangular.

The practice of closing the caves with straight walls had suggested the use of walls, not only to divide up the elliptical house but, long before, to build a square or rectangular house. In the Neolithic Age there was built at Magasa, opposite the rock shelter which was completed by a wall, a slightly trapezoidal house of big unhewn stones. The entrance, set in a corner, divided it into two equal parts, of which one was doubtless the dwelling-room and the other the storeroom or byre. It is therefore impossible to agree with Noack in making the rectangular form a derivative of the elliptical form, as the latter is referred back to the circular form ; this would be squaring the circle by archæology.[3]

The quadrangular type lent itself to every kind of improvement. With it nothing was easier than to add new premises as they were required. So it necessarily drove out the rounded type almost completely. However, this result was not achieved everywhere with equal speed. In Crete the ossuary at Kastri presents a remarkable instance of the simple hut with rectangular walls, still just like the house at Magasa,[4] but

---

[1] **V,** 34 ff.
[2] For the question of the accuracy of this plan see p. 398 below.
[3] Noack, **LXIII,** 51 ff. ; cf. Leroux, **XLVI,** 7–8, 20, 30.
[4] BSA. xi, 270, fig. 4, 2.

there was already a house at Vasiliki in E.M.II which contained more than twenty rooms communicating easily with one another.[1] On the mainland sites, the rectangular plan did not attain such dimensions before the Mycenæan Period, but all the same it was known as early as the third millennium in the townships of Corinthia, it appeared at Dimini and Sesklo in stone houses with two rooms, and it was a characteristic feature of the Third City of Orchomenos.[2] This type had the advantage that it alone was adapted to the juxtaposition *ad infinitum* of rooms to form a house, of houses to form a town, of apartments to form a palace, and it alone could obtain the precocious favour of the Cretans. It still imposed very simple plans on them ; in the palace a central court and small secondary courts determined the direction of all the walls, and in the town the streets and lanes were arranged, so far as possible, on a rectangular plan.

On the mainland, on the other hand, when this type was finally adopted, it was with reluctance. From Thessaly to the Peloponnese for a long time the curvilinear plan forced the rectilinear plan to lend itself to a quaint combination. The apse, adapted to straight walls, furnished a new type. It had a great fortune in pre-Mycenæan Greece, and specimens as late as the XVIth century are found at Thermos in Aitolia.[3] In Crete the half-ellipse plan appears only in the rock tombs, and was perhaps never given to houses.

Among the traditions which went back to primitive times one of those which persisted was the orientation given to houses, and consequently to palaces and towns. Since the entrance of the Neolithic dwelling generally faced east, the same was the case with the *tholos* tomb, and the rectangular house, especially the sanctuary, had its four walls aligned with the cardinal points and the door set for choice towards the rising sun. Thus continuous rows of houses were set along streets running from North to South, or from East to West. The rule of the *cardo*, which was regularly applied in the plan of the Etruscan temple and of the Roman camp, was already observed in the terramare of Italy. Like many other cities, *Roma quadrata* was divided into two equal parts by a big street

---

[1] **XL,** pl. xii, 49 ; cf. **XX,** 71–2.
[2] **III,** 75 ; **LXXXIX,** figs. 18, 22 ; **V,** 53 ff.
[3] **XCI,** 37 ff.; **V,** fig. 9 ; **III,** figs. 110–11; AM. 1913, 86 ; 1908, 188 ff.;
AΔ, i, 225 ff. ; ii, 178 ff.

running north and south, the *cardo maximus*. Each of these halves was subdivided into two quarters by a street running east and west, the *decumanus maximus*. Parallel with the main streets the *cardines minores* and the *decumani minores*, much narrower, cut the quarters up into blocks. In Crete orientation is observed, not only in isolated dwellings like the Neolithic house at Magasa and an old house at Hagia Triada, but in the buildings of Tylissos, the Palaces of Hagia Triada and Phaistos, and the Great and Little Palaces of Knossos (Figs. 19, 21). Slight divergences are sometimes to be noted, either to the North or to the South; but there is nothing abnormal in these. They are due to the variation of the ortive amplitude of the sun, that is the angle made by the direction of the rising sun with the true East; for the ancient peoples, and still more the prehistoric peoples, had neither the knowledge nor the instruments necessary to determine the east with scientific accuracy. When the priests consulted the orb of day in order to determine the axis of the earth, when they wished to mark the *templum* in order to draw the divine blessing on a building or a town to be constructed, the strict observance of rites could not make up the inadequacy of their science. The *cardo* is necessarily subject to more or less deviation in the prehistoric sites. This deviation has enabled the Italian astronomers to calculate the two days in the year out of which we must choose that on which the terramara dwellings were inaugurated. By doing the same for the towns and palaces of Crete,[1] we reckon that their construction must have commenced either between the 22nd February and the 7th April, or between the 6th September and the 21st October, and indeed, for ritual and practical reasons, in the former of these periods, at the beginning of spring. In any case we must admit that the early Cretans had the religious spirit which is implied by the application of the *cardo*.

II CRETAN ARCHITECTURE

The houses of the small folk were generally composed of stone foundations and walls of brick dried in the sun. The masonry of the big walls was reinforced with horizontal beams. A clayey plaster was used as a coating. The floor consisted of

---

[1] I am under a profound debt of gratitude to M. Andoyer, who has kindly supplied me with the data necessary for this calculation.

a pavement of flags, cobbles, or cement, or simply of beaten
earth. The ceiling was made of reeds coated with plaster.
All these materials, except the stone, have disappeared in the
ruins. The bricks have crumbled, dissolved, and merged into
the soil. They are only preserved in dwellings which have been
burnt. In that case the fire has given them the look of calcined
bricks, with a brilliant red tinge, which has earned for the lower
part of Palaikastro the name of Roussolakkos ; but the proof
that they were not baked is that the mortar which bound them
has the same colour to-day. But the Cretans used baked
bricks as well. They have been found at Gournia, Zakro,
Palaikastro, and Phaistos. They are of different types, and
measure on an average 40 by 30 by 10 centimetres. These
dimensions remind one of the big bricks of the classical period ;
there is nothing astonishing in this, since the Greek word for

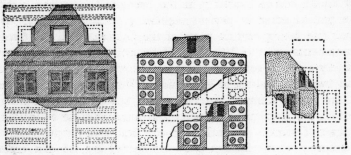

FIG. 18.—Faience plaques representing Cretan houses.

" brick ", πλίνθος, is of pre-Hellenic origin. But the
Cretans began early to build in stone. In the towns of Crete
and at Phylakopi quite simple dwellings and the very humblest
rooms are often made of small stones with a mortar of clay.

The private houses of the big towns are known to us not only
by their actual remains, but, still better, by one of the most
extraordinary documents which Crete has left, about fifty
plaques of faience reproducing in detail so many different house-
fronts (Fig. 18). All these houses, which date from the XVIIIth
century, have several storeys and are lighted by windows.
They are of three types. Some, doubtless of brick, are rough-
cast all over. Others are of freestone arranged in regular
courses and bound by thick layers of clay. But the most
numerous are remarkable for the great use which is made of
wood. Beams are laid horizontally at regular intervals, and

are generally supplemented by cross-beams. These sides and heads of beams, which are left showing intentionally, give the wall a decoration of bands and disks the dark colour of which stands out against the rest of the masonry.

In the large buildings, brick is rare, and choice materials are used. Everywhere the builder has at his disposal a fine limestone, and a homogeneous gypsum which looks like alabaster or marble ; but whereas at Knossos both materials are used for rough work, at Phaistos gypsum is reserved for partition walls, jambs, and decoration. The blocks are beautifully cut, with sharp edges. The usual dimensions attain to a length between one metre and 1·50, a breadth of 50 centimetres, and a height between 50 and 70 centimetres. Laid on a solid foundation, the bottom course sometimes forms a projecting plinth. In the First Palaces bonding is effected by lavish use of mortar ; in the Second Palaces the blocks are put together in perfect regularity without mortar. By their fine facing certain parts of the palaces recall the Greek monuments of the Vth and IVth centuries. For greater variety a plinth sometimes supports three courses of gypsum, and two of limestone in succession. Wood is still much used in the construction of internal walls, sometimes for framing rectangular sections of masonry and sometimes for supporting courses of stone.[1] Sometimes, too, it was used for purposes of economy ; stone facings were connected by wooden cross-beams fixed in mortises and the interval was filled with rubble ; above this foundation the masonry was of stone, supported at intervals by timbers.[2] This method of construction did not spoil the effect, for it was concealed under a coating comparable in its perfection to the best that the Romans have done in this way. This coating was so habitual that it was used even on stone facings. On inside walls it was formed in certain rooms of increasingly thin coats of a mortar of increasingly fine consistency ; the last coat, the surface of which was smoothed with marble polishers, was an excellent stucco on a basis of slaked lime, perfectly adapted to fresco painting. Stucco was used for the flooring in the First Palace of Knossos, and was replaced in the Second Palace by gypsum.[3]

[1] Cf. **XX**, 347 ff., 306, 334, 364.
[2] Cf. **XLII**, 177.
[3] Cf. **XXXVII**, 117 ; **LVII**, 130 ff. ; **XX**, 351.

An essential element in the Cretan house, which more than any other influenced the whole of its construction, was the roofing. The round hut of primitive times had necessarily been given a conical roof. On the rectangular house, the roof still rose towards the centre sometimes, so that with its four faces it was in the form of a pyramidical hat[1]; but as a rule it was laid flat over the surface to be covered. It was so convenient to extend the roofing in one piece over all the rooms, and the terrace was so well suited to a hot climate. The houses of Knossos represented on the faience plaques are cubical, often with a lantern or turret, also cubical, on the roof; while the northern folk at Mycenæ build the gabled roof, the Cretans keep to the southern terrace. Among the former " the skilful craftsman gathers the beams to the ridge of the lofty house so that they may withstand the violence of the winds (and cause the rain to run off easily) " ; among the latter the roof is built so that, as in the palace of Kirké, one can climb up by a stair and sleep there in the cool.[2] We shall find that most of the arrangements peculiar to the Cretan houses are more or less directly related to the flat form of roof.

The Cretan architects built houses with upper storeys from the earliest times. We often find on the ground floor rooms completely walled in without any opening. These are cellars which were reached from the floor above by a trap and a ladder, or by an internal stair. Arrangements of this kind existed in the most ancient houses, at Koumasa, at Vasiliki, and at Chamaizi. Later they are found everywhere, both in Crete and on the mainland. At Gournia, built on a hill, special arrangements are found ; the ground floor is entered by a door at the back, and the principal storey by a door on the level of the street ; an inside stair leads from one to the other. What is much more remarkable is that the private house, to judge from the faience models, frequently had a second storey, and sometimes a third with a lantern. In the palace of Knossos the ground floor was covered everywhere, at the time of excavation, by debris which can only have come from above— fragments of fresco in a cellar, others on a pavement above a porch, column bases which had fallen into a passage, a block of stone which had crashed on to a balustrade. In the western

---

[1] **XXVI**, 96 ; MA. i, 11 ff. ; pl. ii.
[2] *Iliad*, xxiii, 712–13 ; *Odyssey*, x, 554–8.

wing the Sanctuary and the Magazines were surmounted
by at least one storey, which was reached by five stairs from
the courts, and the plan of it can still be seen from certain
walls on the ground floor, the thickness of which would be
excessive if it were not explained by the weight which they
had to carry. The two quarters on the eastern slope could
only communicate with the Central Court by the upper floors.[1]
In the south-east quarter part of the Great Stairway survives ;
a room on the first floor still holds a stone bench at the foot of
a wall, and traces of a sanitary installation corresponding
to the one on the ground floor ; above the great hall stone
door-jambs are still to be seen ; the queen's apartments still
contain the steps of several stairs ; with this evidence Evans
considers it possible to reconstruct the whole plan of the upper
floor.[2] In the north-east quarter, too, we must suppose that
one storey and perhaps more existed, making the two
neighbouring quarters symmetrical.[3] Like the palace, the
Royal Villa had a storey, which was served by four staircases,
of which two had a double turn.[4]

To bear the weight of the upper floor or roof it was not
enough to reinforce the walls below ; the cross-beams too had
to be supported. This was usually the purpose of the
quadrangular pillars set up in the middle of ground-floor
rooms. These pillars have been much discussed. Some of
them, perhaps, never had a structural purpose, and we shall
see what was their religious significance ; but the majority,
even when they are surrounded by ritual emblems, have a
practical object. At Knossos the Sanctuary of the Great
Palace contains two pillars, standing in two communicating
rooms. Both bear the sign of the double axe in more than
one place, and the base of one was surrounded by little libation
cups ; but the other bears notches on its upper face, in which
the tenons of a beam were fitted. In the Little Palace there
was a whole series of pillar-rooms, a crypt filled with sacred
objects ; but it must have supported the storey above. The
pillar had a magical meaning and a structural use. In many
instances there is no trace of sacred accessories in connexion
with its use. A very great number of Cretan houses are known

---

[1] **XX,** figs. 237–8, 245–7.
[2] Ib., figs. 240 ff.
[3] Ib., 382 ff.
[4] BSA. viii, 133 ff., fig. 86.

in which there is no sign that the pillar was anything but a
pillar. That which stands in the palace of Phaistos in the
middle of the Corridor of the Magazines cannot be either a
symbol or a fetish. There is one at Knossos, in a room in the
Royal Villa, the object of which is indicated as clearly as
possible, for notches cut in the walls mark the position of the
beams which it supported.[1]

It would be idle to inquire where the architectural motive
of the column was invented and how it was disseminated.
Nobody invented the column. " Man found it in nature, all
ready to take its place in building. The tree is a column ready
shaped. The first column is a simple tree-trunk sharpened at
the base and planted in the ground like a pile." [2] But this
element, which enters into primitive wood construction
everywhere, bears witness to great originality on the part of
the Cretans.

Among them a fairly clearly marked development can be
followed. At first the internal supports are always square
stone pillars ; then stone pillars co-exist with round columns
of wood ; finally the round form triumphs, first in wood, and
later in stone. This development was completed more rapidly
at Knossos than in the provincial towns or on the mainland.
When the column was of wood its diameter was rather less
at the base than at the top (Pl. I, 1). It seems that this
form of an inverted truncated cone lasted longer in sacred
monuments than in others, as if the architect had been conforming to some religious rule, or else simply because mere
posts would do for chapels of exiguous dimensions and moderate
height. Besides, he knew how to give a good solidity to the
wooden shaft and could get decorative effects from it. It took
its load on a broad round capital and its point rested on a
broad high base of stone. The base was of some polychrome
material, serpentine, porphyry, breccia, or conglomerate, with
strongly marked veining. The shaft was often of cypress
wood and seems to have been coated with brilliant colours.
Towards the end of the XVIIth century, in the new palaces,
a low base of gypsum or plain limestone was preferred, being
sufficient for a shaft of stone. Henceforward, too, the architect
preferred to shape the shaft into a perfect cylinder and to

[1] BSA. ix, 150–1, fig. 90 and pl. i.
[2] Leroux, **XLVI**, 38 ff.

decorate it with the chisel. Already in a sanctuary at Mallia
the columns were octagonal, flat listels alternating with faces
adorned with notches at right angles. Every kind of fluting
was tried, convex, concave, and in spirals.[1]

When Cretan architecture was provided with all its resources,
it adapted the column to arrangements which are found nowhere
else. Among the Greeks the gabled roof and the pediment
which it forms impose upon the buildings a noble symmetry.
Among the Cretans the terrace roof incites to the free play of
asymmetry. Since the door is generally placed near a corner
the columns of the façade need not flank it in twos ; since
the rooms are often open on two consecutive sides the adjoining
porticoes can be at right angles ; since the small courts may
give on to one room or several they can light them by one
colonnade or several. Finally, the presence of several storeys
makes it possible to set numerous columns along the stairways
to support or decorate the flights and landings, either singly
or grouped on balustrades. In consequence of this very diversity
it happens fairly often that the colonnades of the Cretans recall
those of the Greeks by the even number of the columns. Thus
at Phaistos a square court gives on to a peristyle of twelve
columns in perfect symmetry (Fig. 21), at Knossos a small
court has two stylobates, each with two columns,[2] and two-
column porticoes are to be seen on all sides. Sometimes one
might think that one was in the presence of the three sections
of a *megaron* house, and the basilica of the Royal Villa is
divided into three aisles. But the arrangement of the columns
in pairs proves no more than that the Cretan architects were
not exclusive in their tastes and had no mania for unity.
Almost everywhere an odd number of bays and aisles
corresponds—if one can use the word—to an even number of
openings. Small courts with two columns give light to
neighbouring rooms by four bays. We never find, when the
columns are in pairs, that the principal entrance of the room,
or even any entrance, is in line with the space between the
columns. So the pairs of columns were not expected to give
an effect of symmetry, which was even avoided—for example
where the columns on two opposite stylobates were not set
exactly opposite each other.

[1] BCH. 1921, 538 ; **XVIII**, fig. 77.
[2] Fig. 19, North-east Hall.

Moreover, the columns are more often in odd numbers. Columns in pairs are the exception. The rule strikes the eye as soon as one approaches the great palaces, in the shape of a porch with a central column. At Phaistos the breadth of the propylæa is divided by one column, and again by three ; at Knossos there is one column on the steps of a stairway, and there are three pillars in the fore-hall and one on the threshold of the Throne Room. Perhaps the most curious arrangement, which is one of the most frequent, is that of colonnades at a right angle along two sides of a room. In short, the liberty of the combinations to which the column lent itself was not hampered by any tradition or any academic prejudice ; it gave to uniformly rectangular constructions an extraordinary variety. But as a rule the need for supporting the horizontal roof in the middle, and consequently for placing one column in the centre of the façade, governs the whole plan of the building, and imposes the bipartite division upon it.

One of the features which best show how little the Cretan architect cared for symmetry is the position of the entrance. Being thrust aside by the central column, it frankly abandons any claim to occupy the middle of the façade and settles near a corner, generally to the right. This practice is very old, and is to be seen in the Neolithic dwelling at Magasa. The remarkable thing is that it was handed on from the hut and the large house to the assemblage of buildings which constitutes a palace. At Phaistos and at Knossos the porch of the west front is towards the southern end ; in the palace of Gournia and the large house at Palaikastro the porch of the south front is towards the S.E. corner. In the rooms, as we saw when we considered the position of the columns with reference to the doors, the entrance is almost always near a corner.

Lighting was ensured by two methods, often combined, namely, by small internal courts or " light-wells " and by windows. The circular huts represented on the Melos box as grouped round a court could receive light only from the court. The great house at Chamaizi (Fig. 23) may have had openings in the outside wall of the upper floor, but on the ground floor it was lighted only by a court of about twenty square metres. In the palaces the great courts were not sufficient, and numerous small inner courts were built. These light-wells are among the most characteristic elements of

Cretan architecture. Being exposed to the rain, they have
walls of hard limestone, and the cement or flags which form
the floor are slightly sloped to allow the water to drain off.
Usually they are adorned with columns and balustrades,
and a skilful arrangement of doors, windows, and spaces
between columns admits sunlight mixed with shadows into
the suites of vestibules and rooms. (Pl. I, 1.) These effects
of lighting must have been charming. The importance of
the light-wells in the general plan of the buildings may be
estimated from one fact alone—Evans has identified five
within an area of 200 square metres.

This mode of lighting by no means did away with the use
of windows. This is one of the most precious pieces of
information which we are given by the faience plaques from
Knossos (Fig. 18) : there are windows in every house. These
oblong openings are often divided into four by cross-bars
and coloured a bright red, representing panes of some trans-
lucent material, probably oiled parchment. Traces of similar
windows are found all over Crete, for example at Gournia
and Pseira, and indeed all over the Ægean lands, for example
at Thera and Orchomenos. Since windows were not made
on the outside of the ground floor they are only found at
Knossos on the inner courts ; but there they are numerous
and some are three metres broad, so as to give plenty of light
to rooms, passages, and stairs. These openings were repeated
on the upper floors, which also had windows on the outside.

It cannot be said with certainty that the Cretan house
never had a permanent hearth. In some rooms at Gournia
and Pseira there stands in a corner a semi-circular piece of
stonework arranged in upper and lower portions, which is
said to resemble the raised hearth which at this day exists
in many Cretan inns.[1] But, although we may admit that
we have here a type of hearth, yet, since this hearth could be
placed anywhere, it does not impose any definite rules on
architecture like the central hearth of the Mycenæans and
the Greeks. Most of the time, and probably all the time,
a movable hearth was sufficient. Cooking was done out of
doors. For heating, which was necessary only for a few days
every year, there were braziers and " fire-boxes ". In the
house at Chamaizi a hollow tray of clay was found beside

[1] Seager, **LXXXI**, 16, and pl. i, 15, 1.

a pile of ashes. A tripod found at Knossos in a sanctuary was probably used for the preparation of the food offered to the gods. Vessels of various shapes were deposited in the tombs, with coal in them : with these the dead could feed and warm themselves. The living used them in the same way.

In an island where the rain falls in buckets the builder had to give especial attention to the problem of drainage. Below the First Palace of Knossos there was a whole system of drains (Fig. 19). The rain-water from the terraces and the waste water of the different floors descended by large shafts, veritable wells, into underground conduits which were strongly cemented and covered with flat stones. These drains are large enough for a man to walk about in them without difficulty. The system of channels of the eastern wing is fairly well known. Two branches, the combined length of which was 80 metres, met and discharged into a main drain, which descended to the little river, receiving other affluents on the way. In another part there are two stone basins which once excited admiration under the name of oil-presses ; but these, too, are the heads of drains. The water from the neighbouring roofs was carried there by cemented shafts against the walls, and thence discharged into stone conduits with a square section which led it by a zigzag course from terrace to terrace down to a stone spout ; below this spout another channel began, ending in a great well, whence the water flowed through an overflow into the main drain. Finally, along the North Entry there was a branch which carried off the surface-water from the Central Court and the N.E. and N.W. quarters. The same system of drainage was employed in the towns for houses and streets. At Gournia terra-cotta cylinders were used. At Palaikastro the drainage system bears evidence of an inventive and practical spirit in the variety of straight and curved pipes and in the combination of vertical shafts and vats.

Nowhere, either in antiquity or in the Middle Ages, did the science and art of drainage advance so far. Take, for example, the drain discovered at Gezer in Palestine.[1] It is made of jars fitted one into the other, a primitive method. The Melians, it is true, had conduits of rather greater breadth than depth, floored and roofed with flagstones, and walled

[1] **XC,** figs. 46–7 ; cf. **VI,** 9, 104, n. 1.

with rude blocks ; at Tiryns the water was carried from the bathroom by a terra-cotta channel ; at Thebes semicircular gutters were scooped out.[1] But here the influence of Crete is certain. The Minoans alone solved the problem of " everything to the drain " by a variety of ingenious methods which they communicated to their neighbours, only to be lost when they were gone.

And now we come to the finest inspiration of this art of causing the rain-water to carry off waste. At Knossos, in the queen's apartments, there was on the ground floor an installation which was repeated on the first floor. Immediately above the drain is a recess, which communicated with it by two holes. A groove in the wall shows where a wooden seat was fitted, 57 centimetres above the floor. Certain details have even caused some to suppose that there was a balance flap. However it was done, the opening over the underground drains ensured flushing and ventilation.[2] The queen of Knossos enjoyed conveniences which not all the splendours of Versailles were to offer to the queen of France.

Engineers who were competent to deal with the surface-water and the waste water cannot have had any difficulty about supplying the palace with spring water. Did they think of it ? The water of the stream is too full of gypsum to be drinkable ; the wells which had been bored before the construction of the palace had been blocked up at that time, and there is nothing to be seen at Knossos resembling the cisterns found at Phaistos. Now in certain parts of the palace there was a system of channels quite different from that which served for drainage, and it belonged to the time when the wells had ceased to be used. It is made up of terra-cotta pipes. These pipes were manufactured and set in place with incomparable mastery. They are of a fine, well-baked clay, and were joined with a cement of such good quality that it still sticks to the joins. One end being wider than the other, they were fitted one into another, and they were furnished with stop-collars. These pipes are too narrow for drains ; the diameter is 17 centimetres at the wide end and half as much at the other. This difference no doubt increased the pressure, but not enough to save pipes of such

[1] **XXI,** figs. 36, 42, pl. ii ; **LXVII,** fig. 87 ; **XLI,** fig. 192.
[2] **XX,** fig. 172 ; cf. fig. 244.

small capacity from being quickly choked with sediment
if the water was muddy or dirty. We may therefore conjecture that they were used for leading in spring water.[1]
Now some distance north of the palace a Roman road, built
over the Minoan road, has a double system of channels for
drainage and for the water-supply.[2] Why should the Romans
not have copied the hydraulic arrangements in addition
to following the line of the road ? Why should the waters
of Mount Iouktas, which the Venetians and Turks continued
to bring to Candia after the Romans, not have been brought
to Knossos before the Romans ?

It was not by the chance methods of empiricism that the
architects of Knossos obtained such results. In the palace
of Knossos a veritable monument of hydraulic science has been
preserved.[3] Alongside of a stairway which descends towards
the stream there is a runnel. For each step of the stairway
there is a corresponding convex curve in the runnel, so that
the water, instead of falling down a series of vertical steps
in violent cascades, flowed in a succession of parabolas ;
at every bulge the current was broken and by the time it
had reached the bottom of the stair and turned a sharp double
corner it had lost its force. At this point the runnel is deepened
so as to form a kind of basin in which the current was slowed
down still more, and the water left any impurities behind
before turning a right angle and finishing its course. Not one
of the laws which should be observed in order to check and
clarify a flow of water seems to have escaped the builder
of these waterworks.

How could these competent hydraulic engineers and sanitary
experts come to build such unpractical bathrooms as are
often ascribed to them ? If the Cretans were as fond of
baths as the Greeks the places in which they indulged this
taste must have been suitable. In the north-west of the
palace of Knossos a stair of about fifteen steps, with a
balustrade surmounted by columns, descends to a kind of
basin which is almost square, being 2·56 metres by 2·45,
with a depth of about 2 metres. The sides are of limestone
blocks faced with gypsum, and the floor is of gypsum too.

[1] Evans, **XX**, 141 ff. ; cf. Mosso, **LVII**, 90–1.
[2] BSA. x, 53. fig. 18.
[3] Ib., viii, 111–14, figs. 67–8.

In the Throne Room and in the South-east House there are
basins of the same kind, except that one is open to the sky,
and the other has no depth below its four steps.[1] The same
arrangement exists in the Little Palace, in the palaces of
Phaistos and Gournia, and in the houses of Palaikastro.
Are these apartments with basins really bathrooms?
Certainly they were not for taking a complete bath in. For
that there were clay bath-tubs, like those which stood in
the queen's apartments and in the South-east House.[2] Then
were they used for washing the feet in the Oriental way,
or for douches? But how is it, then, that they were not
cemented like the light-wells which were exposed to the rain,
and that they were everywhere lined with gypsum, which
disintegrates so easily, and that this gypsum shows no sign
of suffering from the water? The extraordinary thing at
Knossos is that the bathrooms, the real bathrooms, are not
connected, like the latrines, with the underground drainage
system. There is one at Tiryns of which the purpose is
indisputable, for it contained a bath-tub and it is floored by
one enormous slab of porphyry; now, in one of its corners
there is an escape-hole. Why did the Cretan architects not
think of such a convenient and simple arrangement at Knossos
and Phaistos, when it was perhaps one of them who worked
at Tiryns? Without answering this question we may conclude
that the stone basins were not ordinary baths but were used
for some ritual purpose.

III THE CRETAN PALACES

In Cretan buildings we must not look for grandiose conceptions and imposing proportions. If we take the ground
plans alone we see no essential difference between the humblest
houses and the palaces. One rectangle was added to another
according to requirements. One and the same system of
construction is applied, whatever the size of the area covered.
There is a very second-rate dwelling at Palaikastro which
in the number of its rooms resembles the mansions of nobles
and the palaces of kings. The same arrangements are repeated
indefinitely—room after room, with corridors connecting

---

[1] **XX**, figs. 291–4, 2, 418.
[2] Ib., figs. 418–19, 424; cf. **XXXVII**, fig. 63.

them. There is no attempt to obtain an ordered whole; rooms and quarters are put down side by side or one on the top of the other with an irregularity which is subordinated to practical needs alone. The palace of Knossos itself was only a collection of islands enclosed in a single compound; when the lanes were roofed so as to form corridors it became a whole, but a very irregular one.

To estimate the level reached by Cretan architecture and to enjoy its charm one must first forget those intellectual qualities of order, symmetry, and balance which give Greek buildings their incomparable beauty. The Cretan architect made no effort to offer to the gods temples worthy of them. He wanted to build comfortable houses and mansions and magnificent palaces, in which the master could conveniently accommodate his whole family, an army of servants, and the offices of a complicated administrative system, and display his wealth by brilliant entertainments. The great artistic skill with which all crafts combined their resources at the call of the Cretan architect is clearly shown not so much in the majesty of the general effect or even in the splendour of the external decoration as in the perfect adaptation to climatic conditions, happy distribution of light and shade, and intelligent ventilation and drainage, in the ease of communication between the countless rooms, the arrangements made to satisfy quite modern notions of comfort, and the harmonious opulence of detail, and finally in a sure sense of the spectacular and picturesque which indulges in monumental entrances, the elegant ordering of terrace upon terrace and vistas of noble landscapes on every side.

These are the solid and native qualities which appear in the palaces of Knossos, Phaistos, and Hagia Triada when one tries to imagine them as they were when they had taken on their final form.

A slight eminence overlooks the valley of the Kairatos and the cypresses of the opposite bank; in the distance Mount Iouktas stands against the sky. It is Knossos with its palace. Nothing could be so complicated or so simple. (Fig. 19.) A great Central Court, 60 metres by 29, runs north and south; this disposition determines the direction of the main passages, which run towards the four cardinal points and affects, one after another, the different quarters and all

their rooms. The west wing is cut in two by a longitudinal
gallery which was 100 metres long in the First Palace, and was
reduced in the Second Palace to the length of the Central
Court. On one side of this gallery are the Sanctuary and
reception rooms, with the Throne Room, and on the other
is the treasury with a long row of magazines. The east
wing is divided across its breadth by a corridor which separates
the private apartments from the workshops. The north-east
quarter consists of annexes ; the north-west quarter, comprising a great hall supported by eleven strong pillars and a
hall of purification, is flanked outside by the Theatre, with
a state box overlooking two flights of steps set at a right
angle. A great part of the southern quarter is taken up
by the outbuildings.

On the four sides of this great rectangle there are entries,
generally commanded by guard-rooms. In the North, where
the road from the sea ends, you have to pass between
formidable walls and then through the two successive doors
of a Propylæum, before reaching the inner door. In the
South-west a porch with a single column opens on to a long
corridor with a turn in it, adorned with wall-paintings, which
leads to the South Propylæa. The latter give access between
two columns to a large court, at the end of which a broad stair
rises to the upper floors of the west wing. In the South-east
and the North-east there are posterns opening on to the valley
roads.

The domestic and industrial quarters lie under the slope
and look towards the valley, but all the rest of the palace
is on the level of the Central Court. Stairways give on to
this court in pairs, some rising to the upper floors of the west
wing and others leading on the same level to the upper floors
of the east wing or descending to the ground floor. The
stair in the south-east quarter, which is the best preserved,
is truly imposing, with its columned balustrades and its steps
about 2 metres broad. Formerly it rose in five flights
to a floor above the level of the court, from which it was
entered on the fourth landing. Seen from the stream, then,
the palace presented a series of terraces rising one above the
other so as to conceal the empty space of the Central Court.
Each of the two main wings had its hall of state. In the region
of the Sanctuaries one passes through a fore-hall with four

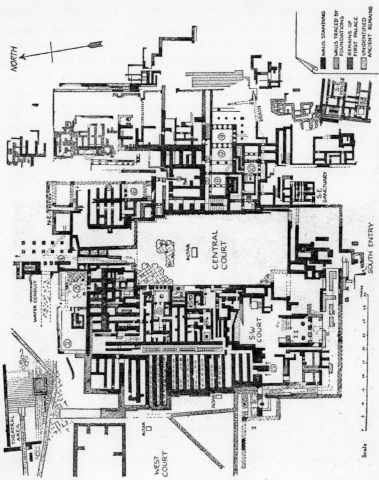

FIG. 19.—PLAN OF THE PALACE OF KNOSSOS,

1. South-west Entry.
2. Hall of Purification.
3. North-west Portico.
4. Drain.
5. North-east Magazines.
6. North-east Hall.
7. East-West Corridor.
8. Hall of the Colonnades.
9. Hall of the Double Axes.
10. Queen's Megaron.
11. South Propylaea.
12. Entrance to Magazines.
13. Altar.
14. Pillar Rooms.
15. Repository.
16. Throne Room.

openings to enter by a double door into the Throne Room
(Fig. 20) ; here Minos, on leaving the lustral basin, takes
his place on his gypsum throne in the midst of priestesses
or ministers seated on low benches and under the eyes of the
gryphons painted on the wall. In the domestic quarter the
apartments of the queen, with their Megaron, bedrooms,
bathrooms, and treasury, are commanded by the great Hall
of the Double Axes ; here the king comes and sits on a throne
against a partition-wall when the evening light filters between
the columns of the little court or the splendour of the sunrise
is softened by the broad peristyle.

FIG. 20.—The Throne Room at Knossos.

As the Palace of Versailles has the Grand Trianon and the
Petit Trianon, so the Great Palace of Knossos has the Little
Palace and the Royal Villa. West of the Theatre is a road
300 metres long leading to a height on which stands the Little
Palace.[1] It has a frontage of 35 metres. On the ground
floor the principal room, with a peristyle in front of it, is
a replica of the Hall of the Double Axes. On the opposite
side, 200 metres from the Great Palace, the Royal Villa,[2]

[1] See Evans, XVIII, pl. vii.
[2] See Evans, BSA. ix, 130 ff., pl. i.

set in a deep hollow cut in the rock, looks down over gardens
to the valley. Two double stairways serve the upper floor.
The great hall, 11·50 metres by 4·55, is supported by two
rows of pillars. It is divided into two unequal lengths by

Fig. 21.—Plan of the Palace of Phaistos.

a stone balustrade with columns. An opening in the middle
of this balustrade gives access by three steps to the back
part. At the bottom of this raised portion, which is lighted
obliquely by a small court, is a recess in the wall containing

a throne of gypsum. It was in this hall, according to Evans, that Minos delivered justice. In any case, with its longitudinal division into three aisles, this hall may well be the distant prototype of the *Stoa Basilike* where the King of Athens sat, and of the basilica which Rome handed on to the Middle Ages.

Phaistos stands at the end of a mountain ridge. Below are the olive-groves of the Messara, and on the horizon the peaks of Ida, seldom without snow. The palace (Fig. 21) is built on an acropolis at four levels.[1] The architect has surmounted this difficulty so triumphantly that he has obtained effects of perspective and symmetry from it. The state entrance, which is on the West, is the most magnificent which exists in Crete. At the end of a broad esplanade, along the side of which the main façade runs, one passes for 25 metres beside the tiers of a theatre before coming to the bottom of a monumental stairway, and then goes up steps, 13·75 metres broad, to the platform of the Propylæa, which are divided into two passages by a central column and lighted at the back by a small colonnaded court. On the same side a more unassuming entrance opens on to a corridor on the second level, which runs east to the Central Court on the same level, passing before a guard-room. The court has exactly the same orientation as that at Knossos, and although less spacious (46·50 by 22·50 metres) it has the same proportions. A large number of stairs lead from one level to another. North of the great corridor lie the Magazines, which are reached from the West of the Court through a colonnaded fore-hall and a passage with one pillar. To the South extends the quarter in which the staff and perhaps guests were lodged ; it ends in a kind of balcony—either a belvedere or a look-out—from which the roads to the sea can be easily surveyed. The eastern wing presents to the court a long portico of columns which are round and square alternately ; at the back it gives on to a large esplanade where there is a potter's kiln. The northern quarter, built on the highest level, is that of the royal family. It has a special entrance on the North, with a monumental gate, and a private stair allows the king to go direct to the bottom of the Grand Stairway and to the Theatre. This quarter

[1] Cf. Pernier, ASI. i, 363 ff.

contains many sets of rooms containing halls flanked by porticoes, and the centre is marked by a fine peristyle court with twelve columns. From up here the lord has a view over his whole palace and all the surrounding country.

While the palace of Phaistos is chiefly remarkable for its exterior, the palace of Hagia Triada [1] is more interesting for its internal decoration and wealth in artistic objects. Nevertheless it supplies an epitome, very happy in parts, of all the features of Cretan architecture. At first it was only the villa of a prince, in a pretty situation resembling that of Phaistos, but nearer the sea. But in L.M.I the neighbouring houses were knocked down, the whole surface of the ground was levelled, and the villa, extended over the entire site, was transformed into a palace. The stairway at the entrance, the porticoes and two wings at right angles, the frequent bipartite division, the pillared rooms, the lightwells, the small court with columns round and square in turn, everything recalls the palaces of Phaistos and Knossos, down to the little apartment which reminds one of the Throne Room and its annexes.

IV CRETAN ARCHITECTURE AND MYCENÆAN ARCHITECTURE

Thus from the history of dwellings, from the analysis of architectural elements, and from the synthesis presented to us in the palaces, we have seen how Minoan architecture produced and developed a new type. Between the Cretan house and the Egyptian house there are obvious resemblances —the cubical shape and the absence of a permanent hearth. But these resemblances are not such that they can be explained by the similarity of the climate. The differences are profound. The Cretan house is not a villa with a court on one side and a garden on the other, but a town house adjoining other houses and standing on the street. It is not full of openings ; instead of three doors it has one or two. It has no awning roofs, on account of the annual hurricanes. It is the dwelling suited to a climate which is already cooler and less equable. Then is the Cretan house of the same origin as the northern house, of which the Mycenæans bequeathed the type to the Greece of the future ?

[1] See Halbherr, MA. xiii, 5 ff. ; MIL. xxi, v, 235 ff.

This is the opinion which archæologists maintained at first, either deriving the Cretan type from the mainland type or *vice versa*.[1] But to-day it is generally admitted that between the two systems there are radical differences, due to the climates in which they had their birth.[2] There is nothing at all Cretan about the purely " Nordic " arrangements which appear in the second half of the third millennium at Troy II and in Thessaly, reappear about 1600 at Mycenæ and Tiryns, and extend during the XIVth century to Melos and even to Crete.

At Troy II, after crossing two courts connected by a porch one finds before one a group of parallel independent buildings with narrow fronts. The largest is thrice as long as broad, and the others are four times. All open on to the court by a square fore-hall entirely open in front. From the vestibule a central door leads into a hall with a central hearth, behind which there is sometimes a smaller room.[3]

We have here the oldest specimen of the type which was subsequently perfected on the European mainland. The porch between two courts became the *propylæum*. The fore-hall still admitted air and light from the court to the rooms inside, while protecting the first of these rooms from rain and sun ; but, since in a wider building the gabled roofing needed more support than the projecting ends of the side-walls, the fore-hall became the *prothyron* with columns between the *antæ*, and this tripartite division was extended to the whole building. Then the inrush of air from the central door created by the central hearth became too strong, and the principal room was not warm enough in winter, so this room was placed at the end, behind the little chamber ; to ensure ventilation and lighting a hole was made in the roof with a louver, and four columns were set on the flags of the hearth to support it. Thus the *prodomos* and the *megaron* were obtained. This was to be the mainland type when the evolution was complete.

It is to be seen, with a single central entrance, in the palace built by the lords of Mycenæ on the top of their Acropolis. But it is at Tiryns that it appears most clearly, in several

[1] Cf. Doerpfeld, AM. 1905, 257 ff. ; 1907, 576 ff. ; Mackenzie, BSA. xi, 181.

[2] Cf. Noack, **LXII,** 19 ff. ; Leroux, **XLVI,** 117 ff.

[3] **X,** fig. 23 ; cf. **LXXXVIII,** figs. 11, 18 ; **XCI,** fig. 137.

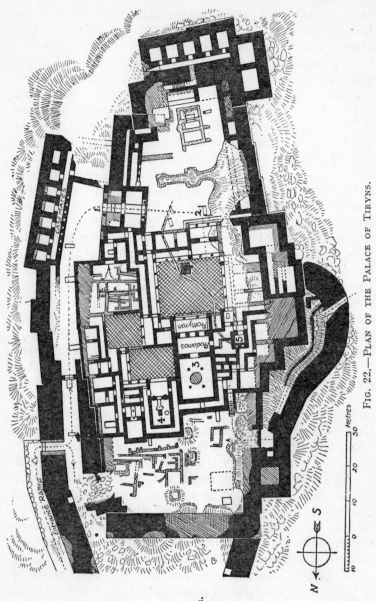

FIG. 22.—PLAN OF THE PALACE OF TIRYNS.

1. Great Propylæa.
2. Small Propylæa.
3. Megaron.
4. Women's Megaron.
5. Bath.

examples (Fig. 22).   Built on the highest terrace of a steep
hill, the palace of Tiryns dominates the whole plain, like an
eagle's eyrie.   To enter it you climb a ramp along the outside
of a formidable circuit-wall, and, having passed the gate,
you go for 75 metres along a passage imprisoned between
the outer wall and another almost as mighty.   In this way
you come to the Greater Propylæum, 13 metres in depth ;
but when you have passed it you are still only on an esplanade,
which you must cross in order to find yourself, on turning to
the right, before the columns of the Lesser Propylæum.   Here
the palace really begins.   After the Propylæum you enter
the Inner Courtyard with colonnades on all its four sides
and an altar near the entrance.   At the back the fore-hall,
with two columns, leads by three doors to the first room,
which is decorated with an alabaster frieze.   A single door
opens on the great *megaron*.   This hall, which can be recognized
by its round hearth and the four columns set about it, is
12 metres long and 10 broad, and has a magnificent floor
painted in a chess-board pattern, which is interrupted at the
middle of the right-hand wall to mark the position of the
throne ;   perhaps it was also adorned with fine frescoes of
life-size figures.   This *megaron* is simply a hall of state with
its ante-chamber.   The others, at the side, are smaller.   Since
each forms a whole by itself, communication is very difficult.
To give direct access from the king's *megaron* to that of the
queen all that was wanted was to pierce a door in the right-
hand wall of the great *megaron* ;   but no such door exists.
There is only one in the left-hand wall of the *prodomos* ;   it
leads to a passage which is forced by the outer walls of the
megara into several right angles, and to a labyrinth of little
bedrooms, in the midst of which a mighty slab of stone,
4 metres by 3, indicates the position of the bathroom.
In this palace, for all the luxury it displays, convenience
of communication is wholly subordinated to the need for
retaining the closed *megaron* with a fixed hearth.

We are now in a position to compare, with some knowledge
of the facts, the palaces of Crete and of the mainland.   The
Cretan palace is composed of rooms grouped round a central
court without any apparent order, but with great facilities
for communication ;   the essential feature of the mainland
palace is the *megaron*, independent and isolated.   The addition

of one new room after another to the original building is hardly possible except with a flat roofing, the terrace on which the dweller in hot lands loves to spend the summer nights ; the long straight line of the *megaron* makes it possible to drain off the water by a roof with two slopes. The immediate consequence is that the terrace needs a central support and, if that is not sufficient, secondary supports on either side of it, so that you have one column or three, and the bipartite division of the façade, while the ridged roof rests on the *antæ*, which are relieved by columns placed symmetrically in an even number, so that you have the tripartite division of the façade and of the *megaron*.

The Cretan house is broad without depth, so as to be open to the air as much as possible, with its two entrance doors in the long sides ; the mainland house is deep, with a single entry in the small side, so as to keep the heat in the cold season. There is no need for a fixed hearth in the small scattered rooms of the southern house ; but the long *megaron* must have in the middle a stone-flagged hearth where the eternal fire burns. This central hearth necessarily entails an arrangement to dispose of the smoke, and on the circle of flags which marks its position four columns set at the corners of a square support the part of the roof where an arrangement of windows creates a draught. Such an arrangement constitutes a serious obstacle to the construction of upper storeys, which is encouraged, on the other hand, among the Cretans by the need for building on slopes and the habit of having many rooms even on restricted sites.

To let air and light into their houses, when the central court does not suffice, the Cretans leave as many small courts as possible open to the sky ; but to avoid violent draughts they prefer to have the rooms open on two consecutive sides, they set the doors near corners and not opposite to each other, and, in suites of porticoes, fore-halls, and rooms, instead of continuing one bay by another in a long aisle, they place the columns of one row opposite the gaps between the columns of the next row as wind-screens. To protect their *megaron* from the weather the Mycenæans resign themselves to having no light in it but what comes through the doors, the central louver, in which the openings are so narrow that they do not prevent the smoke from blackening the ceiling, and the gaps

K

between the heads of the beams supporting the timbers of the roofing.

The outcome of all these contrasts is one certain conclusion. It was all very well for the palaces of Mycenæ and Tiryns to borrow from Crete some subsidiary arrangements and the whole of their decoration, to turn clumsy supports into columns, to treat the entrance court like a central court or a light-well, to offer boxes adorned with double axes to the royal patronesses of spectacles and to display the foreign luxury of frescoes all over their walls ; between the principles of architecture applied in Crete and the mainland system of the *megaron* with a fixed hearth the difference is profound and absolute, and lies in their very origins. It is due to the difference of climates, not between those of Knossos and Mycenæ, but between those of Crete and the distant lands where the Achaians lived before they settled in Argolis. Here men simply adapted to local requirements a method of construction invented much further north ; there they spontaneously created the dwelling best suited to the southernmost island of the Mediterranean.

BOOK II

SOCIAL LIFE

CHAPTER I

THE SOCIAL SYSTEM AND GOVERNMENT

I THE SOCIAL SYSTEM

The Clan, the Family, and the Individual

ON the organization of the social group the remains of prehistoric times leave a free field to the imagination and do not, it seems, supply any information. It is not impossible, however, to form a rough idea of the lines on which the Ægean societies must have developed. There is some likelihood that they passed through the same phases as the Hellenic peoples, who perhaps began over again the whole history of their precursors. We may suppose by analogy that, before the arrival of the Greeks, Greece already knew the system which has left so many traces in the legend and the epic, the religion and the law of future centuries, the system of the *genos*, the clan, the large family, and that gradually the *genos* broke up into smaller families. The fact is so general that it is hardly likely that it did not occur a first time on the shores of the Ægean between the Stone Age and the Iron Age.

It should be possible to confirm this hypothesis by the examination of the dwellings. The poet of the *Iliad* tells us that Priam lodged in his palace all his children, his fifty sons and his daughters with their husbands ; the poet of the *Odyssey* again shows us in the palace of Nestor six sons, six daughters-in-law, and several married daughters.[1] Here we discover the close relationship which may subsist between

---

[1] *Iliad*, xxiv, 495 ; *Odyssey*, iii, 387, 412 ff., 451 ; cf. vi, 62–3.

social organization and architecture. Nevertheless, we must beware of seeing in the great palaces of Knossos and Phaistos anything but royal dwellings. Even if the master lived there in the midst of all his relations, as well as his servants, courtiers, and ministers, it would be nothing more than a dynastic custom. In the same way we have dwellings of princes or nobles which were set up in M.M.III or L.M.I at many places, at Tylissos, Gournia, Mallia, Nirou Chani, etc. But prehistoric Crete reveals to us the existence, in remote corners, at very distant epochs, of houses, about which there was certainly nothing royal or princely, which sheltered a considerable number of persons. They are of great interest to the study of dwellings, but they also deserve a place in social history.

In E.M.II days there was no village at Vasiliki. There was one single house there about the XXVIIIth century, and it was rebuilt about the XXVth.[1] It was of rectangular shape and built of brick and wood on a stone foundation. The ground floor was divided into more than twenty rooms, above which were one or perhaps two storeys. A very numerous family lived there. It was sufficient to itself. It already had its æsthetic needs, for the internal walls were coated with painted plaster and the pottery was of a fine mottled type.

Three centuries later we find at Chamaizi another house, very large, like the first, but very different in other respects. (Fig. 23.) [2, 3] It is in the form of an ellipse enclosing an area of about 300 square metres. The thickness of the external wall and the way in which the entrance-passage narrows inwards seem to have been precautions against sudden attack. The interior is divided by partition walls into a dozen rooms of very varying size, connected by a vestibule and a corridor. One of these rooms is completely walled in, and could only be reached by a ladder from above ; therefore the house had at least one higher storey. The folk who lived there were not rich, to judge by the furniture. They had no comfort, for in the downstairs rooms they walked on beaten earth, and the daylight barely penetrated.

The comparison of these two houses seems to show that at

[1] **XL,** pl. xii, 49.
[2] ’Eφ., 1906, 117 ff., pl. ix, 4.
[3] But see Corrections and Additions, p. 398.

the beginning of the Middle Minoan Period, towards the end of the third millennium, the *genos* of Chamaizi were less numerous than that of Vasiliki had been, and found existence more difficult. Was this the beginning of a development? At all events in later years, in the Late Minoan Period, in the XVIth century, when the site at Chamaizi was once more inhabited, the new-comers did not need such a phalanstery; they built against the outside wall quite small houses. At this time in all the Cretan towns, for example at Gournia, most of the

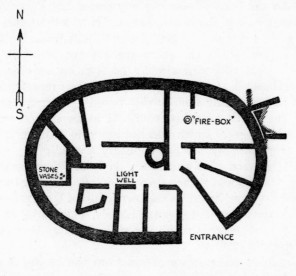

FIG. 23.—The house at Chamaizi (M.M.I).

dwellings consisted of two or three little rooms. The development was complete; the small families had supplanted the large family.

In the Cyclades and on the mainland, the necessity of housing a whole clan together led to the adoption of other arrangements; but the difference is only of an architectural nature, and we can perceive the same process of social evolution. The rotunda or *tholos* discovered in the lower strata at Tiryns has a diameter of 27·70 metres. The foundations of the outer wall are 4·80 metres thick, while the wall of stone and brick above was 1·80 metres thick; this rotunda was therefore a veritable fortress. Inside there are other circular walls intersected by transverse walls, forming all the cells that were needed to shelter the whole swarm in the hive. The great difficulty about collecting many persons in this way under one roof, especially with round buildings, was the problem of roofing. Whatever the solution may have been, the mere fact that one was found indicates a comparatively recent date ; and indeed the *tholos* is built over a stratum containing simple huts. If the huts date, as is probable, from Early Helladic I, the *tholos* can hardly belong to any period but Early Helladic II, that is to say about 2500–2200. Therefore at this epoch, in Argolis, the unity of the clan was still intact ; divisions into families within the *genos* are not yet perceptible from outside. But they can already be seen on an object from the Cyclades ; a stone *pyxis* found at Melos [1] represents seven round huts standing side by side round a court entered by a broad gate with a peaked roof. It looks as if it were the dwelling of a *genos* which was beginning to disintegrate. Yet the *pyxis* probably belongs to Early Cycladic II ; we may place it between 2800 and 2400. It is therefore earlier than the Tiryns rotunda rather than later. But it is natural that the *genos* system, based on the ownership of land, should have been less deeply rooted in small islands, which lived on fishing and sea-borne trade, than in the plains of Argolis or even the country-sides of Crete.

What little evidence we obtain from the houses is supplemented by what is afforded by the tombs. The dwelling of the dead has always been conceived in the same form as the habitation of the living. This rule is remarkably confirmed in the funerary architecture of prehistoric Crete.

In the earliest times collective burial was practised ; the members of the family were gathered together in the life beyond the grave as they had been gathered together in this world. At Palaikastro and at Gournia some tombs have been distinguishable from contemporary houses only by the piles of skulls with which they were filled.

On the model of the round house the circular sepulchral chamber was conceived, the *tholos* or bee-hive tomb of brick on a stone foundation, with a rudimentary dome on top.

[1] **IV,** i, 11.

More than twenty *tholoi* are known. They are all in the South of Crete, in the Messara, where several terra-cotta models of round huts have also been found. As a rule they are isolated, one in each locality. Sometimes there are several together, three at Platanos and as many at Koumasa. The largest have an inside diameter of between eight and nine metres, and even 9·50 metres at Kalathiana and 10·30 metres at Platanos. Almost invariably they are furnished with adjoining cells, supplementary tombs.

At Platanos [1] the oldest *tholos*, which was surrounded by at least fifteen cells of this kind, contained ashes left over from sacrifices in honour of the dead, wonderful ivory seals, over three hundred vases of stone and marble, and some daggers, all Early Minoan objects. In another, the largest, were found a meteoric mass of iron, a Babylonian cylinder, scarabs, over seventy seals, polychrome vases, and daggers of a long type, a rich furniture dating from the end of the Early Minoan Period and the beginning of the Middle. It contained a layer between 40 and 80 centimetres in depth formed of decomposed bones ; during the XXIInd and XXIst centuries it received hundreds and thousands of bodies. At Hagia Triada [2] there are two *tholoi*. The larger is nine metres in diameter, and the passage in front of it is still flanked by ten cells. There were there at least two hundred and fifty skeletons of men, women, and children. Of the objects deposited by the side of the bodies some clearly belong to the most remote period (obsidian blades, pottery incised or painted with clumsy lines, rude idols) ; many witness a more advanced culture (vases of marble and granite, copper daggers, idols of an Egyptian type, and seals shaped like cones, cylinders, and buttons) ; lastly, certain barbotine vases found in the cells can only have been made at the beginning of the Middle Minoan Period, at the time of the small *tholos* and its annexes.

In the spacious *tholos* at Kalathiana, too, a very great number of bones have been found, with the usual offerings which are found over the two last Early Minoan Periods and the first Middle Minoan. The three great *tholoi* of Koumasa, surrounded with annexes, contained fewer skeletons, a hundred each ;

[1] *AΔ*, ii (1916), 25-7.
[2] MA. xix, 213 ff. ; Halbherr, MIL. xxi, v, 249 ff., pls. vii–xi, figs. 16–27 ; RAL. xiv (1905), 392-7 ; cf. Paribeni, MA. xiv, 677 ff., 691.

but their furniture, which is very rich in vases, idols, seals, weapons of bronze and silver, and small plaques of copper and gold, is on the whole of a rather more recent date, for Kamares ware appears among it.[1]

All these tombs, then, present two striking features—the great quantity of the human remains and the chronological diversity of the furniture. But we must not regard them as ossuaries in which the remains of earlier interments were heaped together at a single later date ; they are tombs in which for centuries the same *genos* laid its dead with the objects which they had loved, and came to honour them with solemn offerings. These family tombs must have existed all over Crete. Among those preserved in the Messara some are paltry affairs, of which the contents are redolent of poverty, and the greatest number probably were made of unbaked brick and have disappeared without leaving a trace. But in the long run the *tholos* of the ancestors, filled with their descendants, was not sufficient. It was supplemented by another built by its side, generally smaller, and later by mere annexes. In E.M.III the days of the glory of this kind of tomb were departed. Why ? Because the *genos* tended to disintegrate. In its reduced form it no longer needed such spacious dwellings for the living or for the dead, and the *tholoi* which contain the latest objects contain the fewest skeletons. Then the *genos* began to split up into small families which were content each to lay its own folk to rest in its place in the shadow of its ancestors.

But after the complete disappearance of the social system which had given rise to the collective domed tombs, the latter were hallowed by the veneration of centuries. Towards the XXIst century (the beginning of the Middle Minoan Period) they ceased to be used regularly, towards the XIXth century (M.M.II) they were closed for ever. Yet the more powerful families did not cease in the course of the ages to consolidate and repair the monuments to which their traditions and their claims to nobility were bound, and thus the most distinguished *tholoi* have come down to us in what may be called their secondary state. They were perpetuated as *heroa* glorified by ancient lines. Long afterwards—such was the respect inspired

---

[1] Cf. JS. 1910, 127, 128 ; AM. 1906, 367–8.

by the sacred circles, haunted by the shades of ancestors !—
when a great king or illustrious personage was buried it was
deemed a fitting tribute to raise above his remains a dome
which rendered them sacred. In L.M.I, when it was decided
to build for Minos a tomb the majesty of which should be
worthy of him, a sepulchral chamber was dug in the hill of
Isopata and surmounted with a vault of overlapping courses
of masonry. And just as the princes and chief lords had their
mansions near the palace, they wished their tombs to be of
the same form as the royal *tholos* and in its vicinity ; a number
of these monuments have been found, reduced copies of the
magnificent original.[1] Between these individual tombs and
the collective tombs of distant centuries there is all the interval
which divides family self-government from monarchic
authority.

By the side of the round houses rectangular houses were
built at a very early date ; by the side of the bee-hive tombs
there were rectangular chamber tombs. The tombs tell the
same story of social development as the houses. At Palaikastro
a great quadrangular building divided into parallel compartments is entirely filled with skeletons. At Gournia small
houses with a door are crammed with bones piled pell-mell;
they are true charnel-houses.[2] These examples, it is true,
only belong to the beginning of the Middle Minoan Period ;
but we are in eastern Crete, where the persistence of old
customs justifies us in assigning a very distant origin to the
practice of collective interment. There, as elsewhere, we see it
undergoing transformation. At Mochlos six chamber tombs
of various size and eighteen smaller tombs have been unearthed.
The big chamber-tombs and the smaller tombs all contained
much the same furniture which extends from the Early Minoan
to the Middle Minoan Period.[3] This is one more proof that in
an island of sailors and fishermen development is more rapid
than in an agricultural and pastoral region. Mochlos shows
us a period of transition in which the nobles maintain traditions
of the solidarity of blood-ties while the merchants and smaller
folk, coming from everywhere, already have other ideas.

When family separatism gains the upper hand over the

---

[1] Evans, **XVI,** 1 ff.
[2] BSA. viii, 291–2. figs. 5, 6 ; **XL,** 56.
[3] **LXXXII,** 13–14.

collectivism of the *genos*, individualism is not far off. It makes its appearance definitely in sepulchral architecture in the form of the chest or cist grave in which the dead man, all by himself, is buried in a crouched position between the stone slabs of the sides. This form of grave, which is usual in the Cyclades, appears at Mochlos at the same time as the chamber tomb, of which it is as it were a reduced form. Constructed like the chamber tombs in E.M.II and III, the cist graves were supplanted at the end of the Early Minoan Period and during the Middle Minoan Period by similar graves with sides of small stones instead of flags. Elsewhere than at Mochlos they were supplanted by movable clay chests (*larnakes*) or jars (*pithoi*).[1] Henceforward all interments were in small family tombs or in individual tombs. In the cemetery of Zapher Papoura, in Late Minoan days, there is no tomb destined to receive a large number of dead. The hundred tombs of this cemetery can be divided into three types : (i) the chamber tomb excavated in the rock, for one, two, or three persons (father, mother, and child) ; (ii) the shaft grave, of which the narrow bottom is adapted to one body only ; (iii) the pit cave, in which the corpse was walled up in eternal solitude.[2] Whatever the origin of these three types may be, they show a complete fusion of funerary practices in a civilization with definitely individualistic tendencies.

The Urban System

In order that the practice of collecting the dead in hundreds in one tomb should be abandoned, and that each body should be buried separately in a great necropolis, it was necessary that the living, instead of forming scattered clans, should be grouped as individuals in the towns. The development of the urban system is in fact one of the phenomena which the explorers of prehistoric Crete consider the most striking. Nearly all the sites which have been excavated show crowded agglomerations of houses, intersecting lanes and streets with pavements and gutters, all grouped round a market-place or a small palace. It would never have occurred to anyone to

[1] Examples, from E.M.III at Pyrgos (*AΔ*, 1918, 136 ff.) ; from E.M.III-M.M.III at Pachyammos (cf. **XX**, fig. 94, 110, 429) ; from M.M.III at Knossos (ib., 584 ff.) ; from M.M.III–L.M.I at Mochlos (loc. cit.).

[2] Evans, **XVI**, 393.

go and live on an islet like Pseira, bare, wretched, and waterless, if the opposite coast had not already been very thickly populated. It is certainly not by mere force of imagination that the Cretan artists are so skilful in reproducing the swarming of crowds in their representations of festivals. When the Greek invaders, who had seen nothing of the kind in their own country, landed in Crete, they were stupefied by the spectacle of the multitudes thronging all the cities. The memory of it lived ; Homer could not mention Crete without immediately referring to men beyond counting, and, according as he wished to be accurate or to give a round number, to the ninety or the hundred cities in which they swarmed.

Knossos was not merely a royal residence. The palace was not surrounded solely by the mansions and villas of the great. Beyond the Western Court there was a town with square houses one or two storeys high. It is perhaps a quarter of this town that we see on the faience plaques depicting rows of houses which reach as far as the trees on the outskirts. Phaistos, another capital, cannot have differed greatly from Knossos. But we are able to obtain a clearer idea of the small provincial towns.

Praisos is typical of the purely agricultural little town. Zakro, with its abundance of sealings which were once affixed to bales of merchandise or bills of lading, shows us what a trading centre was like. But let us pause before Palaikastro, a rural agglomeration, which, as time went on, turned more and more towards the sea, and grew rich by commerce. At the foot of hills ending in steep cliffs, it spreads along the coast over a fertile plain covered with olive-trees. During the Early and Middle Minoan Periods its population seems to have lived chiefly on the produce of the fields, the vines and the neighbouring meadows. The women, in magnificent dresses and stylish hats, and the men, shod in half-boots of a light colour, and wearing daggers in their belts, went to perform their devotions at a shrine at Petsofa, further inland, and took with them as ex-voto offerings models of parts of their bodies either in need of healing or already healed, and figurines of domestic animals. There were already landowners rich enough to buy beautiful Kamares vases and to bury them in the tombs or to commission a local artist to execute a cup adorned with a herd of cattle in relief. But it was in the Late Minoan Period, especially L.M.II, that the town reached its fullest development and enjoyed a brilliant prosperity. The main street, which was well paved and well drained, was lined with houses of imposing appearance. One of them had no fewer than twenty-three rooms on the ground-floor. Luxurious dwellings opened upon the very alleys. A set of seventeen prettily decorated *rhytons* was found in one room ; elsewhere some delicate carving on ivory was discovered. The men who took a pride in these works of art were traders and shipowners, as is proved by the presence of weights, jars, and the port hard by.

Other little towns were built on barren islands where there was not even a spring of water. They can only have been the haunt of fishermen and sailors. Nevertheless they contained great wealth and wonderful masterpieces. Such is the case with Mochlos and Pseira. Mochlos, where no houses of any kind have been discovered, but which is celebrated for its necropolis, was flourishing as early as E.M.II. The hundred and thirty vases of mottled, veined, and marbled stone, with their modelling and their glittering colours enhanced by a perfect polish, the rich variety of the painted pottery, the good quality of the copper tools and weapons, the skilled workmanship of the seals, the precocious perfection of the jewellery which included quantities of crowns of gold flowers and leaves, necklaces of crystal or enamel beads, and rings with extraordinarily fine engraving upon their bezels, all these denote the presence of a population with a taste for beautiful and costly things. Where did it find the means of obtaining them ? The technique of the stone vases and the substance of which some are made, namely alabaster, witness relations with Egypt ; a silver cylinder, in a style reminiscent of Babylonia, must have been imported from Asia, perhaps by way of Cyprus. Here is a town owing its prosperity, nay its very life, entirely to sea-trade.

Lastly, we have in Gournia an example of the industrial town (Fig. 24). The houses are crowded together on the arid slopes of a limestone ridge, a few hundred yards from the shore at the end of an isthmus which narrowly separates the north and south coasts of Crete. Not a patch of ground is wasted. It would seem that men were determined on no account to surrender the smallest plot of cultivable land by encroaching upon the valley to make their homes. Into the two main

streets, paved with gypsum, open narrow, tortuous, climbing
alleys, the steep parts of which are scaled by steps. Two

FIG. 24.—Plan of Gournia.

flights of steps at right angles lead up to the little palace.
As far as it can, it resembles the large palaces of Knossos and

Phaistos ; it too has its court, adjoining the magazines, its
hall of state, with two rows of alternating round columns and
square pillars, and its stair-case leading to the private apartments.   The master of the house, who had his own seal and
caused the emblem of the double axe to be painted on his
vases, aped the great king, his overlord perhaps ; but as chief
of a little provincial town he was easily approached.   The
court served as a market-place and the humble dwellings of
his subjects leaned in familiar fashion against the outer walls
of the palace.   Climbing a narrow lane, with flagstones worn
by the feet of the faithful, we reach, in the centre of the town,
a little sanctuary standing in the middle of a tiny enclosure
and consecrated to the Serpent Goddess.   The houses are not
constructed on any fixed plan ; the ground is too uneven for
that.   The blocks have just as much regularity as is compatible
with the exigencies of the slope.   The buildings, of mortarless
stone masonry, touch one another.   They have one storey less
in front on the street than at the back, which is on a lower
level and contains the entrance.   They comprise a small
court, cellars, several little rooms—often as many as six or
eight, but rarely more.   One section of the population is
concerned with agriculture, cattle-raising, and fishing.   But
the neighbourhood supplies clay, stone, and copper ;   thus
side by side with such industries as weaving and shoe-making,
the raw materials for which are obtained from live-stock, we
have building, the manufacture of pottery and stoneware,
and metal-working.   There are no elaborate arrangements,
only small shops and work-rooms set up in the small dwellings.
There we surprise the company of artizans hard at work.
Here is an oil shop with refining-vats and a complete equipment of vases.   There a bench for a joiner whose wife spins
and weaves in the next room.   Near the harbour a blacksmith
casts nails, chisels, and awls of bronze in a four-sided mould
which he has carefully repaired.   So vivid is the impression
made that at the time of the excavation the workmen, on
beholding the site which they were uncovering, called it
μηχανικὴ πόλις, " the industrial town."

The Rights of the Women

In the community of which we have briefly considered the
general transformation, one feature stands out with a certain

clearness—the large part played by women in religious ceremonies and public festivals. The principal divinity of the Cretans is a Goddess Mother. It is the priestesses who bring humanity into touch with the divine powers. Although the women are represented with white skins, and it is true that they live in the shade, they are not recluses. There is nothing corresponding to the harem in Cretan dwellings, even in the palace of Knossos. We must not look for a rigorous division of the house into two parts, one allotted to each sex. The queen's apartments, with their zigzag corridors, are rather difficult of access, but the quarters where the women are lodged are not reserved for their exclusive use. The Hall of the Double Axes, which is quite close at hand, serves for ceremonious receptions. In the Late Minoan Period, it is true, the free communication between that hall and the queen's apartments afforded by a portico was cut off by a wall, and access from one to the other was restricted to a narrow corridor[1]; but as the greater part of the evidence on the mingling of the two sexes is of later date than this alteration, it cannot be supposed that there was a sudden and profound change in customs. Doubtless their ordinary occupations kept the women at home. They spent most of their time in sitting on low benches and spinning wool in the Room of the Distaffs, or in taking the air in a small courtyard. But, gentle or humble, they were not afraid of showing themselves outside their homes. One has only to look at the " Parisienne " (Fig. 6) ; hers is not the face of a woman shut up in the *gynæceum*. From seals of E.M.II, it can be seen that pottery was made by women as well as by men.[2] The Cretan artists are fond of representing high-born maidens standing up in chariots and holding the reins like Nausikaa. Like Atalante they go hunting. On the wall-paintings some of the persons leaping over the bulls and taking part in boxing are white-skinned. Crete had its female toreadors and female pugilists (Fig. 51). With still greater reason the women were present at public shows. Greek legend recalls this custom and on the frescoes of Knossos and Mycenæ we actually behold the ladies of the court flaunting their charms in balconies.[3]

[1] Evans, **XX**, 333.
[2] Ib., figs. 93 *a, b* 2, 3, *c* 1, 2.
[3] Plutarch, *Theseus*, 19. See figs. 48, **55**.

In Minoan society, then, women did not hold that inferior position imposed by the Oriental system of seclusion. This was not without influence upon her legal status. Of course, archæological documents cannot give us a definite answer on a question of this kind. Yet it is well to notice that in a betrothal scene the man and the woman, both of the same height, facing each other as equals, pledge themselves mutually by the same gesture, each raising the right arm for a hand-clasp (Fig. 25).[1] But we have the knowledge of what happened among a neighbouring people with whom the Cretans had constant intercourse, and we may ask ourselves whether we are justified in applying to the Cretans the indications supplied by this contemporary people, in view of the analogy with later examples afforded by peoples supposed to be akin to the Cretans.

FIG. 25.—Betrothal scene. Ivory cylinder from the neighbourhood of Knossos (M.M.I).

Under the Pharaohs, woman occupied an important place in the Egyptian family, both in law and in fact. In primitive art she is represented as of greater stature than man, a convention which seems symbolical of a matriarchy similar to that which Herodotus afterwards found in Libya.[2] By her the sacred seed of the ancestors is propagated and fructified. She is the progenitress by whom the race is perpetuated, and she is portrayed with an enormous development of the hips. The mother is the centre of gravity of the family and descent is reckoned on the maternal side. In order to keep pure the blood of which she is the guardian, she takes a husband of the same blood. Marriage within the tribe is compulsory, and a

[1] **XX,** fig. 145.
[2] Herodotus, iv, 176.

union between brother and sister is blessed by the gods. Thus the queen confirms the authority of the king, and the founder of a dynasty can only win recognition of the legitimacy of his title, or rather of that of his future son, by marrying a daughter of the old dynasty.

It is obvious that ideas of this kind are not borrowed by one nation from another. But it is precisely for this reason that we must take into account the information given by Greek historians regarding the customs of peoples who, they said, came from Crete. The Lycians passed for descendants of Cretan emigrants and were thought to have preserved customs which were partly of Cretan origin. Now they bore the name of their mother, and took her rank and, when stating what was their family, they enumerated their kinsfolk on the distaff side.[1] The Carians equally plumed themselves on their Cretan origin, and Herodotus saw a resemblance between their customs and those of the Lycians. The Carian women of Miletos never gave the name of husband to the men with whom they lived. One Artemisia ruled the kingdom in the Vth century and, a hundred years later, another queen of the same name received the inheritance from her brother and husband, Mausolos, to the exclusion of a younger brother Idrieus. Even the remote Tyrrhenians, if it is true that they came from Asia, bear interesting testimony with their Tanaquil, the creatress of kings.

What conclusions regarding Minoan Crete can we draw from these analogies? The Mycenæans can be contrasted with the Egyptians. Before Cretan customs were adopted the Mycenæan woman seems to have been relegated to an inferior position. In the royal interments of the Shaft Graves only three skeletons out of seventeen are female, a fact which seems to indicate that the chieftains had concubines of lower degree and that they did not habitually bring up their daughters to the rank of princesses. As for the peoples of Asia, they doubtless inherited their family laws less from the Cretans than from the Hittites, among whom the mother of kings, as was fitting in the country of the Goddess Mother and of the Amazons, held the reins of government and had herself styled " Great

---

[1] Herodotus, i, 173. It has been affirmed to-day that the Lycian inscriptions do not corroborate the statements of Herodotus (cf. Sundwall, *Klio*, Beiheft xi, 1913, 257–8) ; but his testimony is too explicit to be contested except for peremptory reasons, and those given are not peremptory.

Queen ".[1] Let us now consider more closely the cases cited. Sometimes the woman has simply civil rights, at other times she enjoys political superiority. The most recent critics of the theory of matriarchy have carefully distinguished between *Mutterrecht* and gynæcocracy, between kinship traced on the maternal side and rule by women. Even in primitive groups, and still more in those that have developed, woman can be the sentimental link between men, and thereby the vital centre of the community, without being the chief. There is one sufficient reason why she should not hold authority; motherhood comes to her too soon. As a matter of fact, it is generally her eldest brother who becomes chieftain. Were a woman's rights then limited in Crete to an important rôle in the family, to great liberty in the matter of conduct, and to an active service in religion, or did they go so far as to secure for her a position of eminence in the State ? It seems incontestable that the Cretan woman possessed the whole range of civil rights that was later to belong to the Lycian. Long after the Dorian invasion the laws of Gortyn were to take woman under their protection once more, and Plutarch observes that the Cretans do not call their country a " fatherland " but a " motherland ".[2] This is no reason for having faith or recognizing a general significance in the words of an obscure historian who speaks of " power fallen into the hands of Ariadne ". There is no necessity to acknowledge an essential connexion between the worship of the Goddess Mother and matriarchy. The vogue of steatopygous figurines and the feminine custom of baring the breast are sufficiently accounted for by the pride of motherhood and its deification. It is unnecessary to see in them symbols of political power. Ariadne is the " very sacred " queen, but Minos is the king.

II GOVERNMENT

The King

The political system in Crete had passed through many vicissitudes before the Minoan monarchy was evolved.

[1] Contenau, *Trente tablettes cappadociennes*, 59 ; cf. Hrosny, *Un Code hittite*, 1923, § 171.
[2] Kleitodemos, in Plutarch, *Theseus*, 19.

At first the whole of Crete was in the power of the clans. That was the time when the most powerful chieftains were buried in *tholos* ossuaries, each with his seal tied to his neck, and his best weapon in his hand. A dozen *tholos* sites within a radius of 10 metres, in the neighbourhood of Koumasa, show how the island swarmed with these petty potentates. The decline of these sites towards the end of the Early Minoan Period marks the dissolution of a social system and the disturbances which resulted. Each family and each locality tried to provide itself with a means of defence. At Kalathiana, a village of a hundred to a hundred and fifty hearths, some of the houses had fronts with redans. The elliptical dwelling at Chamaizi could offer a certain amount of resistance, with its wall a metre thick and its funnel-shaped entrance-passage, which could easily be barricaded at both ends. An enclosure of piled up rocks crowned Mount Iouktas. Eventually a certain concentration took place. In the Messara it was the chieftain perched on the hill-spur of Phaistos benefited by it, and in the valley of the Kairatos it was the chieftain who was established in the keep of Knossos and protected by a strong tower and massive ramparts. Shortly after the year 2000, each of these two kings had his own palace. This did not make for peace. In M.M.I no man of rank as yet went out without his dagger in his belt (Figs. 7, 25). Fortresses and a beleagured town are represented on faience marquetery of M.M.II. About 1750 the two palaces went under in a general catastrophe.

When other dynasties erected other palaces, however, things were different. The northern city began to hold a fruitful intercourse with the mainland, while the southern city did not attempt to trade with the Egypt of the Hyksos. They were no longer equally matched, and it was for Knossos to aspire to hegemony. She had armed herself with strong fortifications, and the road leading up from the harbour was confronted by an entrance bristling with bastions. Yet the struggle was a bitter one, and indeed, about 1600, the west wing of the great palace, where the treasures were kept, was partially burnt and given over to pillage. In the end the majority of the local chieftains recognized the overlordship of Minos. They may even have been replaced by governors. About 1450, Phaistos, Hagia Triada, and Tylissos succumbed ; their palaces were razed to the ground, and the sites abandoned for half a century.

Minos, henceforth undisputed master, could have a new throne
room built in which to receive the homage of his subjects.

Only then, or at the earliest from M.M.III, historical
probability permits us to call the king of Knossos by the
name of Minos. This name does not seem to have been applied
to one personage only. It is less a proper name than a dynastic
title. There were Minoses in Crete, as there were Pharaohs and
Ptolemies in Egypt and Cæsars in Rome. The Parian
Chronicle mentions a Minos in the XVth and again in the
XIIIth century. Another chronicle speaks of two Minoses
and two Ariadnes. Diodorus Siculus makes Minos I the
grandfather of Minos II.[1] Further, the innumerable towns
bearing the name of Minoa cannot all have been called after
one man any more than those named Ptolemaïs, Antioch,
Seleukeia, and Cæsarea. Each Minos, therefore, like each
of the Pharaohs, must have had his personal name and titles
along with his family tree. Out of these the Pharaoh composed
his cartouche, and the Minos, in the same way, combined them
into a device which he had engraved on his seal. The fleur-de-
lys and certain animals, such as the lion, the wolf, the cat,
the owl, and the dove, provided the principal elements of this
official and sacred nomenclature.[2]

Minos was above all the priest-king.   A religious impression
is produced by the whole wing of the palace-sanctuary, where
he presents himself to the general gaze seated on his throne
guarded by gryphons. He is the representative of the Bull
God, the incarnation of the Minotaur, whose image appeared
everywhere on the walls, and dominated the gateway of the
sacred dwelling. When the divine bull had received the name
of Zeus or, as the legend has it, when Zeus had taken the form
of the divine bull, Minos was the son, and, according to the
Odyssey, the " companion of great Zeus ".[3] Once set apart
by the divine will for the veneration of men, he became " king
for a period of nine years ".   At the end of that time the
divine power which had been breathed into him was exhausted
and had to be renewed. He climbed the sacred mountain to
converse, to commune with the god. He entered the awful
grotto of the Minotaur, he penetrated the most mysterious

[1] Parian Marble, 11, 19 ; Plutarch, *Theseus*, 20 ; Diodorus, iv, 60.
[2] Evans, **XVII,** 264–5.
[3] *Odyssey*, xix, 179.

of all labyrinths,[1] he came to render account to his father,
to bow to the judgment of his master. In that hour the island
was in anguish. All those whose fate depended upon the
forthcoming decision made sacrifice, in breathless suspense,
of chosen victims. It was perhaps for these festivals that the
tribute of seven young men and seven maidens, exacted every
nine years, was reserved. If the god was dissatisfied with his
chosen, he kept him, and the king who was thus condemned
was never spoken of again. If the god was satisfied, Minos,
renewed for nine years, came down again into the midst of
his people with a fresh store of power. Translated into modern
language, the legend seems to mean that the priest-king held
his power by a religious investiture, and that he was appointed
for nine years and re-eligible.

The king, like the god, had as insignia the sceptre and the
double axe, the *labrys*. Two thousand years before it became
the symbol of authority in Rome, the axe already held that
position in the palace of the Labyrinth. The kings of Knossos
had perhaps another emblem besides, the fleur-de-lys. Strange
coincidence. Are we to believe that the three-pointed flower
symbolized a religious idea, that of the trinity ? Nothing
either confirms or belies this hypothesis. The fact remains
that in L.M.II the fleur-de-lys appeared in all parts of the
palace of Knossos, and spread over the whole Ægean world.
The figure on the painted relief, with the crown of fleur-de-lys
topped with great plumes and the necklace of fleur-de-lys, is
Minos himself (Fig. 57). The royal flower appears in devices
on seals ; it is painted on walls and on vases (Fig. 77). From
the capital it spreads throughout the island ; at Gortyn it
surmounts a lion's muzzle, at Palaikastro it accompanies a
heraldic bird.[2] It crosses the sea ; in Thera and Phylakopi,
in Mycenæ and Pylos it blooms on frescoes, pottery, arms,
and ivories.[3] It might be said that for foreigners as well
as for Cretans the realm of Minos is the realm of the fleur-
de-lys.

---

[1] Plato, *Minos*, 319 D ; *Laws*, 624 D, 630 D, 632 D ; Strabo, x, 4, 8, 19 ;
xvi, 2, 38 ; Dionysius of Halicarnassus, ii, 61.

[2] **XVII,** 156, p. 34 ; BSA, xi, 285, fig. 14*b*.

[3] **LXVII,** figs. 211–12, pl. xix, 5 ; **XXI,** fig. 64, 163, pl. xxiv, 9 ; AM.
1907, pp. xii–xiii.

The Royal Administration

The whole palace bears witness to a centralized government and an already complex administration. It covers an area of nearly five acres. Hundreds of persons were lodged there. Only one part of it was given up to the royal family and the household. The remainder was not occupied by the princes and nobles ; they had their country and town houses in the quarter between the palace and the city, where the king, too, had a villa built for himself. They were thus able to take part in court life, to attend the festivities arranged by the king, such as theatrical performances, concerts, and rodeos. Since they composed the class from which Minos recruited his high officials, they had easy access to the palace for the execution of their duties. In all probability then, a large number of royal services were installed in the palace. They were at once private and public, for a distinction between the two hardly exists in patriarchal monarchies where natural economy still prevails.

One thing that gives a good idea of Minoan administration is the multitude of tablets bearing inscriptions that have been found in the palace. To the West of the North Entrance there was a regular storehouse of archives.[1] Lying pell-mell among the tablets at the time of their discovery were fragments of gypsum slabs, the remains of coffers in which the tablets were put away. In other places they were packed in wooden chests ; metal handles and clay sealings mark the spot where they stood, and prove that they were scrupulously sealed. It is not impossible, moreover, that the coffers and chests contained leaves of some light substance like papyrus ; for, in Knossos, besides the official writing, they had a kind of cursive which was done with a point dipped in ink. The king, then, had at his disposal an order of scribes. They learned that " court hand " which Evans has recognized in the inscriptions.[2] The signs used in this official writing were doubtless fixed by the rules of public administration. Thus the palace made use of bureaucratic methods of registration and accounting which were handed down from century to century and were perfected in the process.

[1] BSA. vi, 50.
[2] **XVII**, 39.

The principal documents were authenticated by the royal seal. It can be recognized in a number of instances by the " throne and sceptre " sign, and in others by a device containing the name of the king.[1] The king's seal had to be affixed so often that it was necessary to make several copies of it. In the palace a clay mould was discovered which was used to reproduce a seal of which the impression has been found on several tablets.[2] This mould had therefore been manufactured in order that the king's signature might be given more easily. Each administration, moreover, had its own special seal ; from the northern storehouse we have the impression of a ship, a lion from the north-west storehouse symbolizes war, and from the magazines we have an ear of corn. Better still, the high officials had personal seals showing the positions held by them.[3] In the Third Magazine, near some charred corn, a seal was found representing heaps of cereals guarded by gryphons, an eloquent heraldic device of the royal grain-keeper. According to Evans a door signifies a guardian, a leg a chieftain, and an eye a supervisor. Thus the seal with the door and the double axe belongs to the guardian of the labyrinth, and the seal with the eye and the trowel would suit a supervisor of public works. The adze associated with the trowel (like the adze associated with the saw in Egypt) must be the badge of a high office.

The chief mission of Minos on earth is to dispense justice. From the mountain whither he goes to consult his god he brings back, like Khammurabi or Moses, sacred laws and infallible decrees. But besides being law-giver he is also judge. Evans claims to have discovered his court of justice— the basilica of the Royal Villa. Seated on his throne at the back of an apse raised to the height of three steps, and separated from the hall by a balustrade, the king presided over his tribunal, while at the bar (ad cancellos) in front of a large standard lamp stood the chancellor. This conjecture would be attractive if it were not so venturesome. There is less improbability in the supposition that a connexion existed between the king's justice and the " oubliettes of the palace " ; but these subterranean chambers, hollowed out below the old keep to a

[1] Ib., 46, 270.
[2] BSA. vii, 19.
[3] **XVII,** 267–8.

depth of 7 metres, belong to a time when the lord of Knossos
had as yet no palace. It was in this very manner, as pits or
subterranean vaults, that the Jews were to represent prisons,
whether in their own country or in Egypt.[1] Imprisonment
in the beginning always means being walled up. In Knossos
the scene of punishment was an artificial cave, a labyrinth of
the Minotaur. Moreover, the infliction of this penalty is
always traceable to a religious idea ; the guilty are handed
over to the deity to perish or to be kept alive. It is a kind of
ordeal, a judgment of God. Ordeals seem indeed to have
played a large part in Minoan justice.[2] When they did not
take place in the bowels of the earth they were performed—
as befitted a nation of sailors—in the sea. Cretan legend is
full of stories which lend a more or less transparent disguise
to the old idea. Skylla " the she-dog " dies tied to the stern
of a ship, Phronyme " the wise " is exposed to the terrible
test and saved by Themison " the justiciary ". Purity of
maidens, legitimacy of birth, and right of heredity are
established by a leap into the sea. Britomartis throws herself
into the waves because " in that plunge lies the proof of
virginity ". Theseus shows Minos that he is the son of the
gods by going down to the bottom of the sea. The judicial
function of Minos, which grew out of his religious function,
contributed largely to his glory. When his time came, when
he had nothing further to do in this world, he would depart
into Hades to be judge of the dead.

If we could decipher the tablets we should be thoroughly
acquainted with the financial administration of ancient
Crete. This written evidence being withheld from us, we fall
back upon the palaces themselves. Along the ground floor
lie the Magazines—what the Homeric epics were to call the
" treasure ". There, lined up in rows, stand the great *pithoi*
containing grain, wine, and more especially oil, and the subterranean cists or *kaselles* holding the objects of greatest value.
In the First Palace at Phaistos an enclosure measuring 9·75
by 3·60 metres was divided into three magazines, furnished
with niches and connected by doors in a straight line. In these
thirty-one *pithoi* were standing in their places at the moment
of the conflagration. In the Second Palace a corridor 21 metres

---

[1] Jer. xxxvii, 16 ; Gen. xl, 15 ; xli, 14.
[2] Cf. Glotz, *Les Ordalies dans la Grèce primitive*, 55-6, 40, 44-5.

long gave access to ten magazines, five on each side (Fig. 21).
At Knossos there was a large store of oil in the east wing, but
the chief magazines were in the opposite wing. At first fifteen
in number, and later eighteen, they opened on to a passage
60 metres long.   Along the rows of *kaselles* the *pithoi* were
ranged (Figs. 19, 26). Some of these enormous jars are adorned
with rows of handles and of large knobs, the purpose of which
is explained by mouldings in imitation of ropes.   Others are
decorated with a trickle ornament, from which their contents
may be guessed. As for the cists in the ground, from the
XVIIth century onwards, they were insufficient for the king's
riches.   In the corridor itself, an enclave, 30 metres in
length, was formed, and shut off by a solid door.   Here a new
series of compartments, twenty-seven in number, was installed
with meticulous care and elaborate precautions against damp.[1]

FIG. 26.—The Magazines of Knossos.

One can understand this solicitude in guarding precious
objects, but why this accumulation of provisions and liquids ?
The reason is that the king's " treasury " was, in the modern
sense, the treasury of the State.   It was fed by the State
revenues and doubtless also by gifts, voluntary or otherwise.
It did not provide merely for the needs of the royal family
and the large household which took its meals in the south
quarter.[2] In Homer, the king gives official banquets sometimes
for notable strangers, sometimes for " ancients " who have a
right to the " wine of honour ". These royal feasts must have
occurred in prehistoric Crete also.   The Minos had his " table

[1] **XX,** 448 ff.
[2] BSA. vii, 11.

companions " like the Pharaoh.   At all events, out of the
resources of his treasury, in foodstuffs or in other forms, he
supplied the salaries of his officials, defrayed the expenses of
religious celebrations, and paid the craftsmen and the artists
of the palace.

The king of Knossos owned workshops which had to supply
him with objects of art and luxury which were envied among
all, and bore brilliant witness to his glory, all the world over.
Three thousand years before Urbino, Sèvres, and Meissen,
Knossos had its royal porcelain factory, which produced
strange and magnificent pieces of work.   Close at hand, His
Majesty's sculptor fashioned stone vases.   His lapidary mounted
gems and rare substances in settings of precious metal and
of marquetery.   The pottery, fine examples of which were
already being moulded in M.M.II, took up considerable space,
with its warehouses, when stocks of ordinary crockery were
being turned out at the same time as those costly vases upon
which the major-domo placed a seal that was broken by much
use.[1]   A whole staff of workmen and perhaps of slaves was
employed in these establishments under the orders of eminent
masters. With the corps of builders and the officials in charge
of them, they composed a kind of rudimentary Department of
Fine Arts.   The dignitary with the trowel and the adze for
badge may well have been, like his colleague in Egypt, the
superintendent of the royal buildings.

Minos commanded an army.   The royal war administration
had as its emblem the lion with the fleur-de-lys or with the
" throne and sceptre ".   Did it recruit professional soldiers,
or were certain subjects of the king pressed into military
service ?   Cretan artists sometimes represent warriors who
do not wear the national dress.   On the other hand, a seal
belonging to a private individual has on one face a person
holding a spear driven into the ground and on the other two
the emblems of the carpenter and of the cattle-breeder
respectively.[2]   Let us, however, look closely at the Chieftain
Vase (Fig. 27).   Drawn up to his full height, with his chest
thrown out, a triple necklace reaching from shoulder to
shoulder and his head, adorned with long curls, raised
majestically—the king !   In front of the palace gate, he

---

[1] **XX**, 564 ff. ; 568 ff.
[2] Fig. 8 ; JHS. xiv (1894), 338, fig. 56.

stretches out his right arm to its full length and, with an
imperious gesture, plants on the ground a sceptre as tall as
himself. Opposite to him a smaller person, with a single
necklace, stands in an attitude of respect—the leader of the
soldiers lined up behind him. He is receiving orders from
his master, but in what capacity ?   Is he an officer or a vassal ?
With his weapon at the slope, his elbows bent at right angles,

FIG. 27.—The Chieftain Vase. Steatite goblet from Hagia Triada.

his hands on a level with his belt, he grips in his right fist
the rapier that rests against his shoulder. In his left hand
he holds the handle of an object with a sharply curved end
which projects above his helmet. This object resembles
a sceptre-head found in Cyprus and the Egyptian *hiq*. Now
this crook was used by the Pharaohs to invest the princes
over whom they extended their overlordship. At Beni
Hasan the emblem is borne by a Syrian chief.[1] The scene
portrayed on the Cretan vase thus represents the subordination
of the crook to the sceptre, the homage rendered by a vassal
to an overlord. The troops lined up are those whom a petty
chieftain is bringing to the lord of Hagia Triada, or the lord
of Hagia Triada to the king of Phaistos, or perhaps the king
of Phaistos to Minos.

We can see from sealings (Fig. 13) how the warriors of
Knossos were armed as a general rule. They wore a conical
helmet ending in a tail which floated in the breeze, a large
eight-shaped shield and a spear a little shorter than the human
body. With the spearmen of the line marched the companies
armed with bows. The Cretan archers, so renowned in

[1] Cf. **XI**, 264–5, fig. 188, 4.

Judæa and later in Greece, possessed old traditions.   Lastly,
the Minoan army had its war-chariots with two horses, after
this animal had been introduced into the island along with
the Hittite chariot already known in Syria, Egypt, and Cyprus.
This army was, to all appearance, amply provided with the
necessary material.   The arsenal of Knossos was to the
North-West, near the gate from which the road led to the sea.
There, inventory tablets, which were formerly packed in
coffers, have been found in heaps.   At the entrance alone
eighty of them were picked up.   A large number of them,
marked with the sign of the " throne and sceptre ", mention
the separate parts of chariots, which are elsewhere drawn
complete—bodies, with or without pole, and wheels, there
being in all eighty or ninety bodies and 478 wheels.   On other
tablets there are lists of javelins or lances, daggers, and a metal
slug.   A return of arrows, the end of which has alone survived,
mentions two lots, one of 6,010 and the other of 2,630.   The
meaning of these inventories is further established by a seal
which speaks plain language—throne and sceptre, lion,
arrow ; that is to say, kingdom of Minos, war administration,
armament section.[1]

The army, being well organized, did not need to be very
numerous.   Within the island peace reigned ; against enemies
from outside the fleet sufficed.   This explains the fact which
has made so powerful an impression on the explorers of prehistoric Crete but which is only true from the XVIth century
onwards, namely, the absence of substantial fortifications.
The Cretans of the great period nevertheless knew quite well
what a stronghold meant.   They knew Melos, Tiryns, and
Mycenæ.   The siege of a town continued to be a familiar
subject for their artists, who entertained the Achaians of
Argolis with it, and was perhaps a favourite theme with
their poets.   But they had done with all that long ago.   The
entrance to the palace had been made narrower as a measure
of safety in M.M.III, but in L.M.I it was widened again.[2]
They did just leave a few obstacles, enough to prevent a
surprise attack.   The eastern slope only served now to afford
a fine view of the landscape from the hall of state.   Knossos
had been a Vincennes in the old days.   It was now a Versailles.

[1] BSA. x, 57 ff., fig. 21 ; **XVII,** figs. 22, 24, 30, 19.
[2] Evans, **XX,** 394.

The Cretan Thalassocracy

That a people so rich and so expert in every form of art should not have used their skill to protect their riches proves that they felt themselves safe. They lived in complete security, in splendid isolation. They had nothing to fear on land because they had the mastery of the sea. Their ships were their fortresses. At that time it might be said of the Cretans, as Homer said of the Phaiakians, " they care not for the bow nor the quiver but for masts and oars and ships in which they go in gladness over the foamy sea." [1] The first maritime empire that existed in the world, the first "thalassocracy", was that established by the Cretan fleet. In Egypt the name of Keftiu, which stood for the people predominating in the regions of the North, was long reserved for the Cretans. The memory of that domination did not perish. Herodotus and Thucydides, who do not agree about the conduct of Minos towards the Carians, are at one on all other points. According to a tradition which they quote with complete confidence, the Cretans, by means of their navy, dominated the whole Ægean, stamped out piracy, colonized most of the Cyclades and, while exacting from the islanders either tribute or crews for their fleet, brought with them wherever they settled a prosperity hitherto unknown.[2] The mere list of the towns which took the name of Minoa is a sufficient indication of the extent of the Minoan empire. The geographical position of these towns shows that they were at the same time naval bases and trade settlements. There were two Minoas in Crete itself, and others in the islands of Delos, Amorgos, Paros, and Siphnos ; there was one in Laconia and another at the head of the Saronic Gulf ; there were others again from the coast of Syria to Kerkyra and even in Sicily.[3] Within these limits a host of towns, of which the names, ending in " nth " like labyrinth or in " ss " like Knossos, belong to a pre-Hellenic language, were visited or occupied by the Minoans. They were firmly established all over the isthmus of Argolis from Tiryns to Corinth. On the eastern coast of Attica, the plain of Marathon, from

[1] *Odyssey*, vi, 270–2.
[2] Herodotus, i, 171 ; Thucydides, i, 4, 8.
[3] Fick, **XXII,** 27.

Probalinthos to Trikorynthos, always preserved the memory of the Cretan bull whose very name was perhaps kept by the first of these towns.[1]

According to Thucydides, Minos sent his own sons as lieutenants to his foreign possessions. It is not impossible that he sometimes followed a patriarchal policy. In any case, on the mainland the command was in the hands of military chieftains, some of whom must have recognized the over-lordship of Minos. In general, these chieftains, whether independent or vassals, lived upon the peasantry. The more favoured among them, however, were posted at the ports, such as Pylos, or watched the great roads frequented by merchants at Orchomenos, Thebes, Tiryns, Mycenæ, and Vapheio; these became great and mighty dynasts. Each had his retreat on an acropolis surrounded by imposing ramparts. They built themselves palaces with vast colonnaded courts and huge apartments with frescoed walls. There they lived with all their family in joy and luxury, eating and drinking from vases of gold and silver, the men wearing arms inlaid with precious metals and the women sparkling with jewels and admiring themselves in mirrors of carved ivory. In peace-time their greatest pleasure was the chase, to which the ladies followed their lords. When the ruler died they made a mask of his face in gold-leaf, his grave was filled with precious objects, and he was laid in a majestic domed tomb plated with bronze. Such pomp was only possible where the many toiled and moiled for the few. Round the strongholds lived the multitude from whom forced labour could be exacted at will. It was they who, by strength of arm, laid in position the enormous stones from which the ramparts and the bathroom at Tiryns, the Lion Gate and the " Treasury of Atreus " at Mycenæ were built.

These dynasts may have borne the title of τύραννοι, " tyrants ".[2] It is not a Greek word. The Greeks derived it sometimes from Tyra or Tyrrha, a Lydian town, and some-times from the Tyrrhenians or from their eponymous hero Tyrrhenos. They were not mistaken, inasmuch as Tyrrha means a strong place, a tower, and its association with τύρσις,

[1] Hesychius, s.v. βόλυνθος.
[2] See Radet, *La Lydie sous les Mermnades*, 146 ff. ; *Ephesiaca*, 31 ; cf. Ramsay, in Bezzenberger's *Beitraege*, xiv (1889), 309.

which was thought to be " Pelasgic ", makes this name analogous to Pyrgo and Kastro. But the explanation does not fit one town and one people only ; it applies, for instance, to the castle of Tiryns. There must therefore have been " tyrants " in Mycenæan Greece as in Asia, and the mother of one of them took her place in legend under the name of Tyro. From military chieftains they developed into kinglets ; but " tyranny " will always leave the memory of authority which lacks the legitimacy of hereditary right and is not consecrated by religion. It will owe its evil renown to the fact that it stood for the use of force and often, at its origin, of foreign force.

The Cretan thalassocracy did the greatest service. " Thenceforward," says Thucydides, " the inhabitants of the coasts began to grow rich and to own dwellings which were less precarious." Minos had to collect tribute, and one of the paintings adorning his palace represents a train of tributaries, in the Egyptian manner ; but his exactions must have been moderate. Melos, the great intermediate station between Crete and Argolis, seems to have enjoyed complete self-government. At Phylakopi, to judge by the products imported and exported, exchanges with Knossos were carried out on a basis of reciprocity to the advantage of both parties. On the mainland the Cretans did not arrive with their goods, their rites, and their whole civilization without quickening urban life at the same time. But if the great island was to communicate freely with its political or economic dependencies it must have security on the seas and energetic policing. What would have become of foreign trade otherwise can be seen from the tablets from Tell el-Amarna. Here the Pharaoh complains to a Cypriot prince of raids upon the Delta ; the prince replies that he has nothing to do with it, that on the contrary his own land is pillaged every year by pirates, and, on another occasion, he himself claims the restitution of property belonging to a Cypriot merchant who died in Egypt. Piracy, reprisals, absence of any international law—into this world the fleet of Minos brought good order, and it was indeed a blessing.

But the Minos legend has two sides. His name will live to be hated as well as extolled. He appears, according to the country, either as the noble Eitel or as Attila the " scourge of God ". Obviously all peoples did not accept the domination of the " tyrants " with equal readiness. The Cretan thalassocracy had its dark side. The children of Megara always trembled when they were told the story of Scylla, the sea-bitch tied to the ship of Minos. On the plain of Marathon the ravages of the Minotaur and the tribute of slaves which he exacted were never forgotten.

CHAPTER II

AGRICULTURE, CATTLE-RAISING, HUNTING, AND FISHING

ON their island the Cretans found conditions favourable to agriculture, cattle-raising, hunting, and fishing. The plains at the foot of the three mountain-groups, being as fertile as could be desired, were admirably suited to the cultivation of cereals and pulse, fruit-trees, and textile plants. At a time when the forests were vaster and the rainfall, therefore, more copious there was no lack of pasture-land. Heath, copse, and mountain swarmed with game. Bays on all sides teemed with fish.

During the Neolithic Age, however, the Cretans had, in addition to their resources in cattle, game, and fish, only such harvests as wild nature provided. On the mainland of Europe, on the contrary, the tribes of the Neolithic settlements cultivated the land. This does not mean that Crete was behind the mainland in agriculture. It took earlier to metal, not later to the plough. An island, moreover, has no boundless spaces to spare for pastoral life and its migrations. At an early date, as soon as the population of Crete began to increase, it was necessary to resort to agriculture.

So the chief divinity of the Cretans was the Goddess Mother. Their chief festivals were connected with the annual crises of rural life. In spring the firstling flowers were offered up to the deity. At the end of autumn the decay of plant-life was symbolized by the plucking of the sacred tree. (Figs. 38, 39.) The olive-harvest was probably the occasion for a solemn procession. (Plate II, 2.)

One can imagine what a large farm, carried on by a whole family, must have been like at the beginning of the Middle Minoan Period, from the roominess of the house at Chamaizi. (Fig. 23.) But later, to judge by the seals representing various professions, it was rather humble folk who went in for cattle-raising and agriculture. One of the signs used in writing shows that the holdings were separated by hedges.

M

The plough used was a simple wooden swing-plough with the pole and the stock in one piece ; [1] the sickle was made of bronze.

Wheat and barley were grown throughout Crete as in the Cyclades, in Asia Minor, and in Greece proper. Grain was stored in *pithoi*, a considerable number of which have been found in the houses at Hagia Triada and Palaikastro, containing cereals calcined by the fire. There were long rows of them (Fig. 26) in the palace at Knossos and the seal of the royal grain-keeper was picked up near a heap of charred corn. Perhaps bread was made from millet in Crete as in Thessaly.[2] As certain jugs are ornamented with ears of barley in relief, and as, in the writing, cereals are associated with vases of a special shape, it can at any rate be assumed that the Cretans knew how to make beer.[3] Dried pulse was even more important as a foodstuff than cereals. All along the Ægean Sea excavations have brought to light, sometimes by dozens, jars filled with peas, vetches, lentils, and beans. On one beautiful vase there is a design of cultivated peas with short pods, and another variety is called in Greek by a name borrowed from the pre-Hellenes, $ἐρέβινθος$. Plants of the gourd family were likewise cultivated, as we are reminded by the Hellenized name of the pumpkin ($κολοκύνθη$, colocynth).

The cultivation of trees is of interest historically. Since it exacts prolonged care it can only be practised by a completely stationary population who have long been wedded to agriculture. The fruit-tree is one of the most powerful ties by which men are bound to the land. That is why primitive man roots it up or cuts it down in enemy countries and makes a sacred tree of it at home. The Greeks said that their ancestors ate acorns. This was because they came from the North, and in Thessaly, in the Neolithic Age, there were actually stores of acorns in the houses.[4] But the Cretans had other fruits at their disposal.

The olive-tree was of the greatest service to them. In the Homeric poems its oil is only used for the toilet and hygiene. Thus it was believed until quite recently that oil was for a long time a rare commodity in Greece and the olive an

[1] **XVII,** fig. 102, No. 27.
[2] **LXXXVIII,** 360.
[3] **XX,** fig. 299.
[4] **LXXXVIII,** 359.

exotic tree. There was sufficient room to doubt this, for the
olive-tree exists in a wild state from the Punjab to Portugal,
and its oil served the Egyptians and the Semites from the
earliest times for food, anointment, and lighting. Yet nothing
could shake the common belief, not even the discovery in
prehistoric Thera of lava containing olive leaves and twigs.
To-day doubt is no longer possible. The vases full of olive-
stones, which have been dug up in many of the houses, prove
that this fruit was used as food in Crete. There is an abundance
of presses and tanks for refining the oil. Innumerable lamps
of clay, steatite, gypsum, marble, and bronze are a sufficient
indication of the means by which palace and cottage were
lighted. The capacity of the lamps points to an absolutely
luxurious standard of illumination. There was no thought
of economy. Great as the demand was, the supply was
sufficiently abundant to admit of a surplus for exportation.
On certain sealings an olive-bough is associated with a ship.[1]
There is a foundation of truth in the legend which tells that
the olive was brought to Olympia by the Cretan Herakles.[2]

The vine was likewise cultivated in Crete. It spread inland
from the coast. Traces from prehistoric times abound on the
lower mountain-slopes in the vineyards of to-day. In towns,
the wine-presses were installed in the houses ; in the country,
a rock was sometimes adapted for this purpose. The wine
was not decanted ; it contained grape-pulp, as Sicilian wine
does to this day. In the Early Minoan Period the long tubular
spout with which certain vases were furnished was well adapted
for decantation. At a later date too the funnel-shaped
vase or filler, one of the most characteristic forms of Cretan
pottery, was perhaps designed to keep back the lees when
libations were being poured out to the gods. Grape-seeds
and dregs of wine have been found in the ruins of Tiryns,
Mycenæ, and Orchomenos, but it was neither the Greeks
nor any race speaking an Indo-European language who
invented the terms used in those languages for the vine and
wine (οἶνος, vinum).[3] The words were inherited like the
things themselves.

Without man's aid, the fig-tree in its wild state had from

[1] **XX,** fig. 213.
[2] Pausanias, v, 7, 7.
[3] Meillet, *Mém. de la Soc. de Linguistique*, xv, 163.

the beginning of the quaternary period spread along the
Mediterranean. But its fruit became edible only after
caprification. According to a generally accepted theory,
this process was a Semitic invention ; it could hardly have
been known to the Greeks before the day when the poet
described the garden of Alkinoos and the orchard of Laertes
in Ithaka. As a matter of fact, large pots full of beautiful
figs were found in the royal villa at Hagia Triada and at
Pylos, and the fruit was known in Neolithic Thessaly.[1] Again
it was a pre-Hellenic word that the Greeks used for a green
fig (ὄλυνθος).

Side by side with the olive and the fig, the date-palm
(*phœnix dactylifera*) figures among the sacred trees worshipped
in Crete. But long before it was painted in front of a funeral
chapel on a sarcophagus at Hagia Triada (Fig. 50a) it burgeoned
already upon a beautiful jar of M.M.II.[2] Many other fruits
besides figs and dates formed part of the Cretan's diet, among
them the plum, which was copied by the makers of porcelain
at Knossos,[3] and the quince, which by its name recalls the
Cretan town of Kydonia.

Among trees serving an industrial purpose a foremost place
must be given to the cypress, a sacred tree which, according
to Pliny, had its home in Crete.[4] The cypress-wood produced
by the island was of excellent quality. The Minoans made
the doors and columns of their palaces out of it, and later the
Greeks always sought after it for making doors and building
ships. According to a long-lived tradition the Cretans used
the palm-tree for the manufacture of a writing material.

For a plant with textile fibre they had flax. It has been
found in the lake dwellings of Switzerland and Italy and also
in the oldest tombs of Egypt, and Homer's contemporaries
used it for making cords and clothing. The Cretans, too,
doubtless made use of it for twisting the ropes which they
called by a name afterwards inherited by the Greeks
(μήρινθος). They collected oleaginous seeds such as poppy
and sesame, with its pre-Hellenic name (σήσαμον), and also
plants producing colouring matter, such as the crocus or
saffron.

[1] **LXXXVIII**, 359, 360.
[2] **XX**, fig. 190 *a, c* ; cf. fig. 204 *d*.
[3] BSA. ix, 68, fig. 45.
[4] Pliny, xvi, 141.

Most of the aromatic herbs sought after by the Greeks, such as mint (μίνθα), calamint (καλάμινθος), wormwood (ἀψίνθιον), and others, were in demand before their time, as their names testify. The Cretans also brought to notice a large number of simples including *asplenum*, a remedy against the affections of the spleen which were dreaded by runners, *daukos*, which in this country of slim waists was supposed to make the body slender, and *diktame*, imbued by the goddess of Mount Dikte with miraculous virtues which she revealed to women through the medium of the sacred goats.[1]

They collected a certain kind of lichen which has been exported to Egypt ever since. It was placed in the tombs of Der el-Bahri just as it is bought to-day in the bazaars of Cairo.[2] In conclusion, one of the most agreeable surprises offered by Minoan art is the decided fondness shown for flowers and ornamental plants. We must picture to ourselves, in these remote ages, gardens where the royal lily stands side by side with the rose, the tulip, the scabious, the narcissus, the hyacinth, and sweet marjoram. We must even imagine pots of flowers in the houses.[3]

Cattle-raising, after it had ceased to be practically the only resource of the Cretans, maintained an importance equal to that of agriculture. It was the chief business of the population of Praisos and Palaikastro. Milk-food and meat formed a considerable part of the people's diet. Nothing throws a stronger light on this subject than certain sets of earthenware utensils—perforated vessels for draining the moisture from cheese, and condensing and refrigerating appliances for the elaborate business of broth-making.[4] Cattle were indispensable also for clothing, transport, bartering, sport, and sacrifices.

All the occupations proper to pastoral life were reserved for the men, and there was doubtless something noble about this privilege then as later, in the time of Homer. On a bowl from Palakaistro is a relief of a young boy milking a cow in the midst of an enormous herd.[5] A very large number of

---

[1] Cf. Plutarch, *Moralia*, 974 E.
[2] F. Foucart, *Mém. de l'Acad. des Inscr.*, xxxv (1896), 8–9.
[3] **XXXVIII**, 27.
[4] **LVII**, figs. 128, 133.
[5] **XX**, fig. 130 *b*.

seals represent goat-herds and cowmen bearing on their shoulders yokes on which well-filled jars or goatskins are slung. Most of them seem to have some minor calling in addition.[1]

The Cretans, then as now, followed the practice of seasonal migration. After the harvest, which took place early in the year, the herdsmen led their flocks and herds into the mountains for a good part of the year. Thus, their villages were doubled ; they lived on the plains while there was work to be done in the fields, then passed the summer in the uplands. Above the prehistoric site of Kavousi potsherds and foundations of buildings of the Minoan Period have been found on a ridge where lack of space and exposure to winter winds would make a permanent habitation impossible. There a summer hamlet doubtless existed—a *metochi*, as the Greeks call it, inhabited between the reaping and the vintage.[2]

The bovine race contributed largely to the wealth of the Cretans. To be killed for food was not the only purpose for which such beasts were needed ; they were for a long time the only animals available for drawing waggons ; [3] the gods and the dead required bulls and bull-calves as victims, and their horns were consecrated in the temples and chapels ; lastly, the currier needed fine skins, grey, brown, or black, for making into large shields and belts.[4] In addition to all this, the ox was at an early date and for many centuries the unit of exchange. It cannot often have happened that a landowner possessed a herd like the one on the bowl from Palaikastro, 200 beasts crowded together and jostling one another. But cattle were to be found in all parts of the island and it is not surprising that the bull in all his attitudes, whether grazing or raging, and the cow suckling her calf were familiar to artists of keen vision.

Crete possessed several varieties of the bovine species.[5] The primitive type, *bos primigenius*, can be recognized from bones found in a number of sites, teeth, vertebræ, and skulls of vast dimensions and horns measuring as much as 40 centi-

---

[1] **XII,** figs. 36, 55–7, 59, 60.
[2] Cf. **XLIX,** 51–2.
[3] BSA. vi, 108, fig. 39.
[4] **LXX,** 38 ff.
[5] On the fauna of prehistoric Crete see Hatzidakis, 'Εφ., 1912, 231–2 (bibliography).

metres in length and 30 centimetres in circumference at the root. This voracious ruminant haunted the thickets and grassy hollows. A formidable creature, but fitted by its strength to perform all kinds of service, it was a prize to be captured young and could be successfully tamed when its horns had been blunted. The acrobatics customary among cowboys suggested the idea of the *rodeo*, a sport on which the Minoans doted and which served as a process of selection. The mighty beast described above was *par excellence* the sacred animal, the Minotaur. Two other varieties, *bos brachyceros* and the *bos domesticus*, were of particularly sturdy type but, through continual cross-breeding, the second variety disappeared about the XVIth century.[1]

There was always an abundance of the smaller beasts of the field in Crete. Pigs contributed to the food supply in the same measure as sheep and goats. In a pile of bones found at Tylissos thirty-two jaw-bones of sheep and goats were counted as against seventeen jaw-bones of pigs.[2]

The horse was unknown in Crete until the Late Minoan Period.[3] Though mentioned in Asia as the " mountain-ass " in the third millennium,[4] it was not introduced into Egypt until the time of the Hyksos, and made its appearance almost immediately afterwards in Crete, Argolis, and Cyprus.[5] The animal which found its way to Crete at that period is superbly represented on a sealing. (Fig. 28.) It stands with a frisky air beside the ship from which it has just landed. With a short head, arched brow, high neck and shoulders, long mane, graceful crupper, and slender legs, it is a barb, fiery and yet submissive to the restraint of a mere nose-band. The fact that its coat is generally painted yellow seems to point to the prevalence of the chestnut type. The horse was used chiefly as a draught animal, being harnessed to a light two-wheeled chariot with a step and standing room for two persons. Sometimes it was used also as a beast of

[1] Id., ib.
[2] Ib.
[3] Cf. Ridgeway, *The Thoroughbred Horse*, 1905 ; Rodenwaldt, **LXXI**, 27 ; Hatzidakis, loc. cit. Hawes (**XXXIX**, 43) asserts that, according to a seal in his possession, the horse existed in Crete in the Early Minoan Period (cf. **XX**, fig. 89 *a*) ; in any case it was at that time a rare and exotic animal.
[4] LA. i (1908), pl. xvii, 8–12.
[5] On the Tell el-Amarna tablets the king of Cyprus repeatedly wishes the Pharaoh all happiness " for himself, his wife, his children, his country, his horses and his chariots ".

burden, and carried an *amphora* tied on each flank symmetrically.[1] The ass, no trace of which has been found at Troy, but which was known in Mycenæ, as is proved by a wall-painting, certainly existed in Crete at the same period as the horse, for asses' bones have been found among objects of the Late Minoan Period. It is probable, however, that it was there centuries earlier, since the ass's head already appears as an ideogram.

Farmyard fowls were not wanting in the Ægean lands. It was long believed that the cock and the hen made their way there from Persia via Lydia in the VIth century or, according to a more recent view, a century earlier. It is true that these birds are not mentioned in the Homeric poems and that the

Fig. 28.—The arrival of the horse in Crete. L.M.I sealing.

oldest relics on which they appear are coins found at Ephesos which were struck between 652 and 610. But there is probability in the supposition that the cock-god, the Zeus or Apollo Velchanos worshipped by the Greeks in Crete, indicates the presence of birds of that family in pre-Hellenic Crete. It has even been claimed that they can be recognized on a sealing and an engraved stone.[2] Nor did the dove, as was once believed, come from Syria at a comparatively recent date. It is carved on an ivory seal dating from E.M.III. At least 2,000 years before Christ the sacred bird perches on the columns of the temples and invites the adoration of the faithful. (Figs. 36, 42.) The swan and the duck were

---

[1] MA. xii, 118, fig. 47.
[2] Ad. Reinach, An., xxi (1910), 75 ff. ; Pettazoni, ib., 668-9.

familiar enough to be represented on intaglios and to figure
among the ideograms. The peacock, which was afterwards
raised at Samos in the sanctuary of Hera and which set Athens
in a flutter by its appearance there in the Vth century, may
have already supplied feathers for the crown of Minos.
(Fig. 57.)

Bee-keeping was a flourishing occupation, as it is in all
countries where sugar is unknown. From Phaistos we have
a hive of terra cotta.[1] Professional bee-keepers had as an
emblem a bee together with a glove, and they possessed
secrets which they taught to the Greeks.[2] Wax as well as
honey was in demand. It was doubtless used for making
candles, for in rooms without illumination candle-sticks
or sconces have been found with sockets which are too small
to have held torches.[3]

The products of cattle-raising were supplemented to a
considerable extent by those of the chase. Before the Cretan
excavations, the fondness of the Mycenæans for big game
hunting had already been noticed. The frescoes of Tiryns
present a remarkable series of pictures of the chase. Here
are huntresses mingling with the hunters, men armed with
javelins, chariots with two horses, hounds held in the leash
by women, hares, a herd of deer, hunting with the net as
described by Xenophon, and the boar surrounded by the
pack and pierced with spears. (Fig. 56.) The Cretans have
the same taste for hunting and the same enthusiasm. They
hunt to defend their flocks from bird and beast ; they hunt
for spoils of game and precious horns ; and they hunt for
pleasure, for sport. They are aided by thoroughbred hounds
with slender bodies, long legs, and pointed ears.[4] They know
how to train them so well that the tradition is kept up and the
Cretan greyhound is later as highly esteemed as the Laconian.
In marshy ground they take half-wild cats with them. The
Cretan hunter goes after the hare, he surprises the heath-cock
in the long grass and the moorhen and duck in the reeds,
he lassoes the wild goat, he hunts boar, wolf, and stag in the
brake. Among the rocks on the mountain-tops he follows the
chamois and above all the *agrimi*, the ibex with long, regularly

[1] **LVII,** fig. 69.
[2] Cf. Cuny, REA. 1910, 154 ff. (use of κήρινθος).
[3] **XX,** figs. 422, 423 *b*.
[4] **LXXXIII,** fig. 5; **XX,** figs. 203, 204 *c*.

curved horns from which bows of wonderful strength and
suppleness are fashioned. So strong is the Cretan's passion
for the chase that it pursues him beyond the grave. At
Zapher Papoura, in front of the Grave of the Hunter, who
keeps his arrows and large knife within arm's each, one seems
to see, like Odysseus in Hades, "the giant Orion still hunting
through the fields of asphodel the wild beasts he once slew
in the mountains." [1]

The ubiquitous sea offered endless resources in the way
of fish.[2] In Crete, as in the Cyclades, men fished with the
line and the net. This is proved by the fish-hooks and the
weights made of lead or stone which abound in the prehistoric
ports. On a vase from Phylakopi (Fig. 29) [3] we have a picture

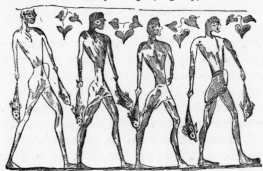

Fig. 29.—Returning fishermen. Vase from Phylakopi.

taken from life of the fishermen's return. Several long,
lean, ungainly fellows are walking in single file, swinging
their arms, with a fish in either hand, all except one of them
who is hitching up his waist-cloth with his left hand. Whereas
the Homeric heroes scorn fish and leave it for the poor, in
Crete it appeared on kings' tables and among the dishes of
the gods. Intaglios, trinkets, frescoes, vases all offer a pretext
for the representation of the creatures of the sea. On a picture
of painted stucco or faience flying fish are portrayed against
a background dotted with shells. (Fig. 54.) Crustaceans
and zoophytes, done in relief with natural colourings, look
as if they had come out of an aquarium, while the octopus
is one of the favourite subjects of the naturalistic painter.
(Plate IV, 2.)

[1] *Odyssey*, xi, 572–4 ; cf. **XVI,** fig. 27.
[2] See Hatzidakis, loc. cit., 232–3 ; Keramopoullos, *AΔ*, iv (1918), 88–101.
[3] **XXI,** pl. xxii.

Besides fishing for mullet, dorado and parrot-fish, the delight of the Cretans,[1] they loved to collect the *frutti di mare* : crabs and sea-urchins, cuttle-fish and nautiluses, oysters and mussels, conches and tritons.[2] Delicacies of this kind were even transported inland along with the fish. If it could be established that certain seals represent the tunny, as is believed by Evans, this would prove that the Cretans went in for deep-sea fishing.[3]

On the east coast the sailors had particularly interesting catches. To-day a fleet of caiques puts out from these parts and visits the neighbouring islands and even the coast of Africa in search of sponges. The same thing must have happened at a time when painters represented the bottom of the sea as carpeted with sponges. But of still greater importance is the fact that the fishing included the purple shell. The murex, the true murex which Pliny describes, exists on the coasts of Crete ; Mosso collected enough specimens in Candia harbour and on a neighbouring beach to extract a few drops of purple. The Cretans made the most of this valuable resource. The vase-painters delighted in portraying the precious shell-fish, with its seven points, surrounded by seaweed and rocks. Immense stocks of broken shells have been brought to light, one on the islet of Kouphonisi and two others near Palaikastro, all three mixed up with pottery of the Middle Minoan Period.[4] Long before the Phœnicians, then, the Cretans carried on the branch of fishing and the industry for which the names of Tyre and Sidon were to become famous. Cretan legend consecrated the type of hero who plunges into the sea, returns laden with its treasures, and thereby crowns himself with the halo of a godlike renown. The secrets of the trade were not lost, but were handed down by the pre-Hellenes to the Greeks, as well as to the Phœnicians. Many centuries after the Minoan manufacturers had piled up the shells which still serve to mark the site of their workshops, the men of Thera, who were seeking a guide to take them to Libya, found at Itanos, close to Palaikastro, a maker of purple who had sailed as far as the African coast.[5]

[1] **XX,** figs. 497–8.
[2] Cf. Bosanquet, JHS. xxiv, 321.
[3] **XII,** fig. 33 *a*.
[4] Bosanquet, loc. cit. ; BSA. ix, 276–7 ; Mosso, **LVII,** 116–17.
[5] Herodotus, iv, 150 ff.

CHAPTER III

INDUSTRY

EVERY nation, even when its life has become highly centralized in towns, has a fair number of industries which are carried on in the home. Such was at all times the custom of Oriental countries. This system was more or less in practice on the shores of the Ægean from the time when the cave-dwellers fashioned implements of stone to the age when the Athenians gloried in the Parthenon. In prehistoric times, from Crete to Mycenæ and from Cyprus to Troy, the work of producing food, clothing, and certain other articles was generally carried on in the houses, in the king's palace as well as in the peasant's hut. But each family had to fill in the gaps in its own production from the surplus of others. Gradually the manufacture of certain objects, particularly those made of wood, bronze, and terra cotta, called for complicated apparatus or a technical training which made it perforce a specialized trade. Wherever there was a sufficiently dense population, the advantages offered to all by the division of labour led everyone to adopt a profession of his own. Only one person could retain the domestic organization, while bringing together the most eminent workmen and artists under his roof. That was the king. Thus pre-Hellenic society presents, as in an epitome of economic history, very varied types of industry.

Certain occupations, in particular those of a rural character, were as yet hardly specialized at all. Among the stock-breeders the Cretan seals show us a potter, a wood-cutter, and a carpenter. Specialists are to be found, however—for instance a potter who is nothing but a potter.[1] It was certainly a carpenter who lived in such-and-such a house, or was buried in such-and-such a tomb with his familiar implements. At Enkomi in Cyprus, a foundry contains, besides lumps of unwrought metal, an assortment of shovels, hammers, and pincers. In Crete, bronze-workers' shops can be recognized

[1] **XII,** fig. 58 ; **XX,** fig. 93 A.

by moulds for casting nails, weapons, and tools. Only an engraver can have used the mould, found at Phaistos, for casting gravers, small hammers, and burins. In front of the potter's ovens, especially when they turned out jars taller than human beings, we must picture professional workers, and we can actually see, from one of the oldest signets in our possession, that some of them were women.[1] A characteristic fact shows us how far labour was divided in painting. The smooth surfaces on which the stucco reliefs were modelled, and the borders of the panels for frescoes were painted in a flat colour before the stucco was adorned with the various colours or the fresco was executed with the swift sureness that such a process demands. In this we cannot fail to recognize the work of two different hands—the common artisan succeeded by the true artist.[2] Another fact to be noted is the appearance of advertisement, the child of competition and professional self-esteem. From the XIXth century onwards certain potters marked their vases with their name,[3] and one faience factory has a trade-mark known from Knossos to Mycenæ.[4]

While the other sites show us isolated workshops, a prehistoric Pompeii offers us the spectacle of what an industrial town could be between the XVIth and XIVth centuries. This town is Gournia. We have already seen it (Fig. 24), with its little houses huddled together along winding alleys, or surrounding a spacious court which served as a market-place. Among the ruins of this " mechanical " town an oil-press, a joiner's workshop and a forge can still be recognized. " At the sight of these stone and clay receptacles, stands of all kinds, tripods, jars and basins for oil, ovens, lamps, tables, weights, hammers, polishers and sharpeners, upper and lower quern-stones, mortars, metal saws, knives, axes, scrapers, pins, hooks, fish-hooks, swords and daggers, in addition to an abundant collection of pottery, both painted and unadorned, one is amazed at the familiar air of all this gear, at the discovery, at a distance of so many centuries, of all kinds of accustomed objects which have survived to our own times, and are

[1] **XX,** loc. cit., c. 1, 2 ; cf. *a* 1, *b* 2.
[2] Ib., 531, 536.
[3] Ib., 242 ; cf. 564–5.
[4] Ib., 483, 485.

found in the hands of the peasants of modern Greece." [1]　It
was in such an environment that the majority of the workmen
and artists summoned to Knossos were formed.

There, all the companies of the various trades were installed
right inside the palace.　Humble workers were housed in mean
quarters with a cupboard in the wall, and a supply of coarse
pottery.　But there was a select body of craftsmen and artists
who rose above the common herd ;　they signed their works,
and had a widespread reputation.　The patriarchal industries
supplied the means of support for the artistic industries.
The women took the corn from the *pithoi* and ground it in
the mortars.　They also plied the distaff and shuttle under
the supervision of the queen.　An oil-press had vast store-
rooms attached.　With such resources the palace possessed
a royal faience factory [2] which turned out quantities of
decorative articles and statuettes of inestimable worth (Fig. 62,
Pl. III, 2).　It also contained a sculptor's studio ; its occupant
had just finished an *amphora* in veined limestone, truly fit
for a king, and was beginning to rough out another, when the
irruption of the enemy caused the chisel to fall from his hands.
In another part we are confronted by a stone coffer with an
ordered array of materials for encrusting ;　steatite lentils
lie about unfinished ;　objects of marble, bone, stone, and
jasper look like pieces of marquetery which were being collected
together to be made into a gameboard.　This is the workshop
of the lapidary.　The king's palace, therefore, held an important
place in the economic life of the country and in the artistic
life of the whole world, in that it grouped together luxury
industries and supplied them with models.

Thus the political and social organization of Crete enabled
it to make use of its natural wealth and of its relations with
other countries for the achievement of great progress in most
industries.　But those which were still carried on in the home
naturally remained behind those which, appealing to the public,
excited competition and aimed at export, and still further
behind those which produced masterpieces for the satisfaction
of a powerful protector.

For this reason industries deriving their raw materials
from the vegetable and animal kingdoms varied very much

[1] Pottier, JS. 1910, 146–7.
[2] See a mould for shells and rosettes, BSA. ix, 65, fig. 42.

in importance. Each house made its own flour for daily con-
sumption, whereas oil and wine were sometimes produced on
the large estates with a view to sale locally or abroad. Spinning
and weaving were done at home, but not dyeing and currying.
The wood industry was not called upon to make the peasant's
plough, but it furnished the townsfolk with timber-work,
columns, and beautiful furniture.

We must, therefore, expect to find, in the food-producing
industries, great differences between the apparatus used for
grinding, and that used for pressing.

In order to grind corn, man at first used two stones in the
form of a fixed table, slightly concave, and a slightly convex
grinder, which was worked by hand. This process, which was
known in all the most ancient sites in Egypt, Canaan, and
Italy, remained in use in the Ægean countries throughout the
pre-Hellenic period. From Troy to Crete grinders are found
together with slabs on all sides. It was the women who handled
these implements. A terra-cotta from Cyprus brings the scene
before us to the life.[1] The table is placed on the ground ;
a kneeling woman, with both arms stretched out, is toiling
over the heavy stone while a child, sitting down, is tilting a
sieve in order to pour grain into it. But at an early stage
they took to pounding the grain in a mortar with a pestle.
This process was likewise prevalent among the Ægeans. The
excavations have brought to light mortars of all kinds of
stone. Many more would have been found had they not been
made for the most part of wood, as in Hesiod's day. Here
again, it was the women's duty to pound the corn. Finally
the mill was devised, consisting of two parts fitting one into
the other. Nothing like it, however, has been found in Crete,
and the existence of the corn-mill is doubtful in the prehistoric
Ægean world as a whole.

Oil, too, was made at home. Everything leads us to believe
that this work fell to the lot of the men, and that the yield
was sometimes considerable. Many appliances for pressing
and decanting have been discovered in Crete and the other
islands. Let us consider their productive power. The
inhabitants of Palaikastro had in their houses troughs, in
which the olives were crushed to begin with, and rectangular

---

[1] **LXIV,** pl. clxxiii, 19 *h*. This terra-cotta dates from the Iron Age,
but recalls an Egyptian statuette of the IIIrd Dynasty (cf. **XC,** 405, fig. 283).

or round presses. One of these presses, in a good state of
preservation, has a pressing surface 28 centimetres in diameter.
It is surrounded on a lower level by a runnel 7 centimetres broad
with no outlet.[1] The capacity of the receptacle is hardly
more than two litres. Such apparatus could not serve for
production on a large scale. In a town like Gournia, with
a working population, there were no presses at all. The oil
came from the country, and the consumer contented himself
with purifying it by mixing it with water in a vat, and
letting the water flow away with the impurities which it had
assimilated.[2]

But at Therasia we are given a glimpse of a rather important
manufacture by a combination of press and refinery. A storeroom, measuring 6 by 5 metres, and provided with an annex
of 2·50 by 2 metres, is separated from the dwelling-house. It
contains a cone-shaped receptacle having an internal diameter
of 40 centimetres at the top and a depth of 30 centimetres.
The inside, worn by friction, shows what it was used for.
It is a mill. It contains a hole communicating with a runnel
which empties itself into a small channel. The oil squeezed
out by the mill came there to be refined, and was then decanted
into the pots which were found near by. A plant of this
kind would be suitable for an industry which was not purely
domestic.[3] There must have been better ones in the palace
of Knossos. If the basins and channels which one admires
in the so-called " Hall of the Oil-Press " are merely part of
a drainage system,[4] it is none the less true that, close to the
quarters reserved for the workmen, the oil was tunned in
enormous jars which, ranged in long rows, filled three
magazines. One of these jars, found in position, is two metres
high and 4·50 in circumference. When we see vessels of
such capacity, we can understand the havoc wrought by the
conflagration in certain parts of the palace, and we gain a very
definite impression of manufacture on a large scale.

The wine-producing industry does not seem to have had
a similar development. In the eastern part of Crete, however,
some of the apparatus seems capable of a greater output than
one family would require. While the cemented base of a

[1] BSA. xi, 277, fig. 8 ; cf. viii, 306, 308.
[2] **XC**, 27–8, pl. i, 14.
[3] **LXVII**, 144, fig. 29 ; 150.
[4] **XX**, 201.

wine-press found at Palaikastro is 1·50 metres square, the rock table at Praisos measures 2·40 by 2·30.[1] At Zakro the accommodation for treading grapes in certain dwellings was confined to three or four basins; but one house contains a special room which has every appearance of being a large reservoir with communicating basins at different levels.[2] Fine wines at least were exported, such as were put in the conical vases. In the palace of Akhenaten at Tell el-Amarna, as in the palace of Minos at Knossos, a fresco represented a cup-bearer carrying one of these vases.

Everything connected with dress, from hair-cutting to needlework, was a domestic occupation. Carding-combs, distaffs, spindles, and weights, notched bobbins with a hole through the axis, pins, stilettos and awls—these objects, of which countless specimens still exist in every material except wood, were to be found in all the houses. The palace of Knossos, which catered for large demands, contained a positive factory for spinning and weaving. Over the queen's doorway a distaff was represented; on the first floor a women's workroom was installed, from which more than 400 weights of spindles and looms were recovered;[3] when it was very hot the work was done downstairs in a gallery which looked on to a shady court. Numerous seals with the spider emblem seem, however, to point to the existence, in the neighbourhood of Milatos, of a textile industry working for the public.[4]

At all events, one can hardly imagine dyeing, comprising, as it does, the manufacture of colours and the colouring of stuffs, as a domestic occupation. The saffron-picker, represented on a fresco, was often a professional, and the flower which served as a raw material for this industry appears on a series of tablets.[5] Purple must have been produced by a fisherman who was also an industrial. Korobios, the manufacturer from Itanos, who as Herodotus tells us, was carried away by a storm while laying in supplies of murex, may have had for an ancestor that other Cretan who, in marking his goods with his seal, professed himself cattle-raiser, weaver, and fisher— in other words manufacturer of purple, producing his own

[1] BSA. ix, 279, pl. vi; viii, 237, fig. 6 and pl. viii, 1.
[2] Ib., vii, 130–1, 135, 140–1, pl. v, 2.
[3] BSA. viii, 64 ff., 94.
[4] **XVII**, 212.
[5] Ib., 213–14, 233, fig. 102, No. 88; **XX**, 265.

cloth and his own dye.   The large deposits of shells found
in eastern Crete, precisely in the region of Itanos, show the
importance and the great antiquity of this industry.   It must
certainly have had a long past to be able to produce the
beautiful materials in three or four colours and of varied
patterns which are to be seen on frescoes and faience.   It is
not surprising that the great ladies of Mycenæ, once they had
seen Cretan materials, would wear no others.   Æschylus was
an archæologist without knowing it, when he had a purple
carpet spread beneath the feet of Agamemnon.

Skins were prepared at an earlier date than cloth among
prehistoric peoples.   It was quite necessary to wear skins and
furs in the cold climate of the Palæolithic Period.   During
the second period of the Stone Age, when the temperature
of Europe was milder, textiles were manufactured.   But in
Crete the traditional skin vestments were always required for
priests and priestesses, likewise huge shields for soldiers, gloves
for boxers, and shoes and belts for everyone.   Leather-dressing,
therefore, could not help being a prosperous occupation in this
country of cattle-raising and hunting.   Moreover, work in
leather was so varied, and required so much technical skill,
that it must be developed into one or more special trades.
The currier, who was called *skytotomos* in the Homeric period,
had his professional emblem long before.[1]

The extent to which wood industries were developed cannot
be gauged from the traces which they left behind, since the
material in question was essentially a perishable one.   We
know, however, that in Crete they had a vast field of action.
In the country it was sometimes the cattle-owner who worked
as a woodcutter or a carpenter, and, doubtless, every farmer
was his own wheelwright, and made his own implements.
But, as a general rule, on the Cretan seals, the emblem of the
tree or the branch is sufficient in itself or else it is supplemented
by the picture of a ship with a mast.[2]   From felling trees to
ship-building there were a great many jobs which, by their
importance or their nicety, called for the hand of a specialist.
The carpenter had a good stock of tools—saws of different
lengths, axes and double axes, hammers, files, chisels, a gouge,
an adze, and an *ascia*, which was a combination of the cooper's

[1] **XVII,** 234, fig. 102, No. 18 ; see, however, 187.
[2] JHS. xvii, 292, fig. 28 *b* ; 293, fig. 29 *c*.

adze and the hatchet.[1] He did a good share of the work of
building, making beams to support the stonework, shaping
columns out of tree-trunks of common species, or out of
cypress logs, and laying the roof-timbers. We can see how
well he knew his business from the Royal Villa at Knossos,
in which beams 80 centimetres in breadth and 60 in thickness
supported cylindrical joists with a diameter of 44 centimetres.
As for the cabinet-maker and the wood-carver, they produced
furniture of a superb style ; for the throne of wood which
adorned the Hall of the Double Axes must have been quite as
fine as the throne of stone which, with its " Gothic " decoration and arched back, exactly recalls a model in wood. We
possess, moreover, thanks to the dryness of Egyptian soil,
some beautiful specimens of Ægean wood-carving, for instance
a box-wood lid which was placed in the tomb of a foreign
priest and was decorated in a style reminiscent of the swords
of Zapher Papoura.[2]

In the matter of extractive industries Crete was vastly
inferior to the Cyclades and the mainland ; she had no marble.
But, to make up for that, she supplied excellent potter's clay,
limestone which was both easy to carve and durable, beautiful
gypsum, which could be split up into big blocks as well as into
thin, flat pieces, slaty schists of light or dark shade, breccias
and conglomerates with veins of many colours and, lastly,
steatite, a soft, soapy stone.

The manual labour at the disposal of the stone industry in
the Ægean countries was more or less plentiful according to
their social system. In none of them do the building materials,
by their bulk, create that bewildering impression which is
produced upon us in Egypt by the Pyramids, or by the archi-
traves of Karnak. The reason is that the Pharaohs, who were
absolute masters, could command forced labour to any extent.
The dynasts of Tiryns and Mycenæ perhaps, but only they,
had in their service gangs of subjects or slaves, in no way
comparable to the Egyptians, but still very numerous.
Pausanias, at Tiryns, went into raptures over the vastness
of the ruins,[3] and we can share his amazement on beholding
the vaulted gallery or the block forming the floor of the bath-

---

[1] See Durm, JOEI. 1907, 44, fig. 12.
[2] **LXVII** fig. 409 ; see also our Figs. 59 and 60.
[3] Pausanias, ii, 25, 7.

room. At Mycenæ the lintel of the Lion Gate is five metres long, 2·50 broad, and more than a metre in thickness. One of the two big stones standing at the entrance of the " Treasury of Atreus " is nearly 9 by 5 metres, and weighs about 120 tons.[1] There is nothing like it in Crete. In the palace of Knossos the largest hewn stones do not exceed 3 to 4 metres in length, 70 to 75 centimetres in breadth, and 55 centimetres in height, which gives them a weight of barely 3 tons. But though the quarries are not worked by an army of labourers in the service of a public administration, the private industry has none the less a certain importance. The methods of quarrying are simple. The tools usually employed are picks, wedges, and saws of bronze, with or without teeth, and sometimes as much as 2 metres long. When attacking very hard strata, the workmen drill holes with an auger, drive in wooden pegs and moisten them so as to split the stone. The timbering is done with care. They have, as yet, neither jack nor pulley for moving the stones ; here, as in Egypt, all the work is done by strength of arms, with the aid of ropes, rollers, and inclined planes.

We have already shown, in connexion with the houses, what the Ægeans and especially the Cretans did with the materials and methods at their disposal. This would be the place, then, to consider what use they made of clay, in an examination of the ceramic industry. When we look through works on archæology we are over-inclined to believe that the potter was almost always an artist. This illusion is nowhere more natural than in Crete, where ceramic factories were installed in the palaces, the site of the one at Phaistos being marked to this day by an oven, and the one at Knossos being known by its specialities in faience and by its particular style. But it must be observed that archæologists make a selection out of the enormous mass of vases and sherds which most of the excavations bring to light. As a matter of fact the potter catered for the humblest needs of all households, and not merely for the luxurious tastes of the richest. This does not mean that a professional was not required for the manufacture of the commonest crockery. The *kerameus* worked for the public long before Homeric times and the palaces contained magazines piled up with common ware.

[1] Perrot, **LXVII**, 266, 289-90, 497-8.

That is why the ceramic industry must be mentioned among the principal ones. Nevertheless, it holds such an important place in the history of art, and its technical and æsthetic qualities are so entirely merged in one, that we shall not attempt to separate them, but shall speak of them further on as a whole. Let us pass on to metallurgy.

A great number of implements were handed on, just as they were, from the Stone Age to the metal ages. Men continued to make weights, grinders, polishers, and hammers of stone. The Ægean metal-workers, however, at the time when they still worked only in copper, already gave proof of great skill in the execution of daggers, tools, and tripods. We can but admire the delicacy and strength of the double axes and the adzes fashioned during the third millennium.[1] No sooner did the Cretans learn of the existence of tin than they appreciated its properties and hastened to mix it with copper. They had now at their disposal an alloy less pliable and malleable than pure copper, but more fusible and, by its durability, better adapted to the manufacture of strong weapons, fine and pointed tools, precious vases, and decorative plaques in relief. It could be made, moreover, in different shades according to the proportion of the metals used ; it was easy to polish and could be given a marvellous patina. The Cretans were masters in bronze-work. Gournia became one of the centres of this industry. A few miles from the town the ground contains copper-ore in quantities apparently sufficient for exploitation on a small scale while, close by, the remains of a furnace bear witness to the presence of an ancient foundry. In the town itself a little establishment has been discovered containing fragments of bronze, scraps of slag, pure copper adhering to smelting vessels, a crucible, and numerous moulds for making knives, chisels, nails, and awls. The man who worked in this shop used copper for round articles of a large size, which needed a lot of hammering, for example a large cup, and for other objects a bronze containing ten per cent. alloy.[2]

Hammering and stamping made great progress. At the beginning leaves of metal were beaten on concave or convex forms, and fastened together with rivets ; but afterwards objects of large size were made from a single sheet of metal

---

[1] **LXXXII,** 106 ff. ; BSA. xix, 44–7 ; cf. **XX,** 194–5.
[2] Cf. Hawes, **XXXIX,** 38.

beaten out on the anvil and soldered at the fire. Casting was
usually done at an ordinary fire. The matrices were cut in
soft stones, sometimes several in one stone ; the rivet-holes
were obtained by means of wooden pegs round which the
molten metal congealed ; the side of the object which remained
uncovered, and therefore flat, had to be finished off by
hammering when it came out of the melting-pot. But casting
was also done in a casting box with two valves or half-matrices
with a smooth surface which were clapped together, into
which the molten metal was poured through a bore.[1] It even
looks as if the *cire perdue* method of casting was known, for
one fails to see by what other process the bronze workers could
have achieved certain *objets d'art*.[2] For the decoration of the
works produced by hammering or casting, the toreutic artist,
or metal-carver, made free use of the punch, the graver, and
the burin.[3]

The transformations of the axe in the countries of the
Ægean are particularly characteristic, with those of the dagger
which we have considered above,[4] of the history of metal-
working. The stone axes in Crete and the smaller islands are
far from being as fine as certain well-polished specimens
with a hole in them which come from Europe and Asia. Troy I,
for example, possesses a good type already ; Troy II, which
inherits the type, is not content to reproduce it in common
stone, but uses nephrite, diorite, hæmatite, serpentine,
porphyry, and jasper, and cuts for its gods or its kings
magnificent articles of lapis lazuli and jade, with knobs of
rock crystal or iron ore for their shaft-heads.[5] But even the
metal axes found in the " Treasure of Priam " still continue,
from 2200 to 2000, to imitate the type of the stone axes.[6]
Only in Troy VI, beginning in the XVth century, is the double
axe known.[7]

Let us pass to Cyprus. Here stone axes are rare. But,
if the Cypriotes soon abandoned stone for copper, they did no
more than change the material ; during the whole Copper Age
and the First Bronze Age, that is for fourteen or fifteen

[1] Cf. **X,** 368 ff. ; MA. xiv, 469–70, fig. 75 *d*.
[2] **X,** loc. cit. ; RA. 1908, ii, 315.
[3] MA. xiv, 466, fig. 73 *f*.
[4] See p. 93 ff.
[5] **X,** 321, fig. 254 ; 338–9 ; 374–5, figs. 323–6 ; 385, figs. 353–6.
[6] Ib., 329–30 ; 346, fig. 267.
[7] Ib., 394, fig. 377.

centuries, so long as their island was not largely subject to Cretan and Mycenæan influences, they kept the forms handed down by the Neolithic Age, only widening the curve of the cutting edge.[1]

Things are very different in Crete. When a fine *simulacrum* of a double axe with holes and great wide edges was found at Mochlos in an E.M.II tomb, no one ventured to give it the same date as the rest of the furniture, and M.M.III was suggested. But since then a double axe of exactly similar shape has been found in the house at Chamaizi, which belongs to M.M.I. Finally, the cave of Arkalochori has yielded a very great number of these implements ; from their size they are only ex-voto offerings, but from the marked curve of their edges they are of the same type as the real specimen from Chamaizi, and from the small proportion of tin which they contain they certainly date from E.M.II.[2] Thus, from the middle of the third millennium, while the Trojans and Cypriotes were still using the axe of polished stone, or just beginning to copy it in copper, the Cretan metal-workers were making a type of double axe which would hardly change at all, and would be gladly accepted as a model by other peoples a thousand years later.

We can only obtain a very faint idea now of the work in copper and bronze done in Crete, for the metal-smiths constantly scrapped and recast objects which had gone out of use, and the invaders fell greedily upon metal. Yet what remains can still give us cause for wonder. The basins, whose name—*lebes*—would long designate the Cretan coins which bear their image, are known to us ; they are hemispherical cauldrons, forged, with cast handles and feet riveted on. They were in their right place in the houses of the mighty, and four gigantic specimens have been found at Tylissos, reaching a diameter of 1·40 metres, and a weight of 52·50 kilograms, kitchen gear fit for a king.[3] The variety of the metal-worker's products is shown in a striking way in a tomb near Knossos ; around a " fire-box " stood a whole apparatus of bronze utensils, a cauldron, flat pans, jugs, ewers, cups, and a lamp with a chain for the snuffers.[4] And the ingenuity of

---

[1] **XI**, 219, fig. 158 ; 222, 257–9.
[2] **LXXXII**, fig. 12, ii, 46 ; **XX**, fig. 141 *e* ; BSA. xix, 46, fig. 9.
[3] **XXXVIII**, figs. 29–30 ; cf. **XXXIX**, pl. iv, 72 A ; **XVI**, fig. 38.
[4] **XVI**, 427 ff., 508 ff., pl. xxxix, figs. 36–7.

the people ! Whereas the Greeks of Homeric times barred
their doors with simple latches or bolts, the Cretans already
had locks—proper locks with keys.[1] Nowhere in the Bronze
Age was the consummate art of the Cretan armourers equalled ;
we have seen how, by lengthening the blade of their daggers,
they obtained, from the XVIth century onwards, beautiful
rapiers with a slender blade, to which they managed to give
a length of 95 centimetres ; we shall see that among these
craftsmen there were great artists.[2]

The bronze-workers owed some of their excellence to the
goldsmiths. The Ægeans, who no doubt obtained gold from
Egypt, must also have brought back models and processes
from that country. The goldsmith taught the bronze-worker
chasing and *repoussé*, the use of the chisel and the burin ;
in return the bronze-worker introduced the goldsmith to the
processes of casting, which, incidentally, were always less used
for silver than for bronze, and still less for gold than for silver.
Probably, too, we must add to all these processes that of
drawing down, without which all the filigree ornaments could
hardly have been obtained. Thus the technical skill of the
Cretans could express conceptions of beauty in every metal.

In sum, in all industries, but above all in the artistic
industries, the Cretans had in the Bronze Age a superiority
which cannot be contested. When to-day the student of
prehistoric archæology passes in review the monuments left
by the second millennium, whether it be in the Mediterranean
countries from Palestine to Spain or in the depths of the
European continent on the banks of the Rhine or the Danube,
every time that he finds an object which marks an advance
he has a right to look for its origin in the workshops of the
Ægean.

[1] **LVIII,** fig. 71.
[2] See pp. 99 and 338 ff.

CHAPTER IV

TRADE

WITH her natural and industrial resources Crete could easily maintain an extensive and profitable trade. She was compelled to look to foreign countries for horses, condiments, hard stones of all kinds, ivory, and, above all, the raw materials required by her metal-workers and goldsmiths. In exchange she offered her surplus oil and wine and the work of her craftsmen—painted vases, dyed cloth, weapons and utensils of bronze, jewels, and precious cups. Opportunities for advantageous transactions abounded and necessarily aroused the spirit of initiative.

The towns, so numerous in Crete, were markets by origin, and became important as such through the development of industry and navigation. Royal residences like Knossos and Phaistos, country towns like Praisos and Palaikastro, agglomerations of small craftsmen like Gournia, centres for sailors and shipowners like Pseira and Mochlos—these were the places where important business was transacted. Zakro, a port splendidly situated between the Ægean Sea and Africa, had large import and export houses ; the five hundred sealings found in one of them had doubtless once been affixed to bales of merchandise or bills of lading. In all these towns shops and workshops jostled one another, particularly round the big square. Communications were ensured by a well-organized roads department. According to the lie of the land, the streets were tortuous or they intersected at right angles. They were carefully built and kept in good repair, being paved with cobbles or flags of gypsum and provided with footpaths and gutters along the sides. When they had a slope to cover they were not built on an inclined plane, but in horizontal sections connected by steps. In Crete they were narrow, their width varying from 1·40 to 2·50 metres and reaching 4 metres as an exception. At Mycenæ the Acropolis had alleys

1·20 metres wide, but the main road up to the palace had a width of 5 metres, and the streets of the lower town broadened out still more at certain cross-roads.

From town to town ran the indispensable roads. It is to be noted that those of Crete and those which converged towards the lower town of Mycenæ conform to the same type and are both 3·60 metres wide.[1] At Knossos, near the North Entry of the palace, is the parting of two roads, one to the arsenal and one to the port. They have foundations of unhewn stone, between 20 and 25 centimetres in thickness, and are covered with a thick layer of concrete. The concrete is left bare for a width of 1·10 metres on each side, forming the two footpaths. It is reinforced in the middle by a double row of flags ; this is the roadway, which had therefore the regulation width of 1·40 metres.[2] Some claim to recognize portions of roads at many other points in Crete, and a stone bridge near Eleutherna is ascribed to the prehistoric period.[3] Mycenæ " of the broad ways " stood at the cross-roads of Argolis ; on one side were the roads to Argos, Tiryns, and the sanctuary which would one day be the Heraion, and on the other three roads ran to Corinth and its gulf. These roads, which climb gradients without diverging and are cut in the rock, are reinforced by retaining-walls of unhewn blocks of stone ; they cross torrents by bridges consisting of a " Gothic arch " with a great slab for a lintel. Like the streets of the towns, these roads climb the gradients by steps which are often very steep. But such as they are they show a very serious effort to facilitate overland travel. The Greeks inherited them later, and used them without improving them.

Travellers on these roads nearly always went on foot. Great personages, however, and particularly women, were doubtless carried in palankeens in the days when the horse was unknown.[4] As soon as that animal was introduced into the Ægean world the use of the chariot spread rapidly. In Crete, in Cyprus, and on the mainland, they used a vehicle similar to the specimens which have been preserved in Egypt. Of very light build, mounted on two wheels with four spokes, and with room for two persons only, the chariot was drawn by

---

[1] Steffen, *Karte von Mykenae*, 10.
[2] BSA. x, 45 ff. ; xi, 1 ff.
[3] S. Reinach, DA. *Via*, 778 ; Petroulakis, 'Εφ., 1914, 230-2.
[4] **XX**, 424.

two horses and, on well-paved roads, furnished a rapid means
of locomotion. But there is nothing to indicate that it was
used for trade. Goods were generally carried on donkey-back
and, from the XVIth century onwards, on horseback. A terra
cotta represents a hack carrying a pitcher on either flank.[1]
In Crete of the Middle Minoan Period, however, they had ox-
waggons also,[2] and the four-wheeled vehicle which figures on
a tablet from Tylissos[3] may well have been drawn by horses.
It goes without saying that the mountain roads with their
stepped levels were not made for wheeled traffic as were
the " carriage-roads " which Homer mentions in the
neighbourhood of Troy. They were practicable only for
pack-animals.

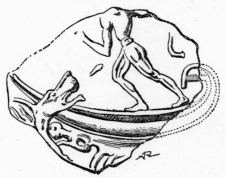

Fig. 30.—Sea-monster attacking a boat. Seal-impression.

To trade with the outer world islanders were obviously
compelled to follow the " liquid roads ". The men of the
Ægean were excellent navigators at a very early date. No
doubt Cretan legend peopled the waves with horrible monsters,
and the mariner paled at the prospect of meeting out at sea
the bitch Skylla, whose grim eye and huge jaws were ever
ready to snap up a victim (Fig. 30).[4] But it is the peoples
who are most familiar with the sea who speak of it with the
most fear. Long before Odysseus Minos vanquished Skylla
and bound her captive to his bark.[5]

[1] MA. xii, 118.
[2] **XX**, 424.
[3] **XXXVIII**, 41, fig. 20, 1.
[4] BSA. ix, 58, fig. 36.
[5] Apollodorus, iii, 15, 8, 3.

The forests of Crete supplied the shipbuilders with very good materials, among others, cypress. Nor was it difficult to obtain the most valued species of tree from other countries. In 1467, Thothmes III commissioned Keftiu to bring timber of Lebanon to Egypt on their vessels of cedar-wood [1]; the Keftiu must therefore have taken wood to their own island as well.

At an early date the Ægeans could build excellent ships. They created a type of boat which has remained in use all over the Mediterranean; unlike those used for Nile navigation it stood the sea well, and had very high bows. In E.M.II terra-cotta models of it were made at Palaikastro.[2]

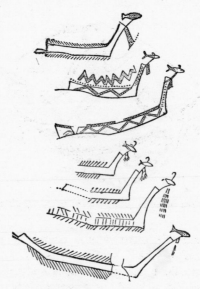

FIG. 31.—Ships painted on vases from the Cyclades.

But at the same period a larger vessel appears, not the massive round cargo-boat but a long slim cruiser driven by oars and sail; this is the "subtle galley". We see her represented on the vases of Syra and Phylakopi (Fig. 31) before we find her again on a Cretan seal; but as soon as she appears in Crete she takes a place among the favourite subjects for engraving and among the characters of writing. She has

[1] *Annals of Thothmes III*, year 34 (Sethe, *Urk. des aeg. Alt.*, iv, 207).
[2] BSA. x, 197, fig. 1 k; cf. **XXV,** 117, No. 3; **XX,** 75; **LXXXII,** fig. 52.

superb lines. The prow, which stands very high, is crowned with symbolic ornaments, a fish and a pennant flapping in the wind. The sides are low on the water, and fitted with a bank of oars each. Above the fish-tail stern is the castle from which the steersman handles the rudder, which is an oar rather larger than the rest. From the central mast stays and guys run fore and aft, supporting rigging which comes almost down to the sides. For want of shrouds a small cruiser of this type could be driven against a head wind only by rowing ; but with a following wind she could make a good speed. She was suitable for carrying goods, and also for piracy, and, consequently, for escaping or catching pirates. She would be capable, when the time came, of policing the seas. At this moment she received all kinds of improvements. The rudder was doubled, instead of one mast there were two or even three,[1] a deck was built over the whole length above the rowers sitting in the hull (Fig. 28), the bows were furnished with a ram, and it seems that a bronze anchor was used.[2]

This is the vessel which the Cretans introduced to the Achaians of the mainland. She is painted on a vase found at Tragana, the Messenian Pylos[3] ; the prow is crowned with a fish and a flag, and protected by a ram, and the castles, open at the sides, are connected by a deck beneath which there are twenty-five holes for the oars. The Achaians thus learned from the Cretans the art of navigation, and no doubt took from them the words which designate the deck ($\mathring{\iota}\kappa\rho\iota o\nu$) and the ropes used for working the sails ($\kappa\acute{a}\lambda\omega s$). They needed to make no changes in the Ægean cruiser in order to make profitable expeditions and to conquer Crete itself. It would be left to the Phœnicians one day, being obliged for their trade to make long journeys without landing, to invent the high-sided type with stem and stern of equal height, broader and rounder in section, no doubt slower, but better adapted to standing the open sea and rolling under the blast of storms.

We know little of the arrangement of the ports in prehistoric times, because the two coasts of Crete have suffered considerable change, having sunk in the North and risen in the South. Evans has observed on the shore near Knossos traces of

[1] **XVII**, 204 ; **XX**, 284.
[2] **XXI**, pl. xl, 37 ; **XX**, 616, n. 1.
[3] 'Eφ., 1914, 108-9, figs. 14-15.

constructions which he declares to be Minoan.[1] In the port
of Candia, where the Venetian quays stand on more ancient
moles, several Minoan blocks can still be seen. To the East,
to a distance of 15 kilometres, not only have many houses
been found containing pottery going back to the Early and
Middle Minoan Periods, but also a mole at Nirou Chani.[2]
To the West there is the same thing as far as Hagia Pelagia,
12 kilometres away.[3] But the Cretan sailors seem to have
preferred the anchorages of the islets near the great island ;
they established themselves at Mochlos and Pseira, on the
islet opposite Mallia, and, 10 kilometres north of Candia,
at Dia.[4] Perhaps there were free ports there, where the
Cretans traded freely with the people of the Cyclades.

In any case this was how they proceeded in foreign countries.
There is reason for believing that before the Greeks came they
occupied the islet of Platea, on the coast of Cyrenaïca, and
that of Ortygia, off the place which was to be Syracuse, and
it has been asked whether they were not the first to pay
attention to the islet on which the town of Tyre arose.[5] But
we may take it for certain that they established themselves
largely on the Egyptian coast, on the isle of Pharos, which
was still frequented by Homer's Greeks, and was one day to
make the greatness of Alexandria. There, from the first half
of the second millennium, a port existed which has been
submerged by the sea, but has been brought to our knowledge
by one of the most astonishing discoveries of our time.[6] And
such a port ! A great basin extended on the West and North-
west of the island, protected on one side by a jetty 700 metres
long, and on the other by a breakwater 2 kilometres long
and 60 metres broad for half its length ; it had an area of 150
acres. In front of this basin another, equally long but less
broad, was protected in the same way. Both were again
served by an outer port. One of the landing-quays is 14 metres
broad. This colossal work can only have been done with
Egyptian labour, but no Egyptians conceived the plan ; they

---

[1] **XX,** 297–9.
[2] Ib., 298 ; cf. *AΔ*, ii, 168 ff. ; **XXV**, 20 ; BCH. 1920, 400.
[3] *AΔ*, iii, 60 ff. ; **XX,** 299.
[4] **XX,** loc. cit.
[5] Raymond Weill, *Bull. de l'Inst. fr. d'arch. orient.*, xvi (1919), reprint,
34 ff.
[6] Jondet, *Mém. de l'Inst. ég.*, ix (1916) ; cf. R. Weill, loc. cit. ; **XX,**
292–7.

felt no need of it, having no fleet. Only one people can have
had the idea and realized it—the people which left its mark
in the redans of a fortified mole, in the rubble filling the walls,
in the pavement of the breakwaters, the people whose presence
in Egypt is constantly revealed by the Egyptian documents,
the Keftiu.

When the Cretans sent goods by sea, they treated them very
well. They knew how to keep them in good condition and
how to protect them from deterioration and from fraud. The
wine-pitchers were closed with a lid of terra-cotta covered
with vine leaves and clay, and held down by strings ; in the
still fresh paste and on the crossed bindings the mark of their
origin was imprinted with a signet.[1] The sealings found in
hundreds at Zakro, Hagia Triada, Knossos, and Tylissos,
are frequently stamped on small lumps of clay pierced with
holes, in some of which the mark or even a few threads of the
strings which were passed through them can still be seen.
They must have served to mark boxes or packages, and these
parcels were passed on from hand to hand, since on the top of
the first seal impression there are sometimes one or two
counter-marks. Now, as later in the time of the Romans,[2]
exporters sealed consignments sent by sea.

No trade flourishes in ever so small a degree without a regular
system of weights and measures. From very early times
the Mesopotamians and the Egyptians had several which
crossed the sea and were adopted in the islands of the Ægean.[3]

The "Babylonian" system, which was already in use
among the Egyptians of the XIIth Dynasty, is a sexagesimal
system, having as unit a light shekel weighing from 7·58 to
8·42 grams, or on an average 8 grams ; its multiples are the
mina of 60 shekels, and the talent of 60 minas (about 28·8
kilograms). This system spread to Crete. A magazine at
Knossos contained a truncated pyramid of red limestone over
the faces of which twined the tentacles of an octopus in relief
(Fig. 32).[4] The weight of this object is 28·6 kilograms ; it is

[1] See BSA. xvi, 9 ff., pl. iii.
[2] Pliny, xxxv, 3, 33.
[3] See Evans, **XV,** 338 ff.
[4] BSA. vii, 42, fig. 12.

perhaps the standard of the royal talent, and the reliefs marked on it may, like the stamp on coins, be intended to prevent any fraudulent debasing. The subdivisions of this talent certainly belong to a sexagesimal system, that is to say, one which is both decimal and duodecimal. A marble cylinder discovered at Siteia [1] weighs 1,140 grams, one twenty-fifth of a talent of 28·5 kilograms, and twelve dozen, or a " gross ", of shekels of 7·916 grams. Certain geese of hæmatite or cornelian,[2] a form of weight well known on the banks of the Nile and in the East, weigh 167·18, 2·6, and 1·63 grams—a fact which seems to indicate a unit of 20 shekels with its sub-multiples of one sixtieth and one hundredth.

FIG. 32.—The standard weight of Knossos, in porphyry.

Another standard, the shekel of about 7·32 grams or the double shekel of 14·64, which already existed in Egypt under the IVth dynasty, spread to the countries round about, whence the name " Phœnician " which is generally given to it. It too turns up in Crete. A cylinder of greenstone with a conical top [3] weighs 43·25 grams, doubtless corresponding to six " Phœnician " shekels of 7·208 grams ; an ingot from Tylissos [4] weighs 26·5 kilograms, or a talent according to the " Phœnician " standard of 7·36 grams.

But at the time when there was the most contact between the Keftiu and the Egyptians, during the XVIIIth dynasty,

[1] 'Εφ., 1906, 151 ff., pl. xi, 14.
[2] XV, 351 ff.
[3] Ib., 347 ff.
[4] XXXVIII, 56–7.

the standard most customary in Egypt was the *kit*. It weighs
from 8·812 to 10·108 grams, 9·46 on the average, and has
the *deben* as a decimal multiple. The *kit* was transmitted to
all the islands. At Enkomi in Cyprus ten olives of hæmatite [1]
weigh two, three, five, or ten times an average weight of 9·26
grams. But in the Ægean world the multiples of the *kit*
belong to a duodecimal system. A dwelling in Thera contained
eleven rounded pebbles, the weights of which are in simple
ratio to each other and form a regular progression in dozens
from 12 to 144 *kit* of an average weight of 8·819 grams.[2] At
Zakro, in Crete, a limestone cylinder [3] weighing 220 grams is
marked with six dots to show that it weighed six times a unit
of 36·66 grams, the equivalent of 4 *kit* of 9·165 grams. In the
cave of Psychro a bull's head of bronze filled with lead was
found.[4] It weighs 73·62 grams or 8 *kit* of 9·20 grams. We
must therefore imagine a system in which the *deben* is worth
12 kit and 12 *debenu* make a " gross ". Does this system go
as far as the talent ? At Serra-Ilixi, in Sardinia, there are
ingots of copper [5] weighing 33·3 kilograms, the exact equivalent
of 3,600 Cypriot *kit*. Thus, on the basis of a larger unit, the
Ægean system of the *kit* corresponds to that of the shekel.

An unusual fortune awaited a fourth standard. Originating
on the banks of the Nile about the year 2000, it was destined
to hold its own for a long time in Greece during the historic
period. This was the gold standard which was in frequent
use in Egypt from the XIIth dynasty onwards. It weighs
from 12·30 to 13·98 grams, averaging 13·14 grams. In the
form of hæmatite olives the weights of this system penetrated
into Palestine, Cyprus, and Crete.[6] A specimen at Knossos
represents a unit of 12·60 grams, a weight almost the same
as that of the stater for which Aigina was afterwards famous.
Now at Kyme in Euboia 19 ingots of copper [7] were found,
all of which, from the smallest to the largest, from 6·93 to
17·64 kilograms, are exact multiples of 6·30 grams, that is
to say, one mina. It is possible that 25 of these minas

---

[1] **XV**, 350-1.
[2] **XXVI**, 118.
[3] **XV**, 343.
[4] Ib., 353, fig. 9.
[5] Pigorini, BPI. xxx (1904), 91 ff. ; Svoronos, *Journ. intern. d'arch.
numism.*, ix (1906), 171.
[6] **XV**, 348 ff.
[7] Svoronos, loc. cit., pl. iii.

constituted a fairly usual multiple, thus enabling us to place
an ingot from Mycenæ [1] which, weighing 23·625 kilograms,
would equal one and a half times that multiple. At all events,
60 minas of 630 grams make a talent of 37·8 kilograms, and it
happens that an ingot from Enkomi [2] weighs 37·094 kilograms.

The use of common systems of weights enabled the Mediterranean peoples to transform the conditions of trade. Barter,
which had the advantages of ballasting the ships for both
the outward and the homeward voyage, had the drawback
of not always bringing to hand wares suitable to the two
parties. A standard commodity which would be acceptable
to all alike was required. The Aryans for a long time reckoned
in heads of cattle. The Ægeans passed through the same phase,
since they afterwards gave the form of an ox's head or a
couchant calf to certain units of weight and value.[3] But they
soon came to use metals in exchange. An ingot represented
great wealth in small bulk ; its homogeneity fitted it for
subdivision and its absolute durability made it possible to
store it in treasuries. Everywhere the first coins were pieces
of metal of fixed weight and the names of monetary denomina-
tions, talent, mina, stater, drachma, shekel, *libra* and *litra*,
recall the universal custom of weighing.

From one end of the Mediterranean to the other, ingots in
the shape of an ox-hide were used for centuries—copper ingots
of fixed weight which formed series of multiples and often bore
a stamp.[4] The princes of Asi and Alashiya (Cyprus) sent some
to the Pharaohs. Thothmes III prided himself upon having
received 108 of them, weighing 2,040 *debenu*, and the paintings
on the Egyptian tombs represent foreigners bringing their
precious gifts of metal (Fig. 35). Elsewhere, we have the
objects themselves before our eyes. At Hagia Triada the
" Treasure Chamber " contained nineteen[5] ; they weigh from
27 to 32 kilograms, but mostly from 29 to 29·5—pretty much
the same as the standard talent of Knossos. The ingots found
in Sardinia are larger talents and the one from Tylissos is
equal to half a " Phœnician " talent. But for copper currency

[1] Ib., pls. iv, vi.
[2] **LIX,** 15, No. 1537.
[3] AJA. 1921, 312 ; **XV,** 355 ; **XXXVII,** 69, fig. 15.
[4] Impressions at Phaistos, Hagia Triada, Mycenæ, Enkomi, and Serra-
Ilixi.
[5] RAL. xii, 334 ff.

preference was given to the system which was to survive
under the name of " Aiginetan ". It is represented by the
Cypriot talent, by the 2,040 *debenu* sent to Thothmes III
which are worth about five of these talents, by the fine series
of sub-multiples found in Euboia, by a series found in the very
depths of Alsace,[1] and perhaps also by the specimen from
Mycenæ. Thanks to the great advantages which they presented, in the ease with which they could be carried about,
subjected to a control, divided up and held in safe keeping,
these pigs of metal had, besides their intrinsic value, value
as a medium of exchange. According to the tablets from
Tell el-Amarna, the kings of Alashiya received gold and
silver in exchange for the copper which they sent to the
Pharaohs.

From this historical instance it is clear that precious metals,
like industrial metal, had an exchange value. A fixed proportion between gold and copper was established in the

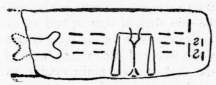

Fig. 33.—Tablet recording the weighing of ingots.

natural course of events. Hence the copper ingots generally
correspond to the gold standard. When the princes of Cyprus
sent copper to the Pharaohs in exchange for precious metal,
in good faith one of the two quantities determined the other.
On an Egyptian wall-painting an officer standing in front of
a balance puts gold rings in one scale and weights in the form
of an ox's head in the other. At Mycenæ, in a tomb which
contained more than seven hundred gold disks stamped with
various impressions, two little balances were found which
had precisely two such disks for scales.[2] When the king of
Knossos caused an inventory to be made of his treasure, his
officials converted the copper talents into gold value. One of
their tablets records the fact that the scales establish the
value of 60 ingots at 52 and a fraction units of the monetary
standard (Fig. 33).[3]

[1] Cf. RA. 1910, ii, 436.
[2] Svoronos, loc. cit., pls. viii, ix.
[3] **XV,** fig. 14.

In the end gold was cut up into pieces of fixed weight. From Mycenæ, Cyprus, and Crete we have series of roundels cut out of gold plates,[1] and conforming to the standard of the half-*kit*. At Knossos there have even been found cast pieces of silver [2] marked with the sign H or the sign Ⱶ, the one being half of the other. As the second, at a later day, stood for the drachma, which was half of the stater, and as the Cretan drachma weighs 3·654 grams, we may infer a monetary system in which the silver stater has the same weight as a " Phœnician " shekel of 7·308 grams.

No less than the evolution of a monetary system out of a system of weights, the use of writing gives a high idea of the organization of trade in Crete. If the first purpose served by writing, here as in Egypt, was to preserve royal documents and public inventories, it was also used in trade, as in Chaldæa, and later in Phœnicia. Merchants and manufacturers had a personal device engraved on their seals. Vase-makers affixed their mark to their vases or wrote with ink in cursive characters. It may even be said that, if writing had an early and rapid development in Crete, it was for the same reason as enabled it to spread over the whole of the eastern basin of the Mediterranean, namely that it was indispensable to transactions carried out on a large scale and at great distances. Though all these signs have come down to us as unsolved riddles, the numerals which abound on the tablets in association with scales, vases, weapons, or utensils, and the inscriptions painted or incised on pottery in Crete, Melos, and Thera, give us a glimpse of the service rendered to traders by the art of writing.

[1] Ib., 354–5.
[2] Ib., 363.

CHAPTER V

INTERNATIONAL RELATIONS

THE Cretans were, then, remarkably well armed to range the seas in quest of profitable business. To what lands were they able to extend their commercial enterprises ?

Certain characteristic objects tell us what distances goods were sent in the very earliest times. Schliemann found at Hissarlik axes of jade and a fragment of white nephrite. Here, then, we have stones which, from stage to stage, have come from the Kuen-Lun Mountains and perhaps still further to the shores of the Troad. Who can tell by what mysterious roads the amber found its way among the pre-Hellenic peoples, and to such an extent that Pylos before Nestor's day contained quantities of it ? Through what hands did the tin pass before it reached the bronze-workers of Knossos ? We see from the Egyptian documents that the ivory followed either the Nile, or the way of the Red Sea, or the land road which crossed the Euphrates to reach the Syrian coast. That an article which had travelled so far should then have reached Crete or Cyprus, the Troad or Mycenæ, is certainly not the most extraordinary thing about these migrations.

In all the exchanges which were effected from one end of the Mediterranean to another, the part played by the Cretans was of great, indeed of capital, importance. Their activity strikes the eye at once. One merchant of the island had his seal engraved with a kneeling camel,[1] a symbol of his relations with the caravans of Central Asia or Arabia. Another had for his badge an ostrich ; now ostrich eggs were used in Crete to make vases, several specimens of which have been found at Mycenæ.[2] On certain weights a hippopotamus was engraved.[3] The silphium plant, which grew only on the plateau of

---

[1] JHS. xiv, 341, fig. 62 *b*.
[2] **XX,** 170, 237, 594.
[3] **XV,** 351 ff.

Cyrenaïca, often appears among the Cretan hieroglyphs,[1] and Cretan art sometimes depicts the negroes who produced this precious spice.[2] Certainly the intercourse between Crete and Africa was regular, for after the Greek invasions, when the people of Thera wanted to go to Libya, they took for their guide a merchant of Itanos.

I CRETE AND THE COUNTRIES OF THE ÆGEAN

The Cyclades were well placed for traffic with Crete and the two neighbouring continents. So long as Crete did not enjoy overwhelming preponderance, the most central island, Syra, sent its ships in all directions and delighted to see them painted on its vases. Cycladic pottery was taken to Manika in Euboia, to Manesi in Phokis, to the Troad[3] and to the ports of Crete, and the Cycladic marble idols went everywhere. In exchange, the Cyclades received pots with a black wash from Hellas, two-handled cups from Troy, and seals from Crete.[4] When Crete had become the great market of the Ægean, Melos, the most south-westerly island, gained the ascendancy. From the earliest times it had exported the obsidian, of which it had the monopoly. It became the great half-way house between Crete and Argolis. While it still imports " Minyan " pottery from the mainland, it soon enters into the commercial orbit of Crete. It borrows from Crete the use of the pillar, wall-painting, and the linear script, and it obtains from Crete pottery of all kinds. It also manages to export in all directions its bird vases, no doubt with wine in them, and even to resist the competition of L.M.I pottery by a clever imitation ; but soon it is flooded with Cretan goods.[5] Thera undergoes the same influences, because it receives the same visitors.[6] Delos welcomes foreign cults, as it did in later times ; the reason is that, as in later times, it is frequented by traders ; from the Middle Minoan Period the Cretans come and deposit their *amphoras* there.[7]

---

[1] **XX,** fig. 216.
[2] Ib., fig. 231.
[3] **LXV,** 3 ff. ; 'Εφ., 1908–87 ; **XXV,** 137.
[4] BSA. xvii, 16 ; AM. 1917, 32 ff. ; **XXV,** 103, 137.
[5] Dawkins and Droop, BSA. xvii, 1–22.
[6] Renaudin, BCH. 1922, 133 ff.
[7] Demangel, ib., 58 ff. ; *Expl. arch de Délos.* v, 68 ff.

From Melos the Cretans had only to continue on their way to reach the Peloponnese by the Argive Gulf or central Greece by the Saronic Gulf. Before the XVIIth century they had hardly ventured to these distant lands. Even the sailors of the Cyclades had only appeared there occasionally, bringing to the petty chieftains a few vases, jewels, or arms. But as time went on the lands about the Isthmus through which the route slanted to the Gulf of Corinth had grown rich. Bœotia lay on the shortest road thither from the northern Ægean and the Troad ; the Second City of Orchomenos knew the *depas amphikypellon* of Troy,[1] and the Third City sent its grey pottery as far as the Peloponnese ; on the hill of the " Kadmeians " at Thebes a palace arose. Argolis lay on the way from the southern Ægean and Crete ; a great road ran across it from Tiryns to Corinth, and Mycenæ, the city " of the broad ways ", became the city " where gold abounds ". The Argive Gulf, stretching south-eastwards, beckoned to the sailors of Knossos, and they came with all speed.

What the great mainland market became is seen in one general fact ; the history of all the industries and all the arts of the Ægean begins in Crete and ends at Mycenæ. Often, indeed, the most remarkable products of the island are known to us from specimens found on the mainland ; this fact alone would show the amount of exchange which went on. To give a detailed account of it, it would not be enough to recall the innumerable objects dug up in the Argive sites, the jewels, the cups of precious metal, the bronze weapons, the painted vases, the ivory, the faience, and the engraved stones. The importance of these transactions was far greater than everything which archæology can show. To what has been preserved we must add the great mass of articles of fragile or perishable material. The ladies of Mycenæ dressed in the Cretan fashion, and they got their luxurious dress materials from Crete. The beautiful vases were so numerous only because they contained fine wine and scented oil ; as for the common pots, the origin of which can never be declared with certainty, they too went about with common products inside them. So Argolis was largely exploited, first by Cretan importers and then probably by colonists, so much and so successfully that Mycenæ became

---

[1] **XXV**, 75, 137.

a considerable market and the *agora* of the Lower Town perhaps robbed the Acropolis of its supremacy. In its turn it became a centre of commercial expansion.

As soon as the Cretans got a landing-place and a staple on the mainland, they disseminated their luxurious articles and tastes, and at the same time their cults, in the lands occupied by the Achaians. They approached the Peloponnese on the south and west, as well as on the north. Their steatite vases had reached the island of Kythera long before their painted vases.[1] The porphyry of Taÿgetos attracted their attention, and they took blocks of it to Knossos.[2] Laconia opened itself to their imports. The princes of Vapheio procured beautiful cups of gold and silver, gems, bronze weapons, and Palace style vases,[3] and took delight in seeing on glass paste or gold filigree the new motive of the flying fish. The west coast saw foreign sailors land at several points. " Many and stout," says the Homeric hymn, " the Cretans from Knossos the city of Minos sailed on their business in a black ship to sandy Pylos, to deal with the men of the country." [4] Not one Pylos but two were visited by the Minoans in these parts. The Pylos in Messenia (Tragana) has preserved many records of these relations, not only faience objects and painted vases, but even, on one of the vases, the portrait of the ship which brought them.[5] The Pylos in Triphylia (Kakovatos) must have especially attracted the Cretans, for it was on the way to Olympia and was in constant relations with the northern seas, as is proved by the great quantities of amber discovered there. The tombs of its princes contained objects which beyond dispute came from Knossos itself, Palace style vases and a bronze rapier 92 centimetres long.[6]

By the two sides of the Peloponnese the current of trade bore on central Greece. In the crags which overlook the Gulf of Corinth south of Parnassos a sanctuary had attracted pilgrims from the most remote ages. At Pylos the Cretans heard about it. Under the guidance of the divine fish attached to their prow, the Delphinian god, behold them landing at

---

[1] *ΑΔ*, i, 191 ff.
[2] **XVI**, 536 ; **XX**, 88.
[3] 'Εφ., 1889, 129 ff. ; JHS., pl. xi.
[4] *Hymn to Pythian Apollo*, 219 ff.
[5] 'Εφ., 1914, 99 ff., pl. ii, figs. 14–15.
[6] AM. 1908, 295 ff. ; 1909, 269 ff., fig. 316, pls. xvi–xxiii ; 1913, 97 ff.

the port which was afterwards called Krissa, and then climbing to the high places which were to keep the name of Delphi. They were missionaries, and brought their goddess, Mother Earth or Ge, their sacred music, their ritual dances, their games, and their calendar, and they left there a corporation placed under the protection of the Double Axe, the Labyadai. They were also merchants, and they did not forget business in the midst of religious ceremonies, nor leave out of sight the fairs which everywhere accompany great religious gatherings ; this is proved by a lion's head of stone, copied from a *rhyton* from Knossos, some votive double axes of bronze and a quantity of idols of terra cotta.[1]

It was naturally on the east coast that most Cretan and Mycenæan goods came to Hellas, either by the Saronic Gulf and Euboia, or by the overland road from Corinth. On this side objects of Cretan origin are not very numerous ; they consist principally of some Palace style vases found at Chalkis and at Orchomenos.[2] Far more frequently the vases of this style are only imitations ; they came from some unknown workshops established on the mainland, and we find them travelling all through Attica, at Thebes, and at Chalkis, and they go as far as the ports of Thessaly.[3] But even the imitations were the work of Cretan immigrants, and it is possible that the same ships carried the vases made at Knossos and those from the branch factories in turn. The port of Megara was given the name of Minoa, and local legend preserved the memory of Minos and Skylla.[4] On the east coast of Attica there are many indications of the same kind. At the time when the mines of Laureion were first being worked,[5] and Thorikos was receiving pots of Cretan style, the sacred hymn tells us that the Goddess Mother landed from Crete at Thorikos itself,[6] and from Probalinthos to Trikorynthos the Cretan bull ranged the plain of Marathon as a master. From the XIVth century the mainland market was extended to Macedonia,[7] and, if it became independent of Crete, it was none the less active.

[1] *Fouilles de Delphes*, v, 1 ff.
[2] **XXV**, 91 ; cf. BSA. ix, 311, fig. 9.
[3] **XXV**, 91.
[4] Pausanias, ii, 34, 7.
[5] **VI**, 117–19 ; 227–9 ; Gowland, *Archæologia*, **LXIX**, 121 ff.
[6] *Hymn to Demeter*, 123 ff.
[7] Rey, BCH. 1916, 277–8, fig. 12 ; 1917–19, 248–9, 269 ff.

II Relations with Egypt

Outside the Ægean the Cretans did business with a great
number of peoples. Of all these relations the oldest and most
lasting were those which they maintained with Egypt. We
know of them not only from the objects manufactured in
the one country and found in the other but from the paintings
and inscriptions of the Egyptian monuments. The only
question which sometimes arises is whether an object is an
article honestly exchanged, or loot brought in by pirates, or
tribute paid to an overlord.

Even in Early Minoan times intercourse between Crete and
Egypt is fairly frequent. The Egyptians confined themselves
to coasting up to Byblos, but the Cretans were not afraid of
long voyages, witness the elephant's tusk found in the lowest
strata of Phaistos. In the third millennium Crete possesses
vases of syenite and diorite which, by their form and by their
material, betray their origin ; they served as models to the
stone-cutters who carved the vases of Mochlos in Aiolian
liparite or native breccia.[1] About the same time the Cretans
obtained from Egypt beads and vases of faience, figurines of
a special type, ritual vessels, and articles of toilet.[2] From
Egypt, too, came the things which Crete itself did not possess—
for example, ivory, and perhaps also the silver Babylonian
cylinder which was found in a tomb at Mochlos.[3] So down to
the end of the VIth dynasty (2390) there was a continual
flow of Egyptian goods and ideas into the isles of the Ægean.
Apparently it was the Cretans who took the initiative in these
transactions. What did they bring in exchange for what
they took away? Oil and wine, perhaps ; for Egypt has not
yielded one Ægean object dating from this epoch. But it is
not impossible that they generally used more violent methods.
They were no doubt included among the Ha-nebu or Ha-unebu,
the " people from beyond the seas ", who caused so much
anxiety to the Pharaohs of the time. In any case the kings
of the VIth dynasty sent envoys " to go round about the
circle of the Ha-unebu ",[4] and who knows but the first seals,

[1] **XX,** figs. 28-32, 54-5 ; cf. 33-6, 58-60.
[2] **LXXXII,** 54-5 ; vi, 22, 35 ; MIL. xxi, v, pl. xi, 27 ; **XXXVII,** pl. xiv,
4 ; **XX,** 80 ff., 101, 83.
[3] **LXXXII,** fig. 36, i, n.
[4] *Rec. de travaux,* v, 37, 161, 176 ; ix, 182, 187 ; x, 1.

which all come from southern Crete, may have been the insignia of fictitious investitures conferred by these messengers ?

In the troublous times which marked the end of the Old Kingdom and only ceased on the accession of the XIth dynasty (2390–2160) relations were necessarily relaxed. But they were not completely broken off. We know this from the amulets of a special shape which exist at the same epoch in Crete and in Egypt.[1] We know it still better from the button-shaped seals which have been found in tombs in the Messara [2] and in Upper Egypt.[3] This type of seal raises many problems ; it indicates borrowings which are far from having been elucidated.[4] But the mere fact of these borrowings is sufficient to establish that the Cretans did not forget the road to the Nile in the second half of the third millennium. If they followed it less than in the past, it was because their civilization was provided with all that it had hitherto sought elsewhere, and because an impoverished country had no longer the same attractions for them.

The XIth dynasty (2160–2000) had hard work to restore order in the kingdom. It had also to defend it against the pirates, " to break the hamstrings of the Ha-unebu." [5] Under the XIIth dynasty the Foreign Office set up a special department for this people ; an official of Senusert I (1970–1935) was able to say that " his stilus (his pen) comprised the Ha-unebu ". Peace reigned. Business recovered. But Crete had gone ahead in the meantime ; the XIXth and XVIIIth centuries were to be for Crete a period of intense activity. It had to be in constant relations with the Department for the Ha-unebu. This is the explanation of the presence at Knossos, in the second part of M.M.II, of a diorite statuette portraying an Egyptian named Ab-nub-mes-Waset-User.[6] This personage was perhaps a high official of the Delta who had given especial satisfaction to the Cretans, a *proxenos* to whom the king of Knossos had sent tokens of gratitude, and of whom he was anxious to keep a souvenir. How intimate

---

[1] **XX,** 125.
[2] MIL., loc. cit., pls. x–xi, figs. 25–6 ; **XII,** fig. 12, 86–7.
[3] **XXV,** 154.
[4] Ib. ; **XVII,** 125 ff. ; **XX,** 103, 122 ff.
[5] Maspero, *Hist. anc. des peuples de l'Orient,* i, 476, n. 3.
[6] **XX,** fig. 220.

and lasting these relations were is shown by the arrival in Crete of religious elements which were of some influence on the development of the cult of the Serpent Goddess.[1] Certain Egyptian scarabs of this epoch, covered with Cretan motives and characters, are in a way symbolic.[2] But we must go right into the heart of Egypt to appreciate the commercial importance of these relations. When Senusert II (1903–1887) and Amenemhat III (1849–1801) built pyramids for themselves, they collected in the village of Kahun, which was founded for the purpose and abandoned about 1765, gangs of native and foreign workmen. All over this village pottery has been found marked with Cretan signs and fragments of good Kamares ware.[3] A tomb at Abydos contained, with cylinders of Senusert III (1887–1849) and Amenemhat III, a magnificent vase which by its shape and its polychrome decoration of dog-daisies resembles the best M.M.II wares of Knossos, Phaistos, and Hagia Triada (Fig. 34).[4] Thus in the XIXth century a

FIG. 34.—Vase from Abydos in Egypt (left), compared with a Cretan vase and fragment.

Cretan colony established itself in Middle Egypt for many long years, and Cretan goods went up the Nile as far as Upper Egypt.

Once again business ceased for two or three centuries. About 1750, the First Palaces of Knossos and Phaistos were destroyed, and from 1675 to 1580 Egypt was occupied by the Hyksos. The need for repairing all these ruins and the dividing up of Egypt led to a rupture of the old relations. Crete when

---

[1] Ib., 199 ff., 291.

[2] Ib., figs. 146–7.

[3] Flinders Petrie, *Kahun, Gurob and Hawara*, pls. xxvii, xxviii; *Kahun and Gurob*, pl. i, figs. 1, 3–8, 10–15; JHS. xi, pl. xiv, 5–8, 10; cf. **XXV**, 107, 156–8; **XX**, 266–7 and fig. 198.

[4] Garstang, LA. v, pls. 13–14; cf. **XXV**, figs. 155–6; **XX**, fig. 199, pl. iv.

reconstituted sought on the mainland in the North the market which was lacking in the South. Its relations with the Shepherd Kings were purely passive. These relations have, however, left a record of very great interest. At Knossos an *alabastron* lid has been found on which is engraved the cartouche of the " good God, son of the Sun, Khian ".[1] This king was the first to take up the tradition of the Pharaohs, to restore the unity of Egypt, and to revive a vigorous foreign policy. He was the " gatherer-up of lands ", and at once posed as the " master of the foreign peoples ". He left the trace of his ambitions at Gezer in Palestine, and he set up on the bank of the Tigris a granite lion ; he must also have drawn Crete into his political combinations. His cartouche at Knossos lay among calcined rubbish in a litter of smashed vases ; are we to see in it the emblem of a conquerer who appeared amidst flame and tumbling walls ? Yet there is nothing to show—and he himself does not venture to say—that he ruled over the sea. It is much more likely that he affected the airs of an overlord, sending to the king of the islanders a vase containing " oil of unction ". In any case, it is the fact that shortly after 1633, the date of Khian's accession,[2] relations at least of a theoretic kind were re-established between Egypt and Crete.

When Egypt resumed the course of its national destiny under the XVIIIth dynasty, Aahmes (1580–1557), the conqueror of the Hyksos, inherited their pretensions and handed them down to his successors. On a stele set up in his honour it ran " Everyone says ' Our lord, it is he ', and the Ha-unebu say ' It is he whom we serve ' ".[3] In reality the foreigners returned to Egypt to do trade or piracy, as circumstances suggested. About 1545, the inscriptions named the Ha-unebu among " the barbarians who are an abomination to God ", and proclaimed the victory of Thothmes III in these words : " To him the isles of the Great Circle are subjected, the whole earth lies beneath his foot-soles." [4] It needed time to restore regular peaceful dealings.

Nevertheless, little by little, we note a significant change in the Egyptian documents. Among all these " people from

[1] **XX,** 418–22, figs. 303–4.
[2] Raymond Weill, *Journ. Asiat., Rec. des Mém.,* iv, 107 ff. ; **vi, 47 ff.**
[3] Sethe, *Urk. des aeg. Alt.,* iv, 17, 21 ; cf. pp. 138, 572.
[4] Ib., 83–6.

beyond the seas ", among the barbarians lumped together
under the name of Ha-unebu, they begin to make distinctions.
They now mention by name the people of Keftiu, that is of the
island which the Bible calls Caphtor, which is Crete, the people
of Alashiya or Cyprus, the people of " the Isles ", and finally
those of " the Circuit ", or the Ægean mainland.

Over all these nations, as over the Ha-unebu in general, the
Pharaoh claims to exercise his right of universal domination.
In the Hymn of Victory of Thothmes III (1501–1447) the god
Amen makes this superb declaration to the king : " I am come :

Fig. 35.—The tribute-bearers.   Wall-painting, Tomb of Rekhmara, at
Thebes.

I grant to thee to crush the western world ; Keftiu is in terror
. . . I am come, I grant to thee to crush the dwellers in the
Isles ; those who live in the bosom of the Great Green are
under thy roaring . . . I am come, I grant to thee to crush
the countries by the sea ; all the Circuit of the great zone
of the waters is bound to thy fist." [1] On the sepulchral
paintings the Keftiu, recognizable by their physical type,
their hair curled into tufts on the top, their decorated waist-
cloths and their high-laced shoes, follow the procession of

[1] Ib., 615 ff.

tribute-bearers. They bring to the king filler vases, *rhytons* shaped like bulls' or lions' heads, goblets modelled like those of Vapheio and adorned with Cretan motives, daggers, ewers of gold or silver, all the most perfect things which L.M.I has produced. Such is the subject treated on the tomb which Senmut built for himself about 1480 [1] ; it was reproduced shortly after on those of Rekhmara (Fig. 35) and Menkheper-re-seneb.[2] It was the official duty of all these dignitaries to receive foreign ambassadors and to take over the gifts or tribute which they brought. The explanatory texts, especially those on the monument of Rekhmara, are quite definite : " Received the gifts of the . . . Keftiu," " Arrive and are welcome the envoys of the chiefs . . . of Keftiu and of the Isles in the midst of the sea." [3] The Egyptian only saw in them bearers of tribute, the representatives of vassal countries. After a procession of this kind one could very well present a gold dish as a reward to the " delegate in every foreign land and in the Isles which are in the midst of the Very Green " for having " contented the heart of the King ".[4]

But we must distrust this unmeaning, high-flown style ; pretensions to world-empire are satisfied, for want of anything better, with the diplomatic exaltation of modest realities. The very persistence of these official formulas for two centuries proves their emptiness. We can judge how much such an affectation of suzerainty was worth by the relations of the Egyptians and Cyprus revealed in the Tell el-Amarna tablets.[5] When he sent to the Pharaoh the products of his mines and forests the king of Alashiya requested from " his brother " in exchange silver, jars of oil which must be " of good quality ", horses, chariots, a bed of precious wood inlaid with gold, female garments, etc. These two noble tradesmen haggled over the price of their consignments. " Why," asked the alleged vassal, " have you sent me no oil ? I sent you everything for which you asked me." Amenhetep III even found himself required

---

[1] BSA. viii, 172 ff., figs. 4–8 ; xvi, 254 ff., pl. xiv ; cf. **XXV**, fig. 176.
[2] **IV,** 257 ff.
[3] Sethe, loc. cit., 1093 ff.
[4] Birch, *Mém. de la Soc. des Antiq. de Fr.*, xxiv, 4.
[5] Knudtzon, *Die El-Amarna Tafeln*, i, 278 ff. On the identity of Alashiya and Cyprus, see the objections of Wainwright, *Klio*, 1915, 1 ff., and the reply of Schachermeyer, ib., 1921, 230 ff.

to restore, contrary to the right of escheat, the property of
a Cypriot business man who died in Egypt.   So the Pharaohs'
dominion comes down to this, and the less real existence
it has the more loudly it advertises itself.   The king of
Alashiya might have done likewise, and had himself represented
as receiving the envoys from Egypt with their bars of silver,
and just at this very time a painter at Knossos was adorning
the walls of a gallery with a long procession of foreigners
carrying vases.   In reality these figures are not vassals coming
to do homage or to pay tribute, neither in Egypt nor in Crete.
They come to effect a free exchange of the products of their
industries against the goods of the country.   At the very
most they take the precaution, like all merchants in early
times who dealt with a foreign country, of buying from the
sovereign the right to trade.   In the *Iliad* the men of Lemnos
offer jugs of wine to the king of the Achaians before exchanging
the rest of their cargo against metal, hides, cattle, and slaves ; [1]
they do not regard themselves either as subjects or as liegemen.
The Keftiu did the same ; in bringing vases to the Pharaoh's
treasury they were actually paying a customs duty to obtain
the protection of the laws.

So the messengers whom the king sent " to the midst of
the Very Green " did not act as governors ; they were rather
ambassadors, sometimes bearers of gifts and always intelligence
agents.   They came home with reports which made it possible
to make a show of a nominal dominion in pompous documents.
A navy would have been necessary to realize ambitions which
were more easily satisfied with words.   The ships of the
Pharaohs never went beyond the region of Syria ; Thothmes
III, who caused his god to give him dominion over the Keftiu,
the Isles, and the Circuit, needed the Keftiu to carry wood from
Lebanon to Egypt.   However, the Pharaohs were well informed
about what went on in distant lands.   When they felt themselves strong and were not afraid of pirates they demanded
fine gifts of the traders, and rigorously levied customs duties ;
this is what Thothmes did with the Keftiu.   When they felt
less sure of their power and wanted to delude themselves with
the belief that they were attaching some foreign prince to
their policy, they themselves sent him those gifts or tokens

---

[1] *Iliad*, vii, 467 ff.

which maintain friendship ; thus a blue glass monkey, a vase, and a faience plaque bearing the cartouches of Amenhetep II, Amenhetep III, and the successor of Amenhetep IV, have been discovered at Mycenæ,[1] and the scarabs of that foreigner-loving couple, Amenhetep III and Tii, are found scattered over Crete, Mycenæ, Rhodes, Cyprus, and Palestine.[2] But at bottom the relations of Egypt with the Ægean countries were chiefly of an economic kind, and down to the beginning of the XIVth century the Cretans secured all the advantages of them for themselves.

It was no doubt in return for presents given to the Pharaohs of the XVIIIth Dynasty that the Keftiu, now better known, obtained authority to build the port of Pharos. From the dimensions of the docks we can estimate the quantity of traffic which was expected.[3] The amount of business done there also explains the fact that the Cretans adopted the weights and measures used in Egypt and all over the East ; they said clearly whence they had them when they handled on their island goose-shaped weights of the Egyptian type marked with a ship or a hippopotamus.

They obtained dried vegetables from the Egyptians ; at Knossos, when Evans' workmen found beneath their spades pots filled with beans, they at once uttered the popular name used in Crete for a dwarf species imported from Alexandria to this day. They got certain oils from Egypt ; the bottom of a Cretan vase contained a residue in which coco-nut oil was identified, which served for the preparation of a varnish ; and a papyrus speaks of an oil manufactured in Egypt which was used " to embalm the great even as far as Keftiu ".[4] But the Ægeans went to Egypt especially for precious materials and certain artistic objects. Cyprus could not be alone in bringing silver and gold from there.[5] Crete seems even to have received Egyptian models for its goldsmiths; for example, pendants in the shape of negroes' heads.[6] Ivory probably went through Egypt before it reached the Ægean lands. The coloured

---

[1] BSA. viii, 188, figs. 13–15 ; 'Eφ., 1891, pl. iii, 3, 4 ; **XXV,** figs. 169–70.
[2] MA. xiv, 733 ff., fig. 33 ; 'Eφ., 1887, pl. xiii, 21, 21 a ; **XXX,** 4, 9, 75, pl. E, 1 ; **LIX,** 21, 36, pl. iv, 608 ; **XXV,** 180.
[3] See p. 190.
[4] Wainwright, LA. vi, 79, 2.
[5] **LIX,** pl. iv, 617 ; pl. v ; pl. iv, 351.
[6] **XX,** fig. 231.

P

glass and the faience of Egypt found markets from Argolis
to Cyprus.[1] The scarabs enjoyed a great vogue.[2] Vases of
hard stone were still being exported under the XVIIIth
Dynasty ; the royal tombs at Isopata, Mycenæ, and Enkomi
contained beautiful alabaster vases, the source and date of
which are fixed by a scarab of Thothmes III and a ring of
Amenhetep IV at Abydos.[3]   Finally, the Keftiu eagerly
picked up ideas for their artists in Egypt, for example the
decorative motive of the papyrus and the scene of the cat
hunting birds. They even carried off or attracted to their
islands experts in rites and music ; when we remember that
the king of Alashiya asked the Pharaoh to send him an exorcist
against eagles we are not surprised to see in a procession of
Cretans singers whose nationality can be recognized from their
physical type and the sistrum brandished by their chief
(Pl. II, 2).

In return the Cretans sold goods of all kinds to Egypt.
For the perishable goods we can only consult the written
documents or make guesses.   The Keftiu, who went to
Egypt for special oils, must have supplied it with great
quantities of olive oil, which was not produced in Egypt, but
filled their own cellars to overflowing. A tomb-painting shows
the Keftiu passing with other bearers of gifts, and the list of
articles recorded includes " wine, cloths, cattle ".[4] A book of
medicine written at the beginning of the XVIIIth Dynasty
gives " the herb of Keftiu " in a formula ; [5] to tell the truth,
there was without doubt an active exchange of medicinal
plants between two countries which were equally reputed in
antiquity for this kind of product.

For articles made of lasting materials we have more information. The ornamented objects which followed the road from
Pharos to Thebes had so much influence that Egyptian decoration was transformed by the Cretan motives of the fleur-de-lys
and the flying gallop.[6] Yet the weapons and the necklaces
which the paintings show in the hands of the Keftiu (Fig. 35)
are not known to us by any real specimens ; the beautiful

---

[1] **LIX,** 34 ff., fig. 62, 1218 ; fig. 63, 1052–3.
[2] Ib. ; cf. **XVI,** fig. 101, 99 a, 1.
[3] **XVI,** fig. 125 ; JHS. xxiv, pl. xiv, e ; **LIX,** 25, fig. 41 ; cf. **XXV,** 173–4.
[4] Sethe, iv, 1906.
[5] *Pap. Ebers,* ix, 18.
[6] **XXV,** 202 ; **XX,** 710 ff.

dagger placed in the tomb of Aahhetep at the end of the XVIIth century or the beginning of the XVIth was engraved after a Cretan pattern, but without doubt by an Egyptian armourer.[1] Of the fine vases of bronze, silver, and gold which were brought by Keftiu or ordered from Keftiu workshops by tributary kings, not one has been found in Egypt.[2] But the evidence of the inscriptions and mural paintings is confirmed by some carved wooden boxes, the work of Cretans or Mycenæans (Figs. 59, 60), by a stone vase bearing the cartouche of Thothmes IV and the inscription " beautiful vase of Keftiu ",[3] and above all by a great quantity of pots which came filled with wine or oil. In the XVth century, the Palace style is represented by a vase and ewer both decorated with nautiluses.[4] Already vases of mainland " ivy-leaf " style came to furnish the tomb of Maket at Kahun,[5] and other Mycenæan vases went up the Nile right into Nubia.[6]

How did these Mycenæan goods make their way into Egypt ? It is probable that the Cretans made themselves the middlemen between the whole Ægean and Egypt during the XVIth century and the greater part of the XVth. We know that they transported wood of Lebanon to the Egyptian ports ; we see them bringing copper bricks which they must have got from Cyprus ; we may suppose, from a sudden fall in white metal, that they gave Egypt its share of the silver extracted in the isles and at Laureion ; it is not impossible that they supplied Egypt with the products of the furthest countries, such as tin and amber. That they acted as brokers between the Achaians and Egypt, as they certainly did between the Achaian cities, is extremely probable.

All those at whose cost this monopoly was carried on must have endeavoured to be free of it. The gifts sent to Mycenæ by Amenhetep II had their political significance ; before 1420, the Achaians were in direct relations with Egypt, and we may believe that the " peoples of the Circuit ", once they took to

[1] **XXV,** figs. 196–7 ; **XX,** fig. 537.
[2] Sethe, iv, 733.
[3] De Mot, RA., 1905, i, 428.
[4] **LXVII,** figs. 485–6.
[5] Flinders Petrie, *Illahun,* 21 ff. ; pl. xxvi, 44 ; cf. **XXI,** pl. xix, 1, and xxviii ; **XXX,** 206–8 ; **XXIX,** pl. xi, 56 ; **LXVII,** fig. 482 ; **XXV,** fig. 77, 161.
[6] **LXIX,** pl. i, 6.

navigation, occupied a site on the island of Pharos by the side of the Keftiu, as later at Naukratis the Aiginetans, for example, by the side of the Milesians. This competition was certainly not unrelated to the catastrophe which ruined Knossos to the profit of Mycenæ about 1400, nor was this catastrophe unrelated to the exchange of gifts which took place between the king of Mycenæ and the Pharaoh ; at the very time when the Cretan empire was going under there arrived at Mycenæ, with a scarab of Queen Tii, a whole assortment of faience marked with the cartouche of Amenhetep III (1415–1380), including a fine " Sèvres " vase,[1] while these sovereigns received in exchange a consignment of Mycenæan pottery.[2] Their son, the heretic Akhenaten (1380–1362), attacked by the national priesthood, gave a great welcome to strangers, kept up regular relations with the king of Alashiya, and ordered for his palace paintings inspired by Ægean art.[3]

So the trade of Mycenæ, once liberated from the hegemony of Crete, poured into Egypt for two hundred years. At Gurob, a town which was largely inhabited by fair-haired men, the tombs and houses are full of Mycenæan stirrup-jars and *amphoras* which are placed by cartouches or scarabs in the last reigns of the XVIIIth Dynasty or in the XIXth Dynasty.[4] At Tell el-Amarna there have been found, with cartouches of Akhenaten and his family, 1345 potsherds, all recalling vases from Mycenæ, Ialysos, and Cyprus.[5] A large number of sites all over Egypt present specimens of the same style. They have been found a hundred miles upstream from Aswan, and still further, in Nubia.[6]

The vogue of this pottery was such that the Egyptians set themselves to copy it in faience in the time of Amenhetep III, and they imitated it in terra cotta in the time of Rameses III (1200–1169), when the great invasions made it impossible to obtain it from the former suppliers.

---

[1] 'Εφ., 1887, loc. cit. ; 1891, loc. cit. ; BSA. viii, 189, figs. 14–15 ; cf. **XXV,** figs. 170–2.
[2] JAI. 1899, ii, 57 ; cf. **XXV,** 99, 163.
[3] **XXV,** 206–7.
[4] Cf. ib., 161–3.
[5] Cf. ib., 164–5, fig. 163.
[6] Cf. ib., 99, 166.

III Relations with Cyprus and Asia

Cyprus was, after Egypt, the market which it was most desirable for the Cretans to conquer. In the interior of the island the copper mines offered inexhaustible wealth. The metal was exported in pigs or worked on the spot. The natives were clever armourers, and made willow-leaf daggers in large quantities. Even before 1550 these daggers managed to find a sale on the neighbouring coast, whence they made their way towards Troy, Thrace, and the Danube. Two cylinders of Khammurabi have been found, one at Hagia Paraskeui, and the other at Platanos.[1] The first proves that Cyprus was in relations with nearer Asia in the XXIst century ; the second may perhaps indicate that it acted as an intermediary between Asia and Crete in M.M.I. Moreover, certain black jugs, known only in Cyprus, Palestine and the Egypt of the Hyksos, bear witness, although we do not know where they were made, to the relations which Cyprus kept up in the XVIth century with at least one of the two other countries.[2] To the Ægeans, above all to the Cretans, it was of first importance to obtain supplies of copper at the source itself, to distribute over the Mediterranean the products of metal-workers who had a great name, and to secure opposite the Asiatic coast an outlet for their own manufactures.

In M.M.II there appear at Cyprus vases with a white ornament of Helladic or Melian type and polychrome vases from Crete.[3] But it is not till 1550 that the island comes into the orbit of the Ægean world. At once industry and trade advance with rapid strides. The mines, the property of the king, supply copper to Egypt, Crete, Euboia, and Argolis. The forests are put under contribution, and wood from Cyprus competes with that from Lebanon. Numerous workshops are built similar to the foundry discovered at Enkomi,[4] and send their daggers abroad. The potters now use the wheel, and their hemispherical bowls with a white wash and black chequers are sold not only in Egypt and Syria, but at Troy VI, Thera and Melos, and in Attica.[5] Suddenly the island grows rich.

---

[1] **LXIV**, fig. 35 ; **XX**, fig. 146.
[2] **XXV**, 104, 158–60.
[3] JHS. xxxi, 110 ff. ; **XXV**, 97, 105.
[4] **XI**, 249–50, figs. 179–80.
[5] **XX**, 104–5, figs. 93–4 ; **XI**, 237–9, figs. 169–71

In exchange for its products it obtains from Egypt stallions and chariots, gold and silver. The Cypriot tombs begin to receive objects of value and for the first time are full of jewels.

Such a transformation was not the result of a spontaneous internal development. The activity of these dealings presupposes a strong navy. Nothing shows that one existed on the spot. It was the Ægeans, and first of all the Cretans, who turned the budding prosperity of Cyprus to account. The sailors who carried the ingots to their own country also sold them to foreign peoples. Among the bearers of presents in the Egyptian paintings who come to lay copper bricks at the feet of the king there are Keftiu ; nor can one see that the metal could have reached Greece by any other intermediaries at the beginning of the Mycenæan Age. For the goods which are sent to Cyprus in return for these exports the Cretans naturally play exactly the same *rôle*. At Episkopi a magnificent bronze vase has been found, which can only have been engraved by a Cretan in the best years of the Late Minoan Period, and deserved to be placed with a golden sceptre in the tomb of a king.[1] At the same time fairly large quantities of mainland pottery arrive in Cyprus. But as soon as the Mycenæans were able to compete with the Cretans on the sea, they followed them to the great island of the Levant. We have reached the time when it becomes hard to distinguish the share of Crete in a more general influence. The whole island is filled with Mycenæan stirrup-vases.[2]

That Ægean traders and craftsmen settled in Cyprus for good is a supposition so much in accordance with the laws of Mediterranean colonization that it is extremely likely. While the Cypriot population preserved its traditional methods of burial, it adapted itself in everything else to Ægean civilization, especially from the XIVth century onwards. For a moment the king of Alashiya seems to have tried to react ; he tightened the bonds of amity between himself and the Pharaoh ; one of his vassals received a scarab of Queen Tii and a ring of Akhenaten.[3] At all events, Cyprus appears more and more as the advanced post of the Westerners. Its potters turn out Mycenæan wares, and paint black chariots and

---

[1] BSA. xviii, 95–7 ; cf. Perrot, vol. iii, figs. 555–6.
[2] **XXV**, 97, 105.
[3] **LIX**, pl. iv, 606, 617.

warriors, bulls and boxers.   Enkomi, whose days of glory begin only after the fall of Knossos, retains the memory of Cretan art ; it possesses carved ivories of excellent style [1] and very fine faience *rhytons* shaped like the head of a woman or of a horse.[2]   A Cypro-Mycenæan school is formed, which in its turn influences Cilicia and northern Syria.   In addition, profiting by Ægean expansion, Cyprus sends the products of its mines and its metal-workers far beyond the Ægean ; its ingots reach the Adriatic and Sardinia, and its flat axes and its scroll-ended pins penetrate to the depths of the European continent.   In later years when the Dorian invasion came and threw the Achaian countries into confusion, Cyprus was all ready to offer a refuge to bands of Cretanized Achaians, who brought to it their religion, their language, and their writing.

From Cyprus, Crete soon extended its relations to Syria and particularly to Palestine.[3]   The recent excavations at Byblos have brought to light silver vases which are certainly Ægean, and are dated by a cartouche of Amenemhat III (1849–1801).[4] One or two centuries later Helladic matt-painted pottery finds its way into Canaan.[5]   The Hyksos invasion must have interrupted these relations.

They were resumed when the XVIIIth Dynasty had restored order in the neighbourhood of Egypt ; the victories of the Pharaohs opened Syria, and the Cretans rushed in.   Whence came the Keftiu ships which Thothmes III, in 1467, found at an appointed place on the Syrian coast, when he had to transport timber to Egypt ?   Did they ply regularly between Crete and Byblos ?   Were they berthed in some Minoa established on the coast of Asia, for example under the islet of Tyre, which might be fitted up for their use like the islet of Pharos ?   However this may have been, the Cretans from the XVIth century, and then the Mycenæans, were constant visitors to the Syrian coast.   The Cretan merchant who had a seal marked with a camel no doubt came every year to confer with the caravans which brought the ivory and perfumes down to the Mediterranean, while the other, who called himself an importer of

---

[1] **XXXVII**, fig. 83.
[2] **XI**, figs. 177–8.
[3] Cf. Welch, BSA. vi, 117 ; Bliss and Macalister, *Excav. a Gezer*, ii, 155 ff. ; Vincent, **XC,** 618 ff.
[4] Pottier, CRAI. 1922, 77 ; *Syria*, 1922, pl. xliv.
[5] **XXV,** 106.

horses, came to seek thoroughbreds in the country which produced them. When they came back to their island, these folk introduced the priestly costume of the East.[1]

Eventually certain Cretans settled down in the country and founded families there. In 1459 a Syrian prince procured a beautiful silver vase, a " work of Keftiu ", to offer as tribute to the Pharaoh.[2] Some years earlier other princes of the same region sent to Thothmes *rhytons* like heads of bulls, rams, or lions, " works of Zahi," that is to say, executed in Phœnicia, but almost certainly by Cretan artists.[3] The newcomers retained the Ægean fashions and made them known ; on an Egyptian tomb of the XVth century, a Syrian princess is represented with the short-sleeved bodice and the flounced skirt.[4]

Finally, at the beginning of the XIVth century, a people which had not hitherto appeared at all in Syria occupied the coast near Byblos ; this people, which according to a later document came by sea, bore the Homeric name of Danauna, or Danaans.[5]

It will be understood then, that the face of Canaan was very much changed in the XVth century. First of all there came, partly by way of Cyprus, a few Early Mycenæan or L.M.I vases.[6] Soon Ægean importing became very active, and the native potters, abandoning their old types, started to copy the foreign models. About the time when the Danauna installed themselves by the sea a great quantity of stirrup-vases arrived in the towns of the interior ; they were imitated with increasing enthusiasm and on the new shapes there appear water-fowl, conventional lilies, spirals and triglyphs.[7] Crete even comes as a competitor of Cyprus in metal-working ; about 1400, a chief of Gezer owned one of the swords of the horned type forged by the armourers of Knossos. Thus Palestine was transformed, and it too was preparing to receive a new wave of western population when the great invasions came.

---

[1] **XX**, 16.
[2] Sethe, iv, 733.
[3] Ib., 718, 722, 732.
[4] **IV**, 261.
[5] Knudtzon, *Die El-Amarna Tafeln*, i, 513 ; Breasted, iv, No. 403.
[6] Macalister, loc. cit. ; **XC**, 448.
[7] **XI** figs. 210–11 ; **XXV**, 98, 106.

At the extreme point of Asia Minor, at the entrance to the straits, there was an important market, that of Troy. Here was the centre of a Thraco-Phrygian people who had natural relations with the interior of the Asiatic peninsula and with the littoral of the European peninsula. From one side came the copper, silver, and gold of the neighbouring regions, and the rare stones of distant regions. From the other came a traffic reaching to the Danubian countries and Thessaly. The sea invited the Ægeans to come and seek their share of these riches. Very early the Trojan two-handled cup appears at Syra and Orchemenos II.[1] At the end of the third millennium and in the first centuries of the second, during the third period of Troy II, everything in that town bears evidence of the importance of its foreign trade. The potters borrow shapes and motives from the Cyclades and the goldsmiths imitate in gold the " sauce-boat " of the islands.[2] There is active business with the Crete of M.M.I, which sends to Troy the steatite vase and gets from it the *cantharus*.[3] What is more, certain objects of bone of quite peculiar shape and decoration have been found both in Sicily and in Troy.[4] How did such objects cross the Mediterranean ? If it was without transhipment we see the Cretan broker turning up again.

Then comes the Mycenæan Age. The Ægeans are now applying their energies to the whole of Asia Minor, and their enterprises leave no gap between Cyprus and the Troad. There appear in Argolis and Crete, at the same time as the cartouches of the Pharaohs, evidences of direct relations with the masters of Asia Minor, the Hittites—a cylinder found at Tiryns and a sphinx discovered at Hagia Triada together with a scarab of Tii.[5]

In the XVth century the Ægeans appear in the islands which bridge the gap between Crete and Caria—Karpathos, Rhodes, Kos, and Kalymna. In all of these Mycenæan vases abound. In Rhodes, Ægeans coming from Crete subdued the native population and founded the three principal cities,

---

[1] **XXV,** 103, 137.
[2] **X,** 271, fig. 158 ; 279 ; 353, fig. 284 ; cf. 'Eφ., 1899, pl. viii, 11 ; **XX,** fig. 82.
[3] **X,** fig. 373 ; cf. **XX,** figs. 138–9.
[4] **X,** fig. 376 ; BPI. xvii, 1 ff.
[5] *AΔ*, ii, ii, 15 ff. ; MA. xiv, 17 ff.

Ialysos, Kameiros, and Lindos, with many minor towns. The part taken by the Cretans in this colonization was recalled ever after in the names given to the port and to one of the phratries of Kameiros. Legend made the hero Althaimenes the son of Kreteus, named Minos as the donor of an offering to Athene Lindia and placed the tomb of Idomeneus in the island.[1] The tombs of the Rhodian cemeteries are of the Mycenæan type with a rock chamber and an entrance passage. Their furniture is in great part dated by scarabs, the oldest of which is of Amenhetep III.[2] The pottery is purely Ægean ; the decoration includes plants, the octopus, the double axe, and the wild goat, and this last motive is bequeathed to the following period.[3] Weapons, carved ivories, glass pastes and seals are in no way different from what is found at the same epoch in the rest of the Ægean.

The Ægeans did not confine themselves to mere trading on the shore of the mainland either. It is true that we have no proof that they did anything else at Telmessos, Assarlik, or Mylasa, or in the majority of the sites of Lycia, Caria, Ionia, and Aiolis where Mycenæan pottery has been found.[4] But it is probable that their settlement in Pamphylia, the dialect of which is related to that of Arcadia and Cyprus, dates from the Mycenæan Period. In any case a complete colony was founded at Miletos, which bears the name of a Cretan city. Here, below the old temple of Athene, near the port which was under the patronage of the Delphinian god, remains of prehistoric houses were found containing great quantities of Mycenæan pottery, and the necropolis hard by is composed of rock chambers with passages.[5] Persistent traditions and confirmatory remains seem to show that at the mouths of the Caÿster Ephesos, with its satellite island, horned altar, and worship of the bull, and Kolophon, with its domed tombs, were both the seats of Cretan establishments.[6] The same may be said of Erythrai.[7]

[1] Strabo, xiv, 2, 7 ; *Chronicle of Lindos*, i, 17 ff.
[2] **XXX,** 4, 9, 75, pl. E 1–3.
[3] Ib., 1–18, 80 ff., pls. i–xi ; Pottier, *Catalogue des vases du Louvre*, i, 129–72 ; **LXVII,** figs. 465–7, 469, 471–4, etc. ; Kinch, *Vroulia*, p. 232 ff. ; 264 ff.
[4] **XXV,** 96 ; but see **XVII,** 63.
[5] Strabo, xiv, 1, 6 ; Pausanias, vii, 2, 5 ; see Wiegand, *Abhandl. der Berl. Akad.*, 1908, 7, ff.
[6] Cf. C. Picard, *Éphèse et Claros*, 313 ff., 416 ff., 517 ff., 540 ff.
[7] Pausanias, vii, 3, 7 ; cf. C. Picard, 430, 541.

North of Miletos, Mount Olympos by its very name proclaims
that the Northern Achaians, the Achaio-Aiolians of Thessaly,
did not allow the Peloponnesians and Cretans a monopoly of
trade and colonization in Asia. But by way of Phokaia
and Pitane, where the pottery marks the passage of the
Mycenæans,[1] we find ourselves back in the Troad.

As Troy II had attracted the attention of the islanders,
Troy VI drew the Achaians of the mainland. The opulent city
of Priam was for two centuries in continuous relations with
the regions dominated by the city of Agamemnon.   While
obtaining daggers and bowls from Cyprus [2] it continued to
deal with Thessaly ; [3] but it turned above all to Hellas and
the Peloponnese for Minyan pottery, other matt-painted
wares and, still more, cups with feet, stirrup-jugs and Mycenæan
craters. [4]

One detail shows how fiercely the potters of Europe at that
time strove to conquer foreign markets ; a vase found at Troy
is of Trojan shape, but of the same clay as the Mycenæan
vases.[5] The Trojan potters, on their side, to resist this
invasion, imitated the matt painting, the spiral decoration,
and all the new shapes.[6] So too the smiths set themselves
to copy double axes of a long thin type known as Gournia,
and ordinary axes on a model from Mycenæ and Tiryns.[7]
We already have the competition described later by Hesiod,
" between potter and potter," but it is international ; it is
already, on the economic field, the Trojan War. And indeed,
when the Achaians, masters of the trade and the coasts from
the mouths of the Nile to the Hellespont, grow tired of seeing
access to the straits barred to them, Agamemnon need only
send out the call to arms and all, from the Rhodians and
Cretans to the Kephallenians, from the men of Pylos to them
of cold Dodone, will come rushing upon the city of Priam.
Quite a small fact, but a significant one, shows what was at
stake in this war ; [8] at the far end of the Euxine, in the *Hinter-*

---

[1] F. Sartiaux, CRAI. 1921, 122 ; **LXVII,** fig. 489, 491.
[2] **X,** 287.
[3] **LXXXVIII,** figs. 199, 204, 210.
[4] **X,** 291, 287, 283–4, 296 ff.
[5] **XXV,** 96, 103.
[6] **X,** 284–7.
[7] **X,** figs. 377–8 ; cf. **XL,** pl. v, 24.
[8] Leonhard, *Hittiter,* 203, 230.

land of Samsun, at a place named Akalan, excavations have brought Mycenæan pottery to light.

IV RELATIONS WITH THE WEST

The Western seas, like the others, were sailed by the ships of the Ægeans. On this side it was not Cyrenaïca which attracted them most, although there was a regular fair wind to take them to the country of that valued spice, silphium, and the Cretans knew the island of Platea long before one of them conducted Greek colonists to it. In another direction they could collect on the coasts still more precious goods, brought from very far by caravans—amber, and above all, tin. Italy, Sicily, and Iberia thus became the Far West of the Ægeans.

The great sea way which led there was followed in very early days. Indeed it must be noted that the idea of adding tin to copper can only have been conceived in tin-producing countries,[1] and that therefore Crete was in relations with the furthest regions of the Mediterranean before it began to work in bronze. Moreover, Greece is only one day's crossing away from Italy, and the mainland peoples of the earliest times were aware of the fact. The importance of Kephallenia [2] and Leukas [3] in the Neolithic Age is significant, and the rapid development of the two Pyloses at the beginning of the Mycenæan Age is a sure sign that the navigators were already following the coast preliminary to sailing straight across to the peninsula of the Iapyges, in the " heel " of Italy.

From one end of this peninsula to the other, from Manfredonia to Taranto, we see the traces left by these foreign merchants. In the Neolithic Age there were on the eastern coast and far inland potteries related to those of Sesklo, and especially to those of Dimini and Chaironeia. It is possible that some of these pots were made locally, for the land of the Iapyges had nothing in common with the rest of Italy, and, on the contrary, came within the sphere of the Balkan civilization,

---

[1] Cf. Piroutet, An., 1917, 55 ff.
[2] Kavvadias, CRAI. 1909, 282 ff. ;   1911, 7 ff. ;   *Πρ.*, 1912, 115 ff., 247 ff. ; **VII**, 355–73.
[3] Doerpfeld, *Briefe üb. Leukas-Ithaka* ; Velde, ZE. 1912, 852 ff. ;   1913, 1156 ff.

like Thessaly.[1] But in that case the existence of commercial relations between the two shores of the Adriatic is all the more probable, and the resemblances are the more significant. Moreover, these associations continue to exist in the Bronze Age and even extend to idols and weapons ;[2] this long duration cannot be explained by parallel unconnected developments. Towards the XVIIIth or XVIIth century doubt is no longer possible, for the highest stratum at Coppa della Nevigata contains a fairly large quantity of matt-painted wares.[3] Later, too, stirrup-vases and other pots from the same source are found at the two ends of Iapygia, and in the interior ;[4] and in the canton of the Messapians, at Taranto where they abound, they are accompanied by idols of terra cotta.

Mycenæans or Cretans, did the men who came so much to this coast confine themselves to trading ? Archæology by itself does not permit us to infer a permanent settlement. But tradition is quite definite on the point ; it tells us that the Cretans, on their way back from Sicily after the death of Minos, founded the city of Hyria on the territory of the Messapians, or—what comes to the same thing—that Idomeneus, the successor of Minos, came and settled among the Salentines in Messapia, or, yet again, that Iapyx was the son of Daidalos.[5] The modern town of Oria, the ancient Hyria, is just one of those at which excavators have found pottery manufactured after the death of Minos, in L.M.III. Even the name of the Messapians is not Italiot, and their dialect has manifest associations with Eteocretan.[6] Long after the Greek colonization the Messapians kept their curls on their forehead and their cloths embroidered with flowers ; the horns of consecration and the double axe were always part of their religious apparatus.[7] The concordance between all these testimonies and all these facts is so striking that one cannot deny the tradition all historical value.

Did the Cretans or Mycenæans go on from the Ionian

---

[1] Cf. Peet, **LXVI,** 135 ff., 184 ff., 217 ff. ; Fimmen, **XXV,** 111.

[2] Cf. Peet, 423 ; Evans, **XVI,** fig. 90.

[3] Peet, LA. iii, 118 ff. ; Mosso, MA. xix, 305 ff., pl. i–iv.

[4] BPI. xxvi, 285 ff. ; Pottier, loc. cit., pl. xxix, D 1.

[5] Herodotus, vii, 170 ; Strabo, vi, 3, 2, 6 ; Virgil, *Æneid*, iii, 400 ; Pliny, iii, 102.

[6] Conway, BSA. viii, 145, 155 ; Fick, **XXII,** 24 ; cf. von Scala, *Hist. Zeitschr.*, cvii, 8 ff.

[7] Athenæus, xii, 24, p. 523 A ; Cook, TCHR. ii, 187-9.

Islands or Iapygia to the northern end of the Adriatic ? The
Mycenæan vases preserved at Torcello in Venetia may have
been taken there in modern times, and the fragments of
statues and stone slabs excavated at Nerazio in Istria do not
justify any conclusion.[1] After noting some analogies between
the dialects of Venetia and of Iapygia [2] and the presence of
an ingot of eastern copper on the Dalmatian coast,[3] all that
one can say is that it is not at all improbable that sailors
from Pylos came to fetch amber at the mouths of the Po.[4]

Sicily offered the Ægeans a vast field for exploitation,
and they did not fail to profit by it. But here too a distinction
must be made between the epochs defined by Orsi. The
incised pottery of the Sikan or Neolithic Period has some
resemblance to that of Crete ;[5] but a vague likeness between
very simple patterns does not justify us in inferring either
import or filiation.   In the First Sikel or Chalcolithic Period
the simultaneous appearance of vase-painting and metal marks
a change which cannot have been spontaneous ; nevertheless
the vases of the Sikel invaders have only the most distant
affinities with those of Chaironeia.[6] There are not yet regular
relations between Sicily and the Ægean ; but already we find
that precious objects are sent at rare intervals. Of the two
known specimens of a bone ornament decorated with relief
globules one was found at Troy II and the other at Castel-
luccio,[7] and at least one of them must have been carried
in a Cretan ship. Lastly, in the Second Sikel Period or Bronze
Age a great part of the island is in constant intercourse, of
increasing intensity, with the Mycenæan world. From the
district of Catania to beyond Syracuse and in the neighbourhood of Girgenti a dozen sites have yielded, sometimes in
considerable quantities, late Mycenæan [8] vases and bronze
daggers equally similar to Ægean types.[9] All these objects
are found in vaulted rock chambers, the most usual form of
tomb in the contemporary Ægean.

[1] Cf. Dawkins, JHS. xxiv, 125 ff. ; Evans, **XVII,** 95.
[2] Conway, loc. cit., 155.
[3] **XV,** fig. 13.
[4] [Aristotle], *De mirab. ausc.*, 82.
[5] **LXVI,** 135 ff. ; cf. **XXV,** 109.
[6] **LXVI,** 217 ff.
[7] **X,** fig. 376 ; **XX,** fig. 3.
[8] See Pareti, *Studi Siciliani e Italiote*, 325 ff. ; Peet, **LXVI,** 425, 434,
439, 474, 479, 490.
[9] **XVI,** 498, 503–4 ; **VIII,** ii, 199, 214 ; cf. 76–7.

In Sicily, then, far more than in Italy, the archæologist finds all sorts of indications which suggest the establishment of colonies rather than the extension of trade.[1] It is objected [2] that the rock tombs of Sicily are not identical with those of the Mycenæan countries, and that even those sites which are richest in Mycenæan pottery present a still larger quantity of local pottery. It might equally well be added that, although the daggers are generally of Ægean types, these types had gone out of use by L.M.III, and that one at least of the vases is decorated with a motive which had been abandoned at that time.[3] But it is just these differences and these survivals which make it probable that colonies existed which traded with the mother-cities, but lived their own life among the natives of the country and faithfully maintained old customs. Moreover, we have no right to disdain the traditions which mention successive migrations of Cretans to Sicily.[4] Daidalos, it is said, came the first, and then Minos, in pursuit of Daidalos. What Daidalos, who personified the industry and art of Crete, brought with him we see in the painted vases, the weapons, and the jewels laid in the tombs; what Minos did, who personifies its political power, we know from the concordance of Cretan and Sicilian evidence, even more than by the name of the Minoa which lay near Girgenti.

Beyond Italy and Sicily the Ægean current flowed, now much weaker, into the western basin of the Mediterranean. It did not go by Malta, for that island received only a pale reflection of eastern influences, perhaps from Sicily.[5] It was through the Straits of Messina, from ports already familiar to them, that the Ægean mariners ventured forth on more distant enterprises; it was by the whirlpools of Charybdis that they once more braved the monster Skylla. The Cretans knew the Lipari Islands. In all times they sought Aiolian liparite, to make vases and lamps.[6] At first they may have procured it indirectly through Italy or Sicily, but there is no

[1] Evans, **XVI**, 497 ff.; **XVII**, 96; Peet, **LXVI, 463 ff.**; Bethe, *Rhein. Mus.*, 1910, 206 ff.; von Scala, loc. cit., 17 ff.
[2] Cf. **XXV**, 110–11.
[3] **XVI**, 498–9.
[4] *Chronicle of Lindos*, i, 27; Herodotus, loc. cit.; Aristotle, *Polit.*, ii, 7, 2. Cf. Pareti, op. cit., 261 ff.; Pais, *Stor. di Sic.*, 231 ff.; *Studi storici*, 1908, 562 ff.
[5] M. Mayer, *Die Insel Malta im Alt.*, 59 ff.; Peet, **LXVI**, 22–3.
[6] **XX**, 23, 86–7, fig. 55 c.

reason why they should not have gone direct to the spot for
it in Late Minoan times.

We do not find the Ægeans sailing north in the Tyrrhenian
Sea any more than in the Adriatic ; for the analogies which
we may descry between the civilization of the Etruscans and
that of the Ægeans, between the Salii of Rome and the Kory-
bantes of Crete, are sufficiently explained by the long sojourn
of the Tyrrhenians in the East.   But the west-bound ship
touched at Sardinia.   The Cretans came there bringing ingots
of copper marked with stamps certifying their origin and
weight, and probably also jewels ;[1] but these relations remained
purely commercial.   Sardinia could only be a port of call.

Still further away they visited Iberia.   This was an important
market, with its caravans which brought the tin from Britain
to the shores of the Mediterranean.   In the mining region
civilizations of some brilliancy grew up.   The district of Argar
has preserved visible traces of relations with the Cretans.[2]
They brought to the country glass wares, the beads which
they had once imported from Egypt, and now imitated for
export.[3]   The Mycenæans, as ever, followed them.   Both
gave the natives a taste for their painted vases, so much so
that, centuries after they had disappeared in the East, the
Ægean motives, come back from no one knows where, were
still used to decorate Iberian wares and spread from Alicante
to Narbonne.[4]   In the Balearic Isles, the religion of the
foreigners must have made a strong impression, to judge by
the symbols in bronze, double axes, doves and bulls' heads,
and by the horns of consecration.[5]   Even Minoan writing,
according to Evans, was taken up by the Iberians.[6]   If there
was no colonization here, there was at least commercial contact.

As it follows the sailors of Minos archæology confirms all
that ancient legend and learning have given us.   Pausanias,

[1] BPI. xxx, 91 ff. ;   **XXX,** fig. 27.
[2] Siret, *Les Prem. Ages du métal dans le S.-E. de l'Esp.* ;   P. Paris, *Essai
sur l'art et l'industrie de l'Esp. primit.*, vol. ii, 1 ff. ;   Déchelette, **VIII,** ii,
78–84, 786 ;   cf. Evans, **XVII,** 96–100 ;   Dussaud, **XI,** 212 ff.
[3] Evans, **XX,** fig. 352.
[4] Pottier, CRAI. 1909, 990 ff. ;   cf. Evans, **XVII,** loc. cit.
[5] RA. 1897, ii, 338 ff. ;   P. Paris, op. cit., i, 157–8 ; Déchelette, loc. cit., fig. 25 ;
cf. Evans, loc. cit., 97–8.
[6] **XVII,** fig. 44, table viii.

standing half-way between the pre-Hellenic civilization and our own day, recognized the works of Daidalos, first at Knossos and then on the mainland, from Messenia to Bœotia ; he described him sailing from Crete to Sicily, he even spoke of Sardinia.[1] It is not of such rare occurrence for the supreme effort of history to achieve a realization of tradition. It was by trade that the Cretans extended their thalassocracy. No doubt they had to occupy certain points in the Cyclades, to send colonies of merchants and craftsmen into certain wealthy cities of the mainland, to organize ports of call, and to create ports in islands well situated for trade with the natives, generally by agreement with the king of the country. But they were masters of the Mediterranean in that no exchange took place there, so to speak, in which they were not concerned. These carriers of the sea were not content with going everywhere to seek the raw materials which they needed and supplying everybody with the products of their industry and their art. They were suppliers of the civilized nations and barbarous peoples, and they were always ready to act as brokers as well. To Egypt they carried the wood of Lebanon and the ingots of Alashiya, and to Argolis they took Egyptian faience and ivory. They took the copper of Cyprus as far as Sardinia, and distributed the tin of Spain to all the countries which, following their example, were making bronze. Every time that we find, in however remote a site, a bit of bronze or a pot-sherd earlier than the XIVth century, and of eastern origin, we may ask whether, to come so far, that article did not at some moment pass through Cretan hands.

However, from the moment when the Achaians of Argolis, who had given the Cretans such a good welcome, joined in their enterprises, these enterprises quickly changed in character. A young, turbulent, pugnacious race did its apprenticeship in sea-voyages under the guidance of Minoan navigators, but at once wanted to augment the profits of commerce by those of piracy and warlike expeditions. On silver vases buried in the tomb of a Mycenæan ruler, and on a gold ring which some lord of Tiryns wore on his finger, we find depicted scenes of siege, battle, shipwreck, and rape. When the Mycenæans could do without their teachers, they

[1] vii, 4, 5–7 ; viii, 35, 2 ; ii, 4, 5 ; i, 21, 4 ; ix, 3, 2 ; 4, 5–7 ; x, 17, 4.

Q

turned against them, and after Knossos was taken Crete became only one part of a world in which trade went hand in hand with violence and pacific colonization was replaced by immigration by force of arms. All the markets which had been conquered in the past centuries by the mercantile and peaceful policy of one single island, passed to the Ægeans in general, and new markets were added, such as the Macedonian. At the same time bands of adventurers established themselves in Miletos, Rhodes, Cyprus, Syria, Italy, and Sicily. Soon, too, the Achaian tribes united to take from the Dardanians the possession of the straits and the monopoly of dealings with the Euxine. Egypt was quick to see that the theoretical supremacy which it arrogated was compromised. Amenhetep III (1415–1380) had perhaps by his encouragement contributed to the Achaian attack on Knossos ; perhaps too, the victory of Rameses II at Kadesh (1295) over the Hittites and their Dardanian allies had not been unconnected with the Trojan War (about 1280). But immediately afterwards we find in the *Odyssey* Menelaos and Odysseus, with the men of Crete, Laconia, and Ithaca, setting forth from Pharos, sailing up the Aigyptos on ventures which were half commercial and half military, and returning with coffers filled with gold. And, indeed, under Meneptah (in 1229) the " peoples of the sea ", among others the Akai-washa, came and pillaged the Delta, " passing the time in fighting to glut their bellies." [1] More than ever the " isles " and all the " Circuit " are " without rest ", for the great migrations have begun.

[1] Maspero, *Hist. anc. des peuples de l'Orient classique*, ii, 432.

BOOK III

RELIGIOUS LIFE [1]

CHAPTER I

FETISHISM

NOTHING is more tempting and nothing more dangerous at the present stage of our knowledge than to try to establish a relationship between the religion of the Ægeans and those of the peoples living at the same time in Mesopotamia and Egypt. Apparent associations with Babylonia and Nearer Asia are not lacking. Certain idols are of the same type; the predominance of a feminine cult and the *rôle* of the axe, the dove, and the bull, are strikingly characteristic of both civilizations. But as we penetrate further into the past the resemblances, instead of growing closer, become vague or disappear. They are only definite at the last, when the Ægeans are planting their civilization upon the coasts of Asia Minor and Syria. As for the Egyptian religion, the Cretans are obviously indebted to it. Some very old idols from Hagia Triada look as if they might have been shaped on the banks of the Nile. The Cretan demons in their shells are strangely akin to Ta-ueret, the Hippopotamus Goddess, and the Serpent Goddess seems to be related to the Waset worshipped in the Delta. The cynocephalus with arms raised in an attitude of worship is decidedly exotic. The designs of the amulets, the forms of the ritual vases, the symbols, including the *ankh*, the use of the sistrum in processions—all these show the influence exercised by " the most religious of men ", as Herodotus called them. But while drawing on the pious imagery and symbolism of foreigners,

---

[1] Evans, **XIII, XVIII**; G. Karo, *Altkretische Kultstaetten*, ARW. 1904, 117–56; 1905, 51 ff.; Burrows, **VI**, 107–16; Lagrange, **XLII**; Hogarth, art. *Ægean Religion*, ER. i, 141–8; H. Prinz, *Bemerkungen zur altkretischen Religion*, AM. 1910, 149–76; Dussaud, **XI**, 327–413; Hall, **XXXVII**, 145–77.

the Ægeans kept the native character of their own beliefs almost intact. Though their religion has some remote analogies with that of Asia, and many points of resemblance with that of Egypt, it has characteristics of its own and deserves to be studied in itself.

All religions begin with fetishism, the worship of natural objects or animals, of weapons or implements. It had a great influence upon the moral life of the Ægeans. Even after they had given a human form to their divinities, they never ceased to worship, at different times, rough or hewn stones, the axe and the shield, and all kinds of trees and animals.

Sacred Stones.—In its crudest manifestations fetishism attaches itself to stones. Unhewn blocks of stone, particularly on the mountain-tops, are believed to be inhabited by spirits. Occasionally man subjects the stones to a certain preparation, rough-hewing them and setting them up on end. Often he chooses rocks to which nature has given a faint resemblance to a human being or an animal. Still more frequently he piously adopts some stone of meteoric origin, and turns an aerolite into a bætyl, the " dwelling of God ".

All these varieties of fetishism have left traces in historical Greece. Zeus Kappotas, the " god fallen from heaven ", and Zeus Keraunos, the " thunderbolt-god ", were merely stones, and the *omphalos* at Delphi was supposed to be the dwelling of a god. Similar instances are to be found among the pre-Hellenes. At Phaistos, a Neolithic idol was discovered near a mass of magnetic iron.[1] The stalagmite niches in the grotto at Psychro were filled with ex-voto offerings.[2] Meanwhile, the Mycenæans were setting up over their tombs steles which perhaps took the place of standing stones ; they saw the demons pouring libations on heaps of unshaped stones or on pillars.[3] Moreover, with the arrival of the Achaians in Crete, beliefs which had acquired refinement relapsed into their old rudeness. In the Little Palace at Knossos stone concretions, resembling animals or human beings, were placed—a monkey, and a mother with a child.[4] It was at that period that the contamination of an anthropomorphic mythology by aniconic religions gave rise to the legend of the infant Zeus devoured by Kronos in the form of a swaddled stone.

[1] **LVII,** fig. 6.   [2] BSA. vi, 100, 109.
[3] **XIII,** figs. 12–13.   [4] BSA. xi, 10, fig. 4.

The Pillar.—While the bætyl is not found anywhere in Crete, and Evans' "bætylic altars"[1] must accordingly be regarded for the present as sacred tables mounted on little columns, it is none the less true that the cult of the pillar and the column was known in Crete.[2] But this cult had nothing in common with that of the bætyls, which possessed divine power in themselves. It cannot even be traced to a single source, the cult of standing stones. Before it was hewn out of stone the pillar was a squared tree-trunk, and in Crete the double axe is often set up on a gnarled post, a tree-trunk still bearing marks of branches. (Fig. 50.) The cult of the pillar has, therefore, a twofold origin—the standing stone and the sacred tree. For that very reason it has a composite character.

FIG. 36.—Votive colonnade with doves. Terra cotta from Knossos.

It seems probable that in Crete the pillar is not sacred in itself, irrespective of its purpose. It is not an aniconic divinity but an object which derives its virtue from the whole of which it forms a part and, above all, from a special rite. It is true that it has not always an architectural purpose in appearance. In the Repository at Knossos three terra-cotta columns on a single base were found, each surmounted by a dove (Fig. 36).[3] On a cylinder from Mycenæ a man makes the gesture of worship in front of a row of columns.[4] Often, for example on the Lion

---

[1] **XIII,** 112 ff. ; **XVII,** 13 ff.
[2] Evans, **XIII, XVIII,** 63 ff. ; cf. Rouse, JHS. 1901, 268 ; Dussaud, **XI,** 350 ff. ; Lagrange, **XLII,** 169 ff. ; P. Foucart, *Mon. Piot,* xviii, 150 ff.
[3] BSA. viii, 29, fig. 14.
[4] **XIII,** fig. 124.

Gate, animals confront each other on either side of a shaft (Fig. 61). But in all these instances the part does duty for the whole. Elsewhere a single column suffices to represent the *palæstra*, here it stands for the sacred building. The columns surmounted by doves represent, in an abbreviated form, the chapel of the doves which appears on a gold plaque, just as the chapel is connected with the Dove Goddess portrayed on another gold plaque.[1] Similarly, the shaft in front of which the lions face one another is often either supported or replaced by an altar, or the goddess herself is substituted for it.[2] To make the gesture of worship in the presence of a column is equivalent to making it in the presence of the goddess seated in front of a column.[3]

Are we then to believe that the pillar has only a symbolic significance ? No. In the first place the sanctity of the sacred object is communicated to its support. This becomes impregnated with the fluid emitted by the table of offerings and the horns of consecration placed upon it. It assimilates the power emanating from the dove perched on its capital or from the double axe set in the echinus. Still more, it has an energy of its own which it exercises on any kind of a building, for it is a vital function, a magic power, which ensures the balance and stability of a building. The Greeks engraved on *cippi* the charm " Herakles dwells there " ; the Cretans for their part believed the column to be " bound " by knots hanging from the abacus or by ropes fastening lions to the shaft.[4] There has been a great deal of discussion about the sign of the double axe carved on the pillars. There are two standing in the Sanctuary of Knossos, each formed of four blocks. One of them has the double axe engraved on each face of every block, and the other has it on three consecutive faces, while both have it once again on the horizontal face of the upper block.[5] One wonders how the sign could have had any religious significance here, since it was hidden by the plaster coating or covered by the story above. But it is precisely when it was covered up that it best kept its full efficacy, unseen, but present. The pillars, like the foundations and the doors, owe their sacred character to the building-rites observed particularly

[1] **LXVII,** figs. 111, 290.
[3] MA. loc. cit., fig. 51.
[5] BSA. vi, 32–3.

[2] **XIII,** figs. 35–45.
[4] **XIII,** fig. 39.

in the sanctuaries but also in the ordinary houses. Since the tutelary power of the pillar needs renewing continually, it is continually surrounded by pious attentions. Idols and pedestals with the double axe, tables for offerings and sacred vases—everything that can serve to strengthen it is placed at its foot.

Utilitarian fetishism, so well exemplified in the cult of the pillar, leads to the cult of weapons, to " hoplolatry ".

The Double Axe.—In the earliest times stone axes were supposed to be thunderbolts fallen from the heavens and visible habitations of a divine power. The Germans call them *Donnerkeile*, and the Greeks, according to the period, either *keraunia* or *astropelekia*. This supernatural virtue is communicated to the bronze axe and above all to the double axe or *labrys*. " Symbol of the thunderbolt which cleaves the trees of the forest," [1] the double axe is first and foremost an engine of death. As a weapon it lends the human arm a superhuman force with which to master and destroy life. As a sacrificial instrument it is imbued with the divinity which, by its means, is brought into communion with men. It is the sacred tool *par excellence*. That is why, long after iron had been discovered, the bronze axe remained in the hands of the sacrificers. [2] Concentrated in the axe, then, lies all that is divine in the storm, in human blood, and in the sacrificial victims. [3]

From the time that the Cretans discovered metal they fashioned double axes for religious purposes. In E.M.II votive double axes of copper and lead were enclosed in tombs. A large number, of copper and silver, were consecrated in a sacred grotto. [4] Anthropomorphism took the fetish inhabited by the divine spirit and turned it into the image of a deity. The double axe appears floating in the air on its way down from heaven. It hovers over the goddess beneath the sun and the moon, while far away, as a modest complement, a divinity appears armed with spear and shield (Fig. 37). It can be seen dominating the worshippers and the bringers of offerings, [5]

---

[1] F. Cumont, REA. 1906, 282.
[2] Carapanos, *Dodone*, pl. liv ; Furtwaengler, *Olympia*, pl. xxvi ; Perdrizet, *Fouilles de Delphes*, v, 5, 120.
[3] On the cult of the double axe see Evans, **XIII,** 106–12 ; Lagrange, loc. cit., 79 ff. ; Burrows, loc. cit., 110 ff. ; Dussaud, loc. cit., 338 ff.
[4] **LXXXII,** 36, ii, 46–7, fig. 12 ; *AΔ*, ii, ii, 25 ff. ; BSA. xix, 35 ff.
[5] JHS. xxii, 78, fig. 5.

and presiding over grand ceremonies. (Fig. 39.) The importance
of the *labrys* in the worship of the gods is manifested on all
sides in the palace of Minos ; its importance in the worship
of the dead is shown by a neighbouring grave, which was dug
in the shape of a double axe so that it might the more worthily
receive the wonted *simulacra*.[1]

The majority of the specimens which have come down to us
belonged likewise to holy places or to tombs. They were
often *simulacra* of a size and sometimes of a substance unfitted
for practical use. They were made not only of lead and silver
but also of steatite. In the grotto of Psychro and in the little
sanctuary of Knossos they were tiny ; [2] in the palace of Niro
Chani there was one which measured 1·30 metres by ·60,
but it was quite flat.[3] These double axes were fixed by the
handle between the horns of consecration [4] or into a small
pedestal which easily developed into a pyramid with steps.[5]

The association of the double axe with the other elements
of the Ægean religion enables us to observe the progressive
degradation by which the fetish became a mere attribute
of the divinity or even no more than a symbol. One of the
most characteristic facts is the union of the double axe with
the pillar, fetish linked to fetish. In the grotto at Psychro
the double axe adorns the stalagmites, the pillars carved
by nature. Elsewhere it is raised on posts, it surmounts
small columns, it is fixed into the mouldings of capitals.[6]
When it is not apparent to the eye, its incised image is hidden
under the coating of the masonry. Even if it does not over-
spread the pillar it forms part of the sacred apparatus
surrounding it.[7] The connexion of the double axe with the
cult of trees, flowers, and fruits, though less frequent, is still
clearly visible. (Figs. 37, 39.) Thus, the post which supports
it is frequently a gnarled trunk and the crocketed shaft in
which it is fitted fairly often ends in a tuft.[8] The vase-painters
associate an olive-bough with it or mount it on a stalk which

---

[1] **XVIII,** figs. 71–3.
[2] BSA. vi, 109 ; viii, 101, figs. 57–8 ; cf. ix, 280.
[3] **XX,** fig. 313.
[4] BSA. viii, 97, fig. 55, pl. xviii ; ix, 115, fig. 71.
[5] **XX,** figs. 314–15, 317 ; BSA. viii, 300.
[6] Fig. 50 ; BSA. viii, pl. xviii ; x, pl. ii ; **XX,** fig. 320.
[7] **XVIII,** fig. 80 ; **XX,** 427.
[8] **XL,** pl. K, fig. 18 ; JHS. xxiii, 255, figs. 23–4 ; BSA. ix, 115, fig. 71.

blossoms into a fleur-de-lys.[1] But still more often the cult
of the double axe is mingled with the cult of animals. In
Cyprus it is suspended above the horse. In Crete it
accompanies the serpent or the ibex, alternates with the
fish or the triton-shell, and serves as a perch for the sacred
bird. (Fig. 50.)[2] Finally, it is especially associated with
the bull.

There is, in fact, almost always a place for it on the *rhytons*
shaped like bulls. Whether they represent the whole bull
or only its head these libation vessels have between the horns
a hole through which they were filled.[3] The shaft of a double
axe was used as a stopper. In this way the *protome* or forepart
of the bull is consecrated on the intaglios,[4] and in a Mycenæan
tomb which yielded a silver bull's head with a pierced skull
heads of stamped gold surmounted by a double axe were
found in dozens.[5] By the same formalizing process which
occasionally reduces the double axe to a St. Andrew's cross,[6] the
bull's head is simplified to a *bucranium* and the *bucranium*
to a pair of horns. Both *bucranium* and horns, however,
keep the traditional adornment.[7] That is why the horns
of consecration are in their turn pierced in the centre and are
so often represented bearing the sacred implement.

Affinity with the bull is the dominant idea of the cult of
the double axe. The Minotaur is the sacred animal *par
excellence*. The weapon by which his blood is shed and his
horns vanquished takes his warlike strength and procreative
vigour and transmits them to men. Thus the idea attached
to it is essentially that of male force. The female figures
bearing the double axe are not goddesses but priestesses
making the gesture of exaltation or offering.[8] Though the
sacerdotal office was held by women as a general rule, it appears
that they shared it with men in the cult of the double axe.
(Fig. 39.) It is true that the double axe has fairly often a re-
duplicated form, with two blades on either side. (Figs. 37, 50.)

---

[1] **LXXXI**, pl. vii ; **XL**, pl. viii, 26.
[2] MA. xiv, 444, fig. 55, 1 ; **XVII**, fig. 76b ; BSA. vi, 104, fig. 34, 2 ; ix,
115, fig. 71 ; **XLVII**, iii, fig. 514 ; DA. art. *Securis*, fig. 6272.
[3] See **XVIII**, 79–94.
[4] BSA. ix, 114, fig. 70.
[5] **LXVII**, figs. 398–9.
[6] BSA. viii, 102, fig. 60.
[7] **XIII**, fig. 3 ; **LXXXI**, pl. vii.
[8] 'Eϕ., 1900, pl. iv ; BSA. loc. cit., fig. 59.

A bisexual fetish, it has been said ;[1] the germinate axe reveals a twofold presence. This is giving a very profound meaning to a detail of shape. Its religious significance made the double axe necessarily an *objet d'art*. It had to be a thing of beauty. It was made of silver or of bronze plated with gold,[2] it was decorated with various designs,[3] and its edges were scooped out.[4] It is quite as probable that the reason for reduplicating the blades was an æsthetic one. In itself, therefore, the double axe does not suffice to prove the union of the god and the goddess. It is, in Crete as in Asia, a male god or the symbol of a male god. But as such it is very frequently connected with the goddess. It stands beside the female idol or hovers above it. (Fig. 37.) The bird of the goddess perches on the axe of the god (Fig. 50) and the votive robe and sacral knot are both associated with it.[5] It is not the cleft double axe which symbolizes the sacred marriage but the double axe tied with a ribbon,[6] which has its pendant in the shield to which a robe is attached. (Fig. 39.)

Worshipped throughout Crete, the axe of the sacred bull had its chosen habitation in the palace-sanctuary of Knossos. There was the proper home of the *labrys*, the *labyrinth*.[7] There reigned the dynasty of the priest-king who served the Minotaur. This dynasty might, like the priestly family of Delphi, have styled itself the Labryadai or Labyadai. It derived its divine right from the same weapon as marked the elect of Zeus Labrandeus in Caria.

This last association deserves some attention. In Asia the double axe keeps its religious significance with extraordinary tenacity.[8] It is in the hands of the god of Caria and Lydia.[9] The Teshub of the Hittites and the Zeus of Doliche, mounted one on a lion and the other on a bull, both brandish it.[10] All these gods thus appear to be related to Adad-Ramman who in his own country, Mesopotamia,

---

[1] Evans, **XIII**, 108 ; BSA. loc. cit., 101–2.
[2] BSA. loc. cit., 101, fig. 58 ; **LXXII**, fig. 368.
[3] BSA. vii, 53, fig. 15 *a–d* ; viii, 117, fig. 65.
[4] **XI**, fig. 250 ; **LXXXI**, pl. vii, fig. 12.
[5] BSA. viii, 102, fig. 59 ; JHS. xxii, 78, fig. 5 ; **LXXII**, fig. 541.
[6] Cf. **XI**, 340–1.
[7] The word appears to be represented on a seal (**XVII**, 164, fig. 64 *c*).
[8] See Evans, **XIII**, 108–9 ; **XX**, 15 ; Cook, TCHR. ii, 184–94 ; Lagrange, **XLII**, 79–81 ; P. Foucart, loc. cit., 145–75.
[9] Herodotus, v, 119.
[10] Perrot, vol. iv, pl. viii, fig. 279 ; cf. Foucart, loc. cit., 158–60.

has the single axe as his emblem.[1]   At this point one might
be tempted to seek the origin of all these cults in proto-
Elamite Babylonia,[2] supposing that the Lydians and Carians
received it from the Hittites and transmitted it to the Cretans.
But it was known in Crete long before it existed, so far as we
know, in the countries which might have served for its transmission.   In order, therefore, to establish a direct connexion
between the Asiatic and the Ægean cult we must acknowledge
the ethnical relationship of the Cretans and the Chaldæans
and trace back their common beliefs to the IVth millennium
at least.   In any case, the Ægean cult developed on
independent lines.   Even in Asia Minor it managed, during
the migrations, to contaminate the parallel cult which was
prevalent there.   The Zeus Labrandeus of Mylasa and the
Zeus Labranios of Cyprus both got their names from across
the sea.   In one legend we are introduced to one of the Cretan
Kouretes, Labrandos, in the neighbourhood of Tralles where,
moreover, *simulacra* of the *labrys* were discovered.[3]   Another,
still more significant, mentions a Zeus Kretagenes at Mylasa
itself.[4]

The Shield.[5]—Though its antiquity was not so great and its
destiny not so brilliant, the cult of the shield is not unlike
that of the double axe.   As the figure-of-eight shield with
the two lobes was the first object of this cult it might be
supposed that it originally represented the " fiddle-shaped "
idol.   But the cold symbolism of a diagrammatic attribute
would have found no place among popular beliefs and it
could never have passed from the goddess to the god.   In
reality, this is merely a special case of hoplolatry.   The
shield is to be seen in front of worshippers, near chapels,
sacred animals, and trees.   It covers the handles of ritual
vases and adorns bull's head *rhytons*.[6]   Models of it serve
as ex-voto offerings or amulets in sanctuaries, houses, and
tombs.   It is set on the bezels of rings and painted on walls.[7]
It hovers in the air above battlefields and can be brought down

[1] **XLII,** fig. 57.
[2] Heuzey, *Découvert. en Chaldée par Ern. de Sarzec*, 3rd book, pl. xlv,
5, 6 ; Scheil, *Mém. de la dé..g. en Perse*, vi, pl. i ; cf. **XLII,** pl. i.
[3] *Etymologicum Magnum*, s.v. Εὔδωνος ; cf. Perrot, vol. v, figs. 204, 206.
[4] Le Bas and Waddington, *Inscr. d'Asie Mineure*, 338, cf. 394.
[5] Ad. Reinach, RHR. 1909, ii, 161 ff. ;   309 ff. ;   1910, i, 190 ff.
[6] BSA. ix, 72, figs. 49, 50 ;   **XVIII,** fig. 87.
[7] MA. xiv, 593, fig. 55 ;   **LXX,** pl. v.

from the sky, when necessary, by incantations and ritual
gestures. (Figs. 68, 37, 39.) Which divinity will appropriate
the shield when we come to anthropomorphic cults ? On
a painted tablet from Mycenæ the deity in question has a
white skin.[1] It is the goddess, akin to the Athene of Troy
who covered the town with her palladium. But on the
seals representing the goddess and god of war (Figs. 45–6) the
latter alone carries the shield. On a sarcophagus from Milatos
it is a god who, with hair streaming in the wind, descends to
the earth carrying a shield of unusual shape.[2] This sarcophagus
which is of late date, comes as herald of the Kouretes who
beat upon the sacred shields and the Salii who did their ritual
dance with the *ancilia* fallen from heaven.

Sacred Trees.[3]—The worship of trees, *dendrolatry*, is of
universal occurrence. A tree to which a peculiar power is
attributed becomes the symbol of vegetative force, the principle
of all existence. The Cretans, who worship all the powers

FIG. 37.—Offering to the Great Goddess. Gold ring from Mycenæ.

of nature, are careful not to neglect the tree of life. A bush
often appears on the altar or in front of it, or else it is associated
with the horns of consecration, the pillars or the heraldic
animals. Pious homage is paid to consecrated boughs.[4]
The demons in the shells water young plants, the Minotaur

---

[1] AM. 1912, pl. viii.
[2] **XIII,** fig. 50.
[3] Cf. Evans, **XIII,** 100–6 ; Dussaud, **XI,** 345 ff. ; Karo, ARW. 1904,
142–5.
[4] **XIII,** fig. 52, 30–4 ; cf. ib., figs. 25, 29 ; **XX,** fig. 470 ; **XXI,** fig. 162.

loves shrubs,[1] and, even in her boat, the sea-goddess sits
beneath thick foliage. (Fig. 41.) Still more often the sacred
trees stand on open ground. At the foot of a tree, the Great
Mother, with a flower in her hair and flowers in her hand,
is receiving yet more flowers and fruit offered by women
and young girls. (Fig. 37.) The sacred trees, whether
standing alone or in a grove, are generally surrounded by
an enclosing wall, which is sometimes flanked by a small
sacred building. (Figs. 38, 50.) It is before such an enclosure
in front of branches overhanging a wall and altar, that the
apparition of the divinity is evoked (Fig. 47) by prayers,
sacrifices, and ritual dances.[2] Certain low walls with no
coating on the inside must once have enclosed sacred trees.
One has been cleared at Hagia Triada at the end of an esplanade
quite close to the sarcophagus on which is painted the scene
which perhaps took place on that very spot. Another at
Goulas is near a cistern from which, it may be, priests disguised
as demons filled their *hydrias* for watering the shoots.[3]

Though the decorated objects do not always make it possible
to ascertain the kind of trees to which the Minoans offered
their prayers, we can, however, recognize the pine,[4] the palm,[5]
and the olive.[6] The fig, in particular, spreads its broad
leaves over the enclosing walls,[7] and this preference seems
to have been inherited by the Greeks in their worship of
Gaia, Demeter, and Dionysos, and perpetuated in the *ficus
ruminalis* of the Roman Forum. The cypress and the plane-
tree had their devotees before they were made sacred to
Rhea and the divine Europé. From trees and bushes the
cult naturally spread to certain flowers. The lily, the emblem
of royal state, would not have assumed a symbolic meaning
if it had not first possessed a religious significance.

Whether or not it was associated with the Great Goddess
or the Minotaur, dendrolatry gave rise to various ceremonies.
Before the sacred trees the faithful did not confine themselves
to the gesture of worship. By ecstatic dancing they urged

---

[1] **XIII,** fig. 1 ; BSA. vii, 18–19, figs. 7 *a*, *b*.
[2] Cf. ib., fig. 2.
[3] Mosso, **LVII,** 167 ; Evans, **XIII,** 100–1.
[4] **XX,** loc. cit.
[5] BSA. viii, 302, fig. 18 ; **XXI,** loc. cit. ; BCH. 1907, 118, figs. 1–2.
[6] Miniature fresco from Knossos.
[7] Fig. 47 ; cf. **XIII,** 102–4, 128, fig. 2.

on the work of vegetation (Fig. 44) ; by the watering of
plants, a demon lustration, they called down rain ; by the
solemn gathering of the fruits of the earth and the offering
of the first-fruits they addressed acts of gratitude and prayer
to fertile Earth.   But of all ritual dramas the most significant
is the plucking of the sacred tree.   In one instance we see this
act performed by a priestess.   Naked and wild with orgiastic
frenzy, she pulls down the branches and, with her leapings,
shakes off the fruit while a dove takes flight from one altar
and a man on his knees leans over another.[1]   Elsewhere
(Figs. 38–9), it is the man who clutches and bends the branches
and the women who serve as acolytes, dancing or leaning
over the sacred table.   The rite has a funerary character.

FIGS. 38 and 39.—Plucking of the sacred tree.   Gold rings from Mycenæ
and Vapheio.

It celebrates the annual death of vegetation, the winter
mourning of nature.   But while the tree is plucked incantations
and magic movements release the spirits which will enable
other trees to reproduce themselves eternally.

    Sacred Animals.—In very varied forms *zoolatry* has left
undeniable traces in pre-Hellenic religion.   Perhaps the most
arresting of these forms is that which establishes a direct
connexion between man and beast and thus resembles
totemism.[2]   A painting from Mycenæ represents a procession
of persons with asses' heads.   These are not monsters created
by the artist's fancy but men dressed up in sacred skins, etc.,
for the performance of a ritual act ; they can be seen on
a small plaque from Phaistos, each holding a cross (*crux
ansata*) in one hand and making the gesture of worship with

---

[1] MA. xiv, 577, fig. 50.
[2] Cook, JHS. 1894, 81–169 ; cf. S. Reinach. An., 1902, 19 ff.

the other.[1] The demons with skins like saurians, standing
up on two legs and sprinkling water over plants or carrying
libation vases,[2] are in all probability priests or believers.
Similarly, in later Attica, Artemis Brauronia was worshipped
by young maidens disguised as she-bears. The original
object of these religious masquerades was to bring about
a communion between man and an animal divinity.

It is useless to go far afield in search of the cradle of these
beliefs. Obviously it is possible that the procession of genii
carrying the *crux ansata* may have been copied from a sculpture
from Karnak and the scaly hide of the two-footed demons
recalls the Hippopotamus Goddess, Ta-ueret. But we must
not draw exaggerated conclusions from such resemblances.
These borrowings were limited to details of secondary
importance which were quickly naturalized. For its essential
beliefs Crete was indebted only to itself. It had no need
to imitate Waset in order to conceive the Serpent Goddess.
It had practised zoolatry long enough to be able to modify
the conception in its own way, while at the same time following
the universal laws of religious evolution.

The different phases through which animal divinity passed
are particularly well marked in the Ægean in the cult of the
dove. From the earliest times in that region many birds
bore a sacred character, but none more so than the most
amorous and prolific of their kind. If the domestication of
animals can be explained by a purely utilitarian conception,
that of the dove, at all events, points to a period when creatures
were spared and taken care of as objects of worship. In
Crete doves were modelled in terra-cotta from the Neolithic
Age to the end of the pre-Hellenic Period.[3] Before becoming
symbolic ex-voto offerings, these figurines were actual idols
to which martens, the enemies of birds, were offered up as
expiatory victims.[4] In those times the dove possessed
sufficient efficacy to serve as a talisman for the dead.[5] In
the Middle Minoan Period it communicates its power to cult-
objects and to aniconic divinities, spreading its wings over

---

[1] **LXVII,** fig. 438 ; **XI,** fig. 285.
[2] **XIII,** fig. 1, 12–14 ; MA. xiv, 519, fig. 10 *c* ; *AΔ*, ɪɪ, ii, 15 ff.
[3] **LI,** i, pl. xxxiv, 33, 44, 50 ; **XL,** pl. xi, 3, 4 ; BSA. **XX,** 217, fig. 6 *a-f* ;
MA. xxii, 73 ; **XVIII,** fig. 45.
[4] **LVII,** 228 ff.
[5] **LXXXII,** fig. 20, iv, 7 ; 'Εφ., 1898, pl. viii, 16–17, 23.

ritual vases or stretching its neck in order to drink out of
them.[1] Of preternatural size, it perches on the sacred tree
or flies away from the altar.[2] It sanctifies the columns
and chapels upon which it rests.[3] But when no longer alone,
when in conjunction with the Great Goddess, it appears only
as an emanation. The goddess-dove is absorbed into the
Dove Goddess.

When the association of animals with aniconic divinities
ceased to have more than a symbolic value, it lent itself to
designs of figures facing each other. If there is one motive
which seems to have come from Egypt, it is this ; and yet
such groups of two opposed figures were unknown in the
Ægean world at the time when they flourished on the banks
of the Nile, under the XIIth and XIIIth Dynasties, and they
had long vanished from Egyptian art when they were in
favour in Crete.[4] In the Late Minoan Period the heraldic
animals appeared on either side of the sacred tree, the pillar,
the pedestal, or the altar. They include stags, ibexes, bulls,
gryphons, demons, sphinxes ;[5] but most often they are lions.
The rampant beasts above the great gate at Mycenæ (Fig. 61)
are well known. Similar figures abound. In one of the most
remarkable the beasts are tied to a column.[6] But, as if to
leave no doubt about the relations between all the categories
of divine beings, the tree and the pillar were finally replaced
by goddess and god, the tamers of wild beasts.[7]

Zoolatry always brings us back to anthropomorphism
because, behind it, there is always a more or less vague belief
that man is of the same nature as the animals. From the
beginning divinities in human shape ranked among the animal
divinities. Then a moment comes when the beast-gods give
way to them. But the same belief in the common nature
of all beings allows the animals to keep their place beside
the great deities. It is enough for them to take up a subordinate position. According to one theory,[8] it would be
easy to draw the line between the anthropomorphic religions

[1] **XX,** fig. 107 ; **LXVII,** fig. 531.
[2] **XX,** fig. 470 ; MA. xiv, 577, fig. 50.
[3] Fig. 36, cf. 50 ; **LXVII,** fig. 111 ; **XX,** 222, n. 2 ; **XI,** fig. 270.
[4] Jolle, JAI. 1904, 27–55.
[5] **XIII,** figs. 12–14, 30–1, 33–4, 36–7.
[6] Ib., fig. 39, cf. 38, 40–1 ; JHS. xxii, 87, fig. 28.
[7] **XIII,** figs. 43–5 ; BCH. 1921, 511.
[8] Karo, loc. cit., 153 ff.

and the remains of zoolatry : the human aspect would indicate
the god, and any being of an animal form would be relegated
to the rank of demon or acolyte. This distinction is too
sweeping not to be artificial, and too arbitrary to be true.
There is no invariable sign by which divinities and demons
may be recognized. Polydæmonism is a part of polytheism.
Transition from one to the other is imperceptible, and confusion
between the two is easy. Below the principal divinities
in the pantheon of Crete there must have been groups of
secondary divinities and a whole race of demons ; but, since
there are countless intermediate stages, they often elude
a strict delimitation by the indefiniteness of their avatars.

On the one hand, there are innumerable genii of more or
less sacred, but not necessarily divine, character. The whole
of Crete was peopled with good and evil spirits. Each locality
and each family had its own special ones. Genii of the caves
and mountains, woods and springs, they were the Oreads,
the Dryads, the Nymphs, and the Sileni of the pre-Hellenic
peoples. In proportion as unions were formed between
the families, the same thing happened to their genii, which
gradually assumed heterogeneous and composite forms.
These hybrid figures shed their strictly religious significance
and had henceforth only a magic virtue. On the signets
they were both talismans and proofs of identity. Each
individual looked to the sacred orders of the animal kingdom
to supply him with his personal badge. Thus the animals
were subjected, limb by limb, to the most fantastic
transformations.

On the other hand, the two great divinities who embody
the male and the female element in nature wear a purely
animal or a half-animal, half-human form, before they become
definitely human, and adopt animals as emblems. The
goddess appears as a goat suckling the divine child under the
auspices of the swastika [1] or as a woman with a bird's head
making the gesture of benediction. Later, we behold her as
mistress of the dove, charmer of serpents, tamer of lions and
ibexes. (Figs. 42, 46, 62.) The bull, which still retains
something of the god in the *rhytons* modelled in its likeness,
becomes the bull-man, the Minotaur, raising his arms above

---

[1] BSA. ix, 88, fig. 60 ; JHS. xxii, pl. vi, 23.

his worshippers.[1] It was with good reason that the names
" Minelaphos " and " Minokapros " were invented to describe
the stag-man and the boar-man who are to be seen with
holy boughs and horns of consecration.[2] Before the time of
the Greeks, Zeus Velchanos was a cock-god. But like the
goddess the god finished by being conqueror of the feline
race and patron of domestic animals.

When zoolatry had become no more than a survival, what
remained was the sacred character which appears to have been
attached to certain kinds of animals. The dove flutters
over the roofs of the sanctuaries with no fear of man. The
bull cannot be sacrificed to the goddess herself without
expiatory ceremonies. Among this nation of sailors shells.
in plenty are deposited in the sanctuaries and tombs, the
image of the octopus is reproduced indefatigably and the
ships, which do not venture upon the waves without a fish
tied to the prow, have no better pilot than the dolphin.

[1] BSA. vii, 18, fig. 7 a ; JHS. xxii, 78, fig. 4.
[2] Evans, BSA. xi, 19.

CHAPTER II

THE ANTHROPOMORPHIC DIVINITIES

I THE GODDESS

AS we have just seen, belief in fetishes did not exclude divinities in human form. The earliest inhabitants of the Ægean world had female idols. In Crete, as in all countries from the Euphrates to the Adriatic, the chief divinity was at first a steatopygous woman. The most typical specimen is one which was found at Phaistos near a block of magnetic iron. Its protuberant breasts, its enormous flanks, on one of which a cross is cut, and the triangle traced on the pubis all indicate, with an intensity which verges upon the horrible, the deification of motherhood.[1]

The earliest steatopygous idols of terra-cotta or marble are in a squatting position. For this reason specimens at vast distances present striking similarities ; for example, a figurine from Knossos is explained by another from Adalia (Pamphylia).[2] This attitude and this fullness of form are rendered, in idols made of hard material, by a flat surface with rounded contours ; when carved out of marble from the islands, the idols are of the " fiddle-shaped " type. Gradually the goddess assumes an upright posture. Her legs take a vertical position and, in the course of time, become separated.[3] She still continues in the same measure to express procreative force, often by the width of her flanks, her enormous navel, and her triangular *kteis*,[4] and always by the position of her arms held against her bosom to support or press her swollen breasts. In spite of the inevitable evolution of beliefs, in defiance of casual innovations which proved more or less permanent, successive generations faithfully adhered to the traditional type.

[1] **LVII,** fig. 117.
[2] **XI,** figs. 264–5
[3] **XX,** 45–52.
[4] **LXVII,** figs. 331, 333–4, 294 ; **XI,** figs. 269–70.

Was the goddess of the Ægeans naked ? This question has always been answered by yes or no from the standpoint of incompatibility between the type of the naked goddess and that of the clothed one.[1] As a matter of fact the two types co-existed from Neolithic times. The idol from Phaistos displays a tattooed flank. The idol from Adalia, though its navel is visible, has outlines of clothing and ornaments on its chest, arms, and legs. Of two contemporary idols at Knossos one is naked and the other is covered with lines and dots which indicate apparel.[2] How does it happen that two such different conceptions prevailed at the same time ? They are not really irreconcilable. The magic emanations from the divine body exercise their fertilizing influence more readily when nothing is interposed between them and the being who comes to be impregnated with them ; but, on the other hand, they preserve their potential efficacy more easily when they are protected against continual wastage. The second of these conceptions accounts for the women's dress and applies equally well to the goddess. The fact that every indication of sex is not hidden is sufficient to prevent the obstruction of all the sources of fruitfulness. That is why the navel of the idol from Adalia can be seen through its drapery. The Cretan style of bodice which leaves the bosom bare would not have been adopted or retained if it had not corresponded to a religious idea. It was invented for the goddess and was a ritual dress before it became a costume of ceremony. From E.M.III the bust of the goddess is wrapped in a stole with two openings in it through which her breasts appear.[3] Later she wears the very low-necked bodice which was copied by the ladies of Knossos (Figs. 42, 62) except when, by a compromise devised for her sole use, she wears the flounced skirt, but is naked from the neck to the waist. (Figs. 37, 40.)

The goddess is, then, above all, the patroness of fecundity. Such is the magic effect or the symbolic significance of her image. Ideas change but she is always there, with her arms folded below her bosom or with both hands pressed against her breasts. A time comes, however, when the idea of the

[1] Cf. S. Reinach, *Chron. d'Orient*, ii, 566–84 ; W. Mueller, *Nacktheit und Entblössung*, 72 ; Dussaud, **XI**, 368–70.
[2] **XLII**, fig. 48, 3, 4.
[3] **LXXXII**, fig. 34.

benefits emanating from her is expressed by a more ideal gesture, by the raising of the arms in benediction. She presents the edge of her left hand and the whole breadth of her open right hand to the faithful. (Fig. 42.) But, as if to show that the gesture of benediction is intimately associated with the gesture conferring fruitfulness, figurines in one attitude or the other were found all together in the chapel of Hagia Triada, and the largest had its left arm bent across its breast while its right was stretched upwards.[1] The goddess spreads happiness around because it is she who gives life to her children and feeds them at her innumerable breasts.[2] She is the Great Mother.

It is she who makes all nature bring forth. All existing things are emanations from her. She is the madonna, carrying

Fig. 40.—The Goddess of the Rock. Sealing from Knossos.

the holy child or watching over him.[3] She is the mother of men and of animals, too. She continually appears with an escort of beasts, for she is the mistress of wild animals, snakes, birds, and fishes. She even makes the plants grow by her universal fecundity. At the season of first-fruits she sits beneath the tree of life adorned with flowers and holding up her breasts (Fig. 37) ; at the fall of the leaf she claims assistance, by the plucking of the sacred tree, in perpetuating the vegetative force of which she is the eternal fountain-head. (Figs. 38, 39.)

The whole earth is subject to her. Her most venerated sanctuaries are the high places, the caverns and the rocks

---

[1] MA. xiii, 71, fig. 55 ; pl. xi, 2. This is the attitude of the pregnant woman on the *rhyton* from Gournia (**XL,** pl. x, 11).

[2] MA. xiv, 725, fig. 24.

[3] **LXVII,** figs. 332, 338 ; **XI,** 366, 368 ; BSA. xi, 10, fig. 4.

on mountain-tops. Standing on a precipitous peak (Fig. 40) [1] she is Our Lady of the Mountain, especially Diktynna, the Lady of Mount Dikte, as in Greek times she was to become the " Mountain Mother " and particularly the lady of Ida. She reigns over the sea. It is perhaps in her honour that such

FIG. 41.—The Sea Goddess. Gold ring from Mochlos.

quantities of shells are deposited on the altars, at the foot of pillars, and in tombs, and that triton shells are used as vases for sprinkling or as instruments of sacred music.[2] At all events our Lady of the Sea can be seen sailing towards a chapel, while over the boat in which she is seated a tree rises above an altar. (Fig. 41.) [3]

It is from the heavens that the goddess extends her influence over the earth. Astronomical mythology was not of the same importance in the Ægean world as in Chaldæa, but it nevertheless reached a certain development. The succession of day and night and the alternation of the seasons are controlled by her upon whom all life depends. When the sun shines above the altar the servants of the goddess worship it and make offerings of flowers to it as if it were the goddess herself.[4] In front of the horns of consecration and the holy boughs the priestesses call upon the moon or upon a star which forms a pendant to the idol.[5] From the highest heaven the sun and the moon, united in a starry firmament, take their share of the homage rendered to the goddess of whose grace they are a manifestation.[6]

[1] BSA. vii, 29, fig. 9.
[2] MA. xiv, 407, fig. 38 ; 555–6, fig. 40 ; **XL,** pl. xi, 17–18 ; **XIII,** fig. 25.
[3] **LXXXII,** fig. 52.
[4] **XIII,** fig. 41 ; 'Εφ., 1900, pl. iv ; **XI,** fig. 288 ; **XX,** fig. 93 A, *b*, 1.
[5] **XIII,** figs. 59, 25.
[6] Fig. 37 ; JAI. 1916, ii, 147–8, fig. 4.

Queen of heaven and of the earth, the goddess descends
from her ethereal abode to bestow her favours upon men.
The apparition of the divinity poised in flight is a favourite
scene in Cretan art. Sometimes the goddess responds in
person to the incantations, and in the apparition evoked by
the orgiastic dances it is she, her very self, whom we recognize.[1]
Again, when passing through the immensity of space, she
often scorns to clothe herself in a human body, and takes the
form of a bird. Is she not the dove, or at any rate, when

FIG. 42.—The Dove Goddess.   Knossos (L.M.III).

she presses her breasts and lays bare her sacred navel, does
she not transmit all her efficacy to the doves which perch upon
her head and take flight from her shoulders ? [2] The dove
is the emanation of the goddess, the spirit that sanctifies
all beings and all objects upon which it rests. Through the
dove divine possession is effected. The dove was a sacred
bird to other peoples besides the Ægeans. The Pelasgians
watched its prophetic flight above the oak-trees of Dodoné
and the Chaldæans took it as a religious attribute.[3] But the
Ægeans linked it closely with the goddess of love and fruitfulness. It is this particular feature which was to predominate
in the East. The Lady of Paphos clasps the cherished bird
to her bosom as the Lady of Knossos carries it on her head
(Fig. 42) ; [4] she, too, sends it forth, under the combined rays
of the sun and moon, to perch upon the roofs and columns of

[1] Fig. 44 ; JHS. xxii, 77, fig. 1.   [2] Fig. 42 ; **LXVII**, figs. 293–4.
[3] Pottier, BCH. 1907, 244.   [4] BSA. viii, 99, fig. 56.

the little shrines.¹ A mould from Asia Minor represents
on one face the goddess and, on the other, some columns
with pigeons billing.² In Syria the sacred bird was adopted
by Derketo at Ashkelon and by Astarte at Hierapolis. When
it took flight, in the wake of the Phœnicians, for Carthage,
Mount Eryx, and Sardinia,³ the madonna of Crete must have
recognized it as it passed by.

From the celestial and terrestrial worlds the care of the
universal Mother spreads to the subterranean world. Her
omnipotence implies a chthonian power. Just as she descends

FIG. 43.—The Repository Hoard from Knossos.

from ethereal regions, she comes up from infernal regions.
She is the dove but she is also the serpent. The serpent
accompanies her at all times, in all places. At Knossos in
both palaces, at Gournia, at Prinias, from M.M.III to the
Hellenic Period, the goddess appears covered with reptiles
that climb up her arms and bust, coil in her hair, and rear
themselves over her head.⁴ The reptile, like the bird, appears
in the hands of the priestesses and the bringers of offerings,

---

¹ Perrot, vol. iii, figs. 20, 142, 179.
² **XI,** fig. 270.
³ Cf. Miss Harrison, TCHR. ii, 155 ff.
⁴ Fig. 62; **XVIII,** fig. 84; **XL,** pl. xi; AM. 1901, pl. xii; cf. BCH.
1921, 511.

on the sacred vases and on the chapels.[1]   In order to estimate
the religious significance attached to the serpent, one has
only to glance at the objects placed round the goddess who
holds it (Fig. 43, Pl. IV, 1)—flowers and fruits, cows and goats
suckling their young, shells and flying fishes ; all the products
of nature.   The ritual dance which calls the goddess down
from heaven brings the serpent out of the earth amid clumps
of lilies.   (Fig. 44.) [2]

FIG. 44.—Ritual dance.   Gold ring from Isopata.

But, from heaven to earth and from earth to hell, the
goddess who creates day creates night also ; the goddess
who brings fertility is she who brings destruction ; the goddess
of life governs birth and death.   She produces and she destroys.
She, and she alone, brings into play all energies, beneficent
or harmful.   Her place is marked in the tombs as in the
sanctuaries.   Men endeavour to turn this deadly power
against their foes.   She is the goddess of war, the Promachos
(Fig. 46) ; she is armed with spear and bow and escorted
by the lion.[3]   Hunting, like warfare, is included in her empire.
She is queen of all the wild beasts, and when she spares them
she tames them.[4]   Yet even in death the Great Goddess
preserves life.   She makes the plants perish only to give
them new strength.   The festival at which the branches
of the sacred tree are plucked is intended to give an impulse
to the growth of all trees, to coax the vegetative force and to
ward off sterility.   The tree of life is planted over the graves,

---

[1] **XX,** fig. 494.
[2] **XVIII,** 10, fig. 16.
[3] BSA. ix, 59, fig. 37.   Cf. our Fig. 40 ;   BCH. loc. cit.;   **LXVII,** fig. 426, 11.
[4] **XXVIII,** pl. xxv ;   JHS. xxii, 77, fig. 3 ;   MA. xiii, 45, fig. 42.   See
Callimachus, *Hymn to Artemis*, 190.

and the holy images that protect the dead are once more those of the procreative goddess. In the infinite sphere of her powers and rights she remains one and the same. She makes the dead breathe again ; she kills and restores to life.

All these powers were only united by degrees in the Great Goddess. It is even probable that she never held them

FIGS. 45 and 46.—The War God and Goddess. Sealings from Knossos.

all at once in the same sanctuary. She combined them in different ways. According to period and place she came forward more especially as goddess of heaven, earth, or hell, of the mountain or the sea, of beasts or plants, of virginity or fecundity, of life or death. By looking at all the scenes in which she appears one can glean some idea of the abundance of myths that sprang up. A few names have survived which seem to have defined the principal aspects of the multiform goddess and to have transmitted to the Greeks her most celebrated legends—Diktynna, Britomartis, and Ariadne.

Diktynna, the goddess of the high places, is essentially the Great Mother. When she descended to the plain she remained none the less Our Lady of the Mountain. The last inhabitants of prehistoric Knossos still worshipped her in the form of an uncarved stone. When the Greeks came to know her they let her keep her old names of Great Mother and Diktynna in Crete and even in Laconia ; [1] but elsewhere they gave her other names, when they did not confine themselves to identifying her with their own Hera or their Demeter. Perhaps it was after her example that the Gaia of Delphi,

[1] *Mus. Ital.*, iii, 736 ; Herodotus, iii, 59 ; Strabo, x, 4, 12 ; Pausanias, iii, 24, 9.

before Apollo took her place, was represented in the form of a dragon and had her seat on the *omphalos*. At any rate, she was called Rhea. This goddess, the ruins of whose "house" were shown at Knossos near a sacred wood,[1] was always Oreia, the Goddess of the Mountain. She still kept her bodyguard of lions and continued to receive the homage of the dancing priests, the Kouretes. Even the stones which represented the Mother and the Child in the Fetish Shrine are strangely recalled to mind in the celebrated myth which tells how Kronos had resolved to devour his sons, and how Rhea, having brought Zeus into the world, hid the new-born child in a grotto and brought the god a stone dressed in swaddling clothes. Lastly, we have every reason to suppose that the Mother Goddess of the Cretans, like the Serpent Goddess of the Egyptians, was the patroness of childbirth, and that it is she who is represented, with details of a realism which would be hideous were it not sacred, by the *rhyton*-idol of Gournia.[2] Thus she became the Eileithyia of the Greeks, she who had a sanctuary, at the time of the *Odyssey*, in a cave near Knossos and was the object of a cult which passed from Crete to Delos.[3]

By the side of their Demeter, the Ægeans had their Kore ; by the side of the divine mother, the divine daughter Britomartis.[4] Her name signifies the "sweet maiden", the "good maiden". Goddess of youth and love, she has, nevertheless, like Diktynna, a twofold aspect, celestial and chthonian. She is already the Kore-Persephone, who dwells alternately on earth and in the underworld. She retained her original personality for a very long time. The Greeks kept her wherever the Minoans had settled, and down to the time of the Roman Empire. They generally assimilated the "sweet maiden" to the chaste Artemis. Nevertheless, a whole cycle of myths shows Britomartis pursued by the amorous Minos, Europé carried away on the back of the Bull God, Pasiphaë yielding to him and giving birth to the Minotaur, and Kore wooed, carried off, and seduced by the divine lover. The essential act underlying this cult was a hierogamy or sacred marriage. This is the link between

[1] Diodorus, v, 66 ; cf. 77.
[2] **XL,** pl. x, 11.
[3] *Odyssey*, xix, 188 ; Demangel, BCH. 1922, 58 ff.
[4] See Glotz, *Les Ordalies dans la Grèce primitive*, 40 ff.

the Cretan goddess and the Aphrodite-Astarte of Kythera and Cyprus and the Syrian Goddess.

This was also the way in which the virgin and the mother were fused into one Britomartis-Diktynna. A myth explained how the one was transformed into the other. Pressed hard by Minos, Britomartis threw herself into the sea and, on being rescued from the waters, received the name of Diktynna. If one admits the ritual significance of the leap into the sea, an ordeal by which virginity is established, the meaning of the myth is clear—the Virgin Goddess is also the Mother Goddess. They are two and they are one. Fused into a single essence they are worshipped under the name of the " very sacred " Ariadne.

II THE GOD

With the Great Goddess, therefore, a god is associated, either as son or lover, and is of a standing inferior to her own. The Egyptians make Isis the wife of Osiris and the mother of Horus. The Phœnicians place Adonis beside Ashtoreth. In Phrygia, Cybele is worshipped with Attis. The pre-Hellenes acknowledged, but not until a fairly late period, a god subordinate to the goddess. He is rarely in evidence and seems specially intended to make plain her character of the fruitful mother. This religion might be called a *dual monotheism*.[1] The expression is incorrect, in that it dissembles the undeniably polytheistic character of this religion, but it aptly fixes the relative positions of the god and goddess.

No male figurine exists which can be said to have been an idol of the Cretan god. It was only in the Achaian period that the people of Knossos placed in the Fetish Shrine a natural concretion in the form of a child with another in the form of a woman. But the god is known to us from representations on objects of the Minoan period and from the myths of the Greeks. Born of Mother Earth, in a grotto, he was fed by the Bee Goddess, Melissa, and the Goat Goddess, Amaltheia. A seal shows, beneath a hand of justice, the divine child being suckled by a goat. On another we see the goat beneath a gammadion.[2] In the side of Mount Aigaion (the Mountain

---

[1] Hogarth, ER. loc. cit., 143. [2] BSA. ix, 88, figs. 59–60.

of the Goat, consecrated to Zeus) is the mouth of the sacred grotto of Psychro, where a vase was found on which goats alternate with double axes.[1]

The satellite god resembles the goddess, feature for feature. He has celestial power and was in later times called Asterios. He descends from heaven to earth with streaming hair.[2] He subdues men and animals. He is the master of the lions, whether he holds them at arm's length like Gilgamesh of the Chaldæans or makes them his escort in war,[3] and when he soars through the air with bent bow, brandished spear, and shield before him (Fig. 47), he brings blindness, terror, and defeat. But chiefly he bears fecundity with him, in himself. He is the beneficent rain that refreshes and quickens the earth. He is moisture, the principle of all existence. He is to become Zeus. He is already Hyakinthos, the father of the virgins who die to secure life. But, for choice, his creative vigour takes an animal form.

As animal, he is the bull ; as man, he is Minos ; as animal, man and god as well, he is the Minotaur. This conception of the divine bull existed in Asia in the IVth millennium. An Elamite cylinder represents him standing with hands with three fingers laid across his breast.[4] In Crete the cult of the bull was of such antiquity that in the Sub-Neolithic Period the animal was already symbolized by the horns of consecration and may already have been represented as a half-human monster.[5] At a very early date, then, and doubtless before the Cock Zeus or Velchanos, the Minotaur was the god full of male force. His chief sanctuary was the palace of Minos itself, and those who crossed the threshold were seized with sacred terror as he rose above them, bellowing and dreadful to behold. Like all divinities he demanded victims. It was not, however, the mythology of the Cretans but the legends of stranger peoples that made him into a god thirsting for human blood. The only sacrifice was the immolation of the god himself by those who wished to commune with him and to receive his force into themselves. To the

[1] Ib., vi, 104, fig. 34, 2.
[2] Figs. 37, 47 ; **XIII,** fig. 50 ; AJA. 1921, 312.
[3] Fig. 45 ; MA. xiii, 44, fig. 40. M. Charles Picard, however, thinks that the animal in our Fig. 45 is a dog.
[4] **XLII,** fig. 66 *a* ; cf. 65.
[5] **XX,** fig. 38 A ; cf. 16 *c*.

Minotaur, therefore, bulls were offered and, since the *labrys* was specially consecrated to him, his dwelling was the labyrinth *par excellence*. But in the great festivals the ritual offering was preceded by a *corrida*, in which the toreadors whose lives were exposed were perhaps chosen from amongst the prisoners and slaves of both sexes.

Eternally young, the procreative god is associated not only with the Mother Goddess who bore him but also with the goddess young as himself. He is the son and he is the lover. As a bull he carries off Europé or, in a union with Pasiphaë, begets the Minotaur. As Minos he pursues Britomartis. Later he was to disguise himself as Dionysos in order to seduce Ariadne. Besides making women fruitful he fertilizes the

Fig. 47.—The apparition of the god. Ring from Knossos.

fields. Together with the goddess he distributes prosperity, since he is the lord of creative love and of eternal life. Nevertheless he dies, and in after times the Holy Sepulchre is pointed out on Mount Iouktas even as the grotto of the Nativity on Mount Ida. He dies, but to be born again, and the Kouretes who protected his childhood help him by their dances and the clashing of their shields to rise from the grave in the rebirth of nature. That is why the Man God, with his hands on his breast, imitates the gesture of fructification, and the Bull God, before the faithful who beseech him, extends or lifts his arms in blessing.[1]

[1] XX, fig. 532; JHS. XXII, 77–8, fig. 4; BSA. vii, 18, fig. 7 *a*; 133, fig. 45.

III THE TRINITY AND THE CROSS

While the subordination of the god to the goddess gives the
Ægean religion the appearance of a "dual monotheism",
the part played by the number three is so important that some
have seen in it a trinitarian character. Without supporting
the daring hypothesis of a religion which should have proclaimed the dogma of the Trinity before the letter, one can
safely note a large number of facts which prove at least that
the number three was held sacred by the Cretans. Is it
because earth, air, and sea, or earth, heaven, and hell gave
a threefold aspect to the divinity? At any rate the trees and
branches and the sacred shields and pillars often appear
in threes, witness the columns planted on one base and
sanctified by doves. (Figs. 36, 47.) On a bronze tablet found
in the grotto of Psychro, a man is worshipping in front of
three horns of consecration.[1] In the sanctuaries, division
into three parts is the rule. The chapels of Phaistos and
Knossos are composed of three rooms in a straight line. The
little sacred buildings in the pictures have three portions.
Frequently, the tables of offerings contain a triple cavity,
or are adorned with three, six, or nine bulls. The libation
vases are made up of receptacles in threes or multiples of
three,[2] and one has been discovered with six receptacles and
three human figures.[3] Since Homer's Achaians still used
similar vases for triple libations,[4] we may suppose that the
pre-Hellenes sacrificed three victims and poured out three
kinds of liquid in honour of the deities. Of all the emblems
proper to the goddess of vegetation, the one which she favours
most is the stalk bearing three flowers, the flower with
three points, the lily with which she adorns her brow and
which consecrates priestesses and kings. Moreover, on the
rhytons the bull's head has a trefoil on the forehead or three
crosses on the forehead and cheeks.[5]

The cross is, indeed, a familiar symbol in Ægean religion.[6]

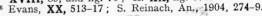

[1] **XX,** fig. 470.
[2] **XIII,** fig. 7; MA. xii, pl. viii, 5; xiv, pl. xxxvi, p. 711; fig. 11; BSA.
xii, 11, fig. 1.
[3] BSA. loc. cit., fig. 3.
[4] *Odyssey*, x, 509; xi, 127; cf. BSA, loc. cit., fig. 1.
[5] **XVIII,** 89, and fig. 70; cf. **XX,** fig. 370.
[6] Evans, **XX,** 513–17; S. Reinach, An., 1904, 274–9.

The Latin cross, the Greek cross, the St. Andrew's Cross
and the gammadion or swastika all exist in Crete. At Knossos
the repository in which the Serpent Goddess was found
contained a marble cross with equal arms, another of faience,
and a seal-impression of an elongated cross. The marble
cross, which is 22 centimetres in length and breadth, is rough
underneath, which shows that it was fixed on some wooden
object or on a wall. (Fig. 43.) There can be no question
here of a purely ornamental design. The cross marks the
forehead of the bull as, in Egypt, it marks the flanks of the
cow Hathor. It divides the sun into quarters or alternates
with it. We see it formed of two double axes placed at right
angles.[1] Here again the mind inevitably turns to Syria.
Must we believe that the emblem of the cross was brought
to Gaza with the worship of Zeus Kretagenes and that it found
its way into Palestine along with so many other elements
of Ægean civilization ? We may hesitate. Cruciform signs
were known in the East, too, at an early date. In Elam
crosses of all kinds have been found,[2] and the swastika appears
everywhere from India to the Troad. But in Crete alone the
cross is more than a mere talisman and appears in close
connexion with the divinity. Twenty-five centuries before
Ezekiel speaks of people who have the *tau* or cross of
St. Anthony cut on their foreheads, the Neolithic idol from
Phaistos bears the sacred mark on its sides. In Cretan
mythology already the sign of the cross is handed down from
the Mother Goddess to her son. The sealing on which the
swastika gleams above the divine goat has its pendant in
another on which the goat is suckling the divine child.[3] Before
it became merely prophylactic, the sacred sign had had a
profoundly mystical significance in Crete. It was only
reverting to its original meaning when, in a new religion,
it came to be the symbol of the Son of God.

---

[1] **XX,** figs. 370–2, 427 *a*, 194 *b* ; **XXI,** pl. xiii, 6.
[2] Gautier and Lampre, *Mém. de la déleg. en Perse*, **VIII,** 59 ff.
[3] BSA. ix, 88, figs. 59–60.

CHAPTER III

PLACES OF WORSHIP [1]

AS long as men worship natural objects the sites of their religion are determined by the actual position of such objects. In Crete they were spaces open to the sky, the ground where sacred trees sprang up, the high places, and the slopes from which fruitful waters gushed. When the anthropomorphic divinities took possession, the original places of worship were consecrated to them with scarcely any outward change. On the summit of Mount Iouktas a thick stratum of ashes marks the spot where generation after generation bowed before the holy rocks and sacrificed victims to them, ere others came who were to erect near by a shelter for offerings dedicated to the goddess, and, later, yet others who believed they were in the presence of the grave of Zeus.

Caves in particular were holy places. They were inhabited by spirits and gave access to the underworld. Their stalagmites were sacred pillars. Each of the mountain-groups which thrust their heads up in different parts of Crete had grottos which attracted the faithful.

Mount Aigaion is compact of mighty masses and weird crags like the scenery of a fairy-tale. It was there that the infant Zeus was to be housed in a cavern and reared by a she-goat. In the Early Minoan Period people climbed up to the grotto of Arkalochori bringing their double axes.[2] From the Middle Minoan Period the cave of Psychro [3] was the most popular. Nineteen metres long and 14 wide, it opened towards the East and ended in the dim gleams of a subterranean lake. Little by little the waters disappeared among the deep fissures, and in the Late Minoan Period one

---

[1] Hogarth, ER. loc. cit., 145 ff.; Dussaud, **XI,** 327 ff., **354** ff.; von Lichtenberg, **XLIX,** 54–7, 120–4; Hall, **XXXVII,** 145 ff.

[2] Hatzidakis, BSA. xix, 35–47.

[3] Halbherr and Orsi, *Mus. Ital.*, 1888, 905–12; Hogarth, BSA. vi, 94–116, pl. viii–xi; Karo, loc. cit., 118–24; Toutain, *Études de mythol. et d'hist.*, 160 ff.; Dussaud, **XI,** 328 ff.

could descend by a precipitous passage into a second cave. This was the holy of holies. The mysterious twistings of this double grotto and its crystalline columns were witnesses of a cult faithfully practised for more than 1,000 years. Round a mass of rough stone the blackish remains of ashes mixed with calcined horns and bones mark the place where oxen, sheep, and goats were sacrificed. The ground was strewn in all directions with little portable altars, tables, and vessels for offerings and ritual vases. In the natural niches formed by hollows in the rock countless ex-voto offerings were placed, such as weapons, including double axes and shields, articles of feminine adornment, gems bearing the likeness of bulls and goats and, finally, hundreds of figurines representing the goddess, worshippers of both sexes, animals, and the chariots to which they were harnessed.

The plateau of Skoteino the Gloomy, 7 miles from Knossos, is riddled by several caves. The largest of them has about its mouth rocks streaked with black and red and, inside, stalagmites pointing up into a spacious vault and a network of ascending and descending galleries. It was likewise visited by pilgrims from the Middle Minoan Period onwards.[1]

Near the centre of the island rises Mount Ida. To the south, in a magnificent landscape easily accessible from Phaistos, the cave of Kamares, divided into two parts, was used for religious purposes from the Early Minoan and throughout the Middle Minoan Periods. Besides vases of the type to which it has given its name, it contained a hearth of stonework and the bones of victims.[2] To the north, facing Knossos, the great cave of Ida was also to serve as a sanctuary but only from the XIth to the IXth century when the Kouretes were to clash their cymbals and shields there, leaping round Zeus.[3]

These are the most celebrated caves. We do not yet know where to place that of Mount Dikte. It must be somewhere on the East side, not far from the rock-shelters discovered at Petsofa and Upper Zakro. Many others existed in Crete, such as, in the neighbourhood of Knossos, the grotto of Eileithyia which was visited up to the time of the *Odyssey*.

---

[1] **XX,** 163.
[2] Taramelli, AJA. 1901, 437 ff.
[3] Fabricius, AM. 1885, 59–62 ; Halbherr, *Mus. Ital.*, loc. cit., 689–768 ; Orsi, ib., 769–904.

The remainder of the Ægean region possessed similar places
of worship.[1] On the island of Amorgos ritual vases and
offerings were placed in clefts in the rocks. On Delos, Kynthos
was hallowed by a rock shrine. On the mainland the caves
of Pan had most of them a prehistoric past.

Remote from the main roads, these grottos were only
visited at solemn festivals when pilgrimages were made to
them. Where were religious celebrations usually held?
There were no great edifices specially consecrated for the
performance of rites and able to accommodate large con-
gregations. Temples in the Greek style have not been
found on any of the pre-Hellenic sites. But it was easy to
arrange places of worship inside or near the inhabited centres,
in the palaces and in the humblest houses.

It sufficed to set up an altar out of doors on an esplanade
or in a court, or indoors in a room. At Phaistos, in front
of the principal entrance to the palace, a heap of ashes,
cinders, and calcined bones, with which a few sacred objects
were mingled, marked the spot appropriated from time
immemorial to a public altar.[2] When the Second Palace was
built, a corner of the Central Court was reserved for a little
construction with steps upon which offering-tables, libation
vases, and statuettes were placed. It was a household altar.[3]
At Knossos the large esplanade in front of the palace was
furnished with two rectangular altars measuring about 1·90
by 1·70 metres; another, slightly larger, was found in the
South-West Court; a fourth, measuring 2·25 by 2·75 metres,
stood in the Central Court. This last one was equi-distant
from the two wings in the First Palace. When in the Second
Palace one of the wings was brought forward they dared
not lay hands on the altar but, scorning symmetry, left it
where the gods had fixed it.

These altars were of various shapes. We have a votive
specimen in terra-cotta in the form of a cube with projecting
mouldings and four pairs of horns on top. In a picture
representing a similar cube ten courses of stone can be seen.[4]
In Argolis the altars placed in the courts were of a different
shape. In the palace of Tiryns a low square of stonework
protects a round pit for offerings like one which was found

[1] Cf. Fimmen, **XXV,** 67.   [2] Pernier, MA. xiv, 345.
[3] Id., ib., xii, 57–62, 126 ff., pl. viii, 5.   [4] **XX,** fig. 166 A; **XIII,** fig. 2.

above a tomb in Mycenæ.[1] Besides altars of stonework the Cretans had others which were quite different. These are known to us chiefly from representations on objects. They consisted of tables mounted on a stand or, more frequently, on five little columns, one being in the middle. If but few stone fragments of altars remain, the reason is that they were generally made of wood. Lastly, in order to facilitate the ceremonies of the cult, there were portable altars for offerings which, for greater lightness, had slightly concave sides. This concave type can be found along with the cube among the ex-voto offerings from Knossos.[2] It appears at Mycenæ under the base of the Lion Gate.[3] Very often simple tables of clay, slightly hollowed in the middle, were considered sufficient. A good proof of the extent to which movable altars were used is the fact that there was one in the rustic house at Chamaizi and that at Nirou Chani one of the many rooms of the palace contained forty-four such altars.[4]

Plots of ground that had been consecrated or struck with a taboo were girt by a little surrounding wall, a *peribole* forming what the Greeks called a *temenos* or an *abaton*. These slender constructions were raised round sacred trees, near springs, along rocks, on mountain-tops, and over tombs. There again wood was constantly used. That is why the unanimous testimonies of countless representations are rarely confirmed by actual relics. Nevertheless, the high places undoubtedly reveal traces of constructions which were made after the ashes from the sacrifices had accumulated on the ground. Certain objects, too, portray enclosures of sacred trees along very steep slopes and perhaps even on the highest point of a mountain.[5] Still more of them existed on the plains, in towns and near burial places. Beside the chapel in Gournia there is a wall only 45 centimetres above the ground. It doubtless served the same purpose as a later rectangular enclosure at Goulas [6] and formed, in fact, the boundary of a *temenos*.

Little covered buildings had to be constructed to shelter

---

[1] Fig. 22 ; cf. **LXVII,** figs. 102–3.
[2] **XX,** fig. 166 H ; cf. **XIII,** fig. 25 ; **LXVII,** 658.
[3] Fig. 61 ; cf. **LXVII,** figs. 102–3.
[4] BCH. 1920, 400.
[5] **XIII,** fig. 2 ; cf. our Figs. 47, 40.
[6] **XIII,** 100–2.

sacred objects and pilgrims' gifts. We can easily obtain
an idea of these little buildings from the frescoes and from
a gold plaque.[1] The foundation was of stone and the masonry
was reinforced by small beams and coated with painted
plaster. The main portion in the centre rose above two
small wings, one at least of which was skirted by a bench.
Each of the three portions had one or two columns set up on
horns of consecration, and there were other horns on the roof.
The little building painted on a fresco from Knossos (Fig. 48) [2]

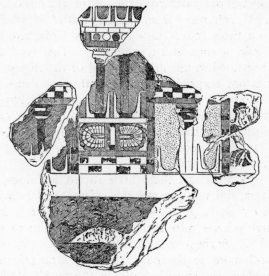

Fig. 48.—Sacred building.   Fresco from Knossos.

is situated within a walled space planted with trees and crowded
with people. The cult required similar constructions on the
heights which were only climbed on the days of the great
festivals. The ex-voto offerings from Petsofa, consisting
of clay figurines, were found at a height of 270 metres on a
levelled terrace. On the summit of Mount Iouktas a *temenos*
surrounded by a " Cyclopean " wall was the repository of
similar offerings and of all kinds of sacred vases.[3]

On these patches of levelled ground we must imagine some
sort of construction like the one outlined behind Our Lady

[1] Fig. 48 ; **LXVII**, fig. 111.
[2] **XIII**, pl. v ; cf. **IV**, 61.
[3] **XX**, 151 ff., 161–3.

of the Mountain. (Fig. 40.) Even in the cities the public chapels were erected on the highest ground. The people of Gournia climbed up a paved road with steps worn by the feet of the faithful in order to arrive at a shrine of rustic simplicity, not more than 3 by 4 metres, with a floor of beaten earth, a tripod for offerings in the middle, and a Serpent Goddess in one corner—a clumsy statuette surrounded by doves, horns, and ritual vases.[1] At Koumasa, beyond the burial-ground and at the top of a hill, there was a little shrine of several compartments, the roof of which was supported by a single column. Here the apparatus of religion was limited to a table of offerings and a few idols, two of which were aniconic, a cone and a cylinder.[2] This type of sacred building remained in use until the end of the Ægean civilization. It is not surprising, therefore, that we come across it again in Homeric Troy. Hector sacrifices victims now on the peaks of Ida, now at the highest point in the city ; the *neos* of Athené on the Acropolis is usually locked, and the priestess opens the door to women who wish to bring offerings to the image of the goddess.[3]

These enclosures and these little sacred buildings, like the public altars, did not prevent the existence of private cults. From the caves the goddess followed ordinary folk into their houses and princes into their palaces. The room in which the tripod for offerings or the libation table was placed became sacred, still more so the halls specially arranged in honour of the goddess, the chapels built on the model of the public sacred buildings, and the pillared crypts. Even in a little port like Pseira the poorest houses have a corner set apart for worship and the richest contain a hall fitted with precious vases, shells, and bull's head *rhytons*.[4] What must it have been like in the palaces of the kings and particularly of the priest-kings ?

At Phaistos [5] the terrace on which the public altar stood gave access to two apartments situated outside the facade wall and communicating at the back with a third, which cut into the wall. It is a chapel with the Holy of Holies, the old

---

[1] Cf. **XXXIX,** 97–8.
[2] JHS. xxvii, 293.
[3] *Iliad*, xxii, 169–72 ; vi, 86–9, 192, 298, 303–5.
[4] **LXXXI,** 22–6.
[5] MA. xiv, 405–12 ; cf. BSA. xi, pl. vi.

chapel of the First Palace. It was provided with an outer
annexe, an independent cell with its own door. The construction of this set of rooms, which are of small stones and
clay, clashes with the monumental entry which rose beside
it when the Second Palace was built. The inner room is
only 3·62 metres by 2·57. Along three of the walls there
are low benches of gypsum coated with stucco, on which
the sacred objects were set out. The bench on the east side
stops short in the middle of the wall before a cache which
contained Kamares vases. Near the middle an offering-
table of terra cotta, 48 by 55 centimetres, hollowed in the
centre and adorned with spirals and oxen along the edges,
was fixed in the ground.[1] Lamps, grinders for preparing
the sacred barley, dishes, stone cups (one of them blackened
by fire) and calcined bones all show for what this place was used.

In the palace of Knossos a large part of the west wing
formed the sacred quarter in which the king exercised his
priestly office.[2] Here, there are two rooms, 3 metres
broad and from 4 to 5 metres long, in which two thick
pillars stand. The stone blocks of these pillars are incised
with the sign of the double axe, seventeen times on one pillar
and thirteen times on the other. In the floor two stone
cists contained the richest ritual furniture which pre-historic
Crete has left us—faience statuettes of the Serpent Goddess
and her acolytes, votive robes and girdles, also in faience,
the great marble cross, shells and flying-fish which have come
off a panel, and a great quantity of vases. (Fig. 43.) Remains
of sacrifices are preserved with care. This repository was
a crypt; the true sanctuary, supported by pillars, occupied
the floor above. The entrance stood on the Central Court,
opposite the great altar. The facade must have presented
the appearance known to us from the fresco from Knossos,
with wings supported by small columns and a central *cella*
from which a door led to the crypt.[3] Before the priest-king
went to the altar or the sanctuary he no doubt purified himself
in the lustral basin of the Throne Room. The people from
outside went up a ramp to the North-West Portico and then,
drawing into line in a fore-hall, entered the hall of purification
by the door on the right and left it by that on the left.

[1] MA. loc. cit., pl. xxxvi.
[2] **XX,** 463 ff., 217 ff.
[3] See the reconstruction proposed by Evans, JIBA. 1911, 289 ff.

Another more unassuming sanctuary served the domestic quarter.[1] Here the hall with a pillar marked with the double axe and the hall with a lustral basin are united. At the foot of the pillar were a libation table and a small pedestal in which a double axe was formerly fixed, and hard by there were vases containing the oil of unction.

Quite close to this a little chapel was built after the destruction of the palace, and it has been found intact with everything in place.[2] It forms a square with a side of no more than 1.50 metres. Nevertheless, it is divided into three sections by steps. Next to the door comes the lowest section, where, on a clay flooring, seven vases were used for aspersion. The central section contains a terra-cotta tripod in the middle and six stone cups in the corners ; here the offerer of sacrifice stood. At the end a ledge about 60 centimetres above the ground formed the holy table ; six rude figurines were placed on it, with two stucco horns of consecration and a minute double axe of steatite. The most remarkable of the figurines represents the goddess on a cylindrical base ; her bodice and her breasts, her bangles and her necklaces, are indicated by patterns of paint ; on her head she carries a dove and she gives benediction with her enormous hands. (Fig. 42.) From the dimensions of this chapel and the space left free by the objects with which it was cumbered up it is clear that it could only hold one or two persons at a time.

About the same period a room in the Little Palace was converted into a sanctuary. On a bench there stood sacred horns, a wild goat, and concretions of stone which more or less resembled a fat woman, a child, and a grimacing monkey. For this reason it has been given the name of the Fetish Shrine.[3]

To all these holy places we might add others, such as the chapels at Hagia Triada [4] and the palace-sanctuary of Nirou Chani. But we have seen enough to show how numerous they were in Crete and how various. By one thing they may almost always be recognized, one thing is found almost without exception on altars, at the foot of trees, pillars and columns, and even on roofs—the sign of the divine bull, the horns of consecration.

[1] Ib., 573 ff.
[3] Ib., xi, 2 ff.
[2] BSA. viii, 95 ff.
[4] MA. xiv, 9, 71-4 ; cf. AJA. 1912, 464.

CHAPTER IV

RELIGIOUS CEREMONIES

THE religious ceremonies and ritual practices of the pre-Hellenes made a deep and lasting impression upon the minds of the Greeks. After the lapse of centuries " the Cretans said that homage paid to the gods, sacrifices, and initiation into mysteries were Cretan inventions which other peoples had borrowed ".[1] These exaggerated claims contain a good deal of truth.

The priestesses long presided over religious practices. Woman was the natural intermediary with divinities, the greatest of whom was woman deified. Hosts of objects represent the priestesses at their duties. It is not always easy, however, to distinguish them from the goddess whom they serve. The Serpent Goddess might be confused with her acolyte (Fig. 62, Pl. III, 2), and divine rank might be attributed to the female personages holding a double axe or flowers in either hand.[2] A close comparison of costumes, attitudes, and attributes is necessary for the appreciation of characteristic differences in certain cases. What is still more difficult and as a general rule impossible is to distinguish priestesses from worshippers or bringers of offerings, and one is reduced to speaking of them all together.

Certain costumes are evidently ritual dresses and the women wearing them must be more than mere worshippers. Such is the skirt with the trouser effect, standing out in stiff puffs, made of spotted skin, and finished off in a point with the animal's tail or an appendage suggesting it. This garment of Palæolithic times, preserved by religious tradition, is worn by women pouring out libations in front of double axes, bringing votive robes or holding the magic wand.[3] Of a

---

[1] Diodorus, v, 79.
[2] ARW. 1904, 146, figs. 27–8.
[3] Fig. 50 *a, b* ; JHS. xxii, 78, fig. 5 ; MA. xiii, 39, fig. 33.

ritual character, too, is the long robe which is in evidence in similar scenes. Occasionally a special head-dress, a tiara, toque or round, flat hat, denotes the priestly character of women who are praying, dancing, or presenting sacred vases.[1] But most frequently the figures performing ritual acts are dressed in the fashion of their time. With the flounced skirt they wear the low-necked bodice, more especially since it probably had, at its origin, a mystic value. In order to resemble the goddess more completely they may on occasion even have shown themselves naked to the waist, for, while it sometimes happens that the bodice is recognizable only by a line on the arms where the sleeves finish,[2] at other times there is no trace of it to be seen.[3]

Very occasionally young maidens, or rather little girls, appear in religious scenes. We see two of them near the goddess seated beneath the tree of life, one offering her flowers and the other about to gather fruit for her. Two more are to be seen dancing in front of a sacred enclosure.[4]

The participation of men in the cult was, like the association of a god with the goddess, a late development. Their part in the religious ceremonies was always a subordinate one even when the king became the high priest of the bull. As if to extenuate their encroachment and to baffle the evil spirits to whose power this act had exposed them, they assumed for divine service the priestly costume of the women.[5] On the Hagia Triada sarcophagus the three men advancing with offerings in their arms wear the spotted trouser-skirt while the lyre-player and the flute-player have the long robe.[6] On a fresco from Knossos there are men wearing stoles over white robes ; on another there are red-skinned persons in flounced skirts.[7] Thus, by the fusion of the cult of the goddess with that of the god, which is illustrated on a seal by the twofold offering of the double axe and the robe,[8] the double axe is actually placed in the hands of the priestesses, and their male acolytes are arrayed in the robe. The Apollo *Kitharoidos*

---

[1] Fig. 50 *b* ; MA. loc. cit., 40, fig. 34 ; ARW. loc. cit.
[2] Fig. 44 ; **XIII,** figs. 53, 57–8.
[3] Fig. 37 ; **XIII,** figs. 25, 59 ; MA. xiv, 40, fig. 34 ; **LXVII,** pl. xvi, 5.
[4] Fig. 37 ; MA. xiii, 43, fig. 37.
[5] Cf. Reichel, JOEI. 1908, 252 ff.
[6] Fig. 50 *a*, *b* ; cf. MA. xiii, 41, fig. 35.
[7] BSA. vii, 20.
[8] Ib., viii, 102, fig. 59.

of later days with his *peplos* was only a replica of the Cretan lyre-player. But as a general rule the men who are praying, and even those officiating in the plucking of the sacred tree, wear the ordinary dress,[1] while the imbricated cassock was donned in exceptional circumstances.[2] Nothing about either the men or the women gives the impression of a priestly caste.

The most frequent of the ritual acts is that of worship. In spite of their progress in art the Cretans, unlike the Egyptians of their own times and the Greeks of the future, never represented their divinities by large statues. They had only small idols which were almost invariably of a clumsy type. Most of them measure only a few centimetres. It has, therefore, been questioned whether these figures were really idols or whether they were merely ex-voto offerings, and Crete never got beyond the stage of aniconic cults.[3] We can, however, take it for certain, that the figurines of the goddess found in position in the domestic shrines, with double axes and horns of consecration, were there to receive homage, offerings, and libations. That being the case, it is surprising to see a goddess of human form constantly represented in religious scenes. Is this mythological imagery? No, the scenes certainly represent open-air festivals in which men draw near to the divinity. What is the origin of this contradiction? There is only one possible explanation. While private worship was performed in front of small idols, in public worship the part of the goddess was played by a woman. It is the high priestess who takes her place on the seat of the goddess, sits at the foot of the sacred tree, or stands on the mountain-peak to receive worship and offerings from her acolytes and from the faithful. That is why it is so often hard to distinguish the goddess from the priestesses in religious ceremonies.

The gesture of benediction is suited to beings filled with the divine spirit and anxious to transmit it to human bodies. The gesture of worship belongs to the priestesses, who are empowered to call down the divine spirit from heaven in the form of the goddess or of the god, or to simple believers who

---

[1] Figs. 7, 38–40, 63.
[2] See our pl. ii, 2 ; cf. MA. loc. cit.
[3] Karo, loc. cit., 139, 142, 155.

prepare themselves to receive it. The first of these gestures
is always the same ; both arms are raised and the palm of the
right hand is spread out to its full breadth with the fingers
apart. (Fig. 42.) The second offers some rather remarkable
varieties. As a rule the person making this gesture raises
one hand to the level of his forehead and often covers his
eyes as if to ward off the glare of too bright a light, of an
apparition dazzling enough to blind him. Often he bends
his free arm across his chest to imitate or provoke the divine
gesture of fructification.[1] Sometimes he raises both arms
in a gesture of prayer and supplication for the purpose either
of urging the divinity to a gesture of beneficence and salvation [2]
or of protecting both his eyes from the brightness which he
invokes but dreads.[3] Occasionally both arms are raised to
the chest (Fig. 7), and the meaning of this gesture is made
clear by the statuette of a man whose right hand touches his
chest while the left comes lower down in front.[4]

The religious ceremonies probably began with purifications.
On ordinary days a simple act of aspersion was doubtless
considered sufficient, the hands being dipped in holy water.
This must have been the purpose of certain jugs with long
spouts, particularly those with a double tube,[5] and a
considerable number of vases marked with sacred emblems.
This too was the purpose of the jugs placed at the entrance
of the little chapel at Knossos. On feast-days people came
to the lustral rooms ; they went down into a little stone
basin and came out worthy to appear before the goddess.
A special solemnity must have attached to the performance
of this rite in the Throne Room when the lord came to take
part in it with the priestesses seated on either side of him on
low benches. In certain cases the purification seems to have
been done by anointing, for not only do we see fine ewers
standing round the basins but also *alabastra* formerly filled
with oil or ointment.

The essential rite, in this as in all religions, was the blood-
sacrifice. A great number of sites have preserved to our own

[1] JHS. xxii, 78, fig. 4 ; MA. xiv, 739, fig. 37 ; BSA. vi, pl. x, 10.
[2] Fig. 44 ; **LXVII,** fig. 440 ; **XIII,** fig. 57, 6 ; MA. xiii, 42, fig. 36 ; xiv,
578, fig. 51.
[3] **LI,** i, pl. xxvi, 3.
[4] **XXI,** pl. xxxvii.
[5] Cf. **XX,** figs. 48, 50.

times the remains of victims sacrificed during the IIIrd and IInd millenniums. On the top of Mount Iouktas, on the rock where religious celebrations were held in the open air and round the building which was the holy place of later days, in the cave of Psychro, on the terrace of Petsofa, in a dwelling at Palaikastro—everywhere horns or bones of cattle, goats, sheep, and pigs have been found in thick strata of carbonized matter, all jumbled up with votive relics and prayer balls.[1]

Artists represent the sacrifice of the boar [2] but they prefer that of the bull. Just as in Egypt Hathor and Apis revealed themselves by infallible signs, by figures marked on the head or body, so in Crete the honours of the double axe were specially reserved for the beasts bearing on their forehead or cheeks the sign of the cross, the shield, or the star.[3] An intaglio shows us the animal stretched out on the table of sacrifice with its tongue lolling out and a dagger planted in the back of its neck.[4] It is the very scene which is painted on the Hagia Triada sarcophagus. (Fig. 50a.) The great offering-table from Phaistos seems to show, by the number of oxen appearing on three of its four corners and along two of its edges, that on great occasions three, six, and even nine bulls were sacrificed.[5]

For the sake of economy but also for the purpose of recalling the memory and perpetuating the effect of the sacrifice, the bull was frequently offered in effigy. Bulls of painted clay were manufactured for the use of the faithful. The potters even had moulds for turning them out in large quantities.[6] The figurine replacing the living animal was often no more than a *protome*, or a head.[7] It was a hecatomb on the cheap. But the question of expense was set aside when bronze statuettes of bulls were dedicated to the goddess or to the dead.[8] Religious fervour alone explains the presence in the tombs of steatite heads which are of exquisite art. A wonderful head hammered out of a plate of silver, with its

[1] Ib., **157** ff., 627 ff.; BSA. vi, 96–7; xi, 287.
[2] **LXVII,** figs. 428, 15.
[3] Cf. Pottier, BCH. 1907, 241–2, Evans, **XX,** 513 ff., See **XVIII,** figs. 70, 87; **LXVII,** fig. 398.
[4] **XVII,** fig. 99.
[5] MA. xiv, pl. xxxvi; cf. **LXVII,** figs. 534–6.
[6] **LXXXI,** 24.
[7] **XL,** pl. xi, 19; cf. **XXXIX,** 153; **LXVII,** 820.
[8] **LI,** i, pl. xxxix, 12–25; MA., xiii, 71; xiv, 748.

ears, horns, and muzzle gilded and its forehead starred with a gold rosette, was buried in a Shaft Grave at Mycenæ, with about fifty smaller heads cut out of small plaques of gold [1]— a holocaust offered for all eternity to the divinities who protected the dead, in imitation of the sacrifices which piled up the bones and horns of the victims from year to year round the altar built above the grave itself.[2]

Bloodless offerings were of far more frequent occurrence than blood-sacrifices. The Hagia Triada sarcophagus (Fig. 50a) represents both the sacrifice of the bull and the offering of fruits. This was the purpose of the low tripods and tables of coarse clay in the holy places and at the foot of sacred pillars. The grain-grinder found with the great table at Phaistos shows what was usually put on them. As the chapels were small and the idols small too, the ritual vessels often consisted of diminutive pots or of painted shells. Hundreds of them have been found in many a sanctuary, even to the Repository of Knossos. (Fig. 43.) What more was needed for the offering of a few grains of corn? The first-fruits being of several kinds, a vase was invented which consisted of a round base and a set of tiny receptacles, one for each kind of offering. This multiple type of vase, which was already in use during the Early Minoan Period and has remained so among the Greeks up to our own times, is called a *kernos*.[3] It was also combined at times with the table of offerings, the receptacles being fastened to a flat base.[4]

Libations and lustrations were constant practices. They were performed in various ways and with different liquids. The watering of sacred trees and plants is often done, on the seals and gems, by demons who advance in a procession with ewers in their hands.[5] Communion with the goddess was effected through the medium of wine, and a drink-offering made from barley [6] may have been poured out to her. If, as is possible, the sacred vases with a triple receptacle contained three liquids, they must have been, then as in Homeric times,

[1] **LXVII**, figs. 398–9.
[2] Ib., 570–1, figs. 102–4.
[3] Dawkins, BSA. x, 221 ff. ; Xanthoudidis, ib., xii, 9 ff. ; cf. **XI,** fig. 80 ; *AΔ*, iv, 76–7, fig. 21, 3.
[4] **LI,** pl. xi.
[5] Cf. **XI,** 346 ff.
[6] See p. 162.

the lower lip.[1] But since the bull was the preferred victim of the Cretans, it had to be represented as completely as possible in the *simulacra*. It was, therefore, filled with blood or at least with wine, the substitute for blood. The Hagia Triada sarcophagus (Fig. 50*a*, *b*) shows us, on one side, a priestess pouring out a red liquid, and on the other the sacrifice of a young bull; it is quite possible that the liquid comes from the sacrificed animal. In any case the *rhyton*, contents and container, symbolizes the sacred being which transfuses itself into the worshippers who seek communion with it.

To do honour to the goddess or to ward off demons, incense was burned.[2] The pomp of religious ceremonies likewise admitted of sacred music. The priestess invoked or announced the divinity with the sound of the conch;[3] players upon the lyre and the double flute rendered hymns while the rites of sacrifice and libation were in progress (Figs. 50*a*, *b*), and the Egyptian sistrum set the time for the choruses of men. (Pl. II, 2.) Further, certain little handbells of terra-cotta, the use of which has not been determined, may have marked the stages of divine service.[4]

Besides the sacrifices and libations performed in common, individual offerings were made by private persons.[5] Dedications were sometimes inscribed on them.[6] All the holy places were filled with these ex-voto offerings. When they could no longer be displayed they were piously buried in underground hiding-places. Such are the repository hoards from which, together with the funerary deposits, we learn most about the religious ideas of the Ægean peoples. All the objects which we have already had in review were placed there—*simulacra* of chapels, of altars, and of columns, horns of consecration and double axes, vases and figurines of all kinds, representations of animals, fruits, and flowers, and panels of stone or bronze painted or engraved with religious scenes. The men for choice brought weapons or ships; the women, in order to add to the fructifying power of the goddess and to their own, consecrated to her real apparel or imitations of it in faience

---

[1] Cf. id., ib., 253–6; De Mot, loc. cit., 214–16; Evans, loc. cit., 85.
[2] **XX**, 568; cf. **XVI**, 13; *A⊿*, iv, 76–7, fig. 21, 3; **XXXVIII**, 35–8.
[3] **XIII**, fig. 25; cf. **XX**, 581.
[4] Cf. **XX**, 175.
[5] Cf. Hogarth, ER., loc. cit., 146 ff.; Dussaud, **XI**, 396–7.
[6] **XX**, figs. 461–72.

or ivory, gorgeous robes, girdles of a traditional type, and above all symbolic knots which transmitted to their wearers the magic virtue derived from the pillar, the bull, the double axe, or the shield.[1]

Besides their daily ceremonies the Cretans had a large number of more solemn celebrations. Their liturgical calendar was rich in special festivals. We are admitted to the epiphany of the goddess, of the god, and even of the fruits and of the double axe.[2] They celebrated the blossoming of the spring-time, the capture of the bull, the olive-harvest, and the withering of the trees in winter. Some of these festivals were accompanied by games, of which we shall speak later. Others were the occasion of processions. The women filed past with caskets, vases, and flowers ; the young men passed before the little sacred building each holding a cup at arm's length ; the men marched two by two, with pitchforks on their shoulders, to the sound of hymns shouted at the top of their voices.[3] On certain days the goddess was carried in a palankeen, like those preserved in the sanctuaries in the form of terra cotta *simulacra*,[4] and, when the *sedia gestatoria* was set down on the ground she, still sitting, looked on the long procession of priests in white robes or servers disguised as demons.[5] In order to excite religious ecstasy and to increase the efficacy of the divine powers, they had recourse to various dances. The dances of Knossos remained famous in Greece. Frescoes, reliefs, and intaglios show us what an important part they played in religion. The Cretans dance before the sacred tree, particularly at the time of the plucking. They dance before the goddess on her seat. They dance in order to draw the virtue out of the magic wand into themselves. They dance to evoke the divinity, to bring the serpent out of the ground and to make the flowers grow.[6] Alone or in groups, men and women, they dance, now with dignity and now with impetuous, orgiastic movements, with the frenzy of the possessed, but without savage fury and without indecency.

[1] Figs. 6, 43 ; cf. **XX,** figs. 308–12.
[2] Figs. 44, 47, 50, 37 ; cf. JHS. xxii, 78, fig. 5.
[3] Figs. 11–12 ; pl. ii, 2 ; cf. BSA. ix, 129, fig. 85.
[4] **XX,** fig. 166.
[5] BSA. vii, 19–20 ; *AΔ*, ii, 14–15, fig. 1.
[6] Figs. 52, 38–9 ; **XX,** fig. 470 ; MA. xiv, 577, fig. 50 ; JHS. xxii, 77, fig. 2 ; MA. xiii, 39, fig. 33 ; **LXVII,** fig. 431, 1.

All that we know of Cretan religion is summed up in two of the pictures executed on the object to which we have referred on many occasions, the Hagia Triada sarcophagus.[1] One of the panels (Fig. 50a) represents the two kinds of sacrifice. Against a blue background we see the blood-sacrifice. The bull is laid on a table, with its feet fastened

FIG. 50a.—The Hagia Triada sarcophagus. The sacrifice.

together, its body bound with a red cord tied crosswise, and its throat above a pail into which its blood flows. Two goats crouching under the table await their turn, while a flute-player in a long robe, with flowing locks and veils, sets a rhythm for the march of the women who, two by two, advance in procession toward the victim with their arms extended and their fingers outstretched. Against a white background we see the bloodless sacrifice. The scene takes

FIG. 50b.—The Hagia Triada sarcophagus. The libations and offering.

place before an enclosure of sacred trees in front of which stand a small sacred building covered with horns, a long shaft into which is fitted a double axe surmounted by a bird, an altar upon which an offering-dish and an ewer are placed, and, lastly, a basket full of fruit floating in the air. The priestess, wearing a spotted skirt with a tail and a low bodice, has her arms stretched down towards the altar.

[1] MA. xix, pl. i, ii.

The other panel (Fig. 50*b*) is likewise divided into two companion scenes. On the left are the preparations for the libation. Between two crocketed tree-trunks sanctified by double axes and birds, and supported by the pedestals of these posts, stands a large urn into which the priestess is emptying a *kantharos* ; an acolyte in a long robe and a head-dress of flowers or feathers is bringing her two more slung on a yoke ; behind, a lyre-player sweeps his seven strings. On the right is the offering to the dead. Standing between a tree and the erection above his tomb, the dead man faces the bearers of offerings who, wearing skirts with tails, bring him a votive ship and two calves.

Let us follow them ; after the cult of the deities, let us behold the cult of the dead.

CHAPTER V

THE CULT OF THE DEAD [1]

THE fetishist belief, the idea that inanimate objects are endowed with life, necessarily entails an instinctive and unconquerable refusal to see in death the annihilation of vital activity. To the group of people among whom he lived, the dead man appears as a good and beloved spirit, whose happiness it is their duty to ensure, and from whom they have the right to expect benefits. But if he had the misfortune to die prematurely, to come to a violent end and to leave none behind him to pay the supreme honours, he is changed into a malevolent demon, a formidable ghost, who must be reduced to impotence. These conceptions, though originally opposed and apparently contradictory, are very largely reconciled in the beliefs and practices of all communities. Among the Ægeans they co-exist more or less definitely from the earliest times.

They might have taken form in two different methods of disposing of the dead, interment and incineration. The former method, in general, represents the wish to prolong the existence of the dead under the ground ; the body may, however, be buried in a crouched position which does not give it room ever to move again. The primary object of the latter method is to prevent ghosts from walking by completely destroying the body ; but a time comes when the body is burned in order to release the soul from its carnal envelope and to open to it the blissful ways of the beyond. What, then, were the actual funerary customs of the Ægean peoples ? Schliemann thought that at Mycenæ all the bodies were burned inside the tombs before they were buried. Doerpfeld has maintained that the bodies underwent a partial cremation, a desiccation, a buccanning, for the purpose of preserving them without

[1] See Evans, **XVI, XVIII ;** Dussaud, **XI,** 28 ff. ; Hall, **XXXVII,** 158–77.

reducing them to ashes and frequently with the object of making them contract.[1] These hypotheses have hardly any supporters now. It is still admitted, however, that incineration and interment were practised at the same time;[2] this is certainly true of Homeric days, when the bodies of the heroes were placed on funeral pyres while poor people were simply put away in the ground. But the alleged cases of cremation, dating from times when burial is an established fact, are to be regarded with suspicion.[3] It is possible that during the Neolithic Age the inhabitants of central Greece occasionally burned their dead ; but, at all events, in no other places, and not even in central Greece itself, from the Chalcolithic Period onwards, is there any trace of funeral pyres before the time of the *Iliad*.[4] The presence in a fair number of Ægean tombs of ashes and skeletons partly blackened by smoke [5] is clearly explained by animal remains or by " fire-boxes " which are sometimes filled with coals ; sacrifices were offered to the dead and the means of warming themselves and of preparing their food were left at hand.

Another fact which certainly proves that there was no intention to destroy the body, but rather the reverse, is the care which was taken to protect it from evil spirits and to preserve its identity. The gold masks which covered the faces of the dead princes at Mycenæ have as a parallel in Mochlos, Mouliana, and Cyprus gold diadems engraved with eyes, nose, and mouth—an indestructible portrait intended to preserve for ever the likeness of the perishable body. In order that his personality might never be effaced the dead man took with him his seal, tied round his neck or placed within his reach.

The first duty of the family was to ensure an eternal dwelling-place for the member who was leaving it. No spot could please him better or consort better with the devotion of his kinsfolk than the place where he had always lived. For a long time the living refused to part with the dead. They were buried in or beside the houses. This custom, which

---

[1] Doerpfeld, *Mélanges Nicole*, 97 ff. ; *Neues Jahrb. fuer class. Philol.*, 1912, 1 ff.
[2] Zehetmaier, *Leichenverbrennung und Leichenbestattung*, 100 ff.
[3] Perrot, **LXVII**, 326–31, 561 ff. ; Fimmen, **XXV**, 65–6.
[4] Sotiriadis, REG. 1912, 264–7.
[5] Skias and Xanthoudidis, 'Εφ., 1912, 22 ; Savignoni, MA. xiv, 659.

was of great antiquity, never wholly died out. In Thessaly
the dwellings are interspersed among the tombs ; in Thorikos,
Aigina, Orchomenos, and Troy they contain skeletons crouching
face downwards in simple holes.[1] But while in these distant
regions the dead, irrespective of age, were accorded burial
within houses, in the remainder of the Ægean world this
was reserved for quite young children. They at least could
not be separated from their parents. At Knossos a new-
born baby was buried in a cavity dug beneath the floor of
a house. At Mycenæ six children's graves were made in two
adjoining rooms.[2] Generally the little corpses were put
into jars, *pithoi*, where, before they had grown stiff, they
were placed in a crouched position with their knees drawn
up to their chins and their hands touching their faces. In
Crete these jars, which were very rarely used for older children
and for adults,[3] were usually taken to a cemetery, but it was
a cemetery of a special kind—a sepulchral nursery. A dozen
of these jars were found in one place near Knossos, fifteen in
Mochlos in addition to the chamber tombs, and one at Hagios
Nikolaos in front of a rock-shelter full of human bones. They
were collected together in veritable necropoles at Sphoungaras
and Pachyammos.[4] But in Melos, stowed away inside houses
on a level with the foundations, eight jars were found containing
children the oldest of whom were only just beginning to cut
their second teeth.[5] The peoples accustomed to indoor burial
were even more disposed to keep the jars containing their
children in their own homes.[6]

Outside the houses the tombs of the Cretans were extremely
varied. It is possible that the ethnical differences which
seem to have existed in Crete in the earliest times were not
entirely without influence upon methods of burial.[7] But when
we consider the extraordinary unity of Cretan civilization
and religion during two millenniums, and when we see the
various forms of tombs developing at a time when the fusion

[1] **LXXXVIII,** 126 ff. ; **XCI,** 132, fig. 80 ; 'Εφ., 1895, 232 ff., 248 ; **V,** 68 ;
LXVII, 562.
[2] BSA. vi, 77 ; **LXVII,** 353.
[3] ΑΔ, iv, 58, 60.
[4] Ib., 60–2 ; **LXXXII,** 14, 16, 87–8 ; BSA. vi, 340 ; **LXXXIV,** 60 ;
LXXIII, 83.
[5] BSA. xvii, 6–9.
[6] **III,** 100, fig. 127 ; **XCI,** 41 ; **LXVII,** 252, cf. 562.
[7] Cf. Evans, **XVI,** 522 ; Dussaud, **XI,** 28.

of the races was already ancient history, we can be sure that the original diversity of those races contributed very little to the subsequent diversity of the types of graves. Other causes operated more forcibly and, at any rate, are more in evidence, namely topographical and geological conditions, architectural practices adopted in the past and maintained through religious scruples and, lastly, social necessities.[1]

In a mountainous country the habitation of the dead, like that of the living, is at first a cavern or, failing a cavern, a mere cleft in the rock of some depth. In Crete *burial caves* must have been numerous in the Neolithic Age.[2] In Early Minoan times there was a Troglodyte ossuary at Pyrgos, and at Mochlos the bodies of the poor were laid in simple clefts in rocks.[3] Even in the Late Minoan Period a sepulchral cave still existed near Gournia.[4] But very soon cavities which were not large enough or too wide at the mouth were transformed into partly artificial grottoes by building up or hollowing out. At Kephallenia, for example, on heights overlooking the sea, Mycenæan interments are found in rock shelters screened by low walls.[5] When tools were made of metal the living rock was cut. *Rock-cut tombs* are common in Eastern Crete from E.M.II to M.M.I. Thirty-three have been found at Pseira. At Mochlos the small tombs are still only one metre by two, while the larger tombs, which were covered over and closed by slabs of stone, are sometimes divided into two chambers and are as much as six metres in length and 1·80 in breadth.[6] These tombs, which were very popular in countries where the stone is soft, were of various shapes until a single type became established, of which the characteristics are an entrance passage or *dromos* and a chamber blocked up with stones and covered with a roof of rock.

But from the first half of the third millennium it was found possible to make tombs large enough to hold all the dead of a clan. It was seldom that a cave was available, like that at Pyrgos, in which hundreds of skeletons could be piled up,

---

[1] Cf. Perrot, **LXVII,** 316–40, 564–650 ; Fimmen, **XXV,** 54 ff.
[2] BSA. viii, 235 ; xii, 267.
[3] *AΔ*, 1918, 136 ff. ; **LXXXII,** 14 ; cf. BSA. ix, 339 ff.
[4] Cf. Fimmen, loc. cit., 55.
[5] CRAI. 1909, 389 ff. ; 1911, 6 ff.
[6] **LXXXI,** 7 ; **LXXXII,** 18 ff., 45–6, 56 ff..

and the most spacious of the tombs cut in the cliff at Mochlos fell far short of the required dimensions. So instead of excavating they started to build. In the Messara the round hut of primitive times furnished a model for the bee-hive or *tholos* tomb. Faithful to tradition, funerary architecture maintained a type which had been abandoned by civil architecture, and adapted the *dromos* to it. In these tombs each stone course projected inwards over the course below, so that the sloping sides rose into a dome of imposing height, and there was usually a small esplanade in front. The smallest tombs had an internal diameter between 4 and 7 metres, while that of the larger was between 9 and 10.

At Platanos there are two which stand in an enclosed court, as if to mark both the independence and the kinship of two clans. The internal diameters of these are 7·30 metres and 10·30 metres, and the walls are 1·30 and 2·50 metres thick respectively. By the very fact that, as we have seen,[1] this type served to re-unite the members of a clan for eternity, its dimensions had to be reduced as the *genos* was reduced, and it disappeared when the system of small families triumphed.

But in the meantime the rock tomb with one or two chambers had been introduced, on the model of the rectangular house. These *rectangular tombs* were more easily adapted to any dimensions than the *tholoi*. They could form large ossuaries, like one at Palaikastro which is divided by parallel walls into several compartments, or they could form annexes which were subsequently added to the *tholoi*, as was done at Platanos and Hagia Triada. At one time and another they were combined with all kinds of elements borrowed from the other types, and they often contained bodies buried in sarcophaguses.

While the breaking up of the clan manifests itself in the progressive reduction of the tombs, whether rock-cut or built, the culmination of this development appears in the evolution of individual tombs. By reducing the rock-cut chamber and the stone chamber to their simplest form the people of northern Greece and the Cyclades had invented the rectangular flagged type of grave, the *cist grave*. The

[1] p. 134 ff.

grave was dug 50 centimetres deep and, since the body
was laid in a crouched position, it was only 1 metre long.
Between the stone slabs of the bottom and those of the lid,
which were laid flat, the four sides were at first formed by
slabs placed on edge, and later by a masonry of small stones
without mortar, which represented a house by a rudimentary
suggestion of the door and threshold. In rare cases the cist
graves were dug deeper and held several dead together;
sometimes they were in pairs, with just a slab to separate
them. From the Cyclades the cist type passed to Crete
and to the Peloponnese, but without success; it must, therefore, have been a case of exceptional imitation and not of
mass immigration. The necropolis of Mochlos contains some
individual cists by the side of collective burial-chambers,
but this is because foreign customs were known on the island
either through the sailors or through resident aliens, and
towards the end of the Early Minoan Period social conditions
began to be the same there as in the Cyclades. In general,
the place of the cist grave was taken in Crete and the Peloponnese by cists of a very different type, in which the body
could be walled up in the same way.

Crete possessed the movable cist of clay, which became the
sarcophagus or *larnax*.[1] This coffin of terra cotta (of stone
in exceptional cases) could be placed, alone or with others,
in any kind of tomb. It represented a house with its gabled
lid, and it still kept the rounded corners or oval form at the
time when it was placed in the funeral caves or the *tholos*
tombs; later it had the rectangular shape. The largest of
these *larnakes*, e.g. those from Gournia and Mallia,[2] are not
more than 1·35 metres long; the bodies were laid in a crouched
position with the legs turned up, the knees bent, and the feet
tucked under the sacrum.

Moreover the cist grave could be deepened. The passage
which led to the rock chambers and *tholos* tombs, instead of
being horizontal, descended gently by a few steps when it
was cut in a hill with a gentle slope; on flat ground it was
vertical. When the body was laid in the hole at the bottom
and protected by a ceiling slab the *shaft tomb* was obtained.
This type which varies in depth between 2 metres and

[1] Hall, **XXXVII**, 162 ff., 172 ff.; Fimmen, loc. cit., 64.
[2] *AΔ*, iv, 74 ff.; BCH. 1921, 536.

3·50, is not very common, although it is represented in Crete, Cyprus, and Amorgos and on the mainland. As a rule the grave itself is just long and wide enough for the body, but at Mycenæ those of the royal family are as much as 8 or even 34 square metres; they are surmounted by relief steles and surrounded by a circular wall.

If the body was laid, not directly at the bottom, but in a cavity at the side, the ground was dug rather deeper, to as much as 5 metres, and the cavity was closed by a wall of masonry; thus the *pit tomb* or *pit cave* was obtained, which is a variety of the shaft tomb and is really a chamber tomb with a vertical *dromos*. When, therefore, the cemetery at Zapher Papoura presents the three types of rock tomb, shaft tomb, and pit tomb, with objects all dating from L.M.II and all revealing the same beliefs, there is no reason for explaining these differences of form by ethnological considerations.

In the Mycenæan world two types were popular, the rock chamber with a false vault and the bee-hive tomb. The *rock chamber*, which is found from Argolis to Kephallenia and from Crete to Miletos, is sometimes round or semi-circular, generally square, and always preceded by a *dromos*. It contains one body or more, usually laid in graves but sometimes crouched in sarcophaguses. Under the same vault there is sometimes also a lateral chamber, and an example of a rock tomb with three chambers is known.[1] In Late Minoan times the Cretans made great use of this type, and the hills were riddled with their diggings, lined with fine hewn masonry.

The king of Knossos demanded a tomb which should be worthy of his glory. He chose for its site an eminence from which the sea could be seen, at Isopata. High dignitaries, perhaps princes, came to bear him company in the neghbouring tombs. In the side of the hill a sloping *dromos* is cut, 2 metres broad and 24 metres long. It leads to a fore-hall, 4·50 metres by 1·60, to which two lateral niches give the form of a cross. The inner chamber, which was carefully closed, measures 7·85 metres by more than 6 metres; at the back it contains a niche similar to those in the fore-

---

[1] Fimmen, loc. cit., 56-7.

hall, and on the right a sepulchral grave of 2˙20 metres by 60 centimetres. The chamber, which is 5 or 6 metres deep in the hill, breaks the surface with a false vault which once rose 3 metres above it. Although this royal tomb had been previously robbed, sufficient precious objects were found there—a silver cup, a gold pin, a bronze mirror, beads of lapis lazuli, vases of porphyry and diorite, Egyptian *alabastra*, and painted pottery—to suggest the accumulated wealth which it once contained.[1]

While the rectangular chambers reproduce the form of the rock tombs of the earliest times, the finest of them, like those at Isopata, by their vault recall the *tholos* tombs and are the forerunners of the great *domed tombs*. But it was on the mainland that the kings built these last to be posthumous monuments of their greatness, and Crete in her decay knew only rare, feeble imitations of them. The most majestic were raised in Boeotia and Argolis. That of Orchomenos, the " Treasury of Minyas ", cut in the virgin rock, is famous for the mighty lintel which surmounts the entrance door, the harmonious proportions of the dome, 14˙20 metres in diameter and 13˙60 metres high, and by the magnificent ceiling which spread like a sculptured canopy above the dead. At Mycenæ the " Treasury of Atreus " surpasses all its neighbours in splendour. It is reached by a passage 36 metres long and 6 broad; the courses of the side walls of this passage rise at the inner end to 14 metres. The door, the leaves of which were of bronze, is 5˙42 metres high and rather narrower at the top than below. The lintel, above which is a triangular relieving-space once masked by light sculptured slabs, is composed of two gigantic blocks, one of which is 9 metres in length, 5 in breadth, and 1 in thickness. On each side an alabaster pilaster adorned with reliefs stood on a pedestal. The dome had a height equal to its diameter, namely 15 metres. Bronze ornaments were nailed on the white stone and made the vault into a starry sky. Off the hall of state was the lateral chamber, in which the lord of this place slept in solitude.

In this extraordinary variety of sepulchres the dominant idea is always that of making life easier for the dead man.

[1] Evans, **XVI**, 526 ff.

Even when he is doubled up in a jar, a cist, or a sarcophagus and thus reduced to impotence this idea is displayed in all kinds of offerings, for logic is the last thing to trouble souls in mourning.

The orientation of the tombs expresses the same beliefs as their shape, and shows as little rigid consistency. In the islands the dead man generally looks toward the sea. In Crete his dwelling as often as possible faces the East. The *tholos* tombs, built on terraces, all have their *dromos* to the East except one, which turns rather to the South.[1] While the rock tombs of Mochlos merely conform with the lie of the ground those of Zapher Papoura and Phaistos are all dug parallel in easterly slopes.[2] At Isopata most of the vaulted chambers have their passage running from North to South, and in one it runs from West to East; but two, including the royal tomb, look on the rising sun. The jars, in which the bodies were placed head downwards, were at first buried upside down, and later they were laid in a hole with the mouth to the West. On the mainland it may be said that there is no rule; however, the *dromos* of the " Treasury of Atreus " faces the East, and so do the mouths of the sepulchral jars in Corinthia.[3]

We have nothing to prove that in Crete the bodies were ever taken to their last dwelling-place in wooden coffins, even when they were not crammed into cists, sarcophaguses or jars. But it is possible that they were placed in this way in the great shaft graves at Mycenæ. Among the precious ornaments which covered the skeletons in these tombs many were pierced with fairly big holes, and cannot have been sewn on to garments; they must have been nailed on to wood. We must imagine an anthropomorphic coffin like the Egyptian mummy-case, with a gold mask showing the face of the dead man, gold jewels wherever it was possible to put them, and gold charging on the rest.[4] But this case is exceptional, as is the size of the tombs in which it occurs.

In the dwelling which shelters him the dead man must have everything which he needs in order to survive. He must

[1] *AΔ*, iv, ii, 15.
[2] **XVI,** fig. 108 ; MA. xiv, 507–8, fig. 2.
[3] **III,** 100.
[4] Staïs, *'Eφ.*, 1907, 31 ff. ; Maurer, JAI. 1912, 208 ff., pl. xii.

have a lamp and a brazier to give him light and warmth in the icy night of the tomb. Since he needs above all food and drink vases of every kind are laid beside him. Before he is shut in for ever victims are brought and their flesh is offered to him (Fig. 50b), and " fire-boxes " are filled with coal for him. The ashes and smoke stains which are so often found inside tombs do not come from the burning of the dead but from the sacrifice of all the beasts whose blackened bones litter the ground.

But it is not enough to deposit shell-fish (a favourite food), clay animals, bull-shaped *rhytons* and full *amphoras* ; these provisions become exhausted and, with them, the strength of the deceased. They must be renewed. On a certain day the family comes back to win the good will of its dead with gifts of food and drink. In front of the sepulchral cavity there is often a chamber which is indeed a chapel, in which the shade can be restored to strength, approached without sacrilege, and evoked without danger. At Mycenæ a ditch for offerings dug across the sepulchral mound communicates direct with the tombs. Through it the living send ritual libations and the dead can take part in the funeral feasts from which bones of goats, bulls, stags, and boars, oyster-shells and olive-stones have survived.[1]

Moreover, man needs companions and maid-servants underground as in this world. The Ægeans do not, like some peoples, burn the women who shall accompany the lord ; they prefer to bury in their place figurines, the purpose of which is explained in Cyprus by certain statuettes of washerwomen. On the mainland, however, piety can be more cruel on occasion. At Chaironeia, above the tomb of a chieftain, the skeleton of a young man lay beneath a thick layer of ash left by sacrifices. At Mycenæ and Argos human bones have been found fairly often, mixed with the bones of animals, before the entrances of rock tombs.[2] In the Achaian country, therefore, human sacrifice contributed to paying the dead their due.

All the gratifications and all the occupations of earthly life were continued in the next life. Toilet accessories such as razors and mirrors were equally necessary over there. In the Cyclades, where tattooing was long practised, palettes

---

[1] **LXVII,** 321–6, 571, figs. 101–4.
[2] REG. 1912, 268 ; BCH. 1904, 370 ; **LXVII,** 572–3.

containing red or blue pigment were placed beside the dead. The abundance of jewellery in the tombs would be incomprehensible did it not show a desire to let those who were departing take with them their most intimate and precious possessions, for, strange to relate, the jewels of the dead are not *simulacra* but the very objects which they used for their adornment on earth, like those diadems with pin-holes in them from Mochlos.[1] In the next life, too, a supply of implements and weapons was necessary. A bee-hive tomb contained an obsidian core from which the dead man could himself knap all pointed and cutting instruments.[2] Although the double axes found in the tombs are too small for real use, and consequently have only a mystic value, this is not true of the tools and weapons. In the cemetery of Zapher Papoura alone Evans has been able to distinguish by their equipment the tombs of a carpenter, a metal-smith, a huntsman, and a military chieftain. Were it not for the funerary deposits, moreover, we should have scarcely any idea how the Ægeans were armed. Whether they had a taste for manual labour, for hunting, or for battle they had the means of gratifying it through all eternity. The sailors had their boat with them, in clay or ivory.[3] Nor was there any lack of amusements. Some loved music, and the lyre-players who had given them delight during the funeral ceremony (Fig. 50) followed them into the grave in the form of statuettes.[4] Others preferred the noble game of chess, and they had the means to play at will.[5] When little children died their feeding-bottles, toy horses, and knuckle-bones were placed beside them.[6] Moreover, the dead continue to have their religious needs. They have to entreat the Great Goddess whose empire reaches to the underworld. She alone can keep them from perishing. For that reason the idols, the votive double axes, and the bulls' heads placed in the tombs are not only talismans but also objects for religious rites. The double axe, painted on sarcophaguses and funerary jars, incised on the stones of sepulchral vaults, and even once reproduced by the plan of

[1] **LXXXII,** 26.
[2] *AΔ*, loc. cit.
[3] **XVI,** 417, fig. 22.
[4] **LXVII,** figs. 357–8.
[5] **XX,** 471 ; MA. xiv, 551, fig. 35.
[6] BSA. xvii, pl. vi, 165 ; MA. xiv, 645, fig. 113.

the grave, is there to assure the dead, as well as the living, of its protection.

No matter how poor they were, then, the Ægeans were installed in their tombs with all possible care. There is something touching in the very poverty which the " tombs of the common people " near Phaistos disclose. A great chieftain, on the other hand, found in death an opportunity to display for the last time on earth and to take away with him the wealth which was his pride. Recognizable under the mask which was to fix his features for all time, with his diadem upon his brow, his rapier by his side, his dagger, ornamented with fleurs-de-lys, in his hand, stiffly clad in his gold-plated dress, aglitter with the chased work of necklaces, bracelets, and broad pectoral, the king of Mycenæ passes before the bowing multitude on his way to his posthumous palace. Once he is stretched upon his couch they pile up around him the gold and silver cups which he drained but a short while ago at the banquet, the weapons with which he so often conquered, ostrich eggs mounted as precious vases, faience sent by kings from beyond the sea, and then jewels and still more jewels. Before leaving him they slay a whole herd of victims to do him honour, and also if need be, when once the door is closed, a faithful servant. From his tomb the king will still watch over his people with a power greater than ever.

CHAPTER VI

GAMES

THERE is no country in the world in which games of all kinds, musical contests, horse-racing, or gymnastics, had such social importance as in Greece. The Greeks made the history of the Attic stage commence in 534, and that of the Olympic Games in 776. The history of both goes much further back ; the theatre and *palæstra* of Hellas did no more than develop the legacy of the pre-Hellenes. The Minoans loved games of every kind. The nobles in the palaces played at chess,[1] and ordinary folk on the tiers of the circus whiled away the boredom of waiting with hop-scotch. But the Minoans had more elevated amusements. In the religious festivals and funerary ceremonies there were contests which were to give birth to a national athletic tradition and to the lyric and dramatic art of later times.

At Phaistos ten tiers, 25 metres long, rise against a back wall and look towards the hills. They overlook a flagged court crossed obliquely by a pathway raised 20 centimetres above the ground. Such is the most ancient theatre known ; it dates from M.M.II. There is another at Knossos, N.E. of the palace. It shows considerable progress, for it has two sets of tiers at a right angle, eighteen tiers, 10 metres long, on one side and six, varying between 6 metres and 16·50, on the other. In the corner stands a kind of bastion, which is taken to be the royal box. As at Phaistos the arena is a cemented floor, with a pathway. Each of these two enclosures could hold between 400 and 500 spectators. These court theatres are perhaps the most original creation of Crete.[2] There was never anything like them in Pharaonic Egypt, and Athens itself had no theatre of stone until the days of its greatest splendour.

[1] **XX,** 124–5, figs. 93 A, *a* 2 ; 93 c ; 472 ff. ; pl. v.
[2] **LVII,** 256.

For what kind of performance were these arenas intended ? The oblique pathway seems to be especially suitable for the evolutions of processions as a prelude to choreographic and musical entertainments. *Choros* is the name which Homer gives to the floor ; the " chorus " or dancing floor is of stone, it resounds under the feet which beat it, it adjoins a palace, and it is supplemented by tiers. And, by a marvellous coincidence, when the poet wants to describe a beautiful ballet, he places it in " the dancing floor which once, in broad Knossos, Daidalos made for Ariadne of the lovely hair ". " There," he says, " the young men and the seductive maidens danced with hands joined. . . . A great crowd stood around, full of delight. A divine bard set the time to the sound of the lyre." [1] Here, we shall say, is the scene which was depicted on many frescoes of the palace, here are the tiers, and perhaps the box where Ariadne sat the day she fell in love with Theseus. An Attic legend tells us that the Pelasgians danced and sang on feast-days at the foot of the Acropolis, in the very place where Dionysos was to cause the verse of Æschylus and Aristophanes to sound. Long before her spouse Dionysos, the divine Ariadne consecrated a " chorus " to dance and music.

Numerous objects testify to the place given to dancing in prehistoric Crete, and to the variety of its forms. A rustic group from Palaikastro shows a musician, male or female, in a long robe, in the midst of a circle of women who, with extended arms intertwined, dance a simple round.[2] This is very different from the miniature frescoes of Knossos, in which the ladies of the court, surrounded by spruce gallants, follow with their eyes the expert steps which women in gay petticoats are dancing in an olive-grove ! In other pictures the measure goes faster ; the music, growing more and more seductive, until it takes absolute possession, lashes the orgiastic dance into a giddy whirl.[3] On a fresco adorning the apartment of the queen the " Dancing Woman " (Fig. 52), with one arm to her breast, the other extended and her curls flying wide, is truly like the maidens whom the poet saw turning. All these dances survived the people which invented

---

[1] *Il.*, xviii, 590 ff. ; cf. *Od.*, viii, 260, 264 ; xii, 4, 318.
[2] BSA. x, 217 ff., fig. 6 ; **IV**, 153.
[3] **LXVII,** fig. 431, 1, 9 ; cf. pp. 851, 847.

them, and thus we have about them, from Greek literature, information which pictures alone cannot give. Besides, Homer is describing a work of art, the shield of Achilleus, when he tells us what the dances of expression were at Knossos. As for the more properly ritual dances, even their name has survived. Even Plutarch [1] knew that the " crane " dance or *geranos* performed at Delos round " the horned altar " had been introduced from Crete and represented the circles which coiled round and uncoiled again in the labyrinth.

A relief from Knossos actually shows the evolutions of the dancers before the horned altar.[2] Another dance, still more celebrated, was that in which the Kouretes worked themselves up by striking on their shields. It may be this which is represented on a sarcophagus of a late period, which shows a figure brandishing a gigantic shield while his rapid movements send his long hair flying.[3]

Music, which accompanies the dance, is, like it, essentially religious. On a relief vase (Pl. II, 2) the sistrum which beats time for feet and voices indicates the sacred character of the procession. The clearest representations which we have of the instruments used at this time are on the Hagia Triada sarcophagus and on two marble statuettes from Keros.[4] At Hagia Triada the musicians are taking part in a sacrifice and wear the sacerdotal costume ; in Keros they were in the presence of the goddess.

The stringed instrument was the lyre. It appears early in Crete as a character in writing.[5] A simple three-stringed type existed. But it was from a normal type with four strings that the seven-stringed classical lyre was derived, which is a double tetrachord with one common note.[6] The instrument the invention of which was ascribed later to Terpander was known to the Cretans more than a thousand years before, and the seven chords are quite clearly drawn on the sarcophagus.[7] The two sides of the frame are shaped like a swan's neck ; the strings are stretched on the box by a band. Such is the *phorminx*, the name of which remained

[1] *Theseus*, 21.
[2] **XIII,** fig. 2.
[3] **XVI,** fig. 107.
[4] Fig. 50 ; **LVI ; XI,** figs. 357–8.
[5] **XVII,** fig. 102, 29.
[6] Cf. Gevaert, *Hist. et théorie de la musique dans l'antiq.*, i, 87.
[7] Fig. 50 *b* ; cf. MA. xix, 170, fig. 21 ; Dawkins, BSA. xii, 7–8.

fixed in the memory of the Greeks, with that of the artists who played it, the *ametores*. It was used on the islands and the mainland. Fragments of lyres with four and with seven chords have been recognized in bits of bone and ivory discovered at Mycenæ and Troy, and it has even been possible to put one together from pieces dug up at Spata.[1]

Certain wind instruments were in use in Neolithic Crete. From the lowest stratum at Phaistos Mosso obtained a reed of bone similar to that of the bagpipe still played by the herdsmen of the neighbourhood, and two tubes of unequal length which formed part of a rustic pipe, the *syrinx*.[2] Later the Minoans were acquainted with the flute. The Greeks said that it originally came from Phrygia. Like the lyre, it comes from Crete, and it is the double flute, without a doubt. It is drawn as clearly as you could wish on the Hagia Triada sarcophagus ; it had a short pipe for high notes and a long one for low notes. Eight holes can be seen, and the hand of the player covers six of them ; we have here without doubt the chromatic flute of fourteen notes, which was to be sufficient for the demands of Greek music.[3] The flute-player is, moreover, a familiar figure in Ægean plastic art,[4] and ivory tubes, the remains of broken flutes, have been found in Mycenæ and Troy with a perfectly preserved reed.[5]

The Cretans had many other musical instruments. We have seen the Egyptian sistrum beating time for a chorus. A pair of cymbals was placed in a funerary tub.[6] The trumpet was sounded—the *salpinx*, as it was called about the Ægean before ever the Greeks came.[7] This instrument was made of a triton-shell or shaped like one. It certainly had a religious value. A woman on a gem is blowing an enormous conch before an altar, and an alabaster triton-shell found in a tomb is cut and bored so as to be able to emit sounds.[8] The shells which are still used in Crete by the rural watchmen were once sacred trumpets.

[1] **LXXII,** fig. 127 ; **LXXIV,** figs. 569–71 ; RA. 1909, ii, 435.
[2] **LVII,** 261–2 ; cf. Cuny, REA. 1910, 154 ff.
[3] **LVII,** fig. 144.
[4] Fig. 64 ; **LXVII,** fig. 357.
[5] **LXXII,** figs. 128–30 *a* ; **LXXIV,** figs. 577–9 *a*.
[6] ’Εφ., 1904, 46 ff., fig. 11.
[7] Cf. Cuny, loc. cit.
[8] **XIII,** fig. 25 ; MA. xiv, 556, fig. 40.

No less than dancing and music, exhibitions of strength and agility were the delight of the Cretans at their festivals. They were the occasion of contests in which both men and women took part. Since they demanded long training, they were certainly not without influence on the physical education of the people. They gave them the wiry suppleness and slimness which are characteristic of them, and they gave everyone the habit of using the strigil [1] and bracing up the waist in a gymnastic belt. The Minoans doted on all sports, which drew crowds. After harmless running matches there may have been gladiatorial combats.[2] But boxing had more patrons.[3]

On this form of contest we possess a precious document : on one of our steatite *rhytons* (Fig. 58) three of the zones represent boxing matches. The stand is indicated in a summary way by a column. The " heavy-weights " have their head protected by a helmet with cheek-pieces and no plume ; they wear a much padded *cestus* which covers them up to the elbow. Here are two at the very moment of the knock-out—one in the warlike attitude of the victor, ready to deliver another blow, and the other laid out on the floor. The " middle-weights " wear the helm with a floating mane. These are pressing each other hard, and one is just about to touch the ground with his knee. The " light-weights " have neither helmet nor gloves. They practise French boxing, a combination of fist-work and the *savate*. When they are down they continue to kick in their defence, waving one leg or both in the air. All these incidents, so full of expressive details which tempted the artist's hand, show how highly developed athleticism was in Crete, and how popular.

But nothing, in their eyes, came up to the *rodeo* or bull-leaping.[4] From immemorial times the sacred beast had his place in the festivals, and the sports in which he appeared had become a national institution. These sports have nothing in common with the bull-fight which ends in the kill. The *corrida* is not made for *aficionados* who are all out to see blood flow ; it has no *matadores* or *prima spada*, nor even *picadores*.

[1] **XXXVIII,** 57, fig. 32.
[2] JHS. xxii, fig. 6 ; **XX,** 691 ff., fig. 512.
[3] Cf. **XX,** figs. 509–10.
[4] See Mosso, **LVII,** 176–90 ; Reichel, AM. 1909, 85–99 ; Evans, JHS. 1921, 247 ff.

It consists of feats similar to those which were the amusement
of ancient Egypt and of Cappadocia in the XXIVth Century,[1]
and to those of which Provence long preserved the tradition,
which are still practised by the bull-baiters of the Landes
and the peasants of Viterbo. It began with the exploits
of cowboys in the grasslands of the plain before it was transported to the arena by professionals. Those whom we have
before our eyes are acrobats, generally wearing the gymnastic
costume of short waist-cloth and high boots. They certainly
need courage and strength to brave the fury and to hang on to
the horns of a bull bigger than the modern bull by a third ;
but still more do they need to be nimble and cool-headed,
and their daring must be founded on self-confident agility.
Is not the calling of a toreador suited to women ? [2]

The terra-cotta bulls found at Koumasa and Porti show,
by the men clinging to their horns, that bull-leaping was in
fashion in Crete at least from the end of the third millennium
or the beginning of the second. It remained so until the end
of the Minoan civilization. It would be impossible to
enumerate all the objects which represent various episodes
of this sport. In Knossos, the sanctuary of the Minotaur, it
is everywhere. At the very entrance it appears in an
impressive manner in the most marvellous pieces of painted
stucco, the famous head of a bellowing bull (Pl. I, 2) and a
man's arm with muscles contracted on a horn. Inside the
palace the " Toreador " fresco explains the vigorous dash
of the ivory " Leaper ". (Fig. 51, pl. III, 1.) If the subject
which Minos loved enjoyed the same favour with the princes
of the mainland, it was not because they fancied themselves
as connoisseurs of foreign art ; they, too, liked to see pictures
of the sport which they enjoyed in reality. On the bezels
of their rings, on the walls of their palaces and on their gold
cups the lords of Mycenæ, Tiryns, Orchomenos, and Vapheio
gazed with rapture at celebrated feats. (Fig. 69.) Even the
little king of Athens had a record of them on a stone box.[3]

The bulls of the ring no doubt lived in freedom on ranches.
It was not easy to catch them. In a mountain landscape
we see a cowboy thrown on the ground by a beast whose tail

[1] Lagrange, **XLII**, 198 ; Pinches, LA. i, 76 ff. ; No. 23.
[2] BSA. vii, 94 ; **LXX**, pl. xviii ; **LVII**, 189 ; cf. Evans, loc. cit., 251.
[3] Reichel, loc. cit., Nos. 2, 10–11, 13–14, 21–2 ; **V**, pl. xxviii. 8.

frisks with joy.[1] The simplest way was to stalk the animal
near the drinking-place and to jump on to his neck while
he had his head in the water.[2] Some of them were broken
in, and we see tamers twisting their heads round by sheer
force of the wrist.[3] Once tamed, they lay down quietly and
allowed the toreadors to take them by the horns and jump
over their hind-quarters ; [4] this was in the acrobats' school.
The shows were given in arenas, near a sanctuary, as we see
sometimes   from   architectural   features.[5] Distinguished
spectators had seats on raised structures ; we know that
the ladies in the Mycenæan fresco who sit in a loggia adorned
with double axes are looking at a *corrida*. (Fig. 55.)

From the pictorial objects we can imagine the movements
of the toreador. Facing the bull just as he is charging with

FIG. 51.—Bull-leaping.   Fresco from Knossos.

head down, the man dodges quickly, leaps back and seizes
a horn. The beast raises his head to shake his adversary
off, and thus lifts him up (Fig. 51) and gives him enough spring
to make a recovery by catching one horn under his knee ·
and the other under his arm-pit. (Fig. 69.) If the toreador
is not of the first order he turns round and, taking off from
the horns or the back of the neck, leaps to right or left.[6] The

[1] **XX,** fig. 310 *a.*
[2] Ib., fig. 274.
[3] Reichel, loc. cit., Nos. 14–15.
[4] Ib., No. 7.
[5] **XX,** figs. 504 *a, b,* 507.
[6] **LXVII,** fig. 426, 13 ; **LXX,** pl. xviii ; *AΔ,* iv, pl. v, 1.

champion does better than this. For a moment he rests on the bull's neck, back to back ; then, with his feet on the hind-quarters, he forms an arch, stands up and jumps,[1] or else, gripping the withers or flanks with his hands, he turns a back-somersault.[2] A comrade, male or female, catches him in his arms to deaden the fall. But now we shall see the triumph of the bull-leaper's art, the special turn reserved for great occasions. As soon as he has leaped on to the beast the toreador lets go the horns with his hands and, holding himself on by his thighs, leans back over the muzzle ; with legs in air and arms outstretched he waits for the moment when the bull will toss him backwards and give him the impetus to take the perilous leap and land on his feet by a vigorous jerk of the loins.[3] We can understand the enthusiasm of a sporting people for exhibitions like this, and the joy which they were to artists who delighted in lovely movements.

The games which, from Crete, spread to all countries of the Ægean were destined to a glorious future. Wherever the Greeks held the great festivals, which by their gymnastic and musical contests had such influence on all education, the excavations and the legends attest the presence of the pre-Hellenes. The Nemeian and Isthmian Games are those whose origin is most obscure ; but their reputation, which was not justified by their importance in historical times, seems to come from the depths of the centuries, and their sites in Argolis and in Corinthia, on the great road of Ægean civilization, is significant. At Delos, the *Hymn to Apollo* sees in the god of Kynthos the lord of the *cithara*, and recalls that his temple-servants imitate the songs and dances of other lands. Plutarch gives details : he relates how Theseus came to the holy island to dance the *geranos* and to hold games in honour of Ariadne.[4] Olympia, near Pylos, the port frequented by the Cretan sailors, worshipped the old deities of Mount Ida, Kronos and Rhea, before it was consecrated to Zeus and Hera. Cymbals found beneath the Metroon, in the lowest stratum, tell how the feasts of the Goddess Mother were celebrated in those days. Furthermore, tradition

---

[1] JHS. 1921, 253, fig. 5 ; **XX,** fig. 504 *a* ; cf. our Fig. 69.
[2] Fig. 51 ; Pl. III, 1 ; JHS. loc. cit., 255 ; **XX,** loc. cit., *c*.
[3] **XX,** loc. cit., *a*.
[4] Plutarch, *Theseus*, 21 ; *Hymn to Delian Apollo*, 131, 160–4.

ascribes the foundation of the contests and games to a Herakles of Ida and to his descendant Klymenos.[1]

It might be expected that Delphi, shut off among its mountains, would have escaped these influences ; but in none of the holy places are they more certain.[2] The *Hymn to Pythian Apollo* says that, to take the place of the goddess Gaia, the god chose for priests Knossians whom he took from Pylos to Pytho. " He went at their head, holding a lyre in his hands ; sweet was his playing and fair and lordly was his gait. The Cretans followed him, beating the ground with their feet and singing the Io-Pæan." [3] All the memories of Delphi traced the musical and poetic contests back to Crete ; when prizes for the *cithara* and for sacred song were instituted the first victor was Chrysothemis the Cretan.[4] There are tales of Cretan missions which came to Delphi and, from there, extended their influence to distant countries ; one of them was said to have left the tradition of choruses in Thrace.[5]

It is obvious that everything in these legends is not historical fact, but taken together they form a solid fabric, a document which cannot be rejected. And here is a counter-check : of the great and ancient shrines of Greece, the only one where games were not held, that of Dodone, is also the only one where nothing betrays the presence of the Cretans.

Yet the most popular sport of Minoan Crete, the *corrida*, disappeared almost entirely from Greece. Legend preserved its memory and distorted it : the young girl who used to leap on the sacred bull and let him carry her with him as she held on by his horns becomes the fair Europé seated on the back of the divine bull, wreathing his horns with flowers. In reality the bull gave place to the horse, which in its turn long served acrobats as a moving spring-board.[6] Only in the remote countrysides of Thessaly and Asia Minor or in the far regions of the West were the secrets of the Cretan *corrida* preserved in obscurity or rediscovered.[7]

---

[1] Pausanias, v, 7, 6 ff. ; 8, 1.
[2] Cf. Swindler, **LXXXVII.**
[3] *Hymn to Pythian Apollo*, 336–41.
[4] Pausanias, x, 7, 2–3.
[5] Plutarch, *Moralia*, 298 F.
[6] *Iliad*, xv, 679.
[7] Cf. M. Mayer, JAI. vii, 72 ff. ; S. Reinach, An., 1904, 271 ff.

The other sports of the Minoans were most carefully taken
over by the Greek athletes. The agility of the Cretan warriors
is well known from Homer.[1] The boxing scenes carved on
the Hagia Triada *rhyton* might illustrate some description
of an Olympic contest, and themselves have a commentary
in the *Iliad* in one of the games given in honour of Patroklos,
the fight of Epeios and Euryalos who go down into the arena
" braced in their belts " and with their fists tied in straps
of wild bull's hide.[2] The Greeks always boasted of what
they had borrowed from the best system of training, like
pupils quoting their teachers. Even in Sparta the rules for
physical education instituted in the name of Lykurgos were
held to have come from Crete.[3]

But the fairest legacy which the Greeks received from their
predecessors was the dance, with its concomitants, already
promoted to high dignity—music and poetry. From Asia,
where Homer sang, to Delos and Delphi, it was known what
was the tie which bound the choruses which performed their
evolutions in the theatre of Knossos to those which performed
the " crane " step or glorified the god of Pytho. In Crete
the Kouretes danced in honour of Zeus and Rhea, as once
in honour of Minos and Ariadne ; in Messenia and in Asia,
where their evolutions alternated with those of women, they
celebrated the divine virgin-mother.[4] All this was due to
the brotherhoods or *thiasoi* [5] of sacred dancers, who perpetuated
the Minoan tradition. Thera and primitive Athens had their
orchestai. At Miletos the guild of *molpoi* or dancers for a
long time had its head recognized as chief magistrate of
the town.

Notwithstanding erroneous stories of the comparatively
recent invention of the large lyre and the double flute, the
old musical instruments were by no means lost. It was said
that Terpander of Lesbos about 676 thought of adding three
more chords to the four chords of the primitive *cithara*, and
that the double flute was invented in Phrygia. Indeed, we
do not know what kind of lyre is played in the Homeric poems

---

[1] *Iliad*, xvi, 617.
[2] Ib., xxiii, 651 ff., 684–5.
[3] Plutarch, *Lykurgos*, 4.
[4] Hesiod, frag. 198 (44) ; Pausanias, iv, 21, 7 ; Sappho, frag. 54.
[5] A word of pre-Hellenic origin (Cuny, loc. cit.).

by Apollo, Achilleus, and the divine bards, nor what sort of
flute is used for commands in Agamemnon's camp.[1] It may
even be remarked that the most ancient representation of
the heptachord which the Greeks have left us is painted,
in the hands of Apollo *Kitharoidos*, on a Melian vase of the
VIIth Century.[2] But it is none the less true that modern
criticism did not wait for the resurrection of the Cretan
civilization before it refused all credence to childish anecdotes.
At the very most Terpander obtained new effects from an
ancient instrument, and it is quite possible that serious music,
driven out of Crete by the invasion, found a refuge on the
coasts of Asia and inspired the singers of Aiolis and Ionia
before it reappeared in Greece proper. But it is enough
to look at the female costume worn by the *cithara*-playing
god and his disciples, to recognize them as the direct heirs
of the long-robed musicians who play the seven-stringed
lyre and the double-flute on the Minoan monuments. It
was on Cretan instruments that Apollo, god of Kynthos,
and Kybele, goddess of Berekynthos, taught the art of sweet
sounds to the lyre players and flute players of Greece.

The dance invokes music and song ; in song the words are
inseparable from the tune. Thus Greek lyric poetry gives us
a faint notion of the lyrics of a people whose language we do
not know. Let us listen to the bard who accompanies the
dancers in the Homeric description of the shield of Achilleus,
and we shall have some idea of him who sang in the theatre
of Knossos ; let us listen to the hymn of the Kouretes in its
Dorian form, and we shall catch an echo of a more ancient
hymn ; let us listen, if we can, to the rhythmical prayers of
the Cretan priests going up to Pytho, and we shall hear the
sounding strophes which accompanied Minos up the holy
mountain.

Song, in the epics, expresses sentiments which are sometimes
joyful and sometimes grave.[3] In the former case song is
subordinated to dancing. The bard Demodokos makes the
young people of Scheria dance to the sound of the *cithara*.[4]
In the marriage ceremony, " by the light of the torches, the

---

[1] *Iliad*, x, 13.
[2] RA. 1908, ii, 282.
[3] Croiset, *Hist. de la littérature grecque*, ii, 17 ff.
[4] *Odyssey*, viii, 260 ff.

ringing hymeneal song resounds ; the young men dance and
turn about ; flutes and lyres mingle their voices." [1] At
the festivals of Delos the temple-servants recalled the long
wanderings of Leto by imitating in voice and gesture the
peoples visited by the goddess. [2] This expressive form, with
its lively jigging rhythm and playful words, is the *hyporchema*,
in which the essential element is a " light dance ". [3] For the
hymeneal song the performers are divided into two choruses
led one by the lyre and the other by the *syrinx*. [4] Generally,
at Delos, for instance, the principal performers, who have more
difficult movements to do, detach themselves from the chorus. [5]
All these evolutions are to be found in Cretan dancing, as the
poet sees it : " Now the chorus quickens its skilful steps and
turns swift as the potter's wheel ; now it divides into rows
which go to meet each other . . . A divine bard enlivens them
with his songs to the lyre." [6] This is the dance in which the
prima donna in the Knossian fresco takes part, turning and
smiling. Tradition made no mistake ; the *hyporchema* passed
for an invention of the Kouretes, and the poet Simonides
called it " a Cretan mode ". [7]

A graver measure is the noble, manly pæan. [8] It too is
known in the Homeric epoch. " The sons of the Achaians
make the beautiful pæan resound " when they placate Apollo
or celebrate the glory of Achilleus. [9] The origins of this
religious song are clearly indicated to us by the *Hymn to
Pythian Apollo*. When the Knossian priests follow the god
singing, these songs, which they accompany on the *cithara*,
beating time with their feet, are " pæans in the Cretan
manner." [10] There is no question now of a dance to which
the song is subordinate ; it is a song with the dance reduced
to the regular step of the procession or military march. A
series of verses, each terminated by a refrain which dissolves
in the cry " Ie Paion "—that is what is meant by " the Cretan

---

[1] *Iliad*, xviii, 492 ff.
[2] *Hymn to Delian Apollo*, 160–4.
[3] Simonides, frags. 29–31. cf. Athenæus, xiv, 30, p. 631 *c* ; 28, p. 630 *e*.
[4] *Shield of Herakles*, 273–8.
[5] Lucian, *On Dancing*, 16.
[6] *Iliad*, loc. cit., 590 ff.
[7] Simonides, frag. 31 ; cf. Strabo, x, 4, 16.
[8] Cf. Croiset, loc. cit., 270–2 ; Swindler, **LXXXVII,** 59–64.
[9] *Iliad*, i, 472–3 ; xxii, 391–4.
[10] *Hymn to Pythian Apollo*, 326–41.

pæans ". The brisk rhythm appropriate to them was impartially called Pæonic or Cretic. Needless to say, it was a Cretan, Thaletas of Gortyn, who first gave a literary turn to the old melodies of his country and caused them to be executed in a richer and more brilliant form, but still with the original rhythm.[1] It was only just that, after other pæans had been formed, one should be discovered in the true home of them all ; chance played up admirably ; we have one which comes from the same site as a group of women dancing to the tune of the lyre—Palaikastro.[2]

[1] Cf. Croiset, loc. cit., 275–8.
[2] Bosanquet, BSA. xv, 338 ff.

BOOK IV

ARTISTIC AND INTELLECTUAL LIFE

CHAPTER I

ART

THE Cretans have had the privilege, rare in history, of
giving both to their contemporaries and to posterity
the impression of an artistic people. In other countries at the
same epoch works arose which still deserve admiration at
this day ; but neither in Mesopotamia nor in Egypt had the
great architects any idea but to gratify the pride of a king by
presenting his glory in material form in a house more beautiful
than those of his predecessors, or to contribute to the majesty
of the gods and to the immortality of the dead by placing
imperishable images in eternal monuments. The Cretans,
too, built fine palaces, pretty chapels, and imposing tombs,
and it is with a description of these works that we should
commence this chapter on art if we had not already seen what
was their civil and religious architecture. But they have this
peculiarity, that for them art extends to everything and to
all men. To the commonest objects in the humblest houses
they knew how to give æsthetic expression, to add those
details of adornment which make them more than mere articles
of use. This instinct affects them from the time when they
still live in simple huts. Even then they preserve unnecessary
articles to which they attach great value, an elephant's tusk
or a whale's vertebra. No sooner have they metal at their
disposal than they make daggers of silver and, without any
transitional stage, execute jewels of incomparable delicacy
and variety. To hold their superior oils and wines they must
have precious vases. At table they want jugs and cups
of graceful form adorned with brilliant painting or fine
engraving. They like to see about them the play of oblique
light in their rooms and, on the walls, the lively images of

all that pleases them in nature and increases their joy in life. Not content with adorning themselves in many-coloured stuffs and jewels, they require their very bodies, braced tight at the waist, to appear as works of art. If ever there was a country in which every circumstance favoured the blossoming of artistic gifts, and the industries which had to meet common needs spontaneously developed artistic industries, it was certainly the Crete of the third and second millenniums.

For genuine masterpieces to be kept in dwellings, which are often very humble, a society must be so organized as not to reserve for some few privileged ones the possibility of rising above material needs. This was the case in the period when Crete was divided into clans or feudal groups ; between all the chiefs there was fruitful emulation. Later, when the power of Minos extended, it did not impair local autonomy or personal liberty. Knossos becomes the centre of Crete, but does not absorb it altogether. Phaistos and Hagia Triada, Tylissos, Mallia, and all the towns of eastern Crete still flourish, and it was at Gournia, Pseira, and Palaikastro that the finest L.M.I. vases were found. Nothing shows better the rights of the individual in Crete and the influence of individualism on art than the innumerable quantity of seals which have been discovered in the houses of every town. They were used by the king and high officials, but also by private individuals, who all stamped contracts or bales of goods with the mark of their personality and all wanted this mark to be beautiful as well as original.

The Cretans also knew how to make the best use of the resources offered by the earth. Marble there was none, and little metal. But they had beautiful limestones, some of which were easily cut, while others could be ground into a lime suitable for making the stucco which was as good as the *gesso duro* of the Italians. On the slope of Mirabello and at Kakon Oros they found breccias mottled or marbled in gorgeous contrasts or delicate gradations of colour which led them on to polychrome. They also had several varieties of steatite, black or green, opaque or transparent, which called out for the chisel, and a yellow clay which fired well and took the colour well. Their palette was rich in firm, brilliant pastes, the brightness of which is still a marvel, where it has not been dulled by the conflagrations of the palaces.

With these material means technique made constant progress
from the day when Crete became acquainted with metal.
The use of fire became a sort of science which was as profitable
to the potter as to the metal-worker. While the one perfected
his moulds and his chisels the other learned to regulate the
temperature of his kiln and obtained mottled ware, barbotine,
and faience. Many inventions were made. The potter ceased
to work with his hands alone ; in the XXIst Century he used
a slow-spinning wheel, and from the XVIIIth the rapid wheel
was in general use. The experience acquired formed into
a tradition without degenerating into rule of thumb. From
father to son processes were handed down which gave the
hand amazing sureness. With soaked fibre and fine sand
or emery they succeeded in converting a block of hard stone
into a vase of perfect shape. Although they knew nothing
of the tempering of bronze they had delicate tools, for example
little turning-saws with double toothing not more than 6·5
centimetres by 4 ; they used these minute implements with
unerring dexterity. The painter saw the effect produced
by the application of colour on stucco while it was still wet,
and with strokes which must be final, without retouching,
only square-ruling his field in order to guide him, he covered
the walls with great frescoes. And, since the various arts
were no more divided off from each other than were art and
industry, what one gained was for the good of all. The
bronze-worker knew the secrets of the goldsmith and supplied
models to the potter ; the wall-painter gradually passed his
subjects on to the vase-painter, the sculptor, and the seal-
engraver and, combining the plastic art with his own, replaced
the flat fresco by the relief in painted stucco. Conscious
of their natural kinship, all artists vied in encouraging and
inspiring one another. By mutual teaching they gave themselves a complete education.

To perfect it they eagerly accepted, especially at the
beginning, lessons from abroad. The influence of the Asiatic
countries was practically nil. The shape of certain Babylonian
cylinders which sailors brought back with them was vaguely
imitated, and the two-handled cup, a speciality of Troy II,
was made in the Cyclades and in Crete. This is not much.
The influence of Egypt was much more fruitful. Egypt
supplied the stone-cutters with models for their stone vases,

and taught the use of seals and the manufacture of faience.
Many subjects derived from its religious traditions were
reproduced for a time or adopted for ever by Crete, such as
the cynocephalus, the hippopotamus goddess, and the gryphon.
Lastly, its painters passed on to those of Crete the
practice of representing men with red skin and women with
white.   The share of Egypt in Cretan art is therefore far from
negligible.   So is that of the Cyclades, for it was through
them that the spiral, which came from northern Greece,
passed on to the great island, there to play an enormous
part in decoration.

But no borrowing ever limited the freedom of the Cretan
artists.   They take good ideas where they find them, without
letting their originality suffer by it.   The processes obtained
from elsewhere are adapted to new requirements.   Motives
hallowed by the centuries and as rigid as religion could make
them grow young and supple and are utterly transformed.
The gryphon of the XVIIIth Dynasty, a lion who did not
know what to do with his wings, dashes off in the flying gallop,
and when he returns to the banks of the Nile they do not
recognize him.   The spiral of the mainland was a poor affair,
with its concentric circles connected by a tangent ; in Crete
it takes on undreamed-of power and variety in superb coils,
clever intertwinings, and happy combinations with linear
and foliate motives.

Freedom in respect of all teachings and all traditions—
that is the most characteristic feature of Cretan art.   It
had its conventions ; none of them ever hampered personal
experiment.   Before the rule laid down that the skin of
a man should be red, since the frescoes at that time had a
background of that colour every other colour was tried to
depict him, even blue, and at the time when the blue background showed off the red of the skin one artist ventured to
portray a king with a yellow skin.   Was this a search after
eccentricity ?   No, but a search after novelty—a novelty
which should be less conventional.   The Cretan artist has the
confidence of youth and an ingenuous audacity.   He feels
keenly the joy of creating.   He brings to his work the gay
heart which is a force.   His fancies are full not of turbulent
pretentiousness but of simple-minded potent joy.

For a long time the Cretan artist delights in feeling his

THE HALL OF THE COLONNADES, LOOKING TOWARDS THE GREAT
STAIRWAY. PALACE OF KNOSSOS

BULL'S HEAD. RELIEF IN PAINTED STUCCO. PALACE OF KNOSSOS

PLATE I

[face p. 306

way in every direction and tastes all the pleasures which
form and colour can give. Then he turns his efforts to design
and polychrome ; while the sculptor still represents life the
painter is content to combine floral elements with geometric
ornament to obtain above all a gorgeous colour-scheme.
When contrasts and blendings of colour have no longer any
secret for him, when he can combine straight lines and curves
so as to form triglyphs, then he is no longer satisfied with
conventionalizing one or two easy flowers and reproducing
the petals of lilies and water-lilies ; he, too, turns to the whole
of nature. The whole of Cretan art plunges into it with
rapture.

The Cretan brings with him the gift which nothing else can
replace, freshness of observation. He loves to watch the
rolling walk of the fisherman on the beach, the airs and graces
of the princess sitting in the royal box, or the excitement
of the crowd on feast-days. He is happy following with his
eyes the furious gallop of the baited bull, the cat stalking
his prey in the long grass, or the chamois leaping in the
mountains. He is charmed by the nonchalance of the bending
tulip and by the pride of the lily on its tall straight stem.
No sight has more fascination for this lover of the sea than the
flying-fish folding his wings in the water or spreading them
in the air, the play of the dolphin as he dives and comes up
again, the tentacles and suckers of the octopus and nautilus,
or all the strange forms, plant and animal, which you can
see in the shallows when the water is clear. Yet the feeling
for nature in Cretan art is by no means brute realism. Indeed,
it is not always a naturalism which selects from reality but
binds itself to be faithful to it. Cretan art seeks the
characteristic line. Men of all ranks must be slim and graceful ;
so they all, almost without exception, have long slender limbs
and such a narrow waist that the torso is almost triangular.
Ladies of high degree must be elegant ; so they often make
dainty gestures with hands lifted and fine fingers parted.

Above all, consequently, movement must be expressed.
The hand essayed it before the eye was trained. The venture
was bold but happy. In the beginnings of naturalism the
human figure and the forms of animals betray inexperience
by faults in the proportions ; but if the static effect is not
all that it should be the dynamic effect is already remarkable.

It will not take long for it to become perfect. The swelling
of taut muscles will be startlingly correct and detailed. The
swiftest motion will be taken, or rather surprised, with an
instantaneousness of vision and a sureness of execution which
are equally infallible. The plastic art of M.M.III shows us
absolute snap-shots. On a vase from Vapheio (Fig. 69) a
cowboy has just caught the bull in full gallop by the ear and
the root of the horns ; he is swinging on one leg in order to
effect with the thigh of the other a recovery on the horns.
The movement lasts the time of a lightning flash ; it would
appear unlifelike, were it not blazing with truth.

This is impressionism, but of the better kind, for it betrays
feeling. And by the feeling which they express the movements
even those of the beasts, even those of the plants, acquire
a pathetic force, one might almost say a moral meaning.
They are scenes of drama, the battle waged before the towers
where wretched women lift their arms to heaven (Fig. 68),
the hunt in which a lion turns on his enemies, fells one and
charges against arrows and javelins. (Fig. 71.) There is
a feeling of elegy in the melancholy of the trees which spread
their naked branches above wintry ponds. One may criticise
the anatomy of the cow and the goat which suckle their young
(Pl. IV, 1), but, as the one turns to lick her calf as it
sucks, and as the other listens to the bleatings of a second
kid waiting impatiently for his turn, they seem truly to
symbolize the dignity of motherhood.

All these artistic qualities were displayed by the Cretans,
as a rule, on objects of small dimensions. They have an eye
for truth and for beauty, but not for size. One might say
that they reduce everything to their own stature, being small
men. Their talent never has need of room ; it is never more
at ease than in a tiny field. The rooms of their palaces are
on the whole rather small. Their largest compositions are
the frescoes and painted reliefs which adorn the walls of those
rooms. Sometimes they depict figures of more than human
size, but very soon, as if repenting this lapse, from inveterate
custom they turn to the miniature fresco. Since their
sanctuaries are only little chapels their cult-images are only
little figurines. Their tallest statuettes do not reach 35
centimetres. It is on seals, gems, ring-bezels, and odd bits
of ivory that some of their most wonderful works are to be

found. They are very close to affectation, but their love
of nature and contact with her save them. The word
" immense " has perhaps never been needed in speaking of
their art, but the word " minute " has, constantly. They
are truly the Japanese of the Mediterranean.

I PAINTING[1]

Painting, and by that we mean painting on the flat, as
opposed to vase painting, is the most precious gift which
Cretan art has left us. This is true not only in contrast with
Græco-Roman art, which has left us so little in this kind
and not one masterpiece. It is, much rather, true in contrast
with all the civilizations of the same epoch, those of Egypt,
Mesopotamia, Troy, and Hellas. We have here, then, a
special taste, a distinctive feature. And, without denying
the Cretans a plastic gift, we must allow them an exceptional
gift for the pictorial.

Already about the middle of the third millennium the walls
of the Cretan houses were given two coats of plaster, the finer
of which received a red wash. When people learned to refine
the plaster and, by burning a certain limestone, obtained
a perfectly pure lime for the upper coat, an artist of genius
had the idea of painting in fresco on the wet stucco. The new
process and the rapid execution which it entailed could only
produce works which were bold, dashing, and exhuberant.
It was impossible to bind such quick strokes by academic
formulas. Each put his whole personality into his work.
The art which blossomed thus was full of charm.

In the First Palaces of Phaistos and Knossos certain walls
had been covered with many-coloured patterns of a liveliness
which recalls the tones of liparite or barbotine.[2] At once
the painter went on to the human figure. The " Saffron
Gatherer " dates from M.M.II.[3] The inexperience of the
artist leaps to the eye, the body is blue all over and too thin,
but the movement of the youth as he clambers over the rocks

[1] See Heaton, JIBA. xviii (1911), 697 ff. ; id., **LXX,** 211 ff. ; Rodenwaldt
LXX, LXXI ; K. Mueller, AM. 1913, 78 ff. ; Evans, **XX,** 524–49 ; Hall,
XXXVII, 178 ff.
[2] MA. xii, 20, p. viii, 6 ; **XX,** pl. i, *k.*
[3] **XX,** pl. iv.

is hit off well, and the bunches of pale flowers are not lacking
in grace.

In the XVIIth century, when the Second Palaces arose,
the fresco painter was in full possession of his mediums.
It cannot be said that he ever made all the progress of which
his art is capable ; he adheres to conventional colours for the
skin, he paints a full-face eye on a profile face, he knows
nothing of light and shade, and he has the most happy-go-
lucky notions of perspective. But his composition is good
and his technique excellent. On purely decorative panels
and friezes he imitates marble, makes labyrinths of interlaced
frets, coils spiral upon spiral, sets out figure-of-eight shields
in rows, and, by framing rosettes between triple bands,
anticipates the triglyph.[1] But all these motives are secondary.
The essential thing is the representation of plants, beasts,
and human beings. The most complete example which we
have is the life-size composition which adorned all the walls
of a room at Hagia Triada.[2] In a landscape dominated by
ivy-clad rocks bunches of crocus, red lilies, and hybrid flowers
of exquisite grace grow all about. A dark bull treads heavily
forward. A hare whisks by. Hidden in a thicket a wild cat
gathers himself up, with head down, eye fixed, and legs tense,
ready to pounce on a heath-cock which shows itself off in
blissful ignorance. (Pl. II, 1.) Lastly, among myrtles
in front of a sacred building a woman clad in a sumptuous
costume dances a mystic step, while a priestess in a long
robe kneels on the ground as if to gather flowers. The man
who could conceive and carry out such a work in M.M.III
was a master, one of the greatest that Crete has produced.

Was it the same man, or others of equal genius, who worked
about the same time for the King of Knossos ? Whoever
they were, they drew on nature and life lavishly, with the
burning freedom of youth. Those who love the beauty
of plants render flowering olive-branches with a nobility
which is none the less simple ; by a few light strokes of the
brush they produce bunches of reeds of charming delicacy ;
they sprinkle a red ground with white lilies, here and there
dropping a petal which has been blown off by the breeze.[3]

[1] Ib., figs. 255–6, 269–70, 343.
[2] MA. xiii, 55 ff., pl. vii–x.
[3] **XX,** figs. 389–90, pl. vi ; cf. fig. 392.

The favourite objects of the animal painter are the bull and marine life. One of them adorned the queen's apartment with two great dolphins swimming among smaller fish over shells and corals.[1] But for a palace the most suitable scenes were those taken from the life of the court and public festivals. The " Ladies in Blue ",[2] sparkling with jewels, enlivened the drawing room in which they sat with their elegant conversation and their noble gestures. The upper floor of the western sanctuary was adorned with a large composition : a superb bull dashes across the foreground, and over his back a toreador takes the perilous leap with his long tresses flying ; at the back we see the shrine of the goddess who presides over the sport ; in between is the crowd, so dense that their heads touch and so curious that they are all stretched in the same attitude.[3]

FIG. 52.—The Dancing Woman. Fresco from Knossos.

In L.M.I this effervescence subsided a little. Experience had created certain traditions. From exuberant archaism a classicism was born which, however, was neither stiff nor narrow. There are no more landscapes ; wall painting treats almost exclusively of scenes in which man plays the chief part. The " Parisienne " with the Watteau back embellishing her bodice has all the appearance of a portrait, with her rebellious curls, big eyes, knobby nose, sensual mouth, pointed chin, and long neck (Fig. 6) ; she formed part of a frieze in which a great number of personages sat in a line. " The " Dancing Woman ", in a clinging chemisette and a bolero, turns and turns in delirium, one arm against

---

[1] Ib., figs. 394–5.
[2] Ib., figs. 397–8.
[3] Ib., figs. 319, 321, 384–5 ; cf. BSA. x, pl. ii.

her body and the other stretched out, her hair flying about
her and a fixed smile on her lips. (Fig. 52.) [1]

Still more extraordinary are the miniature frescoes which
date from the same period. In order to represent larger
scenes someone thought of reducing the scale. With this
process of pictorial shorthand astonishing draughtmanship
was required to give expression to innumerable figures. The
result was brilliantly successful. In one of these pictures
the ladies of the court (Fig. 48), seated near a chapel, look
on from a box or loggia at an open air entertainment. They
are in a gala dress, and they chatter and gesticulate, all in
different attitudes. The spectacle about which they are so
excited is patronized by a dense throng which fills the whole
field. Another time a ceremony is witnessed from the top
of a slope, without doubt that which overlooks the stream
of Knossos east of the palace ; down below a group of women
perform the ritual dance, while behind them the spectators
extend in a seething mass to an olive grove, where some ladies
are sitting in the shade.[2] Needless to say, these genre painters
had a great success and found imitators in the provinces ;
at Tylissos one of these latter painted still smaller figures
which are quite as delicate.[3]

But in L.M.II the painters begin to show signs of lassitude.
They give up the miniature fresco. In life-size painting they
still have new ideas and make happy discoveries. But if
style is maintained it is only by stylization. The drawing
is less sure and less sincere ; the details are simplified and the
principal figures are no longer varied with the same delicacy.
The two couchant gryphons with which the Throne Room
is now adorned (Fig. 20) have a calm majesty, and the
surrounding landscape is not destitute of nobility ; but all
the same this symbolism lacks life, and the repetition of the
subject and the continual reproduction of the same plant
betray a certain poverty of imagination. The famous
Toreador fresco (Fig. 21), on the other hand, is at once
harmonious and spirited. The furious bull charges ; over his
back, in the centre, a toreador is in the middle of a leap ;
a young girl in male dress stands behind the beast and stretches
out her arms to catch the leaper the moment he touches the

[1] BSA. viii, 55, fig. 28. [2] Cf. **LXXI**, 10.
[3] **XXXVIII**, 62 ff., pls. vii–x.

CAT STALKING A HEATH-COCK. FRESCO FROM THE PALACE OF
HAGIA TRIADA

RUSTIC PROCESSION. RELIEF VASE OF STEATITE FROM HAGIA TRIADA

PLATE II

[face p. 312

ground ; another girl has just seized the horns as they were
upon her and is swinging preliminary to jumping on to the
bull's neck. The composition is admirable. But the proportions of the beast are not true and in general the execution
is archaic and at the same time decadent, as if the artist had
been content to copy an old model.

Let us look, too, at the great fresco of the Procession.[1]
Of more than human size, women in long robes and youths

FIG. 53.—The Cup-bearer.   Fresco from Knossos.

in foreign waist-cloths, either tribute-bearers or religious
acolytes, advance by the side of the sea, carrying vases of all
shapes, made of marble and of precious metals in turn.   The
figure to which the name of the Cup-bearer has been especially
given (Fig. 53) is a fragment of the first quality.   The head,
with its fine profile and proud, intelligent eye, is crowned with
curly hair ; the full, supple lines of the body are brought
out by the costume ; the torso leans gracefully backwards
in order that the hands may hold the great *rhyton* upright.
But the other figures have none of this distinction. They
are replicas of one same type, the attitudes are monotonous
and the composition is heavy and careless.   Where is the
alert variety of old ?

Outside Crete there is no mural painting in the countries of
the Ægean before the XVIIth century, and the frescoes which

[1] **IV,** 51–2.

we find suddenly appearing there are at their very first appearance of an advanced style. Everything comes from Crete—technique, style, and often subject.

There is no doubt that this is true of Melos. The finest fresco found there represents a group of flying-fish. (Fig. 54.) [1] Some swim over a rocky bottom covered with shells and sponges while others leap out of the water with spread wings. The curves which they describe and the eddies of blue bubbles which they leave in their wake give a singular grace to the

FIG. 54.—Flying-fish. Fresco from Phylakopi.

whole scene. In another fresco, representing two women, one wearing a richly ornamented dress and the other dropping her arms in an attitude of prostration,[2] the purity of the drawing is only equalled by its simplicity. The origin of the artists who executed these two works is indisputable. It has even been believed that the flying-fish were sent ready-made on a portable panel, but this supposition is unnecessary ; the two frescoes were painted in their place by foreigners.

On the mainland, from Thessaly to the Peloponnese, there is not the least sign of promise, not the smallest fragment

[1] **XXI,** pl. iii.   [2] Ib., fig. 61.

THE BULL-LEAPER. IVORY STATUETTE
FROM KNOSSOS

THE PRIESTESS OF THE SERPENT
GODDESS. FAIENCE STATUETTE
FROM KNOSSOS

PLATE III

[face p. 314

of painted plaster, nothing which could pass for the shadow of a prototype, to herald the great frescos which were to adorn the *megara* of Mycenæ and Tiryns, Thebes, and Orchomenos. Without any stage of transition the fully developed art of Crete appears, the painting of the last years of M.M.III or the first of L.M.I.[1] Cretan painters come at this time and settle in Argolis, and if we at once perceive in their work weaknesses which only appear later in Crete, it is apparently because these emigrants were not the greatest of the masters. But they knew all the secrets of the trade for all that. At Mycenæ and Tiryns the technique and style of the frescoes clearly bear this mark of their origin.

FIG. 55.—Ladies in a loggia. Fresco from Mycenæ.

The subjects are taken indiscriminately from Cretan and from local customs, but they are always treated in the Cretan manner with colours of local origin. On a panel of painted limestone, which might have come direct from Crete, two women in flounced dresses worship the goddess with the figure-of-eight shield near a small altar with concave sides.[2] A miniature fresco (Fig. 55) [3] represents ladies looking on at a *rodeo*. Leaning with their elbows on the edge of a loggia, they are dressed in the latest Knossos fashion and adopt the correct poses ; but it is no good—they are only village princesses giving themselves airs. With these frescoes we find others which breathe quite another spirit. To please

[1] Rodenwaldt, **LXX**, 199 ff.   [2] **LXVII,** fig. 440.
[3] **XX,** fig. 320.

the kings of the mainland, scenes of battle and the chase were wanted. At Mycenæ several friezes show warriors and horses at close quarters ;[1] at Tiryns hunters march one behind the other with two javelins on their shoulder.[2] The men wear the native costume, but often with foreign ornaments. Their hair is long and curly and their face is clean-shaven ; they are not in the least like the masks of the princes buried in the Shaft Graves.

Transplanted on to a new soil, the art of the fresco had had time to root itself strongly. Without losing contact with the country of its origin it had prospered in the new land for two centuries. When the Achaian invasion had destroyed the palaces of Crete and reduced its painters to inactivity the trunk died, but the shoot remained green.

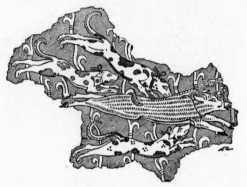

FIG. 56.—Hunting scene.   Fresco from Tiryns.

It was still to bear fruit. No longer having any masters to follow, the painters of Tiryns, Thebes, and Orchomenos go ahead in full independence. In the choice of subjects they freely indulge the tastes of their rude and ostentatious protectors, and thereby attain originality. They prefer large compositions and know how to put life into them. For some time, too, they maintain the good traditions of style. The processions which adorned the palaces of Thebes and Tiryns really deserved this popularity ; to judge by the figures which have been restored (Figs. 11, 12) these life-size figures of women filing round a great hall in two opposing directions, all in glittering dresses, each holding a chiselled

[1] **LXVII,** figs. 241, 437 ; **LXXI,** pl. i ff.   [2] **LXX,** pl. i, 6.

casket, a precious vase, or a bouquet of flowers, must have
had a fine effect. The painted floors of the *megara* of
Tiryns,[1] especially that of the Throne Room, were also works
of which Minoan Crete need not have been ashamed. But
when thrown on his own resources the artist of the mainland
loses purity of drawing and renounces truth of colour. The
painter of Tiryns, wishing to show the bare breast beneath
the bodice, pushes it far in front of the chest and puts the
arms out of joint. In the friezes of stags following each
other and chariots passing each other [2] the rendering of the
animal forms is still excellent in parts, but a prancing stag
has a red back and a white belly, and the horses with their
graceful cruppers have straps instead of tails and are so well
hidden one behind another that each leg counts for two.

The favourite motive, the chase, takes on remarkable
breadth and intense vitality. A multitude of huntsmen
and huntswomen, impatient packs, wild beasts fleeing, and,
in the middle, a boar which has been run down and is bitten
by the hounds until, mad with rage, it runs on to two javelins
(Fig. 56)—the scene is full of wonderful movement. But
the hounds are pink with black, scarlet, or blue spots; as the
boar plunges his hind-quarters taper away absurdly; and
the reeds which appear on the background are like yellow
forks. There is a flagrant contradiction between frenzied
naturalism and polychrome conventionalization. The decline
is manifest. When the painter comes to lose the gift of
making his pictures live it will be incurable. Deprived of
the air of its own country, and then of the light which still
came to it from the South, the shoot was bound in the end
to become etiolated and die.

With their keen sense of the decorative the artists of Knossos
combined painting with the plastic art, and created the painted
relief.[3] This quite special art did not spread outside Crete,
in Crete itself very few specimens have been found outside
Knossos, and at Knossos itself it only lasted for just the time
when painting on the flat was at its height. Its beginnings
date from the XVIIth century and its finest products in high
relief belong to the XVIth and XVth, after which it disappears.
It had a short and brilliant existence.

---

[1] Ib., pls. xix–xxi.   [2] Ib., pl. xv, 6, 1 ; pl. xii.
[3] See K. Mueller, JAI. 1915, 267–73.

The modelling was done on two layers, one on the top of
the other, being roughed out on a clayey plaster and finished
on a fine hard stucco. Frequently certain details, e.g. the
pendants of a necklace, and even a loin-cloth, were painted
on the flat ground. The relief frescoes thus produced are
among the purest masterpieces of Minoan art.

The place of honour must be given to the King with the
Fleurs-de-lys. (Fig. 57.) Of more than human stature,
he advances among reeds and lilies, with his right fist on his
chest and his left arm stretched out behind, holding the
sceptre. His bare chest is adorned with a broad necklace
of fleurs-de-lys, and on his head he wears a crown of fleurs-
de-lys, from the top of which three large feathers rise in a

Fig. 57.—The King with the Fleurs-de-lys. Painted relief from Knossos.

magnificent sweep. His whole being breathes strength and
majesty. Even to-day in the Candia Museum it is a striking
apparition, this portrait of Minos ; when it stood in his palace
it must have filled the beholders with religious awe and made
them carry their hand to their forehead.

But the painted reliefs did not represent single figures,
but large scenes. To what did a remarkable fragment belong
which shows the fingers of a man holding a necklace from
which heads of a negro type hang like medals ? The man
was tying this jewel on to the neck of a woman. Evans

suggests a ritual dressing, a sacred union.[1] The only relief
fresco which does not come from Knossos, that from Pseira,[2]
is known to us by fragments which belong to at least two
figures. They are women, whose contours are given with
a fine fullness, while their clothes and jewels are treated with
wonderful minuteness. They must have been looking on
at a *rodeo*.

At Knossos this sport supplied the favourite subject for
painted relief. In the north-east quarter of the palace piles
of stucco hooves and horns, belonging to several beasts, have
been found together with human limbs, including an arm with
the hand gripping a horn and muscles contracted and veins
swollen in a way which shows a perfect knowledge of anatomy.[3]
This was a fine composition; and they did still better. In
a portico which overlooked the North Entry the traveller
arriving by the road from the sea was confronted by a fantastic
vision. In a colossal group, two bulls at least and several
men were represented on a landscape background. A well-
preserved head of a bull (Pl. I, 2) is perhaps the finest piece
of Minoan art which has come down to us; in any case, the
portrayers of animals in ancient Greece never did anything
so perfect. With his fixed, starting eyes, his wide nostrils
snorting violently, his open bellowing mouth, his quivering
tongue, his brow rising in a movement of pride which is almost
human, he is the divine Minotaur in all his power.

II SCULPTURE [4]

In its technical processes the art of painted relief stands
half-way between painting and sculpture, but in its monumental character and even in its subjects it is only a variety
of fresco painting. It is obviously distinct from all the rest
of Cretan plastic art. There was never any sculpture in the
grand style in Crete. The Cretan sculptor applied his talent
only to small movable objects. He was not required to adorn
the walls of palaces or to carve great statues for temples.

---

[1] **XX,** fig. 383 ; cf. BSA. vii, 26 ff.
[2] **LXXXI,** pl. v.
[3] BSA. vii, 87 ff., fig. 29 ; cf. **XX,** fig. 273.
[4] See K. Mueller, loc. cit., 246–336 ; **LXVII,** 733 ff.

He worked with delight in clay, steatite, faience, ivory, bronze, and the precious metals, but tufa and marble did not tempt him.

In the first half of the third millennium, in E.M.II, the Cretan stone-cutters knew the refinements of their craft. The wonderful collection of vases of many coloured stone found at Mochlos testifies both to their artistic sense and to their manual skill ; [1] men who could find in lumps of unhewn rock such delicate or such vivid hues, and could cut hard blocks, without any other aid than a little sand, into perfectly round jugs with spouts and bowls with handles, supremely graceful little vases, and cups with the fineness and polish of metal were already capable of imitating natural forms. One of them chose out of his materials the softest and most homogeneous stone, steatite, and made a lid with a long-legged greyhound lying across it. [2]

Sculpture in the round appears in an ivory seal shaped like the head of a bird and in statuettes of alabaster, steatite, and even marble. [3] Soon the potters model their vases in the shape of women, birds, and bulls' heads with acrobats hanging on to them in bunches, or else they decorate them with reliefs representing a flying dove or a herdsman in the middle of his herd. [4] The image makers produce innumerable statuettes of men, women, and beasts. [5] The ivory carvers make seals adorned with beasts and later with scenes containing several figures, and make a whole handle into a monkey or a flock of pigeons. [6]

Thus the plastic art, which was inseparable from naturalism, had very ancient origins. It progressed continuously until the beginning of M.M.II. The vogue of polychrome delayed its development for a moment, but did not put a stop to it. And when painting came close to it by its conversion to naturalism it was provided, through the intermediate form of the relief fresco, with all the models which it required, and could thus assume an ever-increasing importance.

Since the plastic art set out to adorn small objects and

[1] **LXXXII,** pl. i–vii.
[2] Ib., 21, fig. 5.
[3] **XXXIV,** fig. 25 A ; **XXXVII,** pl. xiv, 4–6 ; **XX,** fig. 52.
[4] **XX,** figs. 84–5, 147, 137 a–d, 130 a, b.
[5] BSA. ix, pl. viii–x.
[6] **XX,** figs. 87, no. 8 ; 88 b ; 93 A ; 145 ; 87, no. 1 ; 86.

drew inspiration from the painted reliefs, its qualities were above all pictorial and were displayed for choice in reliefs.

Relief on ordinary clay was too fragile, but faience could be made of sufficient consistency. In Crete the faience-worker did not, as in Egypt, stick obstinately to the everlasting reproduction of the same motives. Although he worked for architectural decoration and marquetery, from the outset he adorned his squares with warriors, animals, plants, and houses drawn with documentary accuracy.[1] In M.M.III, when naturalism triumphed, he resolutely took his models from reality; he knew how to render its colours and shapes. On relief plaques destined for decorative panels he represented the goats and cows suckling their young, whose artistic value we have already appreciated.[2] Sometimes the animals of faience or terra cotta which were set in stucco were treated indiscriminately in relief or in the round. Marine subjects were done in this way, with flying-fish, crustaceans, and shells of every kind.[3] The imitation was so perfect that for a moment Evans took one of these creatures for a fossil crab. The plant world also tempted the faience-workers, and they made flowers and fruit in high relief. Among the pretty vessels which come from their kilns there is in particular a flower-vase with the branch of a rose-tree winding over the handle and falling into the interior.[4] There was a Bernard Palissy at Knossos who did not hesitate before any audacity; he made the most effective votive robes and girdles for the goddess,[5] and he even represented the goddess herself in the round.

The best examples of relief which we have are supplied by a series of steatite vases.[6] These vases were much in demand in L.M.I. They are divided into zones or even composed of parts fitting one into the other, a technique borrowed from the metal-workers and goldsmiths. Sometimes they were covered with a leaf of gold on which the reliefs were produced in *repoussé*; but most are so meticulous in execution that the most careful hammering could not have brought their subtleties out in the gold, and some are enhanced

[1] Ib., 301 ff.
[2] p. 308; cf. pl. iv, 1.
[3] **XX,** figs. 379–80.
[4] Ib., figs. 357–8.
[5] Ib., fig. 364.
[6] Cf. K. Mueller, loc. cit., 258–65.

by inlay which was certainly not meant to be hidden. With
or without gold, these carved vases were pure masterpieces.
Mere fragments are enough to give a vivid impression of
artistry.[1] But we have the good fortune to possess three
intact examples, found at Hagia Triada.

They are not all from the same hand ; the relief varies in
height and the anatomy and the way of treating the eye and
ear are different. But all show an equal mastery.

FIG. 58.—The Boxers Vase. *Rhyton* from Hagia Triada.

We have already described (Fig. 27) the scene represented
on the goblet which is generally called the Chieftain or Officer
Vase : it is homage done to the King. Only a great artist
could have so easily overcome the difficulty presented by
a conical field measuring 8 centimetres in height, 27 in girth

[1] See BSA. ix, 129, fig. 85 ; vii, 95, fig. 34 ; 44, fig. 13.

WILD GOAT SUCKLING ITS YOUNG. FAIENCE PLAQUE FROM KNOSSOS

OCTOPUS VASE FROM GOURNIA

PLATE IV

[face p. 322

at the top, and only 12 below, and have rendered within such
a small and inconvenient space the majesty of the King, the
deferential dignity of the vassal, and the force concealed
behind the monstrous shields.

The largest of these vases (Fig. 58) is a *rhyton* 47 centimetres
high. It is divided into four zones, three of which contain
boxing scenes, while one is given to bull-leaping. The precision
of the details makes it an inestimable document for the history
of gymnastic games, and we have already examined it from
this point of view ; but here we must admire the skilfulness
of the composition and the great variety of the scenes and
attitudes in the unity of the subject. The boxers are divided
by age and weight into classes which can be recognized from
their helmets. They advance or break away, parry, punch,
fall, roll on the ground, and triumph. Every incident in
a fight and every position are indicated in a succession of little
dramas which patrons of the ring must have found most
exciting.

There is equally intense movement, though of a very different
kind, in the scene which is unfolded on the belly of the third
vase. (Pl. II, 2.) Solemn and comic, a rustic procession
advances. They have come back from work, well pleased
with themselves, and each carries on his shoulder the long-
pointed fork with which the olives were beaten down. At
their head is the chief of the band, taller than the others,
with a ritual cassock over his upper part ; he smiles, with a
full sense of his importance. In the middle of the procession
march four professional singers. They are giving voice as loud
as they can with their mouths wide open and their chests
inflated, and the chief of the choir brandishes an Egyptian
sistrum to beat time. There is striking resemblance between
this group and that of the blind musicians carved on a tomb
at Tell el-Amarna.[1] But as they go marching in twos,
shoulder to shoulder, one of them makes a false step and falls,
much abashed, while the man in front turns round and the
neighbours are in high glee. Here we have delightful swing
and charming irony with a touch of caricature, combined with
a mastery in the great style shown in the grouping of the
figures.

If nothing survived of prehistoric Crete but these three

[1] See Capart, *L'Art égyptien*, pl. clxxii.

vases we should still recognize through them a highly civilized people, well organized, devoted to sports and festivals, and marvellously gifted for the arts.

Moreover, the steatite vases with reliefs were not exclusively reserved for human figures. They borrowed from vase-painting the motive of the octopus swimming among corals. One example, among others, represents the monster coiling his tentacles with wonderful realism. It comes from Mycenæ, [1] but its origin is certified by a painted vase from Gournia. (Pl. IV, 2.)

Fig. 59.—Carved wooden box, found in Egypt.

Fig. 60.—Carved wooden box, found in Egypt in the tomb of a Syrian priest (end of the XVIIIth Dynasty).

Sculpture on wood and bone, which are fragile materials, has left few traces in the Ægean, but we see what it could do from a fine lid and sides of boxes found in Egypt. (Figs. 59, 60.) [2] Ivory has survived better. From Palaikastro we have a beautiful bird of heraldic type. [3] A roundel which represents a leaping bull turning its head back comes from Cyprus, but it is certainly of Cretan make. [4] The same is true of a high

[1] **LXVII**, fig. 487.
[2] REG. 1899, 176, 178.
[3] BSA. xi, 285, fig. 14 *a*.
[4] **XXXVII**, fig. 83.

relief found at Mycenæ, which shows a woman seated on a rock.[1]
As for the carved mirror-handles which have been found in
many places and the helmeted heads from Mycenæ, Spata,
and Enkomi,[2] their origin is not known.

The Cretan sculptor disdains ordinary stone, and for his
reliefs consents to use only a species of purple gypsum
resembling porphyry, and he uses even this only for articles of
use. He carves spiral flutings and conventional leaves on
the stand of a lamp, and he covers a standard weight with the
tentacles of an octopus (Fig. 32) ; but that is all.

FIG. 61.—The Lion Gate.   Acropolis of Mycenæ.

At Mycenæ, on the other hand, relief on stone is in favour.
Before the expansion of Cretan art simple-minded image-
makers cut the grey-brown limestone of the country into
clumsy funeral steles. One of them [3] represents a warrior
driving his chariot at the enemy. The man is too big ; only
one of the two horses is seen, and it has only two legs and
a thick tail like a lion's curling in the air ; and to fill the
field the artist could think of nothing better than heavy
spirals. The Cretans changed all this. Their influence made
itself felt immediately. Another stele [4] represents a hunting

[1] REG. 1913, 431.
[2] **LXVII,** 815 ff. ; cf. above, p. 86.
[3] **LXVII,** figs. 360–1.
[4] Ib., figs. 359, 364.

scene. The proportions are truer, and the subject is dramatic. A stag flees, a lion defends itself, one of the hunters is laid out near the chariot and covers himself with his shield, and there are even traces of landscape.

But, if the old image-makers learn their trade anew under the guidance of foreign teachers, these masters themselves, who did not know how to carve limestone or to make life-size figures, must apply themselves to it. In the XVth century the development is completed. Were they Cretans or Mycenæan pupils of the Cretans who sculptured the Lion Gate (Fig. 62) and other reliefs in the same style ? One thing is certain, and that is that the style is the style of Crete. The beasts standing above the gate face each other with their feet on concave-sided altars before a single column of a type well known at Knossos, in the familiar attitude of the devices of the Minoan seals. Two fragments seem to have belonged to a big composition ; one represents a lion with a magnificent mane in front of a tree, charging to the right, and the other is the foot of a bull turned to the left. One has only to compare two island seals to be almost able to reconstruct the scene.[1] Even the big reliefs in stone, although they were not known in Crete, show us that Argolis had become a province of Cretan art.

The sculptors of the island had not yet developed their later dislike for stone when, about the middle of the third millennium, they made their first attempts in the round, for the oldest figurines of women or goddesses, those which were found at Hagia Triada and Koumasa, are of alabaster and marble as well as of steatite. These experiments did not lead to anything. A distinction must, however, be drawn. For sculpture in the round, clay, steatite, and even, in rare cases, a hard limestone resembling marble were used for animal representations, but for human figures clay, faience, bronze, and ivory alone were used.

About the end of the third millennium and the beginning of the second the terra-cotta figurines from Chamaizi, Zakro, and above all Petsofa already display a lively feeling for nature and a certain manual skill. We have made use of them in order to describe the dagger of the period, male footgear,

---

[1] Ib., figs. 291, 400 ; cf. **XX,** fig. 539 *a, e.*

and women's clothes and hats.   The legs of the figures are not
made separate, but the elbows stick out and the hands are
raised to the breast in the attitude of prayer.   Since these
figurines were offered *ex voto* they also represented animals
of every kind with their characteristic features.[1]

Being manufactured for humble people, the human figures
of terra cotta show hardly any progress in subsequent years.
Clay was, however, used to make fine *rhytons* in animal form.
Since these vases were *aspersoria* with a ritual purpose they
almost always represented the sacred bull, sometimes the
whole beast, but generally only the head.   Good models
existed.[2]   But clay was too vulgar a substance for the royal
chapels.   From the Little Palace we have a bull's head of
black steatite.[3]   It is of half life-size and of excellent make.
The muzzle is inlaid with mother-of-pearl, the eyes are of rock
crystal with pupils of a red stone, and the horns are of wood
plated with gold ; although the muzzle and hair are conventionalized the expression is quite living.   Another *rhyton*,
of a yellowish-white limestone resembling marble, is in the
shape of the head of a lioness, of life size.   The nostrils and
eyes are enamelled, while the hair is indicated by grooves.
The work is not lacking in spirit.   It was highly valued, as is
proved by the replica which was sent to Delphi and the
imitation which was made in gold for Mycenæ.[4]

Terra cotta is replaced by faience, for modelling in the round
as for relief, when man is to be represented.   The most remarkable products of the royal faience works are the statuettes
of the Serpent Goddess and her priestess.   Everything about
them reveals a liberty which is not restricted by any religious
obligation or any consecrated type.   The goddess (Fig. 62)
is dressed like a lady of the court.   But her big black eyes,
huge ears, and tall tiara give her a strange supernatural aspect.
From the bottom of her apron to the top of her tiara, in front,
behind, round her girdle, over her arms, over her ears, and
everywhere except on the milky whiteness of her breast and
face, long greenish reptiles with brown spots coil about her ; she
is a goddess beyond doubt.   The priestess (Pl. III, 2), who

---

[1] BSA. ix, pl. ix–xiii.
[2] **LXXXI**, pl. ix ; **XI**, fig. 51.
[3] **XVIII**, figs. 87–8, 90 ; cf. fig. 70.
[4] Ib., figs. 91–2 ; Perdrizet, *Fouilles de Delphes*, v, iii, fig. 13 ; for Mycenæ,
see pp. 269–70 and 336.

is rather smaller and more human, wears a more showy costume.
She has prominent breasts and a calm face, she holds two little
snakes in her extended hands, and on the top of her flat cap
sits a little lioness. These two masterpieces show us Cretan
plastic art in full command of its methods in M.M.III; they
are the biggest statuettes which we possess.

To do full justice to the bronzes we must not forget that
the pillagers who gutted the Cretan capitals carried off metal

Fig. 62.—The Serpent Goddess. Faience statuette from Knossos.

more than anything else. We have kept only a small number
of bronze statuettes of the good period of M.M.III and L.M.I;
not one comes from any of the great palaces, and the largest
is only 25 centimetres high, whereas the Serpent Goddess
measures 34 centimetres. Several male statuettes, two of
which were found at Tylissos and in the grotto of Psychro,

represent worshippers, or perhaps priests ;[1] another appears
from the position of the arms and hands to portray a flute-
player.[2] Despite their religious character, each of these
figures has its own individuality. Those which are making
the gesture of adoration have no resemblance to one another.
One (Fig. 63) is short and squat with a bulging stomach which
lifts up his waist-cloth, and looks like the Sheik el-Beled of
Tylissos. The flute-player (Fig. 64) throws his shoulders

Fig. 63.—A worshipper.   Fig. 64.—Flute-player.
Bronze from Tylissos.   Bronze in the Leyden Museum.

back in an attitude of youthful springiness which is not belied
by the rakish cock of his bonnet. These are very living
portraits. The best of the female statuettes, though of
unknown provenance, is certainly of Cretan make. It has
often been called the " Nautch-girl ", but it is really another
priestess of the Serpent Goddess.[3] The material has not

---

[1] 'Εφ., 1912, pl. xvii ; **XX,** fig. 501 ; JHS. xli (1921), pl. 1.
[2] Van Hoorn, JAI. 1915, 63–73, pl. i ; for the attitude see the statuette
from Keros (**IV,** fig. 119) and the Hagia Triada sarcophagus (Fig. 50 a).
[3] **LXVII,** figs. 349–50 ; **XX,** fig. 365.

prevented the sculptor from giving suppleness to the drapery of the flounced skirt, nor is the hair, entwined with snakes, at all heavy.   The head is bent forward, while the right hand

FIG. 65.—The Serpent Goddess.
(Ivory statuette in the
Boston Museum. Front view.)

FIG. 66.—The same.   Side view

FIG. 67.—Head of the same.

makes the gesture of worship and the left takes one of the serpents from the right shoulder.   The movement is graceful and, a great advance, the law of frontality has had its day.

Lastly, we have a group of remarkable workmanship and inspiration [1] : over a great galloping bull a slim acrobat describes a semi-circle from his hair, still flying about the horns, to his feet, which already rest on the hind-quarters.

Of all the figures in the round the ivory statuettes are, with those of faience, the most characteristic and the most precious. It is as if the delicacy and purity of the material inspired and upheld the artist. For the first time we find ourselves in the presence of figurines of children, pretty figures of little naked boys.[2] But nothing comes up to those marvellous products of chryselephantine sculpture, the Serpent Goddess at Boston and the Bull-Leaper. They are hackneyed subjects, made new by genius. The Goddess (Figs. 65–7) holds her arms out stiffly with a golden snake in each hand. Nothing else indicates the sacred character of this figure ; all the rest is pure human beauty. The skirt suggests the slim graceful form below, the belt girds a waist which is slender without conventional exaggeration, and the bodice has none of the rigidity which displaces the bare breasts. The face is treated with particular care and has an expression which is very sweet yet grave. This is not a type, but a woman.[3] The Bull-Leaper (Pl. III, 1) is taken in the midst of the perilous leap. The movement is full of airy lightness. The body is all length and action, the muscles are tense, and the veins are prominent ; it would be impossible to combine more minuteness with more freshness. When we remember that this figure formed part of a group and that there was a bull plunging beneath it, we realize keenly that the highest art is not measured by mere size.

While sculpture in the round thus reached the height of art in Crete it dragged out a miserable existence in the Cyclades. They had marble, but did not know what to do with it. Their only progress consisted in separating the legs of their little idols. When they ventured upon more complicated subjects, flute-players, lyre-players, or the Goddess Mother carrying the divine child on her head, they produced monstrosities.[4]

[1] JHS. 1921, 247 ff.
[2] BSA., Suppl. Paper, No. 1 (1923), fig. 107.
[3] But this figure may be a forgery. See Corrections and Additions, pp. 397–8.
[4] **IV,** 116, 119, 120. The bronze statuette found at Phylakopi (**XXI,** pl. xxxvii) is of Cretan origin.

At Cyprus during the same period, horrible deities were modelled in clay.[1] At Troy the stone idols remained flat and shapeless, and sculpture in metal only gave rise to abortive experiments.[2] Hellas was content to reproduce the figurines of primitive times, only modifying their steatopygous character.[3] It is only after the XVIth century, when the whole Ægean became open to Cretan influence, that we note a change, which takes place without transition. An artist of Amorgos carved a man's head astonishingly like certain archaic Greek types[4]; an image-maker of Mycenæ, turning from relief to the round, produced a figure with a tattooed face in painted limestone (Fig. 1); even in Thessaly they took to making ithyphallic statuettes of clay.[5] But the new school had not time to receive a complete education; sculpture in the round was too difficult an art, and teachers were shortly to be lacking.

For in this art decadence begins earlier and is more rapid than in any other. Already at the end of L.M.I the little bronzes of Hagia Triada are clumsy representations of too thin men and too thick women.[6] There is no question of life or contour; accurate modelling disappears. The legs are absurdly elongated until, in L.M.III, the men seem to be standing on stilts.[7] As for the woman who was the first in the history of Cretan sculpture in the round to show her feet, she would have done better to hide them.[8] Beside bronze only coarse clay is used for human and animal figures, and even bronze is sometimes replaced by lead.[9] In the second half of the XVth century the little Dancing Women of Palaikastro still have the virtue of forming a group and making fairly lively gestures; but, from the XIVth century onwards, the pregnant woman from Gournia, the Dove Goddess from Knossos, and the bull and horse from Phaistos are either repulsively monstrous or childishly barbaric.[10] It is the end of art.

[1] **X,** 379 ff.; 361, pl. xliv, 5, 6; cf. 345, fig. 264.
[2] **IV,** 118.
[3] **LXXXVIII,** pl. xxxii ff.
[4] **IV,** 122.
[5] **XCI,** fig. 30, 110.
[6] **LI,** pl. xxvi, 1–3.
[7] **IV,** 148–50.
[8] Ib., 151.
[9] **XVIII,** 75, fig. 84.
[10] BSA. x, 217, fig. 6; **XL,** pl. x, 11; BSA. viii, 99, fig. 56; MA. xii, 118, 127.

III GOLDSMITH'S WORK AND DAMASCENING

There was great surprise long ago when Schliemann discovered in the Second City of Troy the famous " Treasure of Priam ". Did all this gold and silver plate and all these jewels of beautiful workmanship really belong to a time when warriors wielded stone axes and obsidian daggers ? There is no doubt about it to-day. At the same time and even earlier similar jewels were made in Crete, and the people of Mochlos were at that time wearing diadems adorned with flowers and leaves.[1]

The Cretan goldsmith was thoroughly acquainted with work in gold and in silver, which was rarer and perhaps more valuable than gold, he made use of iron, which was rarer still, he inlaid and overlaid bronze, and he set all the precious stones. He disdained amber alone, and readily left it to the people of the mainland, as the Greeks later left it to the Romans.

In the good period he knew how to give an artistic value to a jewel. We might guess this from the figures on reliefs and frescoes, and we know it from many necklaces and pendants. Quite a special interest attaches to certain little gold trinkets found at Knossos, solid figures of lions, ducks, fish, and the like.[2] These objects are pretty, but the important thing about them is that they prove that plastic goldsmith's work was done at Knossos. The systematic looting of beautiful objects of bronze or precious metal which accompanied the invasions allows and indeed compels us to conclude that this craft was capable of infinitely more artistic productions, and that any which are found elsewhere about the Ægean may be ascribed to the Cretans. For the same reason we have to supplement our information about gold work from that supplied by reliefs and engravings on bronze, which are all too rare. In spite of all, we can see what the bronze-worker could do from finely decorated weapons and certain vases, one of which, decorated with lilies and beads, deserves to be reckoned among the purest and noblest works of prehistoric art.[3] It is enough to give us an idea of the beauty which the bronze-worker and the goldsmith of Crete could attain when they worked together.

[1] **LXXXII,** figs. 8–11.
[2] BSA. viii, 39, fig. 18 ; 80, fig. 45.
[3] Ib., ix, 121–8, figs. 76–83 ; **XVI,** fig. 116.

We have thus a guiding clue with which to traverse Mycenæ, the city "rich in gold". Nowhere, not even in Troy, have such masses of jewels been found as in the Shaft Graves. Some of them are like nothing in Crete, either in form or in decoration. Others clearly bear the stamp of Cretan influence.[1] These two characteristics are shown combined in the largest and most beautiful of the Mycenæan pins. The silver stem is so long that it can only have been used for the old mainland costume, and yet the gold head represents a woman dressed in the Cretan manner.[2] One fact remains certain—in a very short period the style of Mycenæan goldsmith's work became Cretan.

We are driven to the same conclusion by other objects. The famous gold masks which preserve the features of buried kings speak to the imagination, but they are only clumsy impressions stamped by natives. On the other hand, a couchant lion, among other animals of gold, is of a style which need not fear comparison with the standing lion from Knossos.[3] Two gold boxes bear reliefs copied from excellent models, and their origin is proved by the trees of the landscape and by beasts at the flying gallop.[4] There is still much inexperience in most of the plaques hammered and cut out in the shape of women [5] or animals, but the motives are almost always taken from the cycle of Cretan art ; soon, too, the workmanship improves, and we can understand the grace of a flying gryphon and the realism of a nautilus [6] when we see the swallow treated on one of these plaques in the same way as on a vase from Melos.[7] Finally, though there is nothing in Crete at all similar to the roundels of stamped gold,[8] the linear, vegetable, and animal motives of their graceful decoration are of Cretan style, and of the purest.

We come thus to certain works which do not merely indicate the influence of foreign models or masters but were actually executed by those masters and were almost all imported. These are a wonderful series of vases which come for the most

[1] Cf. **LXVII,** fig. 539 ; **IV,** 231, 234.
[2] AM. 1918, 153 ff.
[3] **IV,** 236 *f, a* ; cf. *e.*
[4] Ib., 87–9.
[5] Ib., 237.
[6] Ib., 237 *k,* 238 *a.*
[7] Cf. **XI,** figs. 73–4.
[8] Cf. **LXVII,** figs. 540–3.

part from the Fourth Shaft Grave, one of the most ancient.[1]
They are of very elegant shape and bear decoration of various
kinds—flutings, waving branches, a frieze of dog-daisies,
dolphins, running lions.   One gold cup, with doves perched
on the handles and dipping their beaks into the interior,
is the exact prototype of the *depas* which Homer places in
the hand of Nestor.   One of these vases is quite peculiar :
it is a silver basin with inlays of gold and sulphurous silver
representing the same male head with a pointed beard ; [2]
it was certainly made on the mainland by a Cretan or by a
Mycenæan of the Cretan school.   This may also be true of
the others, but their style is generally so good that it is still

Fɪɢ. 68.—Siege scene.   Silver *rhyton* from Mycenæ.

more likely that they were cut by a master goldsmith in
Crete itself.   One of these vases allows of no doubt whatever.
It is a gold jug from the Third Shaft Grave, with a beak,
a high voluted handle, and spiral ornament ;   two exactly
similar jugs have been found in Knossos, one of silver which,
like that from Mycenæ, belongs to L.M.I, and the other of
faience, going back to M.M.III.[3]

With still more reason must we regard the celebrated
heads of animals modelled in the round as mere variants

---

[1] Cf. **LXVII,** figs. 524–31 ;   **IV,** 205–12.
[2] **LXVII,** fig. 384.
[3] **IV,** 205 ;   **XX,** fig. 356.

of the Cretan *rhytons*. These absolutely first-class works dated from a period when the art of the mainland was in its childhood. A bull's head of silver, with bronze ears plated with silver and gold, gilt horns and muzzle, a double axe on its head and a gold rosette on its forehead, recalls the steatite and terra-cotta heads from Knossos and Gournia by its size, its expression, and even by the way in which the hair has been treated.[1] A gold head of a lioness is of the same type as the stone head of which Knossos sent a copy as far as Delphi.[2]

But there are other *rhytons* from Mycenæ which cannot be referred to known prototypes; these are the silver *rhytons*, the surviving fragments of which represent scenes containing numerous figures. The most famous of these compositions treats of the siege of a city. (Fig. 68.) In a plain planted with trees an acropolis rises. The houses are surrounded with a rampart. On a tower women lean forward to follow the turns of the fray, and their gestures express their agitation. The defenders are making a sally; in front are the slingers, then the bowmen crouching, and in the rear men armed with spears. All are naked, except the spearmen, who wear a short stiff garment fixed over one shoulder. The attackers are armed with clubs and stones. Down below a body of men arrives by sea; a man wearing the long-tailed conical helmet and the short-sleeved *chiton* appears to be handling an oar. What is the historical event celebrated by the artist? Hypothesis here has free play; what we may take for almost certain is that we have two foreign peoples at war, and a party of Mycenæans coming to the help of one side. The *rhyton* clearly glorifies some exploit of the king who ordered it to be made and took it with him into the tomb.

The same may be said of another silver *rhyton*[3] 50 centimetres high, representing a battle scene. The figures, which are very large and well modelled, wear drawers; we see a naked torso, a *chiton*, helmets with crests or tails, and shields of the figure-of-eight type, or cut off square at the bottom. Here again is a tale of war which was told in Argos.

After the *Iliad* we have the *Odyssey*; on a third fragment of a *rhyton* there are shipwrecked men swimming for their

[1] **LXXVII,** fig. 398; see pp. 269-70 and 327.
[2] **IV,** 163; see p. 327.
[3] K. Mueller, loc. cit., 317-25, fig. 31.

lives.[1] Thus all the legend which was to be immortalized
in the Achaian epic was already immortalized in Cretan art.
For the authors of these works, which were buried in the
Fourth Shaft Grave, were not the fellow-countrymen of the
heavy-handed image-maker who carved the stele of the same
tomb. They had come to Mycenæ at the call of a dynast
who had gold and wanted glory. We can imagine them
getting from him the gold which they needed and perhaps
hearing from his lips the story which they were to record.
At every turn they betray their origin. One of them seems

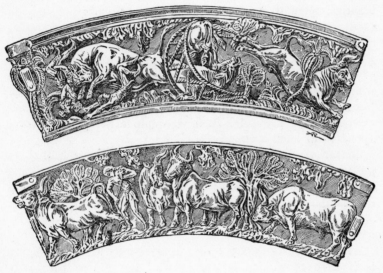

FIGS. 69 and 70.—Wild and tame bulls. Gold cups from Vapheio.

to have taken for the inspiration of his whole composition
a piece of faience marquetery at Knossos, and he might have
copied his fortress from a seal from Zakro. (Fig. 73*d*.) The
other gives his warriors the careful anatomy and light gait
which leave no illusion about his country. The third shows
swimmers threatened by Skylla, the sea bitch of Cretan
legend. These are almost as good as signatures.

The art of the cups from Vapheio (Figs. 69–70)[2] is more
refined and more sure of itself; we pass from the Shaft Graves

---

[1] **XX,** fig. 521, *a, b.*
[2] **LXVII,** 317–25, pl. xv; cf. K. Mueller, 325–31, pl. ix–xi.

to the bee-hive tombs, from M.M.III to L.M.I. The first
of these cups represents the capture of the wild bull, the second
the life of the bull when tamed. The first scene takes place
in the mountains, among rocks and palms ; one bull has been
caught in a net and twists about in impotent rage, another
gallops away in terror, and a third, mad with fury, leaves
the cowboy whom he has just thrown down to charge at another,
who dodges the blow by hanging on to one of his horns.
The second scene takes place in the plain, among olive trees ;
everything breathes peace and idyllic calm ; one bull lets
himself be led by a rope while another addresses amorous
blandishments to a cow. The wonder here lies not only in
the intense expression and the truth of every motion, the clear
outlines, the lively contrasts of light and shade, and the skill
with which the relief is heightened in proportion to the violence
of the movements, but still more in the consummate knowledge
which combines two subjects, similar yet different, in compositions of perfect harmony and order. One really cannot see
where, except in Crete, such complete artistry could have
appeared at such a time.

So far we have spoken almost exclusively of bronze or
precious metal treated by themselves. But the most original
achievement of the Cretan metal-worker and goldsmith was
the combination of materials, various metals, ivory, and rare
stones. Inlay, overlay, and damascening were never done
better.

At a very early date the Cretan armourers had ornamented
their daggers. There is a dagger of the end of the Early
Minoan Period from Mochlos with an alabaster pommel,[1]
and there is an engraved blade of M.M.II representing a boar-
hunt and bulls charging each other.[2] But the wonderful
daggers which are the usurped glory of Mycenæ date from
L.M.I.[3] What a delight they are to the eyes even now !
What a pride they must once have been to the king who wore
them on feast days ! The dark bronze ground gleams with
precious metal laid on in relief plating or set in hollows. Gold
and silver are sharply contrasted or presented by cunning
alloys in a whole series of tones passing from one to the

[1] **LXXXII,** 77–8, xxi, 8, 22.
[2] **XX,** fig. 541.
[3] **LXVII,** pl. xvii–xix.

Fig. 71.—Dagger, of bronze inlaid with gold and silver. Mycenæ.

other. The decoration is extremely delicate. Lions leap forth among rocks. A seed-plot of fleurs-de-lys unfolds the grace of corollas in whitish electron and stamina of burnished gold. By a river where the fish swim in pale gold and great papyrus buds of deep gold rise on slender stalks cat-like creatures with dappled hind-quarters pounce on wild duck, which spread their diapered wings in frantic flight. On the two faces of one blade we see the lion hunting and hunted : on one side an antelope gasps out its last under the tearing claws, while the rest of the herd stampede in panic, and on the other (Fig. 71) two lions flee but the third turns, fells a hunter, and seems to defy spears and arrows. Once more we find great art on a small surface.

From the daggers this wealth of ornament passes to the swords. There are abundant traces at Mycenæ of the luxury with which they could be embellished. The hilts are especially remarkable, being often cut solid out of some precious substance. There is no doubt of their origin. A cruciform hilt of white faience, engraved with wild goats, was found with faience plaques and vases from Crete.[1] Several hilts of agate or onyx, always of the cruciform type which is a kind of Knossian hall-mark, resemble another of rock crystal which was found at Knossos itself.[2]

Moreover, Crete alone presents swords comparable in artistic merit to the daggers from Mycenæ. It was in Crete that the weapons were forged and engraved which excited the greed of kings from afar. The leaf decoration which we see on one blade from Mycenæ is the same as appears on a hilt from Phaistos.[3] The rapier and short sword found in the " Chieftain's Grave " at Zapher Papoura surpass in beauty all that the Bronze Age has yielded of this kind. Down the whole length of the huge rapier, along the rib of the blade, on the edges of the hilt, and on the wings of the guard there are rows of spirals in relief ; five great studs of gold on each side held the precious plating which adorned the hilt ; and the ivory pommel is held by a ring of gold.[4] The short sword[5] is even more magnificent. The spirals on it are of exquisite

[1] Πρ., 1899, 102 ; cf. **XVI,** 500–1.
[2] 'Εφ., 1897, pl. viii, 5 ; **XX,** 500.
[3] MA. xiv, 535–6, figs. 20, 20 a ; cf. **XVI,** 496, n. d.
[4] **XVI,** figs. 58, 110 a ; cf. fig. 66.
[5] Ib., fig. 59.

delicacy. The broad pommel is of agate. The plate of gold which covers the guard and the hilt is divided into two fields covered with chased ornament. Two successive scenes are depicted in a rocky landscape : in the lower are a lion and a wild goat running, and in the upper the lion has caught the hind-quarters of the goat with one paw and is about to pin it to the ground with the other. The combination of the talents of the goldsmith and the bronze-worker, the noble simplicity of the composition, and a skill in execution which is hampered neither by the divergence and inequality of the fields nor by the large studs which encumber them, all reveal the qualities which are the distinctive privilege of Cretan art.

Works in which different substances are ingeniously combined, chryselephantine statuettes, *rhytons*, or weapons set with precious stones or metals, everything which the

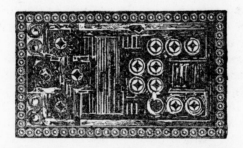

FIG. 72.—Inlaid game-board. Palace of Knossos.

Greeks called *daidala*, have for their symbolic author the Cretan Daidalos. The lapidary installed in the palace of Knossos—he, for example, who was surprised at his work by the irruption of the enemy—had in his work-box copper and gold, rock-crystal, pure and smoky, beryl, amethyst, and *kyanos*, an imitation of lapis lazuli. He wedded stone to metal in mosaics which are masterpieces of the jeweller's craft. An inlaid board has been preserved which must have been used for some game like chess. (Fig. 72.) This royal chess-board was nearly a metre long and over half as broad. The frame was of ivory, with a border of seventy-two daisies with golden petals and eyes of rock crystal ; all the squares were made of the same substances, with silver and *kyanos* as well. No doubt an object of this kind adds nothing to our

knowledge of the great art of the Cretans, but it shows how
far their love of decoration went, and helps to prove that,
if the finest pieces of goldsmith's work were found at Mycenæ,
they must have been taken there from Knossos.

IV GLYPTIC ART [1]

The practice, so widespread among the Cretans, of marking
with a seal certain articles and no doubt also documents
written on perishable material, was of great consequence in
the history of their civilization, and, more particularly, of their
art.   It was this which developed the use of writing ; it was
this which at an early date impelled the artists to give proof
of their skill on minute surfaces.   The glyptic art, that is, the
engraving and sculpture of seals, ring-bezels and gems, therefore held a considerable place in Crete.   The study of it is all
the more important because, in addition to the actual objects
which have come down to us, we have a quantity of seal-
impressions on clay.

As soon as the Cretans were able to express ideas by images
they cut steatite, bone, and ivory into lentil-shapes, prisms,
button-seals, and flattened cylinders, and carved on them by
incision or in relief names, titles, and formulas.   The earliest
monuments of writing are among the oldest monuments of
the plastic art.   Linear designs, such as spirals and mæanders,
might be required ; but generally the artist had to represent
plants, animals, and men.   The result was a spontaneous
blossoming of naturalism, with awkwardnesses which were
soon corrected.   Monkeys squatting, dogs walking, a boat
with fish swimming alongside, potters at work, a goat-hunt, a
betrothal scene—these are some of the subjects treated with
real skill, though still with a fresh simplicity.[2]

When the ideograms became stereotyped into conventional
hieroglyphs a large number of designs passed into the condition
of emblems, graphic signs ; in spite of elegant flourishes the
life went out of them.   Polychrome was all the thing at that
time.   What saved the glyptic art and prevented it from
degenerating into mere heraldry was sculpture in hard stone.

---

[1] Perrot, **LXVII,** 834–62 ; Furtwaengler, **XXVIII** ; Evans, **XII ; XVII,**
32 ff., 130 ff. ; **XX,** 117 ff., 195 ff., 271 ff., 669 ff.
[2] Fig. 25 ; **XX,** figs. 51, 88 *b,* 89 *b,* 87, No. 7, 93 *a.*

The wheel came into general use among the potters, and the lapidaries used the same process, improving it by the use of emery or very fine sand. Seals were soon worn out, as is proved by the impressions ;[1] as ivory had replaced gold, so hard stone replaced steatite. In M.M.I rock crystal was tackled and amethyst was cut in the shape of a scarab.[2] In M.M.II, just at the time when the hieroglyphic script was predominant, these stones and many others (cornelian, chalcedony, agate, etc.) came into general use for engraving. At the same time the advance of the royal power constantly increased the number of administrative seals.

So the new age, far from being unfavourable to the glyptic art, was especially propitious to it, and this was the art which preserved the traditions of declining naturalism. The conventional signs, relegated to a subordinate position, did not prevent the sense of life from coming out in full freedom. Figures of a man and his son, perhaps the King and the Heir-Apparent, are the most ancient portraits known, and we can guess that they are good likenesses. (Fig. 2.) The animals are often of graceful workmanship ; their movements are true—for example, in the boar advancing with snout down and in the bird preening itself. In animated scenes we see the wild goat lying beside a stream, surprised by a dog or fleeing in a landscape of rocks and woods. There is a goat suckling a child. Long before the octopus appears in art on a large scale, engraving shows it being eaten by a large fish among corals.[3]

In M.M.III everything encouraged the glyptic artist to persevere on the path of naturalism. The other artists joined company with him. Moreover, a new change, a revolution this time, had replaced the hieroglyphs by a linear script. This writing, being destitute of æsthetic qualities, was rejected by the engravers. But then a very sharp distinction was set up between the seals. Some, faithful to the past, keeping for choice the old prism shape, are now merely common amulets ; these are crudely engraved with plants, fish, lions' masks, and the like, which often have a fictitious appearance of being hieroglyphs. The others, which were gems perforated in order to be carried on the wrist, are the true seals.

[1] Ib., fig. 410.   [2] Ib., figs. 201–4.   [3] Ib., fig. 147.

Two forms are favoured, the almond shape, which very soon replaces the lentil shape, and the flattened cylinder. There is no end to the subjects cut on these intaglios in the good style of the period. At Knossos a lot of 160 sealings shows 50 varieties, and there are 144 varieties at Zakro on 500 sealings. The reason is that the attempts of forgers obliged private individuals and officials alike to change their seal constantly, and the engravers had to vary their motives as constantly. Egged on by the demands of their customers, the lapidaries vied with each other in talent and ingenuity to render, exact to the last detail, every aspect of flowers and trees, every attitude of beasts, every gesture of men in scenes of war, sport and religion ; and when nature no longer sufficed for their unbridled imagination they took separate elements from it and combined them into creatures of fancy. (Fig. 73.)

If it is true that a list of the hieroglyphs engraved on the seals is like a summary of Cretan civilization before the middle of the XVIIIth century, it is still more true that a classification of the figures engraved on intaglios and bezels would give a faithful and complete picture of Minoan and Mycenæan society from the middle of the XVIIIth century to the XIIth. At first we remain in Crete. We see its landscapes, the mountains, the palms, the great trees bowed by the wind, and the swaying stems of the tulips.[1] But life comes into these landscapes. Rams walk placidly along.[2] The wild she-goat suckles her kid or tries to escape from the buck, but wolf-dogs are growling not far off, and a deadly chase soon begins.[3] Man shows his whole way of living, his house, and his clothes,[4] and tells us of his occupations, his pleasures, and his beliefs. Stock-breeding and the chase are held in highest esteem ; a cowboy leaps on to a splendid bull as it drinks at a pond,[5] and a wild-goat is caught with a lasso.[6] The sea above all attracts these islanders, and one of them returns in triumph from fishing.[7] Here in the beloved arena,

[1] Ib., figs. 519, 518 *l*.
[2] Ib., figs. 503 *a, b, d* ; 518 *a, b*.
[3] Ib., figs. 518 *d, e* ; 539 *d, e*.
[4] Ib., figs. 493–500.
[5] Ib., fig. 274.
[6] Ib., fig. 503 *c*.
[7] Ib., figs. 497–9 ; 518 *g, h*.

beside the toreadors and boxers, we see gladiators.[1] There are not many warriors, and not one scene of battle ; the god and goddess of war appear, but as allegories, accompanied by a lioness[2] and by a lion. (Figs. 45–6.) But we have reached the age of the great adventures overseas, and see a bold skipper defending himself against the monster Skylla. (Fig. 30.)

Moreover, from the Late Minoan Period artistic intaglios are no longer confined to Crete, and the main land has almost a monopoly of bezels. As if to announce that a new age has dawned, the horse makes its appearance by the side of a ship. (Fig. 28.)

FIG. 73.—Seal-impressions from Zakro.

The Cretan engraver no longer picks his subjects with the same freedom, for the very reason that he borrows them from the painter of large pictures, but his composition shows mastery and refinement, and his style, though less bold, is purer. Religious scenes are his favourite subject. He portrays the goddess on the rock, the goddess with the bow, divine apparitions and priestesses.[3] Of two bezels, which are among the most beautiful, one represents the goddess approaching a sanctuary in a boat (Fig. 41) and the other shows four

[1] Ib., figs. 504, 594 (cf. 515, 517, 518 c), 509 ; MA. xiii, 45, fig. 41.
[2] Or a dog. (See p. 253, note 3.)
[3] See figs. 40 and 44 ; cf. **LXVII,** fig. 426, 11 ; **XIII,** figs. 25, 59 ; BSA. viii, 102, fig. 59.

women executing the sacred dance in a meadow dotted with
flowers. (Fig. 44.) The representation of animals from life
is not completely given up, and an onyx is engraved with
two exquisite dragon-flies.[1]   But as a rule the animals themselves become hieratic, e.g. opposed lions in the attitude which
they have on the gate of Mycenæ.[2] When the engraver felt
that he simply must vary his types he went further and created
composite monsters. Thus the sealings from Zakro show
the most fantastic demons by the hundred.   (Fig. 73 a–c, e–g.)

On the mainland the intaglios and rings, whether imported
or engraved locally, are extremely numerous.   A large number
come under the head of religious subjects.   On the celebrated
ring from Mycenæ (Fig. 37) the goddess sits in the shade of
a tree receiving offerings of flowers. Other rings represent
priestesses worshipping, the ritual dance with the plucking
of the sacred tree, and processions of women or demons.[3]
Animals opposed hieratically are also found; lions, gryphons
or sphinxes stand on either side of the goddess, a column,
or an altar ;[4] unearthly genii water sacred branches[5] or are
carried at arm's length by the goddess, tamer of beasts.[6]

But the lords of the mainland want something different—
big game hunting and war.   By the side of the heraldic beasts
there are others, very much alive.   The lion does not appear
only in the conventional attitude ; we see him crouching
or running, felling a bull or rising up against a man.[7]   One
fine composition shows a hunter drawing an arrow at a stag
from a chariot going at full speed.[8]   The Mycenæan consults
the goddess with his spear in his hand before he goes out to
war.[9] He goes, and here he is on his two-horse chariot.[10]
Then come wonderful scenes of battle, a duel in which one
warrior seeks with his sword his adversary's breast behind
the great shield,[11] and a fierce struggle, two a side, in which

[1] Cf. **XXXIX,** 113.
[2] Cf. **XIII,** 153 ff.
[3] Figs. 38–9 ; **XIII,** 56–8 ; *AΔ,* ɪɪ, ii, 14 ; cf. **LXVII,** figs. 428, 15 ;
429.
[4] BCH. 1921, 511 ; **XIII,** figs. 36–9 ; **LXVII,** figs. 428, 22 ; 431, 10.
[5] **XI,** fig. 251.
[6] **XIII,** fig. 44 ; **IV,** 243 *c* ; 248 *e* ; **LXVII,** figs. 426, 14 ; 431, 7.
[7] **IV,** 246 *d, f* ; 242 *b* ; 251 *g* ; 246 *a* ; 251 *e.*
[8] Ib., 251 *d.*
[9] **XIII,** fig. 51.
[10] **IV,** 246 *c.*
[11] Ib., 251 f.

a wounded man lifts himself up and watches his comrade braving with his dagger the sword and spear of the enemy. (Fig. 74.) Or there is a pirate raid, with women torn from their homes and dragged towards a boat which is in readiness to sail.[1]

Works as beautiful as these cannot have been conceived and carried out by Mycenæan artists without Cretan models. The proof is given by one of the most perfect and most ancient rings, that shown in Figure 74 ; it is simply a replica of an almost contemporary seal from Hagia Triada.[2] Even when the subjects are not Cretan, even when the work was done in

Fig. 74.—Battle scene. Gold ring from Mycenæ.

a mainland workshop,[3] the good bezels are products of Cretan glyptic art. As soon as the quickening influence of the island ceased to make itself felt decadence set in, and was soon followed by annihilation ; invaders who knew nothing of writing had no need of seals.

V POTTERY [4]

Cretan Pottery before the Mycenæan Period

Of all the industrial arts which were the glory of prehistoric Crete the ceramic is that which we can best judge to-day. For this art, at least, there is no lack of comparisons. While the Cyclades and the mainland everlastingly reproduced the

[1] *AΔ*, ii, ii, 15 ff.
[2] **XX,** figs. 512–13.
[3] JAI. 1911, 259.
[4] See Hogarth and Welch, JHS. xi (1901), 78–98 ; Mackenzie, ib., xxiii, 1903), 157–205 ; xxvi (1906), 243 ff. ; Miss E. A. Hall, **XXXIII ;** Fimmen, **XXIV ;** Reisinger, **LXIX ;** Fimmen and Reisinger, **XXV ;** Franchet, **XXVII ;** Evans, **XX,** 36 ff., 56 ff., 74 ff., 108 ff., 166 ff., 231 ff., 552 ff.

same types or altered them only at long intervals, without
rising above an industrial technique and an uninspired
geometric decoration, Crete soon learned to give superior
qualities to ordinary pottery, and above all to transform
a utilitarian industry into a luxurious art. The experiments
of the Cretan potters are so numerous and their achievements
so varied that, while we cannot always accept Evans' chronological divisions when we consider them broadly, we should,
on the other hand, be compelled to make even more divisions
than he has done if we wished to examine them in detail.

In the very lowest strata of Neolithic Crete pottery is
already in progress. The clay becomes finer; the baking
produces a uniform black colour, later yellowish; by vigorous
hand-burnishing a brilliant lustre is achieved; the incised
ornament, often of chevrons and sometimes of tree-branches,
is presently filled with a white (less often red) pigment.
Finally painting appears, covering the clay with a black
wash, which gives an effect of fumigation, and timidly replacing
the white fillings by touches of matt white paint. This taste
for a fine polish and for decoration is full of promise.

Towards the beginning of the third millennium the new-
born art of metal-working comes to the aid of the potter.
Seeing the metal-worker heat his fire to 1,200 degrees, the
potter learns to build a kiln in which firing will produce
other results than it did in the pit in which he has hitherto
smoked his goods. Henceforth he will be able to preserve the
natural colour of his clay or to obtain new effects of colour
and vitrification, to use more plastic clays and to vary his
shapes. The potters of Phaistos turn out vases of a fine
glazed red, and the wash, liquefied in the fire, forms a kind
of enamel.[1] But in E.M.II pottery with a dark ornament
on a light ground triumphs; lines of red, brown, or black
glaze stand out on the buff tint of the clay or on a whitish
slip. The design gains in freedom; the paint-brush has
a suppleness unknown to the pointed tool; it forms hatched
triangles like butterflies' wings or perhaps double axes, and
passes from the straight line to the curve. In eastern Crete
the potters use their fire to diversify the red and orange slip
with blotches of black and bronze; this "mottled ware"

---

[1] MA. xix, 201 ff.

is their speciality.[1]   The forms are bold and slow the influence of metal work ; goblets are made, and ewers, and pots with a long high beak, often tubular in form, which has earned them the name of " tea-pots ".

In E.M.III, which brings in the Bronze Age, it is very possible that the method of baking was improved.   A seal representing a potter's workshop [2] seems to suggest this. In any case, the metallic appearance of certain washes indicates that the two fire-using industries were more closely associated than ever.   The potter is not afraid of any technical audacity. He makes jars or *pithoi* of more than human size ; he fits his jugs with enormous beaks ; he turns sculptor as well as painter and gives his pots the shape of a woman or a bird.[3] New experiments lead, especially in eastern Crete, to the rehabilitation of Neolithic ornament ; " dark-on-light " is supplanted by " light-on-dark ", with a white (sometimes yellow ochre) design on a blackish brown glazed surface. So, two thousand years later, the Attic vase-painters were to substitute red figures on a black ground for black figures on a red ground.   Now, too, the noble motive of the spiral appears.   It came from the Cyclades, but the Cretan potter, revelling in the curved line, at once drew endless resources from it.   By simply baking in a neutral atmosphere he was already able to produce effects of colour which his successors need only intensify to create masterpieces.

The princes who built the palaces at the beginning of the Middle Minoan Period gave a great impetus to artistic pottery. A great age was preparing, which reached its apogee in M.M.II. The most renowned masters were established in the Palace of Knossos itself.   A mechanical invention lent skill to the potter's hand : the clay was worked on a revolving disk, turned by hand by means of a primitive winder.[4]   With this apparatus a skilled workman could give more bulge to the belly and make the foot and handles slimmer and rounder. He could fine down the clay with such a sure hand that some-times the walls of the vases are not more than 1 millimetre thick.   A whole class of cups and goblets is called by archæo-

[1] **LXXX,** pl. xxxiv ; **XL,** pl. B ; **XX,** fig. 46.
[2] **XX,** fig. 93 A, *b* 2.
[3] Ib., figs. 84–5.
[4] Cf. **XXVII,** 22 ff., 38 ff. ; **XX,** 168, 189.

logists " egg-shell ware ". Even more than in the past
the potter took ideas from the bronze-worker and even the
goldsmith. At Gournia a silver *kantharos* has been found
with another of clay which is almost a replica of it.[1] There
is even a vase from Pseira which its maker, by an absolute
tour de force in defiance of his material, has copied from a
metal original, with soldered sections, waved edges and riveted
handles.[2] Pottery of this period sometimes seems to be the
prototype of the gold and silver cups of Mycenæ, but it is
because it was itself copied from metal vases. The thin walls,
the curved handles, the division into panels and zones, the
colour effects like glints of light on shiny projecting surfaces,
all constantly give the same impression. But at the same time
the discovery of new colours was to turn the potter definitely
into a painter. He now found on his palette a fat black,
which in firing could take on a purple tone and the brightness
of enamel ; a creamy white replaced the liquid white which
could only be laid on thin and did not stick well ; in addition
to yellow or red ochre he had a pure yellow and the whole
range of the reds. Everything was ready for polychrome.

Just as the light-on-dark of Neolithic times had not
completely disappeared before E.M.III, it had not in its turn
completely driven out dark-on-light ; these were only passing
eclipses. At the beginning of M.M.I, therefore, the vase-
painter could play with his colours freely. He imitated many-
coloured stones, he speckled his goblets with red and black,
and he covered his cups with bands of white and scarlet.
He used every combination with familiarity. Thus was born
the style which has been called after the place where the
first specimens of it were found—Kamares. Sometimes
the painter scatters over the buff surface bright or dark
ornament in a gay variety of shapes and colours. Sometimes
on a brown varnish with metallic gleams he lays vigorous
contrasts in matt colours, white, yellow, brown, orange,
vermilion, and carmine. Often, too, he uses both methods
at once and enlivens the dark surfaces with white dots or
other light details. Then he passes from primary colours
to delicate intermediate tints, and gives no less charm to the

---

[1] **XL,** pl. c, figs. 1, 2 ; cf. **LXXX,** pl. xxxi, 2.
[2] **LXXXI,** 20, fig. 5 ; cf. **XX,** suppl. pl. iii, *b.*

harmony of his colours than power to their contrast. His
linear motives, for choice curvilinear, show an astonishing
variety and mastery ; by curiously seeking out new spiral
forms he achieves an original and refined elegance. (Fig. 75.)
Then he introduces plant motives ; but his hand is accustomed
to the linear decoration, which he only wishes to enliven,
and he does not pretend to reproduce the exact truth. He
paints magnificent scrolls terminating in petals. Those of
his conventionalized flowers which are recognizable—for
example the dog-daisies and the lilies—only have their natural

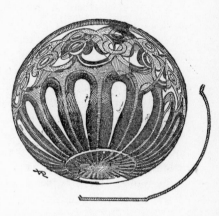

FIG. 75.—Kamares style vase from
Phaistos.

FIG. 76.—Water-lily vase
from Knossos.

colour if it contributes to the general effect of the colour-
scheme ; generally they are red and white in alternation—
palmettes, crocuses, and flowering branches of olive. Every
line, every shade, contributes to the general effect of as ingle
pattern shot with colour.[1] The most typical of these masterpieces, on which the colour is raised in slight relief, is a cup
embraced by the calix of a water-lily, of which the black
sepals veined with red and the white petals spread gracefully
over the red wall. (Fig. 76.)

[1] See MA. vi (1896), pl. ix–xi; xiv, pls. xxxvi, xlii; JHS. xxiii, pls. vi, vii;
xxvi, pl. viii; BSA. xix, pl. iv–xii; **XX,** figs. 181, 186, pl. ii, iii.

These artists who were so enamoured of line and colour
had rivals whose principles were different. Certain vase-
painters could not forget the palaces in which they worked,
and gave an architectural air to their motives, for example,
the man who decorated a vase with arcaded flutings crowned
with fleurs-de-lys, as if he had some Gothic model before his
eyes.[1] Others went more frankly to nature and painted
fish, a heron, wild goats, beetles, and octopuses, or lilies,
crocuses, and white palms with their branches covered with
pink buds.[2] As always in Crete, naturalism leads to plastic
decoration. There are bowls with figurines, a dove or oxen,
inside ; [3] there is a pretty fern-spray of gold inside a saucer ; [4]
there are shells and a cockchafer perched on the sides of
vases ; [5] the enormous sides of the *pithoi* are adorned with
colour dribbling down in imitation of oil or are bound with
imitation ropes.[6] The vase perforated for ritual sprinkling,
the *rhyton,* appears for the first time in the shape of a bull
or of a bull's head.[7]

In this marvellous efflorescence two novelties appear which
truly belong to a time of exuberant colour. The first is
barbotine ware.[8] The patterns are the same as on Kamares,
but more crowded ; the colouring is the same but even more
brilliant—fiery reds and milky whites blaze on a sombre
background. Next comes faience.[9] Even before the middle
of the third millennium a white paste was made on a basis
of silica. The Knossian potters of M.M.II, with Egyptian
objects before their eyes, discovered the secret of a thick
enamel. They obtained a turquoise blue, a blackish or purple
brown, a white, pure or tinged with yellow or lilac, and
lastly a new colour—green. As early as M.M.II the faience-
makers of Knossos produced plaques which were put together
to form a big mosaic composition.[10] They turned out Sèvres
blue vases mounted with gold.[11] The art of faience only

---

[1] **XX,** fig. 183 *a*, 1.
[2] Ib., figs. 131–2, 190–1 ; BSA. xix, pl. x.
[3] **XX,** fig. 130.
[4] Ib., fig. 189 *b*.
[5] Ib., fig. 180.
[6] JHS. xxvi, pl. xi, 21–3.
[7] **XX,** fig. 137 *a–d*.
[8] Ib., 179 ff., fig. 128 ; 239 ff. ; pl. i *a–j* ; suppl. pl. iii *a*.
[9] Ib., 486 ff. ; **XXVII,** 28, 32.
[10] See p. 321 ; cf. **XX,** 301 ff.
[11] **XX,** fig. 189 *a*.

attained maturity later, through the plastic art, but it is in the time of Kamares that we must place its lusty youth.

After M.M.II the Cretan potter was to work in technical and social conditions which were not all equally favourable to him. The quick-spinning wheel, which had no doubt already been tried, came into general use. This invention made it possible to produce the known forms to perfection, to give them finer proportions and a more graceful profile. It facilitated the manufacture of new forms, such as the pot with stirrup-handles which was to have such extraordinary fortunes. It caused the monstrous exaggerations of the spouts to disappear for good, and confined the artist to more sober paths. But, on the other hand, it was fatal to the more delicate processes and drove out the " egg-shells ".

The potter's kiln was so improved that the fire could be raised to an oxidizing temperature. But this advance too brought its penalty. The heat burned the colours or shaded them variously. Black resisted only if it was thick ; if it was thin it became a brown which varied considerably. It therefore disappeared from decoration and was used only for a lustreless wash, generally of a lilac brown tint. White became powdery. The pretty touches of orange, carmine, and vermilion would not " take ".

So the potter, accustomed to polychrome, was faced with two alternatives. Either he must reject the technical facilities which were offered to him, or he must turn out goods of inferior quality ; either he must satisfy a limited but wealthy and refined clientèle, or he must do cheap work. But the choice did not rest with him. It was the day when, between the destruction of the First Palace and the building of the Second, the potters of Knossos were deprived of the royal protection. The great and wealthy no longer confined their passion to beautiful painted vases ; they had the means to procure gold and silver plate, they were attracted by faience, they took up stone, which had so long been neglected, and contented themselves with carved alabaster until the day of the steatite reliefs should come. The pottery trade was therefore simply compelled to cater for less cultivated classes and, since it was beginning to send its goods further afield, to give especial attention to export. So the potters could go on turning out polychrome stuff cheaply as a dull commercial job ; but if they wanted to bring the Palace clientèle back to artistic pottery they must offer it a new style.

There is every sign of decadence in the Kamares of M.M.III, which is really only post-Kamares.[1] *Tours de force* and ingenious experiments are all done away with now. Style in the shape is neglected. The painting, reduced to a dirty black and white, relieved only by yellow or red, has lost all its brilliancy, and the colours often run. The designs have no longer any grace, and the plant motives sometimes tend to become geometric.[2] To impart some slight vivacity to the colouring the painter falls back on the imitation of breccias and conglomerates, or else he amasses straight lines and curves in a feeble design of little strokes of red and white.[3] He is most successful with the " rippled ware ", on which by harder and lighter strokes of the brush he imitates tortoise-shell.[4]

While the style which had once been so fruitful was declining in this way, painters of genius were adorning the walls of princes with frescoes representing plants, animals, and men. Here the potters found models which they set themselves to imitate with energy, in the certainty of obtaining for their own paintings the popularity which the mural pictures enjoyed. Post-Kamares was only a survival ; the true style of M.M.III was naturalism. Even in the preceding period some artists had drawn from nature and had been disposed to monochrome. Henceforward it was the rule. Primary colours ceased to be of use as soon as objects had to be given an appearance of reality. The new school begins by painting in white on a ground of lilac-brown. It renders the beauty of things, without striving for meticulous accuracy, by lively free-hand drawing, often in an impressionist manner. Over an undulating soil rise the slender sprays of decorative plants, tufts of herbs, the thin pointed stalks of grass-plants, flowers of the forest and of the garden, sweet-peas and tulips.[5] The most splendid of these vessels are jars on which the favourite plant, the lily, displays the brilliant whiteness of its long stalk and noble

[1] **XX**, 591–602 ; **XXV**, 137.
[2] **XX**, pl. vii.
[3] Ib., fig. 438, pl. vii ; fig. 437.
[4] Cf. ib., 592 ff.
[5] Ib., figs. 445–6.

flowers against a ground of purple brown. (Fig. 77.) Man
is never represented; no doubt the attempts made in the
preceding period had been too discouraging to the vase-
painters. Even the beasts of the field are neglected. The
marine fauna alone is popular; the spirals are replaced by
the tentacles of the octopus, and dolphins appear swimming
among rocks.[1] The naturalism of the painting is enhanced
by relief; there are terra-cotta vases with barley-stalks, and
fine faience vases with fern-sprays and a branch of a rose-tree.[2]

FIG. 77.—Lily vase from Knossos.

So then M.M.III had been for pottery a period of transition;
but, while the style had changed, the technique had remained
behindhand. Light-on-dark decoration, hallowed by the
success of polychrome, had passed to the post-Kamares
and naturalistic styles. But there was no reason to keep it
when the colours which had made its glory were abandoned.
Already towards the end of M.M.III we notice a tendency
towards a new technique,[3] and in the first phase of L.M.I
zones of white decoration on black alternate on the same
vase with zones of black on yellow. But soon the essentially

[1] Ib., fig. 447 a, b.   [2] Ib., figs. 299 a, b, 357.
[3] See ib., figs. 447 b, 448.

" Mycenæan " technique of black ornament on a light clay ground triumphed. This does not mean that every trace of polychrome disappeared, even then. On valuable vases the clay was covered with a buff coat to which the firing often imparted an orange or red tone, sometimes turning to mauve and red tinged with violet. There is even, at the beginning of the period, a whole class of vases, of which some are among the best, on which the decoration is enhanced by a network of fine lines of matt white or orange red.[1] Nay more, right down to L.M.III certain vessels which were placed in tombs were still decorated in red and black strongly relieved with blue motives.[2] But, with a few exceptions, one may say that in the second phase of L.M.I all accessory colour and all painting of white on a dark ground were abolished.

The naturalism of the Late Minoan potters was seldom a rigid and over-done study of reality. It loved to reproduce forms and movements with effortless skill, accentuating and simplifying. It soon turned to lliusionism and conventionalization, but for nearly two centuries it remained within the bounds of a perfect taste, sacrificing only so much of the truth as was necessary to increase the decorative effect. Thus from L.M.I to L.M.II there is a complete descending scale of naturalistic styles.[3] That of L.M.II was but the last of the series before the fall of Knossos, and it had not yet abolished those which had preceded it. The schools grew in number, living and flourishing side by side.

The marine subjects best enable us to follow the transformation of the style. At the beginning an impetuous naturalism produces marvels. The beautiful steatite relief vase representing a swimming octopus[4] is simply a rather flattened reproduction of a model in painted terra-cotta. The monster is frightful to behold as he appears on a stirrup-handled vase from Gournia. (Pl. IV, 2.) Leaving behind him jagged rocks and sprigs of floating seaweed, scorning shells and sea-urchins, he comes straight at you with all his coiling arms swollen with their suckers and his great glittering eyes, all

[1] See **XXV**, 89–90.
[2] **XVIII**, 26 ff., pl. iv ; **XVI**, 462, No. 66 *h–m* ; cf. our Fig. 14.
[3] Miss E. H. Hall, in **XXXIII**, distinguishes seven classes in the naturalistic style ; cf. Reisinger, **LXIX**, 15 ff.
[4] See p. 324.

fantastically realistic. But presently the coils of the eight
tentacles become symmetrical, and the reefs frame the beast
completely. Then, to allow more room for this frame, the
octopus is replaced by the nautilus with three arms curved
over his back. At first he is still alive, although penned
between the points of rock. But very soon his shell becomes
distorted and round him indistinct masses trail about in
the water.[1] At last, on a fine L.M.II *amphora*, the octopus
with his tentacles in coils forms a pendant to spirals combined
with rosettes and palmettes. (Fig. 80.) So we see dolphins
frisking at regular intervals on a square pattern of rocks,[2]
and star-fish spread out among sea-wrack which is replaced

FIGS. 78–80.—Palace style vases from Zapher Papoura.

later by double axes.[3] The plant world lent itself even better
to conventionalization. Exquisite sweet-peas, pretty crocuses,
lilies rising into volutes, palm-trees with fronds gracefully
bowed, and above all delightful stalks of grass with lanceolate
leaves in pairs [4]—all is preparing the L.M.II vase-painter
to produce superb decorative plants which rise from the earth
on reed-stalks, blossom into lilies, and culminate in palmettes.
(Fig. 78.) [5]

As the motives taken from nature grew more and more
conventional, to become purely decorative in the end, it was

[1] **LXVII,** figs. 485–6; **XI,** fig. 85; **LXXXI,** fig. 13.
[2] **LXXXI,** 29, fig. 10.
[3] BSA. ix, 311, fig. 10; JHS. xxii, pl. xii, 2; **IV,** 184.
[4] JHS. xxiii, 195 ff.; figs. 11–12, 14–17; xxii, pl. xii, 1, 3; **XI,** fig. 30;
LXXXI, fig. 8; **LXXXII,** pl. xi.
[5] **XVI,** pl. ci.

unnecessary to keep them clear of linear motives, which could produce the same effect. Sometimes the potters even exclude all animal or vegetable ornament and paint spirals interlacing in every direction, half-spirals terminated with a charming caprice, chevrons separated by rows of beads, rosettes, and double axes. But far more often the two kinds of decoration are combined. On one *amphora* of flamboyant appearance the secondary zones enclose spirals, ivy-leaves, and double axes, while the principal zone is filled with double axes supported by olive-branches and bulls' heads surmounted

FIG. 81.—Papyrus vase from Knossos.

by double axes with fleur-de-lys handles.[1] This division into zones and this mixture of motives brought vase-painting, at a time when frescoes were covering all the walls of the re-arranged Palace of Knossos, to the " Palace style ", which was a true culmination of everything that had been done for over a century. The decorator of vases let himself be guided by the mural painter, as the latter obeyed the architect. He firmly divided the horizontal zones of the belly into panels and brought all the accessory parts into his scheme of ornamentation. (Figs. 78–80.) If he wished to give a big

[1] **LXXXI,** pl. vii.

place to floral motives he was obliged to add linear decoration to them, and, for the sake of harmony, to conventionalize them to the last degree. The architectonic character of this decoration strikes the eye everywhere, whether it be in two parallel friezes with rows of triglyphs as their sole ornament, or in the stalk and volutes of a lily or iris which perforce suggest the lines of the Ionic column.[1] Sometimes, in spite of all, a feeling for Nature appears amidst this striving for decorative effect and gives it a remarkable power. Nothing could be nobler than the jar, 1·20 metres high and painted on relief, which was found in the Royal Villa (Fig. 81) ; over undulations which represent a running water long branches of payprus are spread in harmonious array. But often by its profusion of heterogeneous decoration, the juxtaposition of conventional forms and the interlacing of curved lines and flowers, the last manner of the Palace style degenerates into rococo.

Pottery outside Crete before the Mycenæan Period

While pottery was making this triumphant advance in Crete, what was it doing in the other countries of the Ægean ? We shall see that its history in the Cyclades, in Greece, and even in Cyprus and the Troad was very different after the end of the XVIIIth century from what it had been before.

The only Ægean country which had, like Crete, a Neolithic culture—Thessaly—easily supports comparison at the beginning of the third millennium.[2] At this time a good ware was made there with red linear decoration on yellow clay or a white slip. The designs vary. When the slip itself has not a strong burnish the ornament contains vitreous ingredients which make it shine ; Thessaly knew the secret of varnish long before the period in which Furtwængler placed the *Urfirnis* of Bœotia. But the Thessalian type, for all the centuries it lasted, only produced local variants and made scarcely any progress. About 2500 northern and central Greece had nothing to show, beside this type, but some wares adorned with white lines and some black vases with a fine lustre and incised ornament. This

---

[1] Figs. 79, 78 ; **XL,** pl. G, 1.
[2] **LXXXVIII,** 157 ff. ; **XCI,** 13 ff.

was not much, at a time when Crete had the dark-on-light
type and the mottled ware. Then Thessaly was isolated by
by invasion and attached to the North. Now it learned
forms which were not without grace, and above all it made
the acquaintance of the spiral before the islands. What did
it do with it? Combined it with straight lines in the most
uninteresting way possible. At the very best a painter in
a moment of delirium ventures to daub eyes on the handles.[1]
This went on until the middle of the XVth century.

In the Troad and in Cyprus, too, pottery developed in
complete independence from the XXXth to the XVth century,
without achieving any very remarkable results. In Troy II
the forms developed, and a tall two-handled goblet (*depas
amphikypellon*) was especially popular; but the potter's kiln
and wheel did not appear until the second period of Troy II;
the spiral was not copied from the Cyclades until the third
period; and Troy VI, after 1500, first rose to painted
ornament.[2]

In Cyprus the wheel and the spiral were both unknown
in the Copper Age (3000–2200) and the first Bronze Age
(2200–1550), and painting first came in with bronze. The
best objects of the former period are globular jugs with a very
lustrous red slip. Having neither wheel nor colours, the
the potter gave rein to his fancy in plastic experiments, making
pots in the shape of animals and adding reliefs, combined with
incised ornament or alone. When this type fell into disuse on
the introduction of painting it was supplanted by a ware with
a linear decoration in matt black on a white wash which was
monotonously poverty-stricken.[3]

Let us pass from these distant regions, which could have
no regular relations with the Ægean civilization before the
XVIth or XVth century, to those which from the beginning
had been more or less continuously connected with Crete,
either directly or through intermediaries.

In the Cyclades [4] the pottery of the Chalcolithic Age was
badly fired, with crude incised decoration. Then the black

[1] **LXXXVIII,** pl. xxiii.
[2] Hubert Schmidt, **X,** 243 ff., 253 ff., 279 ff.
[3] Myres, JHS. xvii, 134 ff.; **XI,** 229 ff.; **XLVII,** 70 ff.
[4] Edgar, **XXI,** 80 ff.; Dawkins and Droop, BSA. xvii, 9 ff.; **XXV,**
80–3, 134–7.

surface took on a vitreous polish ; hatched triangles, herring-
bones and concentric circles were drawn by incisions with
filling ; and special forms were based on marble work, chiefly
pyxides, " sauceboats ", flat pans and palettes. (Fig. 82.)
A little later the island potter got the spiral from the mainland [1]
and adopted a black wash in the place of hand polishing.
But the colour of his varnish was bad and his clay porous,
so that the glaze which he obtained was dull and patchy.
When he started to paint on the top of the wash he adopted
the Cretan dark-on-light technique ; a vase from Syra is
exactly like one from Mochlos.[2] However, he never ventured
to reproduce the bold form of the " tea-pot ", nor anything
like the mottled ware. About the time when the potter

FIG. 82.—Incised pottery from the Cyclades.

of Crete was arriving through light-on-dark ornament at the
beauties of polychrome, his fellow in the Cyclades also began
to paint white patterns on a glazed black or red ground ; he
imported Kamares ware, then copied it, and so we have a
vase from Naxos which shows Cretan influence.[3] But now
the inferiority is flagrant. The Cyclades, which had once
given almost as much as they had received, now content
themselves with belated, desultory, and unfruitful borrowings.

The importance of their pottery lies in the fact that it was
subject to other influences and, inversely, was able to exert
influence and to hand on elsewhere those which it had under-
gone. Syra not only imported Cretan wares but was

---

[1] 'Eφ., 1889, pl. viii, 12 ; cf. **LXXXV**, 219 ff. ; **XXV**, 135.
[2] 'Eφ., loc. cit., 10 ; **XX**, fig. 42.
[3] **XXV**, 136.

acquainted with the *depas amphikypellon* of Troy and introduced the "sauceboat" of the islands to that city.[1] In the other direction Cycladic ware of the incised type reached the Argolid, Attica, Euboia, and even Phokis. The potters of Phylakopi were so little influenced by the forms and colours of Kamares just because they were also importing from the mainland examples of the type which is sometimes called pseudo-Kamares.[2] Late in the day they returned to the primitive method of painting, decorating a whitish ground with matt black ; at the same time the same technique was used on the mainland.[3] As the XVIIIth and XVIIth centuries approached the Cyclades enjoyed increasing intercourse not only with Crete but with the Peloponnese and central Greece. In this rôle of middlemen the more they got from the South the more they sent to the West and North.

From 3000 to 2500 the pottery of Argolis and Corinthia [4] followed the same development as that of the Cyclades, but more slowly. At Nauplia, Tiryns, and Korakou hand-polishing lasts longer, glaze appears later, and incised ornament is the exception.[5] But about 2500 central Greece was detached from Thessaly and thrown on the South, and the pottery of the mainland received a new impulse. From 2500 to 2000 E.H.II and E.H.III produced ware of a new type. Formerly it used to be called *Urfirnis*, on account of its glazed wash, or sometimes *Bœotian Kamares*, on account of certain examples with very thin walls ; to-day it is generally given the name of Hagia Marina, at which place many specimens were found.[6] This type has a dark varnish which was at first monochrome and later ornamented with white lines. It is particularly widespread in Phokis, Bœotia, and Corinthia. It is not impossible that the technique of this pottery was indirectly influenced by E.M.III ware, but it is easier to infer, from certain forms, that the Cycladic tradition continued in the districts nearest to the islands. For example the "sauce-

---

[1] Ib., 137.
[2] BSA. xvii, 16 ff. ; cf. **XXV**, 76, 134.
[3] **XXV**, 83, 76–7.
[4] Furtwaengler and Loeschcke, **XXIX, XXX ;** Wace and Blegen, BSA. xxii, 176–89 ; Blegen, **III.**
[5] BSA. xxii, 176 ; **III,** 4–8, 110.
[6] Sotiriadis, REG. 1912, 253–99 ; cf. **XXV**, 75–6, 132–4 ; BSA. xxii, 176–80 ; **III,** 8 ff., 112–13.

boat " is frequent in the South as far as Attica but does not
appear in Phokis. Of one kind of vase, indeed, it is hard to
say whether it comes from the Cyclades or Argolis.[1] So in
the third millennium it was through the Argive and Saronic
Gulfs that the lands of Hellas communicated with the Ægean
civilization, which for them was represented by the Cyclades.
From Crete they only received a glimmer, much dimmed
by distance.

About 2000, doubtless in consequence of an invasion,
Hellas was isolated, but only for a short time. When it
resumed its old relations it possessed the wheel and was
producing " Minyan " ware with pretty, simple metallic
forms. The " Grey Minyan " of M.H.I (2000–1750) originally
had for its centre Orchomenos III. There it was polished,
but not decorated. But when it spread the potters of Argolis
decorated these northern forms with curved incised lines.
Presently, when they were to manufacture the " Yellow
Minyan " of M.H.II, they would return to the slip, which
had become traditional among them, and would thus create
a vague prototype of " Mycenæan " ware.[2] Moreover, almost
directly after the northern town had made Minyan ware
popular a southern town, probably Aigina, started a rival
type with matt painting.[3] It was a poor kind of painting
at the beginning! On a greenish porous clay a blotchy,
blackish brown was laid without any fixative, and the pattern
consisted of straight lines. But great progress was made;
instead of letting his liquid colour be absorbed by the porous
clay the painter laid it on a white slip, and his pattern became
curvilinear. There is increasing resemblance between the
matt painting of the mainland and that prevailing in the
Cyclades. What is still better, the influence of Crete becomes
undeniable. Two jugs from Drachmani in Phokis are of
the same shape as contemporary jugs from Knossos, and one
of them has exactly the same ornament.[4] The matt painting
becomes polychrome [5]—what more need be said? Minyan
ware itself begins to resemble Minoan models.[6] In the middle

[1] **XXV**, 83.
[2] BSA. xxii, 180–3; **III**, 15–19, 113–14; cf. **XXV**, 79–80, 140–1.
[3] BSA. xxii, 183–6; **III**, 19–30, 114–15; cf. **XXV**, 76–7, 141–2.
[4] **XX**, fig. 117.
[5] **III**, 28–30.
[6] **XX**, fig. 140.

of the XVIIIth century Hellas was ready, like the Cyclades, to open its gates wide to the beneficent influences of the South.

Henceforward the transformations of Minoan pottery are to have their repercussion, soon or late, over the greater part of the Ægean world. The Creto-Mycenæan age begins. The wares of the mainland and of the Cyclades still preserve their individual character, but testify to continual relations with Crete. The vases found at Knossos in the Repository of the Shrine, which are more typical of M.M.III than any others, have their counterparts in the first Shaft-Graves of Mycenæ,[1] and one of them comes from Phylakopi.[2] The result of this connexion can be seen in Hellas. The matt painting, which had already made some progress under the influence diffused indirectly from Crete, suddenly makes giant strides, thanks to the models which come pouring in. A new type of matt painting appears, which borrows many motives from M.M.III and by its two-colour ornament, " red-and-black," prepares the way for Mycenæan ware.[3] For the first time the Helladic Periods begin to correspond with the Cycladic and Minoan.

In the Cyclades the potters of Thera and Phylakopi inscribe Cretan characters on certain vases, as if they wanted to say who their masters are.[4] Hitherto the Melian potter had used matt colours and drawn only straight lines and spirals. Now he becomes a convert to the glazed black-and-red technique, with floral and animal decoration.[5] Even the pots adorned with fat round birds, which are his own special achievement, only show that he has borrowed the naturalistic style from Crete. Moreover, he has only to attempt human figures, for which he is thrown on his own invention, to prove how limited his skill is.[6]

The education of the Cycladic and mainland potters was completed during the two centuries of L.M.I and II. The import of Cretan vases became more and more active all over the Ægean world. Moreover, in many places vases were manufactured which we should call Cretan if certain details

---

[1] Ib., 556 ff. ; **XXIX,** pl. xi, 55–6 ; cf. **XXV,** 138.
[2] **XX,** figs. 404 *h*, 405 *d*.
[3] BSA. xxii, 186 ; **III,** 114.
[4] **XXI,** 177 ff.
[5] Ib., 113 ff., 125 ff., pl. xxi, xxiii.
[6] Ib., pl. xiii, 14, 17, 18.

did not prove their local origin.[1] These can only have been made and painted by Cretan immigrants. The native potters kept up their own types, but they became daily more imbued with a technique and a style which they considered superior. Thus we find everywhere L.M.I and still more L.M.II vases, but this does not mean that the Cyclades were not behind Crete, and Argolis behind the Cyclades. The course of progress is the same, but its speed varies.

At Melos the red-and-black ware remained popular for some time yet; indeed, it was at the beginning of L.M.I that it produced the designs which corresponded most closely to the teaching of M.M.III: crocuses, grasses, and pomegranates.[2] But it did not abandon the traditional bird motive and it still tried to represent human figures, for example, fishermen. (Fig. 29.) Black-and-red, then, merely showed the general influence of Crete, but red-and-black was a conscious, deliberate imitation of Cretan ware.[3] The forms are the same, and so is the technique, but with other colours, while the drawing, pushing the L.M.I reaction to extremes, not only conventionalizes the floral ornament but goes straight to spiral decoration. But the potters of Phylakopi could not go on like this for ever, resisting the competition of Cretan vases by making clever copies to suit the taste of the day. At the end of L.M.I the island was flooded with imports, and the Palace style is represented there by a quantity of vases of which the majority are certainly genuine Cretan products.[4]

A great quantity of L.M.I and L.M.II ware was poured on the mainland. This Cretan pottery not only reached Argolis, Corinthia and Attica; it spread in Laconia, on the western shores of the Peloponnese, and right into Aitolia.[5] Native pottery was revolutionized by it. No more matt painting was done. Mycenæan ware, with its glaze and the spiral decoration of its first style, drives it out for good.[6] The Yellow Minyan ware was itself adapted to the fashion and was given new forms. Presently, in L.H.II, naturalistic

[1] See K. Mueller, AM. 1909, 317 ff.; cf. **XXV**, 91–2.
[2] **XXI**, 126, fig. 96, pl. xxiii; BSA. xvii, pl. iii, 2, pl. viii, 40; **IV**, 185.
[3] Dawkins and Droop, loc. cit., 10 ff., pl. ii.
[4] Ib., 14, pl. xi.
[5] **XXV**, 91.
[6] **III**, 36 ff., 116 ff.

ornament was adopted.   The octopus and the double axe
appeared in the usual ornamentation, leaf and flower motives
were popular, and the ivy-leaf had a success which it had not
hitherto enjoyed.   Imitation was already free.   Skill and
taste were forming.

During this time the Palace style became known.   There
is no doubt of the Cretan origin of some of these precious
vases, which have been found all over Argolis, at Kakovatos,
in Aigina, at Chalkis in Euboia, at Thebes, and at Orchomenos.
(Fig. 84).[1] But others, more numerous, are imitations
(Fig. 83),[2] and these are found still further away, even in
Thessaly.[3] From where do these imitations come ?   They

FIGS. 83, 84.—Palace style vases. The first, from Kakovatos (Pylos), is
of mainland manufacture.   The second, from Mycenæ, is Cretan.

are generally so perfect that it has been very difficult to
distinguish them, and this was only achieved by a comparison
of the kinds of clay and of the ornamental detail.   The native
potters cannot have decorated them ;   the most advanced
of them were still incapable of it.   We must, therefore, suppose
that master-potters from Crete worked on the mainland in
certain centres from which their work was sent far afield.
This fact is important.   It explains how in Melos, Mycenæ,
and many other places the education of the potters was
completed so quickly, and why beautiful vases were not made
in Crete alone.   It also explains the ease with which the
influence of not only Cretan but Ægean pottery was extended
to countries which had hitherto remained almost closed to it.

[1] JHS. xxiv, pl. xiii.   [2] AM. 1909, pl. xxi.   [3] See **XXV**, 90-2.

At the middle of the XVth century, when Palace style vases were arriving at Iolkos, Thessaly awoke from its sleep of a thousand years and learned with astonishment to use the wheel. About 1500 the Sixth City of Troy imported matt-painted pottery of the mainland and hastened to imitate it, using colour for the first time. Even Cyprus did not know the wheel before the time when it set itself to imitate Mycenæan mainland and L.M.II decorations. So, just when the pottery of Crete was at its apogee, Mycenæan pottery borrowed its models, carried off its artists, appropriated its processes, and immensely enlarged its domain. The next thing it did was to take its place.

The Pottery of the Mycenæan Period

When the true Mycenæan period came—L.M.III—Cretan expansion, which had been uninterrupted for more than three hundred years and was increasing in intensity, ceased because it had nothing more to conquer. The unity of the Ægean world was accomplished, and the pottery tells us its area. Local differences do not prevent the identity of essentials. It was the age of a *koine*, like that which was to come a thousand years later.[1]

Having assimilated Cretan civilization the new world no longer needed to look for it in the land of its origin. Knossos lost its supremacy. Pottery had no chosen centre ; its centres were everywhere. Potters' kilns have been found at Tiryns and Thebes, and a workshop at Zygouries in Corinthia ;[2] there were potteries beside the palaces and in the little towns, and they were active in every land. But the clientèle was no longer the same. The general public demanded the commonest goods in large quantities ; the princes and wealthy men who wanted painted vases were numerous but their taste was no longer refined. Moreover, the artistic workshops which supplied the good models were destroyed, and the good traditions were being lost. Pottery became a mere industry. Production was done in mass. Competition was organized, even for export ; a workshop on the mainland manufactured

---

[1] Cf. **XXV**, 92–100 ; see also, for Macedonia, L. Rey, BCH. 1916, 278 ff. ; 1917–19, 177 ff.

[2] AM. 1913, 338 ff. ; Πρ., 1911, 48 ff. ; AMJ. 1921, 298.

Trojan cups to send to Troy.[1] To turn out much and quickly, even if it was of inferior quality, would soon become the rule of the trade.

Nevertheless, the technique was maintained, and spread abroad.[2] For a long time pains were taken to secure a fine clay and wash, nice modelling and uniform, oxidizing firing. Where the matt black had been retained, as in Melos, it gave way to glazed black. Hardly any new forms were invented ; however, the stirrup-handled cup shares its popularity with the " pilgrim's gourd " and the " champagne-glass ", a cup with a fine form. But, although it was not too difficult to learn to set up a vase well, it was another thing to decorate it artistically.

There were plenty of motives. Mycenæan art had an eclectic repertory. It did not renounce naturalism ; it was familiar with plant decoration ; birds (especially water-fowl) fish, molluscs, and shells still supplied it with ample resources ; and in Argolis and Cyprus it used quadrupeds and human figures as well. Under the influence of mural painting the vase-painter even represented complete scenes, hunts, processions of warriors and men in chariots. Lastly, the geometrical patterns of the old native painting in matt colour were revived. But what use was made of all these riches ?

At first some isolated artist in Crete exercises his wits to find a novelty, like the motion of a bird pecking.[3] Generally the consecrated models are copied correctly without personal effort or inspiration ; on vases from Zapher Papoura and Ialysos there are papyrus-branches and octopuses which still have a certain effectiveness. But already stylization has killed style. Even in Crete, where this period of stagnation lasted longest, it could only delay the decline.[4] The day comes, in the XIIIth century, when hasty execution reduces the ornament to infantile simplicity. The undulations set off with stars become feeble zigzags and dots ; all that survives of the octopus is two round eyes in the centre of sets of symmetrical curves ; the shell and the nautilus degenerate

---

[1] Cf. **XXV**, 96, 103.
[2] **XXVII**, 33.
[3] **XXXVII**, 103, 106, fig. 36.
[4] Mackenzie, BSA. xxiii, 198 ff. ; Evans, xvi, 515 ff.

into corkscrew twiddles.[1] Quantity makes up for lack of quality ; motives are mixed haphazard in order to crowd the field. Elsewhere the decadence is still more rapid. The eyes of the octopus have become spirals and his arms are streaks between which molluscs, fish, birds, and beasts are scattered.[2] Floral design is conventionalized into a pattern of lines.[3] The very lines are irregular. At the end, in all parts of the Ægean, the decoration is reduced to horizontal bands with a wretched accompaniment of vague shapes and unrecognizable rosettes. Then even technique goes ; on a porous clay of greenish yellow the varnish is only a thin brown layer, almost without glaze. It is the last phase of a once glorious art, the death agony of a civilization.

[1] **XVI**, figs. 105 A, 116 J.
[2] **LXVII**, fig. 489 ; cf. **XXXIII**, 42–5.
[3] Pottier, BCH. 1907, 137.

CHAPTER II

WRITING AND LANGUAGE

I WRITING

HOWEVER far we go into the past we find man representing objects, ideas, words by signs. Even in the Reindeer Period, on the walls of caves and on implements of horn, bone, or mammoth-tusk, figures with a conventional meaning and mysterious lines are painted or incised. These writings, which have more or less resemblance to each other, are common to the whole of the Neolithic races, and are found from Scandinavia to Africa and from Asia Minor to Iberia. The most ancient Egyptian hieroglyphs and Chaldæan cuneiform signs are derived from still more ancient prototypes. A civilization as complete and as advanced as that of the Cretans —with its highly developed palace administration, its active trade, the hymns which were sung to sacred music and the epics illustrated by the works of art—cannot have been ignorant of the means of propagating thought in space and in time.

Perrot erred by excess of prudence when in 1894 he refused to see on any of the objects discovered at Mycenæ or elsewhere "anything resembling writing of any kind ".[1] Tsountas had already set up a collection of signs drawn on Ægean vases,[2] and Flinders Petrie had found at Kahun in Egypt inscribed vases, the origin of which he at once sought in the Ægean. What was more, as early as 1893 Evans had studied the " pictographs " on the " milk stones " which Greek women tie to their necks as amulets to make them give milk, and had recognized on these gems, which had been attributed before his time to the Peloponnese and the islands, hieroglyphs which in his opinion could only be Cretan. He went to Crete to collect as many documents as possible on the question and came back, in the very year in which Perrot published his volume on the Mycenæan civilization, with a monograph

[1] **LXVII**, 985.
[2] **LXXXIX**, 292.

which established the existence of several Cretan scripts.[1] The excavations have brilliantly confirmed what was only an inspired divination. Thousands of seals, masses of perforated bars and labels, and a great number of stones and pots are covered with various characters. The very conflagrations which destroyed the towns and the palaces have baked and hardened a countless quantity of clay tablets ; fire, fatal to libraries everywhere else, has preserved the archives of the kings and lords of Crete.

Unfortunately these documents are still a dead letter for us and will perhaps remain undecipherable so long as no bilingual inscription is discovered to give the key. All that the penetrating sagacity of Evans has so far been able to do is to distinguish different classes of writing among the *scripta Minoa*.[2] The Cretans commenced with a crude ideographic system which was simplified and conventionalized into two systems of hieroglyphs, pictorial, symbolic, or phonetic, which became more and more diagrammatic. From the hieroglyphs two linear scripts developed, one common to the whole of Crete and the other special to the Knossos of L.M.II ; both possess characters which sometimes designate whole words, sometimes syllables, and sometimes even letters. The development is similar to that which took the Egyptian scribes from hieroglyphic writing to hieratic writing.

The resemblance is not confined to this general transformation, which merely conforms to a universal law; a great number of Cretan signs present a striking resemblance to Egyptian hieroglyphs. Thus a very complicated question arises—what was the relation in the second millennium between Egyptian writing and the writings of the contemporary peoples ?

Students at all times have sought for the origin of the Phœnician alphabet. In agreement with the Cretans of the Hellenic epoch, who had preserved very definite memories of their predecessors, the historian Diodorus declares that the Phœnicians did not invent letters, but took them from Crete.[3] In our own day Champollion and Rougé have maintained that the Semitic alphabets are of Egyptian origin.

[1] XII,
[2] XVII ; XX, 195–6, 271–85, 612–46.
[3] Diodorus, v, 74.

While the Cretan excavations and the studies of Evans for some time restored the Cretan theory to favour, the examination of an inscription found in Sinai has caused the Egyptian theory to prevail. This theory was at once extended from the Semites to the Cretans. But one may still ask whether the Phœnicians, after having collected the basis of the Semitic alphabet which was created between 1788 and 1580, did not then introduce certain elements borrowed from the Ægeans. In any case, the solution of the problem in respect of the Semites leaves the whole question untouched so far as the Cretans are concerned

There is no doubt that the Cretan scripts recall those of Egypt in a large number of hieroglyphs and, subsequently, of linear signs. Some of these resemblances prove nothing, for they lie in the very conditions of primitive writing ; in every country man begins by choosing for his signs, which he draws in almost exactly the same way, the human body, the hand and the eye, a tree or beasts, the moon's crescent and the star, a weapon such as the arrow, and very simple implements such as the wedge and the pestle. In other cases borrowing is certain, in view of the peculiar shape and the political or ritual meaning given to the objects represented— the man seated and speaking, the door and the palace, the saw and the adze, the royal bee, the throne and the *ankh* or sign of life. But on the other hand many Cretan hieroglyphs have no parallels in Egypt ; it is enough to mention those which are most obviously native, the lily and the crocus, the branches of palm and olive, the double axe and the dagger, the plough and the lyre, with three strings or eight.

According as they attach greater importance to one of these categories or the other, scholars arrive at different conclusions. According to Sundwall,[1] the Cretan scribes copied most of their pictorial, hieroglyphic, or linear signs from Egyptian prototypes, and were only independent so far as difference of language made it necessary. According to Evans and Hall,[2] the great mass of Cretan signs is autochthonous. It is at least certain that, of the 135 hieroglyphs in Evans' list, Sundwall has examined only 44, to which he has added, it is true, nine signs known from the linear script.

---

[1] *Acta Academiæ Aboensis*, i (1920), 2 ; ii (1921), 3 ; cf. JAI. 1915, 41–64.
[2] Evans, **XVII**, 236–41 ; **XX**, 280 ff. ; Hall, **XXXVII**, 216 ff.

As for the resemblances which he notes, they are often of a kind which proves nothing (the crescent, the cross, etc.). More frequently the drawing of the same object, even of the eye and the hand, and still more of the vase, the arrow, or the ship, rather brings out the difference between the two writings. Moreover, Sundwall is himself the first to recognize the originality shown by the Cretan scribes on important points. The Egyptian hieroglyphs had a consonantal value which was given to them by the acrophonic principle, that is by the initial of the word designating the object represented. The Semites of Sinai confined themselves to giving to the Egyptian signs corresponding names on the same principle, just as the Semites of Akkad had done with the Sumerian signs. The Cretans went further. They expressed sounds which the Egyptians did not possess, for example, the letter L. Moreover, since Sundwall believes with the German school that Egyptian writing was purely consonantal, he gives the Cretans the credit of having added to their characters a value as vowel sounds.

In that case the simplest thing is to admit, not only that the Phœnicians drew from the Cretan source as well as from the Egyptian, but that the Cretans and Egyptians both drew equally from the primitive source of the Neolithic writings. The Phœnician and Cretan scripts are not branches of one same trunk. The one is a relatively late product, and it owes more to Egypt than to Crete. The other was not taken ready-made from outside, but developed spontaneously, in complete independence, and only later certain religious conceptions, certain political institutions, and perhaps too the exotic signs expressing these new ideas, were borrowed from a foreign country. Two fundamental peculiarities of Cretan writing suffice to prove that it is not of the same descent as the Semitic scripts. It runs from left to right, sometimes returning from right to left (*boustrophedon*), and presents the figures of living beings with their back to the reader, whereas the writing of the Egyptians runs from right to left, like those of the Babylonians, Hittites, and Semites, and presents the figures with their face to the reader. Cretan writing was living its own life when it passed from the purely pictorial stage to that of the hieroglyphs, which grew more and more conventional, and finally to that of the linear characters.

As for Asiatic influence, it appears nowhere in Cretan writing. There is an outward likeness, it is true, between the clay tablets used in Crete and those of Babylonia. One might at first admit, if necessary, that the material form was borrowed, and that only, as in any case the Cretan signs have no resemblance whatever to the cuneiform characters. But even that is very unlikely. In Crete the tablets appear fairly late ; none existed before M.M.II. The round shapes which are drawn on them for choice were not created by the stilus. Pen and ink were used ; we have the proof in the inscriptions on two cups, done in a sepia which does not wash off and in characters which in places show the double mark of a split reed.[1] But even this process was not invented for writing on vases before the final baking. It was used on a perishable material ; a Cretan tradition speaks of a paper made of palm-leaves, similar to the Egyptian papyrus. Perhaps, too, wooden tablets coated with wax were used in Crete long before clay tablets.[2] We must therefore suppose that the documents which have come down to us were not of the kinds most extensively used. The religious and literary writings have disappeared, and of the commercial and legal papers, the stamped documents, nothing remains but the seal-impressions which were attached to them.

Not only did the signs which were incised on the clay tablets exist long before, but they were previously incised on other clay objects, and thus we see the very beginnings of the tablet in Crete itself.[3] First *graffiti* were made on the sealings while they were still fresh, on labels of every shape and, for example, on the four faces of oblong bars bored with a hole. The oldest Cretan tablets, those with hieroglyphs, have far more likeness to the faces of these bars than to the Babylonian tablets. They have neither the thickness nor the noble dimensions nor the square shape of the Babylonian article. They are narrow and oblong like the bars, and they even have a hole in order to be strung in bunches or attached as labels. It is only after a long time, by an independent transformation, that the Cretan tablets come to have some slight resemblance to those of Asia. Those which bear the linear script of Class A

---

[1] **XX,** 613–14.
[2] See *Iliad*, vi, 169 ; cf. **XVII,** 64–5 ; **XXXVII,** 217–18.
[3] **XXXVII,** 220–1.

remain oblong when they grow larger, or remain small when they are almost square ; even those bearing the script of Class B, though of respectable size, vary in form and are generally broader than they are high, such as the fine examples which measure 15 centimetres by 12, 19 by 10, or 27 by 15½, and bear 8, 13, or 26 lines.[1]

In all this there is no trace of imitation and, to tell the truth, if the scribes had looked for their models in Asia would they not have at least baked their incised tablets ?   If Cretan writing owes little to the Egyptians it really seems to owe nothing at all, not even a material process, to the Babylonians.[2]

It is at the beginning of Middle Minoan times that the

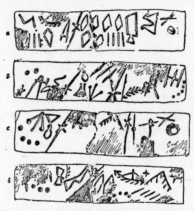

FIG. 85.—Bar with four faces with hieroglyphs of Class B (M.M.II).

ideographs of the preceding period, with their distorted and monstrous forms, are stereotyped into a hieroglyphic system consecrated by official calligraphy. The hieroglyphs of Class A [3] are only known from seals and their impressions. The drawing is regular, but stiff and archaic, especially in comparison with the Egyptian hieroglyphs of the same epoch. The hieroglyphs of Class B [4] appear with M.M.II. They appear on a great number of hard stone seals, labels, perforated

---

[1] **XVII**, 48 and fig. 26.

[2] It was of the Cretan tablets that Hall (**XXXVII**, 221) was able to say : " No culture of the ancient world appears so absolutely un-Babylonian, so completely uninfluenced by the ideas of Euphratean civilization, as does that of prehistoric Greece."

[3] **XVII**, 134, 149 ff.; **XX**, 195–6.

[4] **XVII**, 138 ff., 144 ff., 152 ff., 263 ff. ; **XX**, 271 ff.

bars (Fig. 85) [1] and small oblong tablets. They testify to an advanced art ; the forms are harmonious and picturesque, the human faces, in the case of great personages, are absolute portraits, and the animals are delightfully naturalistic.

Evans places 91 hieroglyphs in the first class and 95 in the second, but 51 of these signs are common to both classes, with very slight differences of style. Thus 135 are known in all, too few for a purely pictorial or symbolic writing and too many for a purely phonetic one. Therefore certain series manifestly retain an ideographic meaning. The seals often bear the emblem of a public office or a profession ; for example, the signs " throne and lion " represent the royal war administration, and the crafts are designated by a characteristic tool. A ship beneath two crescents is easy to understand—a sea voyage lasting two months.

But the example of the Egyptian hieroglyphs teaches us to beware of such interpretations. The body of hieroglyphs, far from becoming more realistic at the time when realism triumphs in art, grows more conventional ; this fact alone would suffice to prove that the signs also represent, in the punning manner of a rebus or picture-puzzle, not an object or the idea which it awakes but the sound or sounds or the initial part of the sounds which express its name. Thus reduced to a phonetic or even syllabic value, the hieroglyphs lend themselves to every possible combination. To make the sense definite the Egyptian practice is adopted in certain cases—to the word. which is written phonetically, a determinative ideograph is added.

The hieroglyphs, then, marked a very decided tendency towards a type which grew less and less pictorial and more and more syllabic, when they were swept away by the whirl-wind which destroyed the first palaces. As soon as new dynasties established themselves in the Second Palaces, in M.M.III, the materials borrowed from the old scripts were introduced into a script which was definitely linear. An artificial selection was made, not only from the most advanced hieroglyphs, but from all which had been in use from the most distant times. The new system, perhaps enforced by the royal authority, was alone taught henceforward. It corresponds to the hieratic of the Egyptians.

[1] XVII, 170.

The linear script of Class A is composed, so far as we know, of 90 signs, or of 76 if we do not count certain variants.[1] So they are much fewer than the hieroglyphs. This diminution enables us to estimate the advance of phoneticism, but it is not so great but that a large proportion of the signs, perhaps a score, retain an ideographic value under a conventionalized form. We have not yet arrived at the purely syllabic alphabet, like that which was derived from the Cretan writing in Cyprus. When we see on a tablet (Fig. 33) an ingot accompanied by numerals, and then a pair of scales followed by another numeral, we can translate without fear of making a mistake : so many

Fig. 86.—Tablet with linear script, Class B, giving a list of women (L.M.II).

ingots weigh or are worth so much. For proper names above all it seems that figures expressing a word or an idea were used ; the ship, for example, formed part of a name of the same kind as Naukrates.[2] But the great majority of the signs are adapted to various combinations of phonetic value ; they are syllables, and sometimes perhaps letters. Certain signs look as if they were roots which come into the composition of words ; the sign " hand " appears thus with thirteen varieties.[3]

This system remained in general use all over Crete. But

---

[1] Ib., 28 ff. ; **XX,** fig. 476 ; cf. Sundwall, loc. cit., iv, 1923.
[2] Evans, **XX,** 644.
[3] Ib., 645.

at Knossos at the end of L.M.I the chancery brought about the predominance of a script which was doubtless reserved for the royal documents, the linear script of Class B. This script cannot be called a mere derivative from Class A ; only half the characters are common to both classes. A new amalgam was invented, certain elements of which seem to be nearer to the hieroglyphs than are their linear equivalents in the rival class, and are therefore taken direct from prototypes which had been preserved no one knows where ; the pig's head, for example, is not recognizable in the Class A character derived from it but is so in the Class B character.[1] The principles were not changed. The palace inventories more than ever record, in pictorial signs, ingots with scales, and also daggers, chariots, horses, vases, cereals, cattle, and houses. On the lists of persons the sex can be recognized by the determinative following the name ; so we have on the one hand soldiers or sailors and on the other women, probably the slave staff of the court. (Fig. 86.)[2]

Thanks to the inventories made out on quantities of tablets we at least know the numerical signs of the Cretan scripts. Here they are [3] :—

	Hieroglyphic, Class B.	Linear, Class A.	Linear, Class B.
Units . . .	Ɔ or |	|	|
Tens . . .	●	● and, more often, —	—
Hundreds . .	\ or /	O	O
Thousands . .	◊	-O-	-O-
Fractions { ½ (?) .	V	L	L
⅓ or ¼ (?)		7	7

The use of writing is known to us especially from documents of an administrative kind. But far from being the monopoly of official or professional scribes it was very widespread. There was great talk once of a school which was said to be installed in the heart of the palace of Knossos. Nothing

[1] Ib., figs. 476–7, no. 87.
[2] **XVII,** fig. 25. On this tablet each name ends with the sign " woman " and is separated from the next by a small upright stroke.
[3] **XX,** 279, 617–18, cf. Sundwall, loc. cit., 1920, 8.

proves that the room containing the benches which suggested
the idea was really used for this purpose, but it does not
matter ; schools and writing-masters must have existed all
over Crete.

Religious life involved much writing. Many ex-voto
offerings bear dedications.[1] The libation-tables, the ritual
vessels, and in particular the spoons of clay or stone are often
covered with characters, and a certain group of four signs
which is repeated on several of these objects seems to represent
a consecrated formula or the name of a deity. The name of
the dedicator is perhaps engraved on a bronze plaque above
a man dancing before a holy place, and on a clay figurine
found at Tylissos.

In Crete, as in Phœnicia, trade seems to have made full
use of the advantages offered by writing. Everywhere there
were tablets similar to those of the royal archives ; everywhere
they were inscribed with signs representing goods of all kinds
and with those of the ship, the ingot, and the scales, and
numerals were placed beside the sign ⊣, which, long before
it took the form ⊦ and had the sound *ta* in Cyprus and the
meaning " drachma " in Greece, perhaps designated in Crete
the talent, the unit of weight and of value. Certain clay
roundels bear inscribed signs in the centre and the prints of
different seals all round ; [2] these were probably contracts
and may have been commercial contracts. The thousands
of sealings found in the palaces and houses served no doubt
to authenticate documents written on a perishable material.
At Knossos they were documents of the royal administration ;
in a port like Zakro they were private documents. The
cursive writing which appears in all these business documents
was sometimes used by the potters to inscribe whole sentences
in ink on the bottom of a vase ; but more often they painted
a few linear signs, a word of consecration or perhaps their own
name or that of the buyer.[3]

There is reason for believing that the fresco-painters
accompanied their pictures with explanatory text.[4] But
certain details show better than all the rest to what an extent
writing was in general use. At Hagia Triada, as at Pompeii,

---

[1] Evans, **XX**, 625–36.
[2] Ib., 624–5.
[3] Ib., 550, 613–14, 616–17 ; cf. **XXXVIII**, 66.
[4] **XX**, 637.

we see *graffiti* scrawled on the walls by idle passers-by.[1]   The
humblest folk could read and write.   A stone-cutter, in order
not to get his incised characters out of line, rules horizontal
lines to guide himself.[2]   In the first half of the XIXth century
Cretan workmen who had emigrated to Egypt write the
characters of their own country on the pots which they make
for their own use.[3]

Since the Cretans took their system of writing with them
it is not surprising that they caused it to be adopted all over
the Ægean.   At Melos the potters draw the signs of the linear
script of Class A not only on the vases which they export to
Crete but on those which are to remain in the island, even on
common crockery.[4]   Those of Thera do likewise.   Everything
seems to show that in the islands it is the Cretan language
which is expressed in the Cretan script.

But on the mainland we do not find things presented in
such a simple fashion.[5]   While certain vase inscriptions
conform to the linear Class A, others appear to mark a
transitional stage between hieroglyphs and linear characters.
At Mycenæ an example of each kind has been found.[6]   At
Delphi and at Orchomenos, on a bronze axe and on a stirrup-
vase belonging to the end of the Mycenæan Age, linear
characters of Class A are mixed with hieroglyphs, and numerals
are indicated as in Crete at the time of the hieroglyphic script
and of the beginning of linear script A.[7]   In Bœotia particularly
the archaic system prevailed.   The famous " Kadmeian "
letters of which the Greeks spoke were indeed used on the
Kadmeia, as at Orchomenos, and it is these no doubt which
were engraved on the bronze tablets which Agesilaos found
at Haliartos in the " Tomb of Alkmene ", and took for
Egyptian hieroglyphs.[8]   This reappearance of ancient characters
recalls the substitution of the linear system B for the
linear system A at Knossos ; but it is still more extraordinary in the Greece of the XIIIth century than in the
Crete of the XVth.   We must admit that the primitive

[1] Ib., fig. 473.
[2] Ib., 621-2.
[3] Flinders Petrie, *Kahun, Gurob, and Hawara*, pl. xxvii, xxviii.
[4] **XXI**, 177-85 ; **XVII**, 35-6.
[5] See **XVII**, 56-9, figs. 31-5.
[6] Ib., 58, figs. 33-4.
[7] Ib., figs. 35, 31-2.
[8] Plutarch, *Moralia*, 579 A ; cf. BCH. 1921, 515.

hieroglyphs led an obscure and mysterious existence in the different countries of the Mediterranean and that in this way, despite manifest borrowings from Crete, the writing of pre-historic Greece already presented all kinds of variants.

The same phenomenon, a number of different alphabets with common elements, is to be seen in almost all the eastern countries visited or colonized by the Cretans. Certain of these countries, however, needed to take nothing from the Ægeans, because they already had an established system of writing. We have one striking example of absolute independence ; it is furnished by a terra-cotta disk found at

FIG. 87.—The Phaistos disk.

Phaistos. (Fig. 87.)[1] Whence did it come ? How did it come to Crete ? No one knows ; but it is certain that there is nothing Cretan about it. The clay is not of the island. The hieroglyphic characters with which its two faces are covered coil in a spiral from the circumference to the centre, running from right to left and presenting the figures of living beings with their face to the reader. They were printed by means of stamps ; the scribe had a set of movable types, one for each sign, and his work was more allied to printing than to writing. Furthermore, this disk dates from a time when Phaistos, like the rest of the island, had abandoned

[1] Pernier, Au., 1909, 255 ff. ; della Seta, RAL. 1909, May ; A. Reinach, RA. 1910, i, 1–65 ; Evans, **XVII**, 22–8, 273–93 ; **XX**, 647–68 ; Cuny, REA. 1911, 296–312 ; 1912, 95 ff. ; Sundwall, loc. cit., 1920.

hieroglyphs ; in fact, it was found together with M.M.III
pottery and tablets bearing linear script of Class A.

Of the 45 signs represented, a few only, such as did not
allow of great differences, like the flower, the tree, or the
fish, resemble the ancient hieroglyphs of the Cretans. There
is nothing Minoan about the others, either in the type of the
human figures or in the form of the objects ; there are men
in short tunics, fat women in double skirts, children in shifts,
and houses like the Lycian pagodas. All these hieroglyphs
are of a very specialized kind, much more so than those of
Crete ever were ; the men, for example, have racial peculiarities,
tattooed cheeks and stiff feather head-dresses. Here development has been in the pictorial direction ; the ideographs
have grown more precise, instead of becoming diagrams,
and, although often grouped in a quasi-syllabic " disematism ",
they are not mingled with phonetic elements enough to become
a true linear script. Certain groups still show the predominance of the image over the sound, such as the succession
of warrior, shield, and captive with his hands tied behind
his back. One-third of the signs appear to have an ideographic
value in this way. Thus the mere sight of such hieroglyphs,
in addition to which there are manacles, the bow, the arrow,
the ship, and the bird of prey, suggests the idea of an expedition
undertaken by one of the " peoples of the sea " mentioned
by the Egyptian documents. Perhaps some tale of adventure
could be read on the disk. From this point onwards a free
road lies open to hypothesis.[1]

Each of the two faces is divided into sections, which sometimes end with a punctuation-mark. On one 122 signs are
divided into 31 sections and 10 groups ; on the other 119
signs form 30 sections and 9 groups. If we allow that on the
first face the first group, which takes up the whole first section,
is an exordium, each face bears 30 sections and 9 groups.
Thus we obtain a remarkably symmetrical arrangement which
is governed by the number 3. We may, therefore, suppose
that we have a metrical composition and, since the same
group of signs appears thrice on the same face, a song with
a refrain. Might it not be a hymn of victory ? As we said,
on the road of hypothesis one can go far. Let us confine
ourselves to one certain fact : the Cretans of the XVII century

---

[1] See Cuny, loc. cit. ; Evans, **XX,** 659 ff.

were in relations with a people which possessed a national and native-born system of hieroglyphs. Moreover, this fact is not unique; the *graffiti* at Troy would furnish another example.[1]

But in places where the Cretans and Mycenæans founded permanent establishments the native scripts changed. We have the proof in Cyprus.[2] The oldest inscriptions found there have no relation with the Egyptian hieroglyphs or with cuneiform. Two-thirds of their characters are identical with the linear signs of Crete, and the others are very nearly so or resemble the Cretan hieroglyphs. Cyprus, therefore, had first a hieroglyphic script, borrowed from the primitive store of the Mediterranean peoples. This writing had perhaps already become linear to some small extent on its own, when it adopted a large part of the characters which the Cretan traders and colonists brought with them.

This local form of the Cretan writing followed its proper destiny. When it was reduced to a syllabary Achaians from the Peloponnese adapted it in a rough and ready way to their own idiom; but it always showed, by its inability to denote certain gradations, despite its 54 characters, that it had not been created to express the Greek language. The Cretan script plays a similar part in the southern portion of Asia Minor. In the historical period the Lycian and Carian alphabets contained a certain number of characters which had nothing in common with the Greek alphabet. From tables drawn up by Evans[3] it is quite clear that these heterogeneous signs are the most ancient, and that they have affinities with all the systems of writing practised in Crete; some, it seems, come direct from linear scripts A and B, while others go back to the common source, the ideographs, not without the intervention of Ægean hieroglyphs. By a curious coincidence, which has an allegorical value, the only passage in which Homer clearly mentions writing is that in which Bellerophon, leaving Argos for the shores of Asia, hands to the king of the Lycians tablets covered with signs.[4]

If we examine the question of the Phœnician alphabet

---

[1] **LXVII,** 206–8; cf. Evans, **XVII,** 67.
[2] Evans, ib., 68–77; Dussaud, **XI,** 428–32; Hall, loc. cit., 223 ff.; cf. Meillet, *Aperçu d'une hist. de la langue grecque,* 88.
[3] **XVII,** 66, fig. 36.
[4] *Iliad,* vi, 168 ff.

in this historical context, we shall shed much light on it.[1]
In the XIVth century, when the princes of Syria corresponded
with the Pharaohs they used cuneiform, and their successors
maintained this system of writing until the end of the XIIth
century. But in the meantime the Kheretim, swelled by the
Pelesati, had come from Caphtor to Canaan. Palestine
had been converted to the Ægean civilization. The immigrants
had established in their new home their agriculture, their
industry, their military practices, their religion, and their
writing. In the smallest towns the chiefs had archives and
scribes, like the kings of Knossos; when, about 1117, the
Egyptian priest Unamonu presented himself among the
Zakari at Dor, Prince Badira asked him for his letters of
credit and showed him the lists of presents sent to his ancestors.[2]
From this time onwards the peoples established in the neighbourhood of Canaan merited the name of Keftiu, which the
Egyptians still gave them in the Ptolemaic period, and that of
Phœnicians, or " Red-Skins ", by which the Greeks always
designated them.

To meet the needs of their trade they made themselves
an alphabet which, going to the very end of the development
hitherto followed by all other scripts, broke the word up into
simple sounds and extracted twenty-two letters from the
syllabaries. Now one-third of these characters bear names
which cannot be explained in any Semitic language and have
forms known from the linear and hieroglyphic systems of
Crete.[3] As for the other characters, the objects which they
are supposed to represent from their Phœnician names are just
those which the hieroglyphs, both Egyptian and Cretan,
reproduced pictorially. In consequence, the greater part
of this alphabet may be an extension of the Semitic scripts
borrowed from Egypt, but may also be derived from the
Cretan hieroglyphs through linear scripts A and B; in any
case, all the letters which have kept their foreign name
untranslated have an appearance of having been transmitted
to the Phœnicians by the Philistines, the heirs of the Cretans.
Even the Phœnician alphabet comes into the class of local
systems which, despite differences of greater or less degree,

[1] S. Reinach, An., 1900, 497–502; Evans, **XVII**, 177–94; Dussaud,
XI, 433–4. See Corrections and Additions, p. 400, for later evidence.
[2] W. Max Mueller, *Papyrus Golenischeff*, 25.
[3] **XVII**, fig. 41.

are connected one with another and all with that of Crete.
But it is the latest of these systems and the most perfect.
The Phœnicians have shown no inventive genius here any
more than in other things ; but they will have the glory,
as they go about the Mediterranean on their business, of
giving to the writing which the Greeks have almost allowed
to die a new life to all eternity.

II LANGUAGE

Of the language which lies hidden beneath the Cretan
inscriptions we know, alas, very little.[1] Judging by the
regularity with which writing develops from the end of the
Chalcolithic Period to the Greek invasions, we have the
impression that the same language is transmitted to successive
generations, with inevitable changes. This speech was
neither Indo-European nor Semitic. From certain groups
of signs it seems to have had alterations of suffix in which
we may see word-endings and inflexions ; this characteristic
makes it similar to the Aryan languages, but proves nothing.

How can such vague evidence be supplemented ? It is
true that inscriptions have been found in Crete and Cyprus
which give in scripts which can be read, the Greek alphabet
and the Cypriot syllabary, texts in a language which is not
Greek. But these dialects, which were still spoken, well
within the historical period, by the Eteocretans of Praisos
and the people of Amathus, have not yielded up their secret
to the most learned investigation.[2] Egypt gives us two
most interesting documents on the subject. (i) A schoolboy
who was given as his task " Say the names of Keftiu which
you know " wrote four on his board, one of which, Akashau,
suggests the Philistine name of Achish.[3] (ii) A book of medicine
gives a formula in the Keftiu language for exorcizing a malady,
and in the three or four words of this formula some believe
they recognize that of *tirkka* or *tarkka*, which recalls the name

---

[1] Kretschmer, *Einleitung in die Geschichte der griech. Sprache*, 370 ff. ;
Fick, **XXII, XXIII** ; Conway, BSA. viii, 125 ff. ; x, 155 ff. ; Burrows,
VI, 150 ff. ; Cuny, REA. 1910, 154–64 ; Meillet, *Mém. de la Soc. de linguistique*,
xv, 161–4 ; *Aperçu d'une hist. de la langue grecque*, 63 ff. ; Dussaud, **XI,**
437–42 ; Hall, **XXXVII,** 229–31 ; Autran, " *Phéniciens*," 11 ff. ; cf. Vendryes,
Mém. de la Soc. de linguistique, xviii, 271 ff.

[2] See Conway, Vendryes, loc. cit.

[3] W. Max Mueller, *Assyr. Zeitschrift*, ix, 394.

of a Cilician god and perhaps that of the Etruscan King Tarquin.[1] But, for all their interest, these documents cannot, with one or two proper names, dispel the darkness which envelops the Keftiu language.

All that we can do for the moment—and it is not without use—is to draw up lists of Cretan words with the aid of various methods. Certain word-endings preserved in Greece and Asia are characteristic. First there is the termination *-inth-os*, which reappears in the Asiatic languages in the form *-ind-a* or *-and-a*, and perhaps also in Etruscan in the form *-uns*. There is too the termination *-sos* or *-ssos*. Both indicate the pre-Hellenic character not only of place-names like Corinth and Tirynth-, Koressos and Knossos, but also of a great number of common nouns. The *sigma* at the beginning of a word or between two vowels is not Greek either ; it enables us to recognize in the Greek language a number of words which it has inherited, and even gives us ground for considering Messapian, which no one has understood so far, as having associations with the Ægean or Asiatic languages. Many Greek words cannot be explained by Indo-European roots ; one is the more justified in ascribing them to the pre-Hellenes because some of them are frequently used in the Homeric poems and disappear from common speech almost immediately after, e.g. μέροπες (mankind) and δέπας (cup). Many related words in the Greek and Semitic languages have no acceptable etymology on one side or the other, nor do they conform to the ordinary laws of derivation on either side ; they can only descend from a common source. Related Greek and Latin words show the same abnormalities, and lead us to the same conclusion. Finally, we are so fortunate as to know a certain number of words preserved by the Cretan dialects of histoiical times, of which ancient writers, particularly Hesychius in his *Lexicon*, give us the meaning.

It is well worth while to classify the words thus known ; let us make the attempt.

Men : μέροπες, men ; μάλκενις, virgin ; πάλλαξ, concubine ; ἀκάρα, legs ; κόρυμβος, tuft of hair.

Animals : βόλινθος, wild bull ; νεβρός, fawn ; δίβαν or δίφας, snake ; σίαλος, fat hog ; κίραφος, fox ; σμίνθος, mouse.

---

[1] Wreszinski, *Londoner Med. Papyrus*, 192 ; cf. Hall, loc. cit., 230.

Edible plants : σῖτος, corn ; κυρήβια, straws ; πίσος, pea ; ἐρέβινθος, λέβινθος, ὀδολινθος, chick-pea ; σήσαμον, sesame ; σίκνος, cucumber ; κολόκυνθα, pumpkin ; σέρις, chicory ; οἴσαρον, rampion ; μῶλυ, orach.

Aromatic plants : μίνθα, mint ; καλάμινθος, calamint ; ἀψίνθιον, wormwood ; σέριφος, sea-wormwood ; σίσυμβρον, water-mint.

Medicinal plants : δίκταμνον, dittany ; δαῦκος, parsnip.

Trees and shrubs : οἴνη, vine ; ἐλαία, olive ; κυπάρισσος, cypress ; τερέβινθος, terebinth ; πτελέη, lime ; ὕσσωπος, hyssop ; ἰόβας, reed ; κάννα, cane ; ἀσπάλαθος, broom ; γάρσανα, brushwood.

Fruit : ὄλυνθος, fresh fig ; σῦκον, dried fig ; βότρυς, bunch of grapes ; σίδη, pomegranate.

Drink : οἶνος, wine ; ἔλαιον, oil ; βρῦτον, beer.

Bee-keeping : σφήξ, bee ; σίμβλος, hive ; κήρινθος, propolis, bee-glue.

Perfume : χαλβάνη, aromatic resin.

Flowers : λείριον, lily ; σισυριγχίον, iris ; ῥόδον, rose ; ὑάκινθος, hyacinth ; κήρινθον, bee-bread ; νάρκισσος, narcissus ; ἀκακαλίς, flower of narcissus ; σάμψυχον, sweet-marjoram.

Dress : ὀθόνη, cloth garment ; βύσσος, βυτίνη, very fine linen ; σισύρα, garment of skin ; σάνδαλον, sandal, shoe.

Building : λέσχη, portico ; πλίνθος, brick, plinth ; χάλιξ, limestone ; σωλήν, pipe, gutter.

Pottery : κάδος, jug ; δέπας, cup ; ἀσάμινθος, bath-tub.

Metal-working : χαλκός, copper ; κασσίτερος, tin ; μόλυβδος, lead ; χρύσος, gold ; σίδηρος, iron ; κίβδος, dross ; λέβης, caldron.

Arms and armour : σάκος, shield ; σφενδόνη, sling ; οἰστός, arrow ; ξίφος, sword ; κόρυς, helmet.

Fortification : τύρσις, tower.

Navigation : θάλασσα, sea ; νῆσος, island ; ξάλη, storm ; ζέφυρος, zephyr ; κέλης, ship ; ἴκριον, deck ; κυβερνάω, take the helm ; μήρινθος, line ; κάλως, cable ; σίφαρος, sail ; ἄσπαλος, fish ; σφόγγος, sponge ; πορφύρα, purple.

Trade : σάκκος, sack ; πείρινς, basket-body of chariot ; ἀρραβών, earnest-money ; μνᾶ, mina, weight ; κάπηλος, retailer.

Political and social life : βασιλεύς, king ; ἄναξ, prince ; ὄλβος, rich, powerful ; κίμβιξ, niggard ; λαός, people, crowd.

Religion : Βριτόμαρτις, Britomartis "the good maiden " ; Ἐλχανός, Velchanos the cock-god ; λάβρυς, the double axe ; λαβύρινθος, labyrinth, sanctuary of the double axe (in Asia Labranda); βωμός, holy place, altar ; θάμβος, sacred terror.

Games, athletics, dancing, music and song : στλέγγις, strigil ; νῦσσα, post of race-course ; κίθαρις, cithara ; φόρμιγξ, lyre ; σῦριγξ, flute ; σάλπιγξ, trumpet ; ἀμήτωρ, cithara-player ; θίασος, band of dancers and singers ; παῖαν, pæan ; διθύραμβος, dithyramb ; θρίαμβος, triumphal hymn.

Æsthetic sentiment : δροιόν, beautiful ; ἀβρός, pretty, dainty, delicate.

The bare list which we have here before us is a summary of all that the archæological documents have taught us, a faithful picture of a very advanced civilization. Everything is there ; under a strong government we see thriving agriculture, prosperous industry, sailors and traders whose activity covers the whole Mediterranean, then a taste for beautiful flowers and beautiful vases, gorgeous dresses and perfumes, and finally the religious ceremonies in which the goddess, surrounded by the sacred animals, lends a kindly ear to the hymns which extol her to the tune of the lyre. That is what the few words which have survived tell us.

It is enough to permit us to imagine that the Cretan language was capable of expressing every sublety of poetry and o satisfying the demands of literature and science. When Homer describes the dances which were performed in the theatre of Knossos he authorizes us to think that the bards who sang in the palace of Alkinoos had their forerunners in the palace of Minos, and that the Greek epic, with its artificial language, was inspired by poems far more ancient. If in the Egypt of the XVIIIth Dynasty the books of medicine take certain formulas textually from the Keftiu, we must suppose that these formulas were not spread about by oral tradition alone, and the reputation of certain prescriptions, containing ceterach (*asplenum*), parsnip (*daukos*), and mountain simples (*diktame*), proves that the Cretan medical treatises combined with tricks of sorcery genuine studies of natural history. Without going so far as to make the legendary Ikaros the pioneer of aviation, we see clearly that the artistic and industrial processes known to the Cretans, the inventions ascribed to Daidalos and the " bronze man " Talos, were not mere lucky experiments but the result of research and teaching which must have been conveyed in writing and must have created a technical vocabulary. Do not let us forget the hydraulic science testified by the drainage of the palace of Knossos ; let us remember that the astronomical knowledge which was required by the architects in order to observe the *cardo* and by the sailors to count the moons was codified in the " calendar of Minos ", which transmitted at least the names of the months to the Cretans of historical times. There is no doubt of it, Cretan writing expressed a highly civilized language which shed its influence far and wide, and survived.

CONCLUSION

SURVIVALS OF ÆGEAN CIVILIZATION

WHEN the Dorians came the great civilization which the Cretans had made and the Achaians had inherited was carried away by the storm. It had expanded during more than a millennium ; one inroad of barbarians, and it was gone. Without any transition we see a world dissolving and a new world born. The Dorian invasion is the *Drang nach Osten* of a continental civilization, that of Hallstatt. The Iron Age commences. The first iron sword from the Ægean was found at Mouliana in a tomb of the very end of L.M.III.[1] It proclaims a revolution. Costume changes, and *fibulæ* are used to hold hanging draperies. The burning of the dead replaces burial. Although disfigured, the motives of Minoan art had been maintained in the Mycenæan Age ; now by a retrogression which takes the nations of the Ægean back to the morrow of the Neolithic Age only geometric ornament is known. All that has been done by generation after generation without number during the Bronze Age perishes.

No, Ægean civilization did not perish utterly. It offered so many material advantages and still had such a power of attraction that the invaders themselves, who after all had not been drawn only by the amenities of the climate and of the land to be had, preserved at least such elements as a gross temperament could assimilate. Moreover, in the days of its glory this civilization had prepared for itself distant refuges, which the Mediterranean, ever kindly, held open to it in the day of its distress. After the great shipwreck the survivors, thrown up on the shore here and there, could at least collect some wreckage.

To make an inventory of this salvage it would be sufficient to run through the list of the pre-Hellenic words which passed into the Greek language. The index which we have attempted to form a few pages back not only gives the balance-sheet of

[1] 'Εφ., 1904, 22 ff.

Ægean civilization but also shows the first assets of Greek civilization. Of what did these consist ?

Even in the countries permanently occupied by the Dorians —the Peloponnese, Crete, and the other southern islands— we must not suppose that they made a clean sweep. No doubt the story which archæology tells is deplorable, and it is perhaps where the break with the past is not complete that we best see the incapacity of the newcomers for understanding it. They still have stirrup-vases, but they change the portion to which the handles are fixed into a neck ; they think that the *dromos* before a rock tomb looks very fine, but (for example, at Plati) they make it lead to a pit-grave at the bottom of which they lay a funerary tub. But do not let us forget that they did not exterminate the old population. On a stele at Prinias we see a warrior of gigantic stature, recognizable as a Dorian from his greaves, round shield, and long spear ; before him a very small figure, dressed in Ægean costume, raises his arms in the attitude of the suppliant ; he is the vanquished whose only hope lies in the mercy of the victor. The victor spares him ; he will have one serf the more, he will turn the Minoan into a Mnoïtes, and he will be able to sing the song which has come down to us : " My wealth is a great spear, a sword, and a fine shield to cover my body. With these I plough, with these I reap and harvest the sweet wine of the vine." What does that mean ? The land in Greece is still worked by those who once owned it. Agricultural methods do not change. The Cretans, and after them the Mycenæans, had found which cultures best suited the soil and climate of their country. From them the Greeks and all the peoples of the Mediterranean would learn to make figs edible and to harvest not only " the sweet wine of the vine " but the good oil of the olive. That is no small lesson.

But the better to trace the survivals of the old civilization we must cast an eye over the whole of Greece and more especially over those countries in which the Achaians, mingled with Cretans, and the Aiolians continued to live in independence. During all the migrations which had led them to explore so many lands in quest of new homes they had not forgotten the art of navigation. They handed down to historical Greece the rules and the technical vocabulary of the Cretan fleet. There was no longer any question of the

impoverished Achaians and Cretans, and still less of the Dorians
with their habits of violence, carrying on regular business with
distant countries. Piracy became an acknowledged and
honourable profession. It at least had the advantage that it
did not allow men to forget the old routes, the " liquid roads "
of Mediterranean navigation. Like the Akaiwasha of
Meneptah's day, the Cretans of the *Odyssey* go to Egypt after
plunder, and Odysseus offers himself as one of their captains.
In the footsteps of Minos and Idomeneus the people of Ithaca
sailed as far as the island of the Sikels to sell or obtain slaves.
New bands went and joined the Danauna on the coast of
Syria. Nay more, since the Trojan War had opened the door
of the straits, men ventured upon the dangerous sea by which
they could fetch iron and win the golden fleece. In the
meantime the Greeks did not abstain from all peaceful exchange
among themselves, or even, on occasion, with foreigners.
The weights and measures used among the Ægeans were
maintained in the cities of Asia Minor and facilitated
commercial relations with the countries which had hitherto
been subject to the dominion of the Hittites and were becoming
more and more open to Western influences. While the peasants
all over Greece fixed values in heads of cattle, Phokaia,
Ephesos, Miletos, and all the ports where the roads of Lydia
ended continued to use the metal unit, and, through them,
the Aiginetan system of weights would reproduce that of the
Cretans and Cypriots.

The invaders of Greece brought with them a very different
religion from that which had been predominant in the Ægean.
A great god prevailed over the great goddess of the Cretans.
Apollo took the place of Gaia on the *omphalos* at Delphi,
and in Crete itself Zeus was henceforth lord of Ida. But
Diktynna and Britomartis were never forgotten ; they often
transmitted their power to Rhea and Eleithyia, and they even
held the first rank in a large number of countries which escaped
the Dorians. Prinias in the VIIth century worshipped
a serpent goddess identical with her whose cult was once
celebrated at Knossos and Gournia. Arcadia always remained
faithful to female deities. Attica was always devoted to
the Goddess Mother and to her rival Athene. In Asia Minor
the most venerated shrine was still that of the Ephesian
Artemis. In Cyprus the Dove-Goddess took the name of

Astarte or Aphrodite without changing her nature or form.
The attributes and sacred animals of the old gods passed to
the new. The pious legends and images which were passed
long since by the Cretans to the Achaians are the explanation
of the apparent rapidity with which Greek religion assumed
its essential features, almost absolute anthropomorphism and
exuberant mythology.

One of the features which give the Ægeans such an original
aspect is just one of those which distinguish the Greeks from
the other peoples of Indo-European race, that is the liking
for the gymnastic and musical contests which accompany
the great festivals. Here again is a precious legacy. Let us
consider the geographical position of the sanctuaries where
the Pan-Hellenic games are held. Only at the time when the
great merchants' and pilgrims' road ran from Tiryns to
Corinth can the tradition have become established of general
gatherings at points so close to each other as Nemea and the
Isthmus. Olympia is the place, at first consecrated to the
Great Goddess, where Cretans and Achaians arrived by the
road from Arene or from Pylos. Delphi is the height to which
the priests from Knossos, starting likewise from Pylos and
landing at Krissa, climbed as they sang the Cretan hymn.
Delos is the island where people from Ionia and from Attica
met before the horned altar and watched the evolutions of
the *geranos*. The imprescriptible tradition of these solemnities
kept alive the national athletics of the Cretans and their
dances and their music and their hymns. There is as direct
a connexion between the boxing-matches carved on the
rhyton from Hagia Triada and those at which Achilleus and
Alkinoos preside as between the games described by Homer and
the Olympic games. The Lesbian lyre with seven chords is
the very same as is played by the musician painted on the
Cretan sarcophagus, and the pæan carved in the Greek language
on a stone from Palaikastro is derived from that very one
with which the Knossians waked the echoes in the Phaidriades.

This was the preparation, in that Aiolis where Terpander
would one day gloriously revive the heptachord, for the finest
of all the works bequeathed by ancient times to modern,
the epic. Even at the beginning of the XVIIIth century
a large composition in faience plaques at Knossos represented
a city surrounded by warriors. At the end of the XVIIth

century Mycenæ produces a *rhyton* of silver showing the siege
of a stronghold, men arriving by sea and women on towers
following the turns of the fight with gestures of encouragement
or anguish. (Fig. 68.) At the same date we see on a seal
from Knossos a boat attacked by the horrible Skylla (Fig. 30),
and on another *rhyton* from Mycenæ shipwrecked men
struggling in the waves and threatened by the monster.
These Iliads and Odysseys no doubt already had their singers.
When the days of trial came the last of the great victories
won by the Achaians, the taking of Troy, assumed legendary
dimensions in the imagination of the peoples who inhabited
the neighbouring region, and gradually the Aiolian bards
attached all the warlike epics to that which most flattered
and best consoled the new generations. Then, when the
migrations in their turn receded into the past and took on
a marvellous colour, all the tales of sea-journeys were fitted
into the " Returns " from Troy, and especially into the
adventures of Odysseus.

Whatever may be the date of the final versions, the basis
of the Homeric epics dates from the Sub-Mycenæan Period
in which bronze still prevails, though iron is gradually coming
into greater use. The *Iliad* mentions bronze fourteen times
more often than iron, and the *Odyssey* only four times. The
Catalogue of Ships gives a faithful picture of Achaian Greece
on the eve of the Dorian invasion. But the memory of past
glories and vanished cities lives on. Crete is still the isle of
a hundred cities. Knossos may lie buried beneath the ground,
but men still know the " chorus " which Daidalos built, where
the young men and maidens danced to the sound of the *cithara*,
and the palace of Minos with its gardens seems to have been
the model for the imaginary palace of Alkinoos. The splendours
of Mycenæ haunt men's minds, and they remember that the
ancestor of the Neleïdai, before his race came to Asia, owned
far away in Pylos a cup with doves drinking from it. Need
we be surprised if the language of such poems is artificial
and contains very ancient words no longer in common use ?

Let us extend our range of view still further. Ægean
civilization had had time to spread outside the Ægean. In
the most distant countries it survived, in some for but a
moment, and in others with sufficient vigour to produce
lasting results.

Cyprus kept very clearly the imprint of Cretan and Achaian colonization, with its Dove Goddess, its alphabet badly adapted to the Greek language, and the exotic traditions of its industry and art. It was able to take the place of Crete as metallurgical centre of the eastern Mediterranean; from its forges came the damascened cuirass of Agamemnon and, no doubt, the shields dedicated in the cave of Ida.

Southern Syria was completely transformed by the Pelesati and Zakari, the *arrière-ban* of the Ægean emigration. The Philistines were Kheretim or Cherethites, according to the Hebrews, and the Jewish legend which relates how they broke the resistance of Samson is a doublet of the Greek story in which Minos took Megara and caused its king, Nisos, to be shorn of his one golden hair. With the sure instinct of first-class men of business they occupied the country where the caravans arrived from Egypt and Arabia. They were good farmers, and acclimatized the vine and olive in Canaan. They were excellent smiths. They brought with them their architecture with the column-base and the capital or *kaphtor* of the Ægean type. Gaza was consecrated to Zeus Kretagenes, who took Britomartis for his companion ; Ashkelon had for its goddess an Astarte of the dove. An especially remarkable detail is that, at a time when the Dorian invasion had almost caused Ægean writing to disappear, these Ægeans who had become Asiatics continued to use it largely. In 1117, when the prince of the Zakari received an envoy from the Pharaoh, he asked him for his letters of credit and drew from his archives the inventories of presents received by his ancestors. We appreciate the full importance of the historical fact when we see that the Zakari were settled in the North of Palestine, on the borders of Phœnicia.

In sum, the history of Ægean civilization deserves more interest than as a mere archæological or even æsthetic curiosity. It is full of the seed of the future. The Cretans, who created it, made a gift of it to the surrounding peoples, thanks to the facilities offered them by the Ægean Sea, and at once communicated it to many other peoples, thanks to the obliging ubiquity of the Mediterranean. While the civilizations of Egypt and Asia retained a local and terrestrial character, an island civilization was sending its light far and wide. By the attraction which it exercised it tempted the warlike nations. When it had spread over the circuit of the Ægean, the supremacy passed from the Cretans to the Cretanized Achaians, from Knossos to Mycenæ, and there was a falling off. When its frontier was the North of Thessaly it drew the barbarous Dorians, and there was ruin. But the seeds cast so lavishly in so many different lands were not all lost. Through the long winter of the Greek Middle Ages they slept, to rise again in a splendid Renaissance. Greek civilization, the mother of the civilization of Rome and the West, is the daughter of Ægean civilization.

CORRECTIONS AND ADDITIONS

THE favourable reception accorded to this work should impel the author to make it the worthier of such kind treatment by certain revisions. Nobody is more conscious than himself of all its deficiencies. When one has spent nearly twenty years in meditation upon so vast and thorny a subject one remembers how one hesitated upon a thousand points before adopting each time an opinion which must always be provisional, and one knows by experience that, from day to day, new discoveries and new publications force the least conscientious painter of the most imperfectly known communities to continual recantations. If it is true of history that, in the words of Fustel de Coulanges, it is a science never completed, ye gods! what can be said of pre-history? Even now this book, which appeared only four months ago, needs considerable amendment.

Unfortunately, the author's good will is hampered by practical necessities which prevent any changes entailing the resetting of the type. I have endeavoured at any rate to make as many corrections as possible. The majority of these consist in the elimination of misprints, but some are of a radical nature.[1] As for the corrections, reservations, and additions which could not be incorporated in the text, the reader who wishes to keep himself *au fait* will find them summarized further on.

Concerning two of the objects which I have reproduced and used as examples, namely, the sceptre-handle representing a bearded personage (p. 65, Fig. 5 ; cf. p. 49) and the Boston statuette of a woman of Anglo-Saxon type (p. 330, Figs. 65–7 ; cf. p. 331), I had for a long time cherished misgivings. However, on receiving assurances that seemed well-founded, I had

---

[1] Page 243 (cf. Dussaud, **XI**, p. 361). Adalia is not in Lycia but in Pamphylia, as Monsieur G. Radet has pointed out to me.

Pages 260 and 264. In the palace of Nirou Chani it is not the rooms which are forty in number, but the altars piled up in a single room (communication from Monsieur Charles Picard).

Pages 386–7. Five words have been withdrawn from the list of pre-Hellenic words in consequence of objections raised by Monsieur Meillet.

decided to take them into account. To-day I owe it to the truth to confess that certain information regarding a factory established in Crete for the production of forgeries has renewed and strengthened my early doubts as to the authenticity of these two objects. The reader should also be warned that the fresco representing the King with the fleurs-de-lys has been largely restored, as is apparent in our illustration (p. 318, Fig. 57). It must be noted that this restoration, the work of Monsieur Gilliéron, has been a good deal contested. Lastly, Monsieur Charles Picard has informed me that my plan of the Chamaizi ruins (pp. 104 and 133, Fig. 23) is scarcely in agreement with that published by Mr. Xanthoudidis, which has been copied by most authors and was apparently generally accepted.

Our bibliography needs completing. For excavations at Mycenæ in 1920–21 (p. 17) see Wace, *Annual of the British School at Athens*, xxiv, pp. 185 ff., plates vii–xiv ; for excavations at Schoinochori (p. 17) see Renaudin, *Bulletin de Correspondance Hellénique*, 1923, pp. 190–240, plates ii–iii. For the transmission to the Hellenes of pre-Hellenic rhythms (pp. 299–301, cf. pp. 388, 393), A. Meillet, *Les Origines indo-européennes des mètres grecs*, Paris, 1923, must now be consulted. Monsieur Cuny, *Revue des Etudes Anciennes*, 1924, pp. 1–29, has made a new study of the Phaistos disk (pp. 381–2). In classifying a certain number of pre-Hellenic words that passed into the Greek language (pp. 386–7) I was unaware of the existence of a complete study of this subject, the work of J. Huber, " De lingua antiquissimorum Græciæ incolarum " in the *Commentationes Ænipontanæ*, fasc. ix, Vienna, 1921. For the excavations of Xanthoudidis (p. 16) see his *Vaulted Tombs of Mesará*, London, 1924.

In his 1923 campaign in Crete (see *The Times* of 28th August, 1923) Sir Arthur Evans made particularly interesting discoveries. He explored a private house at Knossos dating from about 1600. He discovered a great many fragments of frescoes, some portraying a warrior with a horned helmet leading black mercenaries into battle and the rest representing long-tailed Soudanese monkeys with blue turbans on their heads. These are valuable documents not only for Cretan painting (p. 311) and for the Egyptian influences which may be perceived in them (pp. 210, 306), but also for the relations between Crete and Africa (p. 198). An intaglio from the same source displays in a satisfactory manner a whole collection of the divine attributes (p. 250). The goddess is represented with serpents twining from her skirt up to her bosom (see p. 328, Fig. 62). In one hand she holds a sword and in the other the emblem of spiritual authority (see p. 155, Fig. 27, middle). Thus the Serpent Goddess and the Goddess of War are here united in one person.

Among the evidences of the influence of Crete upon Egyptian ornamentation, particularly at the time of Akhenaten (pp. 210–12), we must number to-day the presence of the spiral on a chariot found in the tomb of Tutankhamen.

For want of precise information, I have, to my great regret, been unable to make adequate use of the splendid results of the excavations which Monsieur Renaudin has been conducting at Mallia since 1921. But I am able to add, from letters from Monsieur Charles Picard and Monsieur Renaudin, which were read by Monsieur Pottier at the meetings of the Académie des Inscriptions held on 9th and 10th November, 1923 (see the *comptes rendus* of the Académie ; cf. BCH, 1923, 523–4), information supplementing several passages in this book. The north-west quarter of the palace (cf. pp. 16, 38, 40), which is the only one cleared so far, shows certain new arrangements which do not, however, appear to be entirely unrelated to the west wing of the palace of Knossos. It has furnished an abundant harvest of objects of different kinds, including fine vases and broad leaves of gold stamped with decorative patterns. Some distance from the palace, in the town, a small shrine has been discovered with a lustral basin (cf. pp. 117–18) and, near by, the chief sanctuary where worship was celebrated (cf. pp. 263–4). To judge by the numerous repairs made to the original walls and the variety of the finds these monuments must have been long in use. The first contained an idol of the type known at Petsofa in M.M.I together with the remains of a fresco representing a worshipper bearing a mark in the shape of a swastika (cf. p. 256). But the second building afforded the most interesting discoveries. Two sacred stones (cf. pp. 228–31) remain standing, one upon a rectangular base and the other between the still distinguishable traces of two round wooden columns. Upon the second of these, which is the more recent, is engraved a trident, a sign frequently found in the palace in M.M.II. In front of the base of the more ancient and hence more venerated stone was an accumulation of ex voto objects of terra cotta (cf. p. 273), including vases of all shapes offered between the beginning of the Early Minoan Period and the end of the Middle Minoan, one of which bears an inscription, medallions engraved with animal figures (e.g. a dove and a dog) with an inscription on the reverse and, most important of all, a large number of " tablets", more than thirty of which are intact and all covered with inscriptions. These " tablets " are rectangular parallelepipeds of the old type illustrated by our Fig. 85, p. 375. The signs, sometimes engraved on all four sides, are hieroglyphs of the advanced class and of the type which was apparently used more especially in eastern Crete. The Museum at Candia has had casts taken of these " tablets ", and is to send specimens of them to the Louvre. It is clear that, though the French School at Athens for a long time lagged behind in the exploration of prehistoric Crete, it is now making up brilliantly for lost time.

French excavations in Syria have just produced results of great importance. They show that the origins of the Phœnician alphabet go back to a much earlier period than could have been imagined a few weeks before. Hitherto one had to suppose that the Ægean elements contributing to its formation had been transmitted to Palestine by the Pelesati and the Zakari, that is to say about 1193, and that they had later spread northwards (pp. 383–5; cf. p. 394). To be sure Monsieur Salomon Reinach had already noticed certain signs engraved prior to that date on the pottery of Lachish in Canaan and had identified them with Ægean signs, but practically no attention had been paid to this fact. Now, however, Monsieur Pierre Montet has just discovered at Byblos a tomb contemporary with Rameses II (1300–1234) upon the lid of which the epitaph of King Ahiram is inscribed in Phœnician characters.[1] Thus the Phœnician alphabet was completely formed by the XIIIth century. But it is none the less true that it combined Ægean and Egyptian signs. It must therefore be acknowledged that the appearance of Ægean characters in Syria is connected, if not with the influence exercised by the Keftiu over those regions at the time of

Thothmes III (see pp. 214–16), at least with Mycenæan influences, more especially perhaps with the presence of the Danauna in the neighbourhood of Byblos after the beginning of the XIVth century.

In conclusion I shall add a valuable piece of information regarding the survival of pre-Hellenic cults at Delos (pp. 251 and 392). I received it from Monsieur Charles Picard, to whom I owe special thanks for his obliging communications. This eminent archæologist has in the course of the present year reconstructed from fragments of sculpture belonging to the Artemision two rampant lionesses attending the goddess, and he supposes that the position of this group was near the horned altar, the Keraton. Thus archaic Greece apparently possessed the counterpart of the Cretan image of Our Lady of the Mountain (p. 245, Fig. 40).

G. G.

27th February, 1924.

¹ Discussed by M. Dussaud in an excellent article in *Syria*, vol. v, pp. 135-57.

FURTHER ADDITIONS

THE year 1924 was particularly fruitful in the Ægean world. On two points it has yielded new data which add greatly to our knowledge of Cretan civilization, and are of capital importance for the history of the Achaians.

In Crete, Evans—once again !—had a successful campaign which he described in *The Times* of 16th and 17th October, 1924. At Knossos, beneath the court of the palace, he excavated two rectangular houses of the Sub-Neolithic Age. In the principal room of each was a fixed hearth of stone and clay. Since similar arrangements of a later date have been found at Pseira and Gournia (see p. 114), it must be admitted that, though the fixed hearth is rare in Crete, it was known there from the earliest times. Each house contained a series of store cells, a modest prototype of the magazines which later kings were to build quite near. One of these cells contained, with a Neolithic pot, a flat copper axe and fragments of flat-necked vases of hard stone, of a type known in pre-dynastic Egypt. The association of these objects throws remarkable light on Ægean chronology. Egyptian vases of this kind had been found before, but the stratification was always doubtful (p. 24) ; to-day—unless we allow that these new fragments belong to vessels which were long preserved before they were buried with their last home—we are obliged to make the Cretan Chalcolithic Period, at least its beginning, coincide with the pre-dynastic Egyptian period, at least with its end ; i.e., to make it begin about 3400—3300 at the latest. (Cf. pp. 27, 31.)

At the same time, Evans discovered the port (cf. pp. 189–90) which ensured communication with Egypt in L.M. times, and the road which connected this port with Knossos (cf. p. 186). The port is that described by Homer (*Od.*, iii, 293 ff.) : " On the borders of Gortyn there is a smooth, steep rock, which stands in the spray of the sea. There Notos drives the great waves to the left of the headland towards Phaistos, until the great waves are broken by a little line of stones." The headland where the south wind raises the waves is the southernmost cape of Crete, Lithinos ; the little line of stones which breaks them is a point running west, so as to protect the harbour of Komo. This site was occupied from the beginning of E.M. to the Homeric period ; the population, who first dwelled in an acropolis, came down to the shore in L.M., and rows of *pithoi* show where the Cretan ships came to load the oil exported to Egypt.

It was from Komo, then, that the road ran northward across the broadest part of Crete. Evans has identified sufficient portions of it to describe its construction and to indicate its line. Between Komo and Knossos it had to scale the heights overlooking the plain of the Messara on the north, and to turn the western slopes of Iouktas. Above and below the sections on the hillsides were ' Cyclopean " terrace walls.

The actual point at which the road arrived at Knossos was determined by excavations which Evans describes as " dramatic ". Opposite the South Propylaea which once formed the monumental entry of the palace (p. 120), on the other side of the torrent, blocks marking the line of the road had been noticed before. They had been thought to rest on the rock itself. What had been taken for rock was an accumulation of earth hardened by the water of the neighbouring springs, which was strongly impregnated with gypsum. Attacking this petrified mass, Evans disclosed eight courses, forming the piers, of a viaduct, for a length of 21 metres. At the end of the viaduct, behind a triangular court, was an elegant pavilion containing an alcove and flanked by a bath-chamber. The inside walls of the pavilion were coated with stucco and brilliantly adorned with painting—orange pilasters with red bases against a white ground, and above them an excellent frieze of partridges and hoopoes, rendered naturalistically in a conventional landscape. Preserved by the petrified strata, strong colours and delicate tints have kept all their brilliancy and freshness. This fine specimen of L.M.I reminds Evans, with reason, of certain Dutch dining-rooms. East of the pavilion were stalls for beasts and store-rooms, as is proved by remnants of bins and grain. A stone channel brought water from a plentiful spring situated above the building ; an elaborate system of pipes served the bath-chamber (see pp. 117–18), and one pipe fed a watering-trough. Lastly, there was an underground basement, reached by steps, in which a sacred fountain was arranged. Outside this chamber were remains of sacrifices. Inside, lamps set on all sides illuminated a basin filled with votive vases, including bowls containing food offerings, such as olives. When Evans cleared the basin of the deposits which blocked it, the water sprang as it had done long ago, a striking resurrection of the past. By the side was a round terra-cotta hut, in which the great goddess, Our Lady of the Source, stood with her hands raised in benediction. But the fountain chapel dates from the last Minoan period and the first Hellenic period. The rest of the building is much older, and had no religious purpose ; Evans sees in it a caravanserai or hostel for the use of the travellers who came by the south road.

Let us pass to Asia Minor. All that we have said about the drive of the Achaians to the East (pp. 51 ff., 214 ff.) has received detailed confirmation for which one could not have hoped. The German scholar Herr Forrer has written a wonderful chapter of history in deciphering a series of Hittite documents ; [1] our time has been rich in surprises of a scientific kind, but it has seen few to match these. The Akaiwasha, whom the stele of Meneptah mentions in the company of Asiatic peoples, such as the Lukki (Lycians), about 1229, are now seen mingling with those peoples more than a century earlier. In Cyprus and Pamphylia, where the Achaians left their dialect, we can follow their roamings. The Achaian-Aiolians who made and sang the Trojan War are found in the neighbourhood of the Troad as early as the fourteenth century. These are the facts :—

About 1336, Antaravaas, king of Akhiawa or Akhaiwa (Achaia) and Laaspa (Lesbos), having been attacked by the chieftains of Arzawa (Cilicia) and those of Millowanda (Milyas, N.E. of Lycia), is aided by the king of the Hittites, Mursil II ; the Achaia in question can only be Pamphylia. About 1325 the successor of Andreus, Tavagalavas the Aiavalaas (Eteokles the Aiolian) asks Mursil for the title of king as the price of the help which he is to give to Lugga (Lycia). About the middle of the reign of Dudhalia III (1263–25), the king of Akhaiwa, Attarissijas (Atreus or an Atreid), makes war to the west of Tlos, in Caria, and tries to force the prince of the country to recognize him as suzerain. The Great Hittite boasts of having

---

[1] E. Forrer, " Vorhomerische Griechen in den Keilinschrifttexten von Boghazkoï," in *Mittheilungen der Deutsch. Orient. Ges.*, March, 1924 ; " Die Griechen in den Boghazkoï-Texten," in *Orientalische Literaturzeitung*, vol. xxv, March, 1924, 113–8. Cf. P. Dhorme, " Les Achéens dans les textes de Boghaz-Keui," in *Revue Biblique*, October, 1924, pp. 557–65.

resisted him ; nevertheless, he calls the vanquished man
" brother " in a letter, and is not above treating the king of
Akhaiwa as an equal, just as he does the kings of Egypt,
Babylonia, and Assyria. So at this moment Akhaiwa is a
great power in Asia. From Hellenized Rhodes expeditions
set forth against Lycia and Caria ; Achaian-speaking Pamphylia tries to expand eastward or westward ; Cyprus has its
Akhaiwa, the " Achaians' Shore " ; Lesbos already has settlements of Northern Achaians, Aiolians mixed with Minyans,
the first Argonauts to sail from Iolkos. I am even prepared to
believe that there was an Akhaiwa in Africa. The Akaiwasha
who invaded Egypt in 1229 with Libyans and Asiatic peoples
may perhaps have had a footing on the Libyan coast, where
they succeeded the Cretans and were to be succeeded by the
colonists of whom history tells.

They tried to take in too much ; by scattering itself about
the circumference the race weakened itself in the centre. The
attack on Egypt fails. About the same time (1230–25), the
Atreid returns to the attack against Caria with a fleet of a
hundred ships ; but he is defeated in a great battle by the
generals of Dudhalia. Soon, under Arnuanta (1225–10), the
Hittites, masters of Arzawa and Seha (eastern Pisidia), drive
the Achaians back into their Pamphylia, and refuse their
chief the title of king, allowing him only the rank of *kurievanies*
(κοίρανος in Homer). However, the Atreid is still strong enough
to seek compensation in Bigzaia (Sphekeia, Cyprus) ; he
ravages the island and leaves a vassal prince there. The
Aiolians are still capable, by calling the forces of the whole
Achaian world to their help, of carrying off surprise attacks on
the unsubdued parts of Lesbos, and even, after long efforts,
of taking Troy.[1] But it was the last ray of glory. The Dorians
were coming.

[1] The Greek chronologists gave the Trojan War a date varying from about
1280 to 1180. The later date is usually accepted. We preferred the earlier
(p. 53), for several reasons, but chiefly because the *Iliad* mentions an expedition of Achilleus to Lesbos, and the settlement of the Greeks in that island
seemed to us to be earlier than the twelfth century. The Hittite texts justify
us on this particular point, more than we could have imagined ; they show
that there were Greeks in Lesbos before 1337, and therefore before the Trojan
War, whatever its date was. In that case, we must suppose that Andreus
called himself king of Laaspa long before the island was completely conquered ;
Achilleus' expedition to Lesbos is similar to that of Attarissijas in Cyprus
before its complete Achaïzation. In that case, too, the date of 1180 no longer
offers the same difficulties ; the completion of the conquest may as well have
lasted two centuries as one.

We see the inestimable value of the documents translated by Herr Forrer. They throw much light on the identity of the dialects spoken in Arcadia, Cyprus, and Pamphylia. They show how right we were in placing the Achaio-Aiolian colonization of Asia and the arrival of the Achaians in European Greece several centuries earlier than was usual. New Iliads rise from the darkness. And, when we note that the names borne by the kings of Akhaiwa and Laaspa are given by Greek tradition to the two first kings of Orchomenos, Andreus son of Peneios and Eteokles son of Andreus, when the name of Atreus appears in a text of the thirteenth century, legend suddenly acquires an historical value beyond all expectation.

G. G.

20th April, 1925.

BIBLIOGRAPHY

PERIODICALS, DICTIONARIES, AND COLLECTIONS

American Journal of Archæology . . . . . . AJA
Annals of Archæology and Anthropology of the University of
    Liverpool . . . . LA.
Annual of the British School at Athens . . . . . BSA.
Annuario della Scuola Italiana di Atene . . . . . ASI.
L'Anthropologie . . . . An.
'Αρχαιολογικὸν Δελτίον . . . . ΑΔ
Archiv fuer Religionswissenschaft . . . . . . ARW.
Ausonia . . . . Au.
Bulletin de Correspondance Hellénique . . . . . BCH.
Bullettino di Paletnologia Italiana . . . . . . BPI.
Comptes Rendus de l'Académie des Inscriptions . . . CRAI.
Dictionnaire des Antiquités : Daremberg, Saglio, Pottier, and
    Lafaye . . . . DA.
Encyclopædia of Religion and Ethics : Hastings . . . ER.
'Εφημερὶς 'Αρχαιολογική . . . . 'Εφ.
Jahrbuch des Deutschen Archæologischen Instituts . . . JAI.
Jahreshefte des Oesterreichischen Archæologischen Instituts . JOEI.
Journal des Savants . . . . JS.
Journal of Hellenic Studies . . . . JHS.
Journal of the Institute of British Architects . . . . JIBA.
Mémoires des Antiquaires du Nord . . . . . MAN.
Memorie del Istituto Lombardo di Scienze e Lettere . . MIL.
Mittheilungen des Archæologischen Instituts in Athen . . AM.
Monumenti Antichi dell' Accademia dei Lincei . . . MA.
Πρακτικὰ τῆς 'Αρχαιολογικῆς 'Εταιρείας . . . . Πρ.
Realencyclopædia : Pauly and Wissowa . . . . . PW.
Rendiconti dell' Accademia dei Lincei . . . . . RAL.
Revue Archéologique . . . . RA.
Revue de l'Histoire des Religions . . . . . . RHR.
Revue des Études Anciennes . . . . REA.
Revue des Études Grecques . . . . REG.
Transactions of the third international Congress for the History
    of Religions . . . . TCHR.
Zeitschrift fuer Ethnologie . . . . ZE.

SPECIAL WORKS

NOTE.—Where an English translation is mentioned in addition to the
the French or German edition of a work, the references in the text do not
refer to the English pages except in the case of **LVI.**

ALY (Wolf), *Der kretische Apollonkult, Vorstudie zu einer Analyse
    der kretischen Goetterkulte*, Leipzig, 1908 . . . . **I**

BELOCH (Julius), *Griechische Geschichte*, 2nd ed., vol. i, 1,
Strasburg, 1912 . . . . **II**
BLEGEN (Carl W.), *Korakou, a Prehistoric Settlement near Corinth*,
Boston and New York, 1921 . . . . . . **III**
BOSSERT (H. T.), *Alt-Kreta, Kunst und Kunstgewerbe im
Ægæischen Kulturkreise*, Berlin, 1921 . . . . **IV**
BULLE (Heinrich), *Orchomenos, I* (Abhandlungen der Bayerischen
Akademie der Wissenschaften, I. Klasse, vol. xxiv, II),
Munich, 1907 . . . . **V**
BURROWS (Ronald M.), *The Discoveries in Crete*, 2nd ed., London,
1908 . . . . **VI**
CAVVADIAS (P.), *Προϊστορικὴ ἀρχαιολογία*, Athens, 1909 . . **VII**
DÉCHELETTE (Joseph), *Manuel d'archéologie préhistorique*, vol. ii,
I, pp. 31–64 (Bronze Age), vol. ii, II, pp. 517–29 (Iron Age),
Paris, 1910, 1913 . . . . **VIII**
DEONNA (Waldemar), *Les Toilettes modernes de la Crète minoenne*,
Geneva, 1911 . . . . **IX**
DOERPFELD (Wilhelm), SCHMIDT (Hubert), and GOETZE (Alfred),
Troja und Ilion, Ergebnisse der Ausgrabungen, 1870–1914,
vol. i, Athens, 1902 . . . . **X**
DUSSAUD (René), *Les Civilisations préhelléniques dans le bassin
de la mer Égée*, 2nd ed., Paris, 1914 . . . . . **XI**
EVANS (Sir Arthur J.), *Cretan Pictographs and Præ-Phœnician
Script* (extract from JHS., vol. xiv, 1894, pp. 270 ff.), London,
1895 . . . . **XII**
—— *Mycenæan Tree and Pillar Cult* (ibid., vol. xxi, pp. 99–204),
London, 1901 . . . . **XIII**
—— *Essai de classification des époques de la civilisation minoenne*,
revised ed., London, 1906 . . . . . . **XIV**
—— *Minoan Weights and Mediums of Currency* (Corolla
Numismatica in honour of Barclay V. Head, pp. 336–67),
Oxford, 1906 . . . . **XV**
—— *The Prehistoric Tombs of Knossos* (extract from
Archæologia, vol. lix, II, pp. 391–562), London, 1906 . . **XVI**
—— *Scripta Minoa*, vol. i, Oxford, 1909 . . . **XVII**
—— *The "Tomb of the Double Axes" and Associated Groups,
and the Pillar Rooms and Ritual Vessels of the "Little
Palace" at Knossos* (extract from Archæologia, vol. lxv,
pp. 1–94), London, 1914 . . . . . . **XVIII**
—— *The Nine Minoan Periods*, London, 1914 . . **XIX**
—— *The Palace of Minos*, vol. i: *The Neolithic and Early and
Middle Minoan Ages*, Oxford, 1921 . . . . **XX**
Excavations at Phylakopi in Melos, conducted by the British
School at Athens (T. D. ATKINSON, R. C. BOSANQUET,
C. C. EDGAR, A. J. EVANS, D. G. HOGARTH, D. MACKENZIE,
C. SMITH, and F. B. WELCH), London, 1904 . . . **XXI**
FICK (A.), *Vorgriechische Ortsnamen*, Goettingen, 1905 . . **XXII**
—— *Hattiden und Danubier in Griechenland*, Goettingen, 1909 **XXIII**
FIMMEN (Dietrich), *Zeit und Dauer der kretisch-mykenischen
Kultur*, Leipzig, 1909 . . . . **XXIV**
—— (and REISINGER), *Die kretisch-mykenische Kultur*, Leipzig,
1921 . . . . **XXV**

FOUQUÉ, *Santorin et ses éruptions*, Paris, 1879 XXVI

FRANCHET (L.), *Rapport sur une mission en Crète et en Égypte* (1912–13) (Nouvelles Archives des Missions scientifiques et littéraires, vol. xxii, fasc. i), Paris, 1917 XXVII

FURTWAENGLER (A.), *Antike Gemmen*, Leipzig and Berlin, 1900 . XXVIII

FURTWAENGLER and LOESCHKE, *Mykenische Thongefæsse*, Berlin, 1879 XXIX

—— *Mykenische Vasen*, Berlin, 1886 XXX

GRAEF (Botho), *Die antiken Vasen von der Akropolis zu Athen*, i, Berlin, 1909 XXXI

GROPENGIESSER, *Die Græber von Attika*, i, Athens, 1907 . . XXXII

HALL (Edith H.), *The Decorative Art of Crete in the Bronze Age*, Philadelphia, 1907 XXXIII

—— *Excavations in Eastern Crete, Sphoungaras* (Anthropological Publications of the Pennsylvania University, vol. iii, 2), Philadelphia, 1912 XXXIV

HALL (H. R.), *The Oldest Civilization of Greece*, London, 1901 . XXXV

—— *The Ancient History of the Near East*, London, 1913 . . XXXVI

—— *Ægean Archæology*, London, 1915 XXXVII

HATZIDAKIS (Joseph), *Tylissos à l'époque minoenne*, translated from the Greek in collaboration with L. FRANCHET, Paris, 1921 XXXVIII

HAWES (Charles Henry) and HAWES (Harriet Boyd), *Crete the Forerunner of Greece*, London and New York, 1909 . . XXXIX

HAWES (Harriet Boyd), WILLIAMS (Blanche E.), SEAGER (Richard B.), and HALL (Edith H.), *Gournia, Vasiliki and other Prehistoric Sites on the Isthmus of Hierapetra (Crete)*, Philadelphia, 1908 XL

KERAMOPOULLOS (A. D.), Θηβαϊκά, Athens, 1917 . . . XLI

LAGRANGE (Fr.), *La Crète ancienne*, Paris, 1908 . . . XLII

LANG (Andrew), *The World of Homer*, London, 1910 . . XLIII

LEAF (Walter), *Homer and History*, London, 1915 . . . XLIV

—— *Troy, a Study in Homeric Geography*, London, 1912 . . XLV

LEROUX (Gabriel), *Les Origines de l'édifice hypostyle*, Paris, 1913 XLVI

LICHTENBERG (R. von), *Beiträge zur ältesten Geschichte von Kypros* (Mitteilungen der Vorderasiatischen Gesellschaft, 1906, No. 2) XLVII

—— *Einfluesse der ægæischen Kultur auf Ægypten und Palæstina* (ibid., 1911, No. 2) XLVIII

—— *Die ægæische Kultur* (in the series Wissenschaft und Bildung), Leipzig, 1911 XLIX

LOLLING, *Das Kuppelgrab von Menidi*, Athens, 1880 L

MARAGHIANNIS (G.), *Antiquités crétoises*, with introduction by L. PERNIER and bibliography by G. KARO, 2nd series, Vienna, 1907, 1911 LI

MEYER (Eduard), *Ægyptische Chronologie*, 1904 ; *Nachträge zur Ægyptischen Chronologie*, 1907. Translated by A. MORET as *Chronologie égyptienne* (Annales du Musée Guimet, vol. xxiv, ii), Paris, 1912 LII

—— *Geschichte des Altertums*, 3rd ed., vol. i, ii : *Die ältesten geschichtlichen Voelker und Kulturen bis zum sechzehnten Jahrhundert*, pp. 759–808, Stuttgart and Berlin, 1913 . LIII

MILANI (L. A.), *L'Arte e la religione preellenica alla luce dei bronzi dell' antro ideo cretese e dei monumenti hetei* (Studi e materiali di archeologia e numismatica, vol. i, pp. 161–234 ; vol. ii, pp. 1–96 ; vol. iii, pp. 1–142), Florence, 1899–1901, 1902, 1905 . . . . **LIV**

MODESTOV (B.), *Introduction à l'histoire romaine*, Paris, 1907 . **LV**

MORGAN (Jacques de), *L'Humanité préhistorique, esquisse de préhistoire générale* (L'Évolution de l'humanité, vol. ii), Paris, 1901. Translated as *Prehistoric Man* (The History of Civilization, No. 2), London, 1924 . . . . . **LVI**

MOSSO (Angelo), *La Preistoria*, I : *Escursioni nel Mediterraneo e gli scavi di Creta*, 2nd ed., Milan, 1910. English translation as *The Palaces of Crete and their Builders*, 1907 . . **LVII**

—— *La Preistoria*, ii : *Le Origine della civiltà mediterranea*, Milan, 1910. English translation as *The Dawn of Mediterranean Civilization*, 1910 . . . . **LVIII**

MURRAY (A. S.), SMITH (A. H.), and WALTERS (H. B.), *Excavations in Cyprus*, London, 1901 . . . . **LIX**

MURRAY (Gilbert), *The Rise of the Greek Epic*, 2nd ed., Oxford, 1911 . . . . **LX**

MYRES (John L.) and OHNEFALSCH-RICHTER (Max), *Catalogue of the Cyprus Museum*, London, 1899 . . . . **LXI**

NOACK (Ferdinand), *Homerische Palæste*, Leipzig, 1903 . **LXII**

—— *Ovalhaus und Palast in Kreta*, Leipzig, 1908 . . **LXIII**

OHNEFALSCH-RICHTER (Max), *Kypros, die Bibel und Homer*, 2 vols., Berlin, 1893 . . . . . . **LXIV**

PAPAVASILEIOU (Georgios A.), Περὶ τῶν ἐν Εὐβοίᾳ ἀρχαίων τάφων, Athens, 1910 . . . . . . **LXV**

PEET (T. Eric), *The Stone and Bronze Ages in Italy and Sicily*, Oxford, 1909 . . . . **LXVI**

PERROT (Georges) and CHIPIEZ (C.), *Histoire de l'art dans l'antiquité*, vol. vi : *La Grèce primitive, l'art mycénien*, Paris, 1894 . . . . **LXVII**

REICHEL (Wolfgang), *Ueber homerische Waffen*, 2nd ed., Vienna, 1901 . . . . **LXVIII**

REISINGER (Ernst), *Die kretische Vasenmalerei vom Kamaresbis zum Palast-Stil*, Leipzig, 1912 . . . . **LXIX**

RODENWALDT (Gerhart), *Tiryns*, vol. ii ; *Die Fresken des Palastes*, Athens, 1912 . . . . **LXX**

—— *Der Fries des Megarons von Mykenai*, Halle, 1921 . **LXXI**

SCHLIEMANN (H.), *Mykenæ*, Leipzig and London, 1878. English translation as *Mycenæ*, 1878. French translation by J. GIRARDIN, Paris, 1879 . . . . . **LXXII**

—— *Orchomenos*, Leipzig, 1881 . . . . . **LXXIII**

—— *Ilios*, Leipzig, 1881. Translated into French by Mme. E. EGGER, Paris, 1885 . . . . **LXXIV**

—— *Troja*, Leipzig, 1884 . . . . . . **LXXV**

—— *Bericht ueber die Ausgrabungen in Troja im Jahre 1890*, Leipzig, 1891 . . . . **LXXVI**

—— *Tiryns*. English translation, 1886. French translation as *Tirynthe*, Paris, 1885 . . . . . **LXXVII**

SCHMIDT (Hubert), *Schliemanns Sammlung trojanischer Altertuemer*, Berlin, 1902 LXXVIII

SCHUCHHARDT (Carl), *Schliemanns Ausgrabungen in Troja, Mykenæ, Tiryns, Orchomenos, Ithaka*, 2nd ed., Leipzig, 1891. English translation as *Schliemann's Excavations,* with an appendix on later discoveries at Hissarlik by SCHLIEMANN and DOERPFELD, 1891 LXXIX

SEAGER (Richard B.), *Vasiliki* (Transactions of the University of Pennsylvania, Department of Archæology, vol. ii, iii), Philadelphia, 1907 LXXX

—— *Excavations on the Island of Pseira* (Anthropological publications of the University of Pennsylvania, vol. iii, i), Philadelphia, 1910 LXXXI

—— *Explorations in the Island of Mochlos*, Boston and New York, 1912 LXXXII

—— *The Cemetery of Pachyammos, Crete* (Anthropological publications of the University of Pennsylvania, vol. vii, i), Philadelphia, 1916 LXXXIII

SERGI (G.), *Europa, l'origine dei popoli europei*, Turin, 1908 . LXXXIV

STEPHANOS (Clon), *Antiquités cycladiques* (Comptes-rendus du Congrès international d'archéologie à Athènes, 1905, pp. 216 ff.) LXXXV

STERN (E. von), *Die " præmykenische " Kultur in Sued-Russland*, Moscow, 1905 LXXXVI

SWINDLER (Mary Hamilton), *Cretan Elements in the Cults and Ritual of Apollo*, Bryn-Mawr (Pennsylvania), 1913 . . LXXXVII

TSOUNTAS (C.), *Αἱ προϊστορικαὶ ἀκροπόλεις Διμηνίου καὶ Σέσκλου,* Athens, 1908 LXXXVIII

TSOUNTAS (C.) and MANATT (J. A.), *The Mycenæan Age*, Boston, 1897 LXXXIX

VINCENT (Father Hugues), *Canaan d'après l'exploration récente*, Paris, 1907 XC

WACE (A. T. B.) and THOMPSON (M. S.), *Prehistoric Thessaly*, Cambridge, 1912 XCI

WALDSTEIN (C.), *Excavations at the Argive Heræum*, 2 vols., Cambridge, 1902, 1905 XCII

INDEX

This index does not as a rule give references which may be found from the list of Contents. Objects have not been indexed under sites when it has been more convenient to place them independently or under the headings Vases, Seals, Frescoes. For objects representing the God, Goddess, and tree (sacred), see under these headings.

H. T.= Hagia Triada, K.= Knossos, Myc.= Mycenæ, Phyl.= Phylakopi.

Printed in Great Britain by Stephen Austin & Sons, Ltd., Hertford.